Voting Rights—And Wrongs

Voting Rights—And Wrongs

The Elusive Quest for Racially Fair Elections

Abigail Thernstrom

The AEI Press

Publisher for the American Enterprise Institute

WASHINGTON, D.C.

To Amy Thernstrom and Michael Callahan,
two wonderful people who married into our family.
With much love.

Distributed to the Trade by National Book Network, 15200 NBN Way, Blue Ridge Summit, PA 17214. To order call toll free 1-800-462-6420 or 1-717-794-3800. For all other inquiries please contact the AEI Press, 1150 Seventeenth Street, N.W., Washington, D.C. 20036 or call 1-800-862-5801.

NRI NATIONAL
RESEARCH
INITIATIVE

This publication is a project of the National Research Initiative, a program of the American Enterprise Institute that is designed to support, publish, and disseminate research by university-based scholars and other independent researchers who are engaged in the exploration of important public policy issues.

Library of Congress Cataloging-in-Publication Data

Thernstrom, Abigail M., 1936-
    Voting rights—and wrongs : the elusive quest for racially fair elections/ Abigail Thernstrom.
       p.cm.
    Includes bibliographical references and index.
    ISBN-13: 978-0-8447-4269-4 (hardcover)
    ISBN-10: 0-8447-4269-4 (hardcover)
    ISBN-13: 978-0-8447-4272-4 (pbk.)
    ISBN-10: 0-8447-4272-4 (pbk.)
    1. African Americans—Suffrage. 2. Elections—United States. 3. Voting—United States. 4. Election law—United States. I. Title.

    JK1924.T47 2009
    324.6'208996073—dc22

                                                              2009016284
13 12 11 10 09   1 2 3 4 5

Printed in the United States of America

Contents

Acknowledgments

This book would not have been possible without the support of the American Enterprise Institute for Public Policy Research (AEI), and I am grateful to its long-time president, Chris DeMuth, and his recent successor, Arthur Brooks, for their confidence in my work. Kim Dennis, former director of the National Research Initiative (NRI) at AEI, provided the financial support and encouragement essential to the book's inception. Her successor as head of the NRI, Henry Olsen, drew on his deep knowledge of American politics to make perceptive suggestions that helped shape the book in important ways.

Samuel Thernstrom, director of the AEI Press, not only provided incomparable editing, but also talked through almost every substantive point, enriching my own understanding of the subject in the process. Whatever strengths this book possesses are due in great part to his indispensable help. I am indebted as well to his assistant, Laura Harbold, who provided inestimable assistance with production of the book, to Lisa Ferrarro Parmelee for her meticulous editing, and to Susan Burnell for her careful review of my legal citations.

Several people generously read the manuscript in whole or in part. In their swift but painstaking reviews, J. Christian Adams, Michael Carvin, Roger Clegg, Daniel Lowenstein, and Hans von Spakovsky caught errors and made valuable suggestions, for which I thank them.

I learned a great deal from the many excellent scholars whose work is discussed throughout the book. When I wrote *Whose Votes Count?* more than twenty years ago, there was very little academic writing on minority voting rights; today a rich and varied literature exists, from which I drew extensively. Richard Hasen's immensely useful ElectionLaw listserve has been a great source of information and insight, and I am indebted to

Rick for his indefatigable energy in posting the latest election law news every day.

As always, Stephan Thernstrom read every word and then read them again . . . and again. He is my wonderful colleague, and a husband without whom life would be unimaginable.

Foreword

Juan Williams

It is a simple but revealing joke: Even paranoids have enemies!

That one-liner is pretty accurate in revealing a common mindset among black Americans. Yes, we now know a black man can be elected president in this white-majority country. Yes, even the head of the overwhelmingly white Republican Party is currently a black man. And, yes, a vigilant Congress, on the watch for any sly tactic to diminish black voting rights, has repeatedly extended an emergency provision of the 1965 Voting Rights Act, long after it was intended to expire.

But . . . even paranoids have enemies.

So, when the last extension of that provision—section 5—of the Voting Rights Act was about to expire in 2006, it sparked a frenzy of fear on black talk radio, in black newspapers, and, particularly, on the Internet. The basic message—just two years before a black man won the White House—was that black people faced the possibility of losing their right to vote.

Section 5 was originally intended as short-term insurance against any sleight-of-hand changes by racist election officials looking to subvert newly established protections for minority voters. In a nation where blacks had been kept from voting with bogus literacy tests and interpretive questions from registrars that had no real answers—such as the infamous, "How many bubbles in a bar of soap?"—section 5 gave the government a way to deal with new forms of such blatant attempts to deny black people their voting rights. It was targeted at the nine states of the Old Confederacy with their history of voter intimidation and poll taxes. Now, more than forty years later, in response to a simple debate about the need for yet a fourth extension of section 5, dire voices claimed that any thought of doing away with it or trimming it back amounted to the end of the whole Voting Rights Act. Some announced that black people would be kept from voting.

Please keep in mind that the most important protections of the Voting Rights Act do not require reauthorization. And note that the Fifteenth Amendment to the Constitution, establishing the right for black men to vote, is also chiseled in stone into American jurisprudence. The Voting Rights Act and the Fifteenth Amendment are fixtures in law.

The rumor of the death of the Voting Rights Act often was tied to charges of voter suppression during the 2000 election. The Clinton administration's Justice Department investigated and did not find the evidence to make a case based on voting rights violations or voter suppression. But that did not quash the conspiracy theory. It fell into line with other racial conspiracy theories, including such enduring whispers as the one that has the government giving AIDS to black people.

Nervousness about the end of section 5 also led to questions about Republican efforts to pass laws requiring voters to have government-issued identification. While there have been few extensive cases of voter fraud under existing law, federal courts have generally found voter identification to be a reasonable safeguard against the possibility of it. Nevertheless, that move was seen by the conspiracy-minded as a cagey way for Republicans to depress votes for Democrats by turning away older, low-income, mostly minority voters who are more likely to be Democrats and less likely to have such identification.

To anyone but those most absorbed with this fight, there is the temptation to dismiss all the racial paranoia as just a collective mania. You could write it off as a sad reminder that black Americans have had real enemies at their backs for most of American history. A touch of paranoia is understandable when past generations of your people have been literally hounded, enslaved, and even lynched. Recent elections in the United States have seen fliers arrive in black neighborhoods with the wrong date for voting or inferences about bill collectors waiting to see who votes so they can have people arrested.

When it comes to paranoia, we black people know about ghosts as we pass along stories of Night Riders and the KKK.

You might even explain current outbreaks of paranoia as the cost of ongoing twenty-first-century stereotyping, in which blacks are most often seen on TV, in music, and in movies as hyper-violent criminals, rappers who imitate those gangsters and glorify their lifestyle, or comics who think it is fall-down funny to use the N-word. That barrage of negativity is enough to inspire my own paranoia about the way the rest of America sees black people.

So, all this paranoia can be understood as a leftover psychological discomfort erupting out of America's troubled racial history, and nothing more.

But there are large costs to indulging this particular paranoia, as Abigail Thernstrom shows in this detailed and compelling examination of the history of the Voting Rights Act. Thernstrom sees well-intentioned legislators signing up to extend, even strengthen, section 5 without considering that it may be lessening the impact of black and minority political clout in the U.S. Congress and in state government. She points to other cowardly politicians who, for fear of being labeled racist, prefer extending a provision that is now clearly anachronistic over taking on a complex racial conversation. And she reminds us of still other politicians who profit from encouraging racial bloc voting. They have no interest in discussing the topic, either. Thernstrom is on a brave mission to end the silence that allows politics to distort the Voting Rights Act.

In 1965, when the Voting Rights Act was written and passed into federal law, its authors aimed to get the government to enforce the racial integration of voter registration, voting, and vote counting. Integration was also the goal of the 1964 Civil Rights Act. These laws, along with the 1954 *Brown v. Board of Education* decision ending legal segregation in public schools, are the pillars of the modern civil rights revolution. Their goal was to create equal opportunity for black Americans to go to school, hold jobs, stay in hotels, and become part of the political ruling class, with its coalitions and power players.

Leaders in civil rights, from Thurgood Marshall to Roy Wilkins and Dr. Martin Luther King Jr., never intended to create a separate and contained universe—a political ghetto for blacks. Throughout American history the push from civil rights activists has always been for inclusion. Even when it came to fighting the Civil War, civil rights leader Frederick Douglass pressed President Abraham Lincoln to open the door to black men who wanted to wear the Union-blue uniform and fight to end slavery.

At no point in American history did black leaders endorse separatism that would have black politicians elected to Congress from a seat that was labeled "blacks only" and then consigned to some racially exclusive caucus that remained on the edge of deal makings and deliberations at the heart of the government.

To repeat, the goal was integration. The unstated aim was a political structure in which Americans of all colors could find common political goals and join as allies across color lines to make good things happen, such as changing harmful policies, ending misbegotten wars, and creating programs to deal with entrenched poverty.

In December 1960, the Supreme Court ruled that bus terminals and restaurants for people traveling on buses going across the country had to be open on an interracial basis. The following summer, James Farmer of the Congress of Racial Equality wrote to President John F. Kennedy demanding protection for the Freedom Riders—the young men and women, black and white, who risked their lives riding those buses through the South together in defiance of segregation laws. When Freedom Riders were beaten and some of the buses bombed, a national crisis threatened to spread the violence. The Kennedy administration was put on the spot as southern white politicians—most of them elected as segregationists—refused to acknowledge the rights of black people. A Mississippi court convicted and then jailed the Freedom Riders as having violated trespassing laws.

As the administration struggled to deal with the crisis, the president's brother, Attorney General Robert Kennedy, concluded the civil rights movement needed to focus less on provocative confrontations with segregationists and more on getting black people registered to vote so they might help oust the politicians who kept segregation in force on buses, in schools, and in housing.

"If they registered and participated in elections," Robert Kennedy told an interviewer, "even half of them . . . they could have a major impact" on getting southern politicians to change their opposition to integration. Out of that crisis, the Kennedy administration helped start the Voter Education Project to get more blacks to become voters. This was the seed of political efforts in Washington that later gave life to the Voting Rights Act.

Again, the goal was integration.

These integrationist goals are also part of the legal history of the civil rights movement.

Let me tell you a story. I was once interviewing Justice Thurgood Marshall in his chambers at the Supreme Court when he began to tell me about what he called his "greatest" case as a lawyer. I assumed the former lead lawyer for the NAACP Legal Defense and Educational Fund was talking about the 1954 *Brown* case on school segregation. I was wrong.

He told me about a case called *Smith v. Allwright*, in which a black Texas doctor sued a Houston election judge who had denied him the right to vote in a primary election. Marshall represented the plaintiff, Lonnie Smith. In Texas, blacks voted in general elections but the Democratic primary was closed to them. That meant that white candidates ran on segregationist platforms in the primaries. By the time the general election came around, blacks really had little choice about the kind of politician they wanted to represent them. As a result, several Texans in Congress, responding to their white segregationist political base at home, could close their eyes to abuses against black people, ranging from the brutality of lynching to the terrorism practiced by the KKK.

Marshall told me that he argued the Texas case as a violation of the Fifteenth Amendment's protection of black voting rights. The other side argued that the Democratic Party was a private club that was free to decide who its members would be and who could vote in its primary. Duke Ellington, the famous bandleader, stopped his group from touring so he could spend several days in the Texas court watching Marshall argue the case. But Marshall lost there and appealed to the U.S. Supreme Court; and in Washington, in April 1944, the high Court ruled that any primary open only to whites was a violation of the Fifteenth Amendment because it "endorses, adopts and enforces the discrimination against Negroes."

Later, in August 1965, when President Lyndon B. Johnson signed the Voting Rights Act into law, Marshall was given a front row seat, along with Dr. King and Rosa Parks, in the President's Room adjacent to the Capitol rotunda—the very same room where President Lincoln had signed the Emancipation Proclamation. The president talked to him at length, Justice Marshall recalled, about the power of the right to vote as the key to full integration in American life. Here is part of what Johnson said in public that day:

The vote is the most powerful instrument ever devised by man for breaking down injustice and destroying the terrible walls which imprison men because they are different from other men . . . [The Voting Rights Act is] one of the most monumental laws in the entire history of American freedom.

Again, the animating idea behind the law was racial integration. And Johnson was right. The law led to tremendous growth in black political participation, and doors began opening to black people. New opportunities led to the historic expansion of an educated black middle class in America.

But, over time, distortions also appeared in the law. To some the measure of success of the Voting Rights Act was not protecting the right to vote, but rather the number of black politicians who won election as mayors, state legislators, and U.S. representatives and senators. Any and every politician is interested in gaining power and keeping it. Not surprisingly, black politicians wanted to protect their personal rise to power by arguing for safe seats under the act. But that thinking took the law far away from its roots as an instrument that served racial equality by ensuring black people could vote and run for office.

The number of black politicians is an important indicator, given that blacks had been intentionally excluded from political power as part of the larger strategy to maintain segregation and white power over black people. But it is not the only measure of success. The true goal is making politics work for America's racial minorities as well as it does for America's white majority. In this book Abigail Thernstrom makes the case that the Voting Rights Act was never intended to be measured for success on the basis of how many black or Latino politicians should be in Congress. Specifically, she contends, section 5 was never intended to be used to start an endless debate about voter dilution or discriminatory voter impact. Protections to halt obvious violations already exist elsewhere in the Voting Rights Act and in other laws.

She notes that Justice Clarence Thomas, the lone African American currently on the Supreme Court, is the one justice who has penetrated to the heart of this matter. He has said that different people of good will can have different definitions of concepts such as an "equal opportunity to be elected" and what constitutes a racial group's "undiluted electoral power." Thernstrom quotes Justice Thomas as writing in one Voting Rights Act case that

> The matters the Court has set out to resolve in vote dilution cases are questions of political philosophy, not questions of law. As such, they are not readily subjected to any judicially manageable standards that can guide courts in attempting to select between competing theories.

And yet, the Voting Rights Act is used as a tool by the politically expeditious in their attempts to advance varied theories of redress for social problems—theories that may be profitable for them, but are far beyond the scope or the intent of the law. And it can be used by the politically expeditious of another stripe to strengthen their political power by keeping blacks out of the political mainstream.

Thernstrom is not alone in posing these questions. In a 2003 paper for *The Journal of Politics* of the Southern Political Science Association, professors David Lublin and D. Stephen Voss wrote about the tragic consequences of making the election of black officials the bottom line for judging the efficacy of the Voting Rights Act. They concluded that while mapping congressional districts in the south to create black majority districts did give black politicians a better chance of winning and keeping safe seats in Congress, it "decimated the southern congressional districts once represented by centrist Democrats." The professors pointed out that a sole focus on racial outcomes "helped polarize the South's congressional delegation into a mixture of [black] Democrats and right-wing Republicans, creating a more favorable environment for conservative legislation."

In other words, white political moderates in both the Republican and Democratic parties found themselves forced out. That left blacks in Congress—overwhelmingly liberal Democrats—isolated. White southern moderates became an endangered species. Meanwhile, conservative Republicans grew in power on the basis of newly drawn congressional districts that were distorted into white enclaves by the absence of black and Latino voters. That inevitably led to a political dynamic in which "black [political] interests suffered as a result of this public policy."

In a separate 1998 paper in the *Stanford Law Review* that touched on the same subject of redistricting with the sole aim of raising the number of black elected officials, Lublin and Voss wrote, "One cannot help but wonder if the election of greater numbers of blacks who have little influence will only increase African American frustration with government institutions." The frustration would result from seeing black elected officials marginalized while the overall politics of Congress became more conservative on social issues that are viewed in the black community as critical to the well-being of minorities struggling for economic and social stability.

All of this leads back to the historic election of Barack Obama. His political rise did not take place by developing a racially separate political base. By necessity he mastered the art of speaking to both white and black voters. His most famous speech, at the 2004 Democratic National Convention, was essentially an attack on the idea that any good comes from dividing the nation into racially distinct groups. His credo was that there is no red-state America or blue-state America, and there is no white America and no black America. He created a national political following by making the case for one America.

When Obama began his campaign for the Democratic presidential nomination, the older black political base of voters and most of the Congressional Black Caucus did not support him. He was black, but they did not know him well. And, like most black voters, they doubted that a black candidate could win. That left his campaign to get support from younger and mostly white people. They went to work for him in early caucus and primary states, creating a model of a cross-racial political coalition.

The reality of President Obama is a powerful counter to paranoid racial politics that invite some to distort the Voting Rights Act by arguing it is necessary to use insidious racial groupings to advance racially diverse political representation in the United States.

Abigail Thernstrom is at the cutting edge of the new possibilities of cross-racial unity with the arguments she presents in this book. Her goal, it seems to me, is protecting honest, nonracial competition of political ideas and leadership in service to America's democratic ideals.

Yes, even paranoids have enemies but the wise among us acknowledge when times have changed and old patterns of paranoia are no longer in our best interest.

Introduction

Over time, the Voting Rights Act has evolved into one of the most ambitious legislative efforts in the world to define the appropriate balance between the political representation of majorities and minorities in the design of democratic institutions

—Richard H. Pildes, professor of law, New York University[1]

As I write, Barack Obama has just become the first black leader of the free world, winner of an election in which his race was clearly no barrier, and may well have been an advantage. He won a larger share of the white vote than the previous two nominees of his party, and, for the first time in history, African-American turnout at the polls may have been higher than the rate for whites. President Obama's victory is unmistakably the end of an era and the welcome beginning of a new one. Whatever one thinks of his politics, his stunning success is a historic turning point. Integration was the aim of the civil rights movement in the 1950s and much of the 1960s, and, by the ultimate test, American politics is now integrated. Blacks have been a major force in American politics for decades—and now they have reached its highest peak.

Obama's victory contradicted everything most black voters had long been led to believe. Even as his candidacy began to take off, the word on the street was still that most whites would never vote for a black. America in black and white, separate and unequal—that was still the conventional wisdom, particularly in African-American circles. By any meaningful measure, it was no longer true—and had not been for many years. Yet civil rights spokesmen, the mainstream media, and politicians in both parties continued

1

to poison the racial climate by feeding the deep distrust and alienation that remained ubiquitous among blacks, despite decades of racial progress.

On November 4, 2008, it became clear how dated that picture was, as fears of the "Bradley effect" gave way to returns that closely matched pre-election predictions. Tears flowed, *Washington Post* writer Kevin Merida reported, not only in response to Obama's victory, "but because many were happily discovering that perhaps they had underestimated possibility in America." In Milton, Massachusetts, novelist Kim McLarin told Merida that she had stood at the polling place overwhelmed. "I've been forced to acknowledge . . . there has been a shift—it's not a sea change. But there's been a decided shift in the meaning of race," she said.[2]

Countless other such stories were heard in the days after the election. Blacks and whites alike acknowledged that their fears of racist resistance to a black president had been misplaced. While Obama's election marked a dramatic turning point, his victory was the culmination of a quiet revolution in racial politics that had begun many decades before with the passage of the 1965 Voting Rights Act. The story of that act—its evolution and impact—is the immensely complicated subject of this book. It is a story that should interest not only anyone who cares about race relations in America, but also students of American law and politics. The issues raised by the Voting Rights Act's long and sometimes tortuous story speak to fundamental questions about the U.S. Constitution and the nature of democratic government.

The passage of the Voting Rights Act marked the death knell of the Jim Crow South. The exclusive hold of whites on political power made all other forms of racial subjugation possible. For ninety-five years after the passage of the Fifteenth Amendment, southern blacks had been kept in political chains; the 1965 act was an indispensable and beautifully designed response to a profound moral wrong. Its enactment was one of the great moments in the history of American democracy.

Over time, the Voting Rights Act morphed in an unanticipated direction—a change that has had both benefits and costs. The act's original vision was one that has become all but universally shared: racial equality in the American polity, so blacks would be free to form political coalitions and choose candidates in the same manner as other citizens. But in the racist South, it soon became clear, that equality could not be achieved—as originally hoped—simply by giving blacks the vote. Merely providing access to the ballot was insufficient after centuries of slavery, another century of segregation, ongoing white racism, and persistent resistance to black political power. More aggressive measures were needed.

In response, Congress, as well as courts and the Justice Department, in effect amended the law to ensure the political equality that the statute promised. Blacks came to be treated as politically different—entitled to *inequality* in the form of a unique political privilege. Legislative districts carefully drawn to reserve seats for African Americans became a statutory mandate. Such districts would protect black candidates from white competition; whites would seldom even bother to run in them.[3] The new power of federal authorities to force jurisdictions to adopt racially "fair" maps was deeply at odds with the commitment to federalism embedded in the Constitution, and the entitlement to safe black seats was equally at odds with traditional American assumptions about representation in a democratic nation. But it quickly became clear that southern whites would not relinquish power without the imposition of race-conscious maps.

Today, the Voting Rights Act arguably serves as a brake on black political aspirations and a barrier to greater integration. While the country has moved steadily, if unevenly, toward racial integration, the law has created a black political class too isolated from mainstream political discourse. That isolation has further exacerbated the tendency of African Americans to see themselves as a permanent minority separated from the American dream. Race-based districts have worked to keep most black legislators clustered together and on the sidelines of American political life—precisely the opposite of what the statute intended, and precisely the opposite of what is needed now. With Barack Obama as president, America is ready for a Voting Rights Act premised on the belief that racial animus is a marginal element in American politics.[4]

The emergency of racist political exclusion waned over time, but the interpretation and enforcement of the Voting Rights Act never recognized the reality of racial change. Racial progress rapidly outpaced the law, and the voting rights problems that are now of greatest concern—hanging chads, provisional ballots, glitches in electronic voting, registration hassles, voter identification, and fraud prevention measures—bear no relationship to those that plagued the South in 1965. Nevertheless, the most radical provisions of the statute live on, addressing yesterday's problems.

Barack Obama has become our forty-fourth president. Parents will tell black children that they can follow in his footsteps. He carried the majority of white votes in almost a third of the states. And yet the central provisions of the 1965 statute, which still rest on the assumption that massive disfranchisement remains a danger, continue to reinforce old notions that blacks are fungible members of a subjugated group that stands apart in American life, requiring methods of election that recognize their racial distinctiveness. Such convictions are a roadblock to true political equality, which can only be built on recognition of citizens as individuals with fluid identities, free to emphasize their racial and ethnic identity as they wish and to coalesce in any manner they may choose.

Unconquered Territory

It seems almost unbelievable today, but in 1961, the year Barack Obama was born, most southern blacks were still disfranchised—unable to enjoy the fundamental right that ensures the preservation of all other rights. At the turn of the twentieth century they had been driven from the polls and their voices ruthlessly silenced, and in 1940 an appalling 97 percent of the five million southern blacks of voting age were still denied the vote. That figure did drop dramatically over the next two decades, but ten years after the Supreme Court had signaled the end of Jim Crow in *Brown v. Board of Education* in 1954, the majority of blacks remained unable to cast a ballot in almost every southern state.[5] Disfranchisement was particularly acute in Mississippi and outside of major urban areas throughout the region.

Legal barriers prevented black voter registration, but economic and social coercion directed at blacks who were so "uppity" as to try to vote was also important in maintaining white control over politics. African Americans bold enough to insist on exercising their right to register might find themselves without a job or credit at the store. Or they might end up as James Chaney did: murdered by the Ku Klux Klan. He, along with Michael Schwerner and Andrew Goodman, two northern whites, were volunteers in a Mississippi registration drive in the summer of 1964.[6] These three idealistic young men became the most famous—but by no means the only—martyrs in the drive for Fifteenth Amendment rights.

By 1965, the civil rights movement had been in full swing for a decade. The Montgomery Bus Boycott had started in 1955, when Rosa Parks famously refused to move to the back of a bus. The lunch counter sit-ins (which quickly spread to public libraries, swimming pools, and other facilities in southern cities) had begun in 1960. The 1961 Freedom Rides had desegregated interstate transportation. And the 1964 Civil Rights Act had outlawed segregation in every facility that served the general public. Voting rights alone remained largely unconquered civil rights territory.[7]

Violence in the service of racial exclusion, however, was the white South's fatal error. Selma, Alabama, was a small town in Dallas County where only 1 percent of eligible blacks were registered to vote. On March 7, 1965, police and state troopers attacked blacks and whites marching peacefully for black voting rights. Among the participants who were severely beaten was a future congressman, John Lewis, who suffered a fractured skull. The pictures seen in living rooms across the nation could not be ignored; these were citizens "willing to be beaten for democracy," in the words of one black minister.[8]

The violent resistance of the white South—in marked contrast to the non-violence of those who marched and sang—spelled its defeat. The balance of power shifted in the struggle between Alabama governor George C. Wallace and those ready to die to realize the most fundamental of constitutional rights; Wallace lost. Eight days after that "Bloody Sunday"—as it came to be known—President Lyndon B. Johnson went on national television urging new legislation, and five months later, on August 6, he signed the Voting Rights Act into law.

The Constitutionally Daring Design

No civil rights statute has been more important than the Voting Rights Act. Scholars still disagree on the wisdom and legitimacy of parts of the 1964 Civil Rights Act, but even in 1965, those who raised serious questions about the Voting Rights Act were primarily southerners who, with the notable exception of Justice Hugo Black, had no credibility.[9] In 1997 the Supreme Court depicted passage of the original act as an occasion on which Congress understood precisely its power to enforce the equal protection clause of the Fourteenth Amendment.[10]

Nothing short of radical federal intervention would have enfranchised southern blacks. The 1964 Civil Rights Act had left basic voting rights to the mercy of the South's "tough judges"—generally tough, that is, in their opposition to federal attorneys bringing Fifteenth Amendment complaints.[11] The 1964 "Freedom Summer," in which Schwerner, Goodman, and Chaney had participated, had been a bust. Roughly a thousand students came to Mississippi to join the campaign, and while this young army did persuade 17,000 blacks in the state to attempt registration, a mere 1,600 were able to do so. Moreover, half of those who succeeded lived in Panola County, where a federal court did act to protect them.[12]

The passage of the Voting Rights Act, however, had an immediate impact. In 1963, Martin Luther King Jr. had described Mississippi as "sweltering with the heat of injustice, sweltering with the heat of oppression."[13] In 1964, black registration in the state had been the lowest in the region, under 7 percent. Two years later, its percentage of African-American registered voters (roughly 60 percent) was the highest in the South. In every southern state, the gains were striking.[14] Sometimes good legislation works precisely as initially intended.

The power of the statute flowed from its ingenious—indeed, constitutionally daring—design. A solid statistical formula identified states in which blacks had been disfranchised, and an appropriate remedy was applied: Those southern states lost their traditional prerogative to set rules for registration and other aspects of the election process—a prerogative long assumed to be vital to the notion of states as entities with powers independent of the national government.[15] As Columbia University law professor Nathaniel Persily has noted, the law "stands alone in American history in its alteration of authority between the federal government and the states. No other statute applies only to a subset of the country and requires covered states and localities to get permission from the federal government before implementing a certain type of law."[16]

Persily was actually describing not the entire law, but one provision—section 5—that demands prior federal approval (preclearance) of all changes in election procedure in states and counties that have been designated racially suspect by virtue of having met the conditions of the act's carefully designed statistical trigger. In the original statute, that provision applied only to Alabama, Georgia, Louisiana, Mississippi, South Carolina, Virginia, and most counties in North Carolina.

Jurisdictions in those suspect ("covered") states could not alter "any voting qualification or prerequisite to voting, or standard practice or procedure" without first obtaining consent from the U.S. Department of Justice or the District Court for the District of Columbia. Moreover, the normal burden of proof was shifted from those who charged wrongdoing to the defendant: To obtain preclearance, jurisdictions were required to prove that their actions were untainted by racism. It was an extraordinary shift in the legal burden of proof—one justified only by the particular context of the battle to destroy the Jim Crow South.

While most of the Voting Rights Act is permanent, section 5, which became the centerpiece of the statute, was initially envisioned as an emergency measure with a life of only five years. Beginning in 1970, however, it was repeatedly extended, most recently in 2006 for another quarter-century; the new expiration date is 2031. The emergency of black disfranchisement has come to be treated as near permanent—even in an era when an African American can be elected president.[17]

Racism Wanes while Federal Power Expands

When the Supreme Court signed off on the constitutionality of section 5 and other emergency provisions of the Voting Rights Act, it was with a clear understanding that they were both precisely targeted and short-lived. "The Court has recognized that exceptional conditions can justify legislative measures not otherwise appropriate," it stated in 1966.[18] But the extraordinary nature of preclearance—constitutional only under "exceptional conditions"—was quickly forgotten. Every renewal became an occasion for amendments that strengthened the act; never did Congress stop to consider whether the statute's unprecedented powers should, in fact, be pared back in recognition of its success. Thus, as black political participation was steadily and dramatically rising, federal power over local and state electoral affairs was paradoxically expanding.

In 1970 and 1975, changes in the statistical trigger brought under control of section 5 new states and counties, none of which had a history of minority disfranchisement analogous to that experienced by southern blacks prior to 1965. As a result of these amendments (which will be discussed in chapter 1), Texas and Arizona, as well as scattered counties in New York, California, Florida, and elsewhere, became "covered" jurisdictions requiring prior federal approval for all changes related to the election process. Moreover, blacks were no longer alone in their protected status under the statute. Hispanics (as well as American Indians, Asian Americans, and Alaskan Natives) acquired the extraordinary federal protection that had previously been given only to African Americans.[19] Hispanics were by far the important group in this list. This book focuses mainly on blacks because they are the group that has the greatest moral claim to special protection for their voting rights.

In 1982, section 5 was renewed for the third time, this time for twenty-five years. In addition, the civil rights community successfully lobbied for an amendment to a permanent provision, section 2, which was originally an innocuous preamble. That preamble was rewritten to heighten dramatically the power of federal courts throughout the country to insist on districting maps that protect against methods of voting said to be discriminatory in "result." The amended provision made jurisdictions beyond the reach of federal preclearance permanently vulnerable to suits challenging districting and other aspects of the electoral environment that were said to "dilute" the power of the black or Hispanic vote. Votes were "diluted," it turned out, whenever a method of election did not result in minority officeholding roughly proportionate to the minority population.

In time, section 2, with its nationwide reach, came to overshadow section 5, but the preclearance provision had important advantages: It provided for swift administrative action, and it placed the burden on the jurisdiction to prove its racial innocence—a burden that made findings of suspected discrimination almost inevitable wherever minority officeholding was disproportionately low in relation to the minority population. Section 2, a permanent provision of the act, provided heavy artillery for voting rights advocates when needed, but they nevertheless remained wedded to preclearance as an important tool to attack methods of election that impeded the "ability of minority groups to participate in the political process and to elect their choices to office."[20]

Section 5, which Congress had never dared make permanent, was up for renewal once again in August 2007. Congressional Democrats and

Republicans alike, however, were eager to put themselves on record as true supporters of civil rights well before the presidential election. Congress renewed and amended section 5 in the summer of 2006, passing the "Fannie Lou Hamer, Rosa Parks, and Coretta Scott King Voting Rights Act Reauthorization and Amendments Act" (VRARA) with almost no dissent.[21] This renewal extended the life of the "temporary" emergency provision for an additional twenty-five years and "clarified" the legal standards by which it was to be interpreted.

By the new expiration date, electoral arrangements in the South, the Southwest, and a collection of arbitrarily selected counties elsewhere will have been under federal receivership, in effect, for as much as sixty-six years. The act's proponents believe that, well into the foreseeable future, minority voters in the jurisdictions targeted by section 5 will remain unable to "pull, haul, and trade to find common political ground" (in Justice David Souter's words) with likeminded white voters, and consequently unable to participate in American political life without the benefit of electoral set-asides.[22] In 2006, voting rights activists were still fighting the last war, doing battle with Governor Wallace more than forty years after his famous pronouncement, "segregation today, segregation tomorrow, segregation forever."[23]

In 1965, the Voting Rights Act had been simple, transparent, and elegant. Its aim was to secure basic Fifteenth Amendment rights in a region where they had been egregiously denied. But the cumulative effect of these amendments was to turn the law into a constitutionally problematic, unprecedented attempt to impose what voting rights activists, along with their allies in Congress, the Justice Department, and the judiciary, viewed as a racially fair distribution of political power. Majority-minority legislative districts that ensure the election of black and Hispanic candidates became a federal mandate. These districts protect minority voters' "candidates of choice" from electoral defeat, giving these voters a sheltered status enjoyed by members of no other groups. It is a troubling detour on the road to racial equality.

A Disconnection from Reality

A disconnection from reality surrounds the Voting Rights Act today. By every measure, American politics has been transformed since the 1960s. Blacks hold office at every level of government, and have reached the pinnacles of virtually every field of private endeavor; racial prejudice has fallen to historic lows. Yet the passage of the 2006 VRARA was preceded by a sustained, meticulously organized campaign by civil rights groups to persuade Congress that race relations remain frozen in the past, and that America is still plagued by persistent disfranchisement. An extensive effort to organize support for the VRARA among every conceivable group, from black churches to the business community, was based on wildly misleading claims of catastrophe if section 5 were to expire.

For instance, H. Lee Scott Jr., the president and CEO of Wal-Mart, wrote to President George W. Bush on June 7, 2005, expressing alarm that the temporary provisions of the act might actually be treated as temporary. "On behalf of Wal-Mart Stores, Inc. and our more than 1.2 million associates in the United States," Scott wrote to urge the president "to fully support and reauthorize the enforcement provisions of the Voting Rights Act of 1965 that are set to expire, if not extended, in 2007. . . . I think you will agree that the more Americans are disenfranchised, the more our democracy is at risk—both here and abroad."[24]

In fact, there was no danger that any Americans would suddenly be disfranchised and our democracy put "at risk" if the temporary provisions of the act were allowed to expire. In 2005, the issue was not a return of racist arrangements that made political participation the prerogative of whites only. The question was the wisdom and legality of a fourth extension of the temporary emergency provisions of the original act that had been initially slated to expire in 1970. Activists were determined to garner such overwhelming support for the act's renewal that no one would dare stop to consider whether these provisions were still appropriate in the twenty-first century—and they succeeded. Congress passed the VRARA in July 2006 by votes of 98–0 in the Senate and 390–33 in the House.

In passing the VRARA, Congress signed on to the picture that Scott had drawn—a picture that reflected conventional wisdom in the civil rights community and the media. "Discrimination [in voting] today is more subtle than the visible methods used in 1965. However, the effects and results are the same," the House Judiciary Committee reported.[25] "Vestiges of discrimination continue to exist . . . [preventing] minority voters from fully participating in the electoral process," the statute itself read.[26] Discrimination in 2006 was just "more subtle" than it was in the South in 1965? Every member of Congress had to know that was absurd. It was irresponsible campaign rhetoric.

It cannot be said too strongly or too often: The skepticism of those, like Georgia representative John Lewis, who cannot forget the brutality of those years, is understandable. But the South they remember is gone. Today, most southern states have higher black registration rates than those outside the region, and over 900 blacks hold public office in Mississippi alone.[27] Between 1970 and 2002, the number of black elected officials in the seven southern states originally covered by section 5 in the 1965 act jumped from 407 to 4,404, nearly double the rate at which black representation increased nationwide. Covered and noncovered states in the South are almost indistinguishable by the measure of African Americans elected to state legislatures. Massive disfranchisement is ancient history—as unlikely to return as segregated water fountains. America is no longer a land in which whites hold the levers of power and black and Hispanic political representation depends on the exercise of extraordinary federal intervention, constitutionally sanctioned only as an emergency measure.

No one believes that racial inequality in America has ended. Black poverty and crime rates are still too high; the gap in academic achievement remains as wide as it was twenty years ago. But the congressional record created in the summer of 2006 to pass the VRARA reflected a deeply misguided consensus that nothing important had changed since 1965. Such pessimism is, in fact, deeply dangerous: If four decades of hard work had gone to waste, what was the point of continuing the effort on behalf of racial equality, when that effort was likely to bear such meager fruit? What hope was there for black America? Skepticism about racial change warped not only the Voting Rights Act, but also other race-related areas of public policy. The message hurt blacks and whites alike—a point to which I will return.

The Constitutional Order Distorted—By Necessity

In 1965, a century of Fifteenth Amendment violations demanded what might be called federal wartime powers, and, as on other occasions when wartime powers were invoked, the consequence was a serious distortion of our constitutional order. It was fully justified in 1965, I have already suggested; it is not today.

In the literature on minority voting rights, that distortion is too seldom acknowledged. The long history of pervasive southern racism justified a temporary abrogation of the traditional right of states to govern their own political processes within constitutional boundaries. Yet the Constitution contains no provision for group representation, "no matter how shamefully treated [its members] were nor how tragic their history," as a number of witnesses pointed out at the 1982 Senate hearings on the amendment of section 2.[28] "This is not India," Henry Abraham, professor of government at the University of Virginia, testified. "There is no right to be represented on the basis of group membership." In a community of equal citizens—one in which identity is fluid, and the horizons of trust extend beyond the ethnic, racial, or religious community—individuals, not groups, are the unit of representation.[29]

The principle was right, but there was a problem: In 1965, southern states and counties were not communities of equal citizens. The South, with its racial caste system, *was* Abraham's India, and its long history of group exclusion justified concern that methods of election ensure black inclusion.

What was the measure of inclusion, however? The conviction that the franchise alone would not suffice—that further steps had to be taken to destroy an entrenched caste system—put the enforcement of the statute on a proverbial slippery slope. Ensuring that black and Hispanic ballots carried sufficient political weight became the expanded goal of the act; from there, it was but a short slide down that slope to a constitutionally problematic system of reserved seats for minority group members, even in settings with no history of racist exclusion; and from there, another short slide to proportional racial and ethnic representation as the only logical standard by which to measure true electoral opportunity.[30] Congress, the courts, and the Justice Department could have planted their feet firmly at a point well short of proportionality as an entitlement. But civil rights advocates saw results as the proper measure of opportunity—in employment, education, and contracting, too—and those who wrote, interpreted, and enforced the law consistently took their cues from these advocates.

"Distinctions between citizens solely because of their ancestry are by their very nature odious to a free people whose institutions are founded upon the doctrine of equality," Justice Harlan Fiske Stone said in 1943, but the Supreme Court has never prohibited all race-conscious public policy.[31] Such policies have been treated as morally right when they are essential to opening the doors of opportunity—when the alternative is the perpetuation of all-white (or overwhelmingly white) legislatures, for instance.

The emergence of race-driven districting as an entitlement coincided with a dramatic change in white racial attitudes in the South. In 1982, five black candidates won seats in the North Carolina State House of Representatives, although they ran in districts ranging from 79 to 64 percent white. Nevertheless, the Supreme Court dismissed that record of success in a landmark 1987 decision in which black electoral opportunity in the state was described as generally "impaired."[32] It rested that conclusion mainly on the district court's findings that whites and blacks tended to vote for different candidates—with the court making no distinction between racial and partisan voting. The lower court had acknowledged that it had now "become possible for black citizens to be elected to office at all levels of state government in North Carolina," but the high Court dismissed such black success as "perhaps too aberrational" to be taken seriously.[33] At what point, however, should that possibility have suggested racial inclusion? What was the measure of sufficient racial progress, so that questions about a method of election could be entrusted to elected representatives?

The Importance of Black Legislators

Congress, the Justice Department, and, intermittently, the courts have coped with the question by playing down racial progress. Blacks live in a world of largely arrested time, they have suggested. Without race-conscious districts gerrymandered to elect blacks to public office, "you're not going to have minority representation in Congress. It's just that simple," North Carolina representative Mel Watt stated in response to a 1993 Supreme Court decision allowing constitutional challenges to egregiously race-driven districting maps.[34]

But it wasn't "just that simple." In the 1990s, plaintiffs prevailed in a series of constitutional challenges to racial gerrymandering, but the decisions that struck down what the American Civil Liberties Union (ACLU) once called "max-black" districting plans in Georgia, Louisiana, Texas, and elsewhere did not halt the impressive growth in the number of black elected officials.[35] By the end of the decade, the Congressional Black Caucus was stronger than ever. It is important to note, however, that its enhanced strength was in great part due to the creation of fourteen new black-majority districts after the 1990 census. All but two were in the South, and the impact was a jump in the number of southern blacks in the House from five to seventeen.[36]

More than twenty years ago, I wrote a book on the Voting Rights Act entitled *Whose Votes Count? Affirmative Action and Minority Voting Rights.* I did not argue (as my critics alleged) that blacks needed nothing more than access to the ballot to ensure electoral equality. Some southern states and localities, bent on minimizing the impact of the new black vote, were changing the rules of the game to keep blacks from gaining political office. They were determined to maintain the racial caste system in which whites were born to govern. It was not possible to turn a blind eye to such efforts, I argued, although I did emphasize the substantial costs that flowed from providing protection from such racist maneuvering—the price paid by a reinterpretation of the act to guarantee a racially fair distribution of political power.

In *Whose Votes Count?* I also recognized the importance of descriptive representation—blacks representing blacks. It was a point that should have been clear, although numerous readers ignored it. The history of whites-only legislatures in the South made the presence of blacks both symbolically and substantively important. Racially integrated legislative settings work to change racial attitudes. Most southern whites had little or no experience working with blacks as equals and undoubtedly saw skin color as signifying talent and competence. When blacks became legislative colleagues, their presence inhibited the expression of racist sentiments, and conversations in the public arena changed.

Tom McCain, the first African American since Reconstruction to run for office in Edgefield County, South Carolina, put the point this way:

> There's an inherent value in officeholding that goes far beyond picking up the garbage. A race of people excluded from public office will always be second class. I know it, and the people who keep Edgefield County government all white know it.[37]

Shared political power, as I argued in my 1987 book, was integral to respect and self-respect. And, in recent decades, black electoral success never dissipated that yearning for both—which was surely one reason African-American tears were flowing when Barack Obama actually won the 2008 election.

In returning to the subject after an absence of more than two decades, I reiterate this and many other points I made back then. Much new voting rights law has been made in the intervening years, and I started this book in the belief that a review of recent developments might be of interest. But in the process of writing it, I came to a greater appreciation of the benefits of race-conscious districting in the South, as I have suggested above.

I have not altered my view that such districting carries a stiff price, which has gained in significance as white racism has decreased. But in this work I place more emphasis on the need to protect black candidates as long as southern hostility to black aspirations perpetuated a regime of political exclusion. White hostility—which had more of an impact in some jurisdictions than in others—was not the only problem. Southern blacks came to politics after 1965 with almost no experience organizing as a conventional political force. Race-based districts in the region of historic disfranchisement were arguably analogous to high tariffs that helped the infant American steel industry get started: They gave the black political "industry" an opportunity to get on its feet before facing the full force of equal competition.

The North was not the South. Certainly, it had its share of racial problems, both past and present. For instance, exit polls suggest clearly that a substantial number of whites were unwilling to vote for Harold Washington in 1983, when he was first elected mayor of Chicago. Blacks had, however, a long history of involvement in Chicago politics. The extraordinary measures to protect against disfranchisement contained in the original Voting Rights Act were rightly confined to the region that had kept the majority of blacks from the polls.

A Partial Truth

"In order to get beyond racism, we must first take account of race. . . . And in order to treat some persons equally, we must treat them differently," Justice

Harry Blackmun famously wrote in 1978.[38] He was arguing for racially preferential admissions at the medical school at the Davis campus of the University of California. I have long been a critic of Blackmun's formula, but it always contained a partial truth, recognized by the Supreme Court in decisions that are hard to argue with.

For instance, fourteen years after *Brown v. Board of Education*, the school systems of the Deep South were still deliberately segregated, and the Court finally lost patience and signed off on race-conscious remedies.[39] As Justice Antonin Scalia explained in 1989, the Court had permitted states to take race into account "where that [was] necessary to eliminate their own maintenance of a system of unlawful racial classification." The continuing "'effects' of previously mandated racial school assignment . . . justify a race-conscious remedy," he wrote. Those effects "perpetuate a 'dual school system.'"[40]

If school districts had a duty to dismantle dual school systems, surely southern states had a duty to dismantle electoral arrangements that privileged whites and allowed them to maintain control of legislative power on governing bodies both small and large. Moreover, as Justice Scalia noted with reference to schools, effective dismantling had to include race-conscious remedies to eliminate the continuing effects of the pernicious race-conscious policies of the past.

Race-conscious districting to end a long history of black political exclusion in the South had much in common with race-conscious school assignments to create unified school systems. But other policies that involve racial sorting can be sharply distinguished. Context matters. The racial preferences used by the University of Michigan in admitting college and law students, for instance, were not dismantling a dual system.[41] Moreover, institutions of higher education compare candidates on the basis of criteria such as SAT and other scores, grade-point averages, and teacher recommendations, for which there are no equivalents in public office. Admitting students by racial double standards, I have long argued, is demeaning, patronizing, and unfair to the students themselves.[42] In addition, university policies are clouded in secrecy and dishonesty, while districting maps are public documents.

Also in marked contrast to the educational context, in judging the attainment of racial equality in the electoral process, there are available benchmarks—high black turnout and white racism unmistakably infecting the electoral process, for instance. Pockets of racial intolerance undoubtedly remain in parts of the rural South, but they do not justify keeping election-related decisions throughout an entire region (and in scattered counties nationwide) under preemptive federal supervision. With limited, marginal exceptions, it seems fair to say that the nation has long since crossed the boundary that separates black exclusion and electoral opportunity.

It is not necessary to decide precisely when that transition occurred; different people will give different dates. Suffice it to say that in 2009, the president is black, and blacks and other minorities hold important positions of power at every level of government, as well as in virtually every area of the private sector. The caste system that originally justified taking race into account in structuring elections is gone; further racial progress demands that we now *cease* to take race into account and treat African Americans as Americans, entitled to the same political rights and opportunities as other citizens.

Doing so with respect to districting and other aspects of the electoral process is not likely to have a significant negative impact; in fact, the shape of districts would probably change very little, at least initially. Today, African Americans are a constituency no Democrat can afford to ignore, and black legislators wield considerable power on mapmaking committees. Without federal help, they would protect their "opportunity-to-elect" districts—with one important difference. The configurations of these districts would reflect the priorities of democratically elected state legislators—black and white—rather than those of federal bureaucrats or judges, often with an agenda of their own. Thus, they would square with constitutional expectations about the locus of power in deciding most election-related matters. And they would reflect, as well, those legislators' assessments as to the level of black concentration needed to elect black candidates in particular settings.

Expected and Unexpected Results

America has changed dramatically over the course of my adult life; the conversation on race and representation should have changed as well. By and large, it has not. I came of age when segregation still ruled the South; I have lived to see the election of Barack Obama as the nation's forty-fourth president. Yet the profound racial pessimism of voting rights advocates has continued to define the parameters of debate on voting rights. For example, in the 2006 congressional hearings on the VRARA—particularly in the House—few witnesses outside that community were asked to testify.

In state legislatures, however, the stifled debate had been quietly erupting among southern black politicians, who themselves began to ask whether having a maximum number of safe African-American districts always enhanced minority representation. These politicians understood clearly a long-apparent tradeoff between safe black districts and the strength of the Democratic Party in the South, and they did not want the seats of white Democrats sacrificed in the drive to ensure the election of black candidates.

The North Carolina challenge to race-based districting mentioned previously was not unique. Representative John Lewis, the Democrat from Georgia who played such a heroic part in the drive for racial equality in the 1960s, testified in a 2002 case involving a challenge to race-based districting for the Georgia Senate. He argued for allowing the state legislature to lower the black percentages in majority-minority districts, placing more African Americans in majority-white settings where they could help elect white liberals. If Democrats became the minority in the legislature, he explained, black representatives would lose important committee chairmanships. "I happen to believe that it is in the best interest of African American voters . . . to have a continued Democratic-controlled legislature," he said.[43] Almost every African-American member of the state senate, including the majority leader, shared his concern.

These prominent spokesmen for black interests were identifying themselves as Democrats first, and *black* Democrats second, which was precisely what the framers of the Voting Rights Act hoped would happen in time. As of 2001, Democrats held every southern congressional district that was at least 40 percent black, a testimony to black political power in the new South.[44] But districts drawn to guarantee the election of African-American candidates—districts with much higher black concentrations—were a gift to Republicans. In that more conservative region, concentrating African-American voters increased the likelihood that Republicans would be elected in the surrounding "bleached" areas.[45] Racially gerrymandered majority-minority districts, black leaders concluded, had unwelcome partisan consequences.

The Voting Rights Act irrevocably changed American politics in both expected and unexpected ways. Majority-minority districts initially worked to integrate blacks into mainstream American culture, but, as suggested earlier, by now they may be having quite a different impact. The entire point of racially gerrymandered maps is to give minority voters political territory they control, and, in this sense, separate political space. Thus, they suggest an equation of separate and equal—one that was explicitly rejected by the Supreme Court's 1954 decision in *Brown v. Board of Education.*

It is an equation that has become familiar in recent decades. As Stanford University law professor Richard Thompson Ford has pointed out, in other contexts multiculturalists have often embraced the notion that equality demands separation. They want black college dormitories and black studies programs, which culturally isolate blacks and encourage them to talk only to each other. "Students who have distinctive racial and cultural backgrounds require educational environments tailored to their group," advocates argue.[46] They require "tailored" educational environments and, for political purposes, race-conscious districting lines.

Such "tailored" districts would seem to be poor training grounds for black politicians who have larger ambitions and need experience in building biracial coalitions in majority-white settings. That may be the reason no black members of the U.S. House of Representatives have moved up to the Senate. They have been elected from constituencies in which the normal pressures that encourage candidates to move to the political center are unusually weak. Illinois Democrat Bobby Rush won his 2000 race against Barack Obama for a House seat by emphasizing his racial bona fides, his commitment to representing black interests, and his leftist politics. His political profile was not atypical. As of 2006, the entire Congressional Black Caucus was more liberal than the average white Democrat, limiting the appeal of its members to white voters, particularly in the South.[47] If, as a consequence, these black lawmakers don't have much success in getting their bills passed, their presence becomes largely symbolic.[48]

Politicians outside the mainstream can play an important role in shaping legislative debate. But when a group that has been historically marginalized as a consequence of deliberate exclusion subsequently chooses the political periphery, it risks perpetuating its outsider status. The danger is particularly great in the more conservative South, where whites may be more inclined to see blacks through a stereotypical lens. Reinforcing the sense of difference compromises the goal of the Voting Rights Act.

The point should not be overstated; not all black politicians have been trapped in safe minority districts. President Obama's political career actually began with his successful bid for the Illinois state senate, running from a majority-black district. But Obama was a uniquely gifted political entrepreneur with the skills to reach across racial lines. Thus, he created, saw, and seized opportunity where others have not. Other black politicians have succeeded in majority-white settings. The (very liberal) constituencies of U.S. Representatives Keith Ellison, a Democrat from Minnesota, and Emanuel Cleaver II, a Democrat from Missouri, are over 60 percent white. Journalist Gwen Ifill has described a number of such "breakthrough candidates," as she calls them. Mike Coleman was elected in 1999 as the first black mayor of Columbus, Ohio. His strategy, as she describes it: "Woo the white voters first . . . then come home to the base later."[49]

Nevertheless, "breakthrough candidates" remain the exception. The Voting Rights Act was meant to level the political playing field, so that blacks would become a political faction with the ability to enter and exit coalitions as other citizens do—that is, if they chose to define themselves as members of a like-minded political interest group. Its ultimate goal was full political assimilation. But the law itself now appears to frustrate that goal. Black political progress might be greater today had the race-based districting been viewed as a temporarily needed remedy for unmistakably racist voting in the region that was only reluctantly accepting blacks as American citizens. Instead, as a consequence of the amendment of the statute's permanent section 2, elections nationwide have become more or less permanently structured to discourage politically adventuresome African-American candidates who aspire to win political office in majority-white settings.

This list of the possible unwelcome consequences of race-conscious districting can be greatly expanded and, indeed, will be in the chapters that follow. But I do not draw a simple picture. I share with voting rights advocates a common commitment to a political landscape in which elected blacks and Hispanics are a significant presence. No civil rights legislation has been more important than the 1965 Voting Rights Act. But we do not honor it by perpetuating political arrangements that once served the purpose of combating racial exclusion and today, in a radically different context, work against the integration of American politics. Preclearance has outlived the emergency to which it was a response. By now, in treating blacks as politically helpless wards of the federal government, the statute inhibits progress.

A Medley of Normative Questions

In the Georgia redistricting case in which John Lewis had sided with the state senate's black leadership in opposing a plan that would have maximized the number of safe black seats, the Supreme Court held that whites elected with minority votes could represent black interests—a decision later superseded by the 2006 VRARA. But did the question belong in judicial hands in the first place? It was certainly appropriate for Congress, in the course of renewing the emergency provisions and amending the act, to address the meaning of fair representation, even if congressional deliberation came to misguided conclusions. Neither courts nor the Justice Department, on the other hand, had the skills or the authority to judge whether blacks and Hispanics were so separate from mainstream American culture that only members of the group could represent them. In part, the story of the Voting Rights Act reveals the limits of judicial and administrative power to decide complicated normative questions, as well as the unintended consequences that can flow from the failure to recognize those limits.

Once ensuring equal electoral outcomes became the goal of the act, decisions interpreting and enforcing it involved a medley of judgments involving basic American values. "Over the past fifty years, the steady march of civil rights . . . continues but the demands have changed," Judge Patrick E. Higginbotham wrote in 1993.

> Relatively clear lines of legality and morality have become more difficult to locate as demands for outcomes have followed the cutting away of obstacles to full participation. With our diverse ethnic makeup, this demand for results in voting has surfaced profound questions of a democratic political order . . . questions Congress has provoked but not answered.[50]

These "profound questions of a democratic political order" carried those who interpreted and enforced the statute far beyond their homes in the law—just as they had carried Congress into territory where it stumbled badly. What does a multiethnic, multiracial democracy look like in practice? When are racial and ethnic groups on equal electoral footing? What kind of inequality between minority and white voters demands a revised method of voting? Do whites elected with crucial minority support qualify as representing minority interests, or do black representatives have to be black themselves?

Furthermore, in a nonracist society, would blacks and Hispanics necessarily hold office in numbers reflecting their population strength, and is proportional representation therefore the proper measure of political inclusion? Do these two groups share a common political disadvantage so that, for districting purposes, they can be combined? How do we distinguish contests in which minority candidates lost for normal political reasons (including a political profile unlikely to appeal to voters outside the group) from those in which race was decisive?

Justice Sandra Day O'Connor in a 1993 decision described race-conscious districting as "an effort to 'segregate . . . voters' on the basis of race."[51] As such, she said, it threatens "to stigmatize individuals by reason of their membership in a racial group."[52] How, Justice Byron White asked in turn, could a plan designed to "provide a rough sort of proportional representation" be wrong?[53] Neither the Constitution nor the Voting Rights Act could settle that argument, which—like so many others involving minority voting rights—was driven by very different assumptions about white racial attitudes, persistent exclusion in contemporary America, the nature of representation, the importance of race to individual identity, and the moral legitimacy of sorting Americans on the basis of race and ethnicity. To write about the Voting Rights Act is to write about race in America.

In 1944, the Swedish sociologist Gunnar Myrdal famously called race the "American Dilemma."[54] Of all race-related issues, minority voting rights is perhaps the most important and the most difficult to resolve. Richard H. Pildes, quoted in the epigraph, has called the Voting Rights Act one of the world's "most ambitious legislative efforts . . . to define the appropriate balance between the political representation of majorities and minorities in the design of democratic institutions." It is an effort that has involved courts and the Department of Justice, as well—and one that has largely failed, with profound consequences.

It is time for Congress, judges, and the Department of Justice (DOJ) to move on. Their "ambitious" effort has become more futile with every passing year. Arriving at an "appropriate balance" was only possible in the relatively simple context in which it was easy to identify "minority" representatives by the color of their skin. Even black legislators have come to worry about the tradeoff between safe black seats and overall Democratic power, as noted earlier. Those who are concerned with the further integration of blacks into the political mainstream should be rejecting the familiar remedies for "disfranchisement" (a misnomer today) and shifting their gaze to the costs of the race-conscious arrangements designed to ensure black officeholding that have inadvertently placed a ceiling on black political aspirations.

As Pildes himself has suggested, the Voting Rights Act was a blueprint for an earlier time. It was pure antidiscrimination legislation aimed (at the outset) at ending disfranchisement in only one region. As such, it protected the election process from racist contamination. But, as Pildes puts it, "The Congresses that enacted and amended the VRA over the last forty years recognized that Section 5 and its unique elements should remain responsive to ever-changing circumstances"—and, by every measure, circumstances have changed. Blacks are no longer excluded from political participation, and the most important voting rights dispute in 2004 was in Ohio, not Mississippi.[55] The 1965 Voting Rights Act was designed to ensure black political progress, but today it has become a bulwark against further progress in a racially changed America.

Pildes confined his remarks to the question of the contemporary relevance of section 5, but I would further extend the point to encompass section 2 as well. In 1986, the Supreme Court read the provision to contain an entitlement to proportional racial representation, Justice O'Connor noted in a concurrence. Where majority-minority, single-member districts could be drawn, they were a mandate. Where the black population was too small or too dispersed to permit their creation, plaintiffs alleging black vote dilution could not prevail.[56] By now, section 2 is also out of date, and its defenders have resorted to increasingly bizarre arguments. The waning of white racism, one scholar has argued, should extend the provision's reach to districts in which whites are a majority—as long as those whites have had a record of supporting black candidates. In the face of increased racial tolerance, she contends, this permanent provision of the act should be strengthened to provide even greater federal power to micromanage methods of election.[57]

From Selma to tortured attempts to define black and Hispanic electoral entitlements in the face of black political success beyond the wildest dreams of those who marched across the Edmund Pettis bridge—it has been quite a journey into what Judge Bruce M. Selya has called a "Serbonian bog" of unanswerable legal, social, and political questions.[58] The story of that journey and its impact on politics and racial equality in America is the subject of this book.

1

The Fundamentals

This act flows from a clear and simple wrong. Its only purpose is to right that wrong. Millions of Americans are denied the right to vote because of their color. This law will ensure them the right to vote.

—President Lyndon B. Johnson, signing the
Voting Rights Act, August 6, 1965[1]

The Voting Rights Act that Lyndon B. Johnson signed in 1965 was a model of simplicity and transparency, and even though it was clearly a constitutionally unprecedented intrusion into the rights of states and local governments, the justification for such extreme remedies was well understood. That clarity has long since disappeared. By now, the act's provisions are barely comprehensible to all but a small circle of voting rights scholars.

In 1965 only the morally obtuse could fail to understand the degree to which the widespread, deliberate disfranchisement of African Americans in the Jim Crow South threatened the legitimacy of American democratic government. But more than four decades later, African Americans are enfranchised—and maximizing the number of safe black legislative districts, even in jurisdictions with no history of electoral discrimination, has become the central goal of a thoroughly revised statute. What do these districts, which protect minority candidates from white competition, have to do with the Fifteenth Amendment right to vote unimpeded by "race, color, or previous condition of servitude"?

Black enfranchisement turned out to be a much more complicated process than the original Voting Rights Act envisioned, and thus the 1965 act was altered. Unexpected problems arose; perceptions changed; new questions demanded new answers. But while early statutory revisions, made in response to southern efforts to diminish the impact of black enfranchisement, were legitimate, other changes were not. And those changes that were initially on sound footing did not necessarily remain so.

This chapter provides a guide to the basic structure of the Voting Rights Act as it began and evolved.[2] The process of rewriting the original act began almost immediately with a 1969 landmark Supreme Court decision that responded to efforts on the part of Mississippi and other states to alter the method of voting to keep political power in white hands.[3] In the wake of that decision, judges, Congress, and Justice Department attorneys charged with interpreting and enforcing the statute embarked on a series of revisions and interpretations that changed the act in directions that could not have been imagined in 1965. The result, four decades later, is a complex, confusing mess of an answer to a difficult question: What is the definition of racially fair representation in a multiethnic democracy?

The Original Design

In 1965, the Voting Rights Act had one simple purpose: to provide ballots for southern blacks.[4] The extraordinary power the legislation conferred on both courts and the Department of Justice, permitting an unprecedented intrusion of federal authority into local electoral affairs, was meant to deal with an extraordinary problem: continued black disfranchisement ninety-five years after the passage of the Fifteenth Amendment to the Constitution, which protected "the right of citizens of the United States to vote," against denials or abridgments "on account of race, color, or previous condition of servitude."

By 1965, racial attitudes and practices in the South were changing, but much too slowly. An appalling 3 percent of the five million southern blacks of voting age had been registered to vote in 1940; by 1964, the figure for Georgia was 27.4 percent and for South Carolina 37.3 percent.[5] In fact, in every state except Mississippi, white supremacists were losing ground. But they were far from beaten. In 1964, ten years after the Supreme Court exposed the fiction of separate but equal schools and signaled the end of Jim Crow, Florida and Tennessee were the only southern states in which as many as half of all voting-age blacks were registered—and, in many places, resistance seemed to be hardening. Drastic federal action was clearly needed.

The single aim of combating black disfranchisement dictated the entire structure of the statute in 1965. It contained both permanent and temporary provisions, with those that were temporary consisting of radical measures justified by the civil rights crisis. It was expected that the application of overwhelming federal power would force the South to quickly enfranchise its African-American citizens, and that the temporary powers would be allowed to expire five years after their enactment. Protection from disfranchisement on the basis of race or color is a permanent provision of the act, although Congress must periodically renew the sections of the statute that provide for the most aggressive, preemptive federal oversight of all electoral decisions. The distinction between the temporary and permanent provisions of the act is fundamental, but too often forgotten. For instance, when Congress was considering (in 2006) its fourth renewal of the act's temporary provisions, some advocates stirred old fears that blacks could "lose the right to vote once again"—when, in fact, basic Fifteenth Amendment rights were totally secure.[6]

The opening provisions of the Voting Rights Act, sections 2 and 3, are permanent.[7] Section 2 restates in stronger language the promise of the Fifteenth Amendment, while section 3 gives federal courts permanent authority to appoint "examiners" (registrars) or observers where necessary to guarantee Fifteenth or Fourteenth Amendment voting rights. Those federal officers can be sent to any jurisdiction in the nation.[8]

The temporary, emergency provisions of the act made the statute the exceptionally effective instrument for racial change that it became. Section 4 contained a statistical trigger designed to identify the states and counties targeted for the extraordinary federal intervention. No southern state was singled out by name; instead, jurisdictions were "covered" by the act if they met two criteria: the use of a literacy test to determine eligibility to register, and total voter turnout (black and white) below 50 percent in the 1964 presidential election.

The logic of the statistical trigger was clear. Literacy tests were, in fact, constitutional, the Supreme Court had held in 1959, but the framers of the act knew the South was using *fraudulent* tests to stop blacks from registering.[9] Blacks were being tested on such questions as the number of bubbles in a soap bar, or their ability to read the *Beijing Daily*. Endless litigation over which tests were legitimate was time-consuming and often only temporarily effective, at best. Nothing could be easier than for jurisdictions to devise another, equally discriminatory test.

Thus, those who designed the legislation took the well-established relationship between literacy tests and low voter participation in the South and used the carefully chosen 50 percent turnout figure as circumstantial evidence indicating the use of intentionally fraudulent, disfranchising tests. Critics complained that "fair and effective enforcement of the 15th amendment call[ed] for precise identification of offenders, not the indiscriminate scatter-gun technique evidenced in the 50 percent test."[10] But the 50 percent turnout test *was*, in fact, "precise and effective"—it meant that the act covered exactly the states where it was most needed, and no others.

From the inferred presence of egregious and *intentional* Fifteenth Amendment violations in any state that had both a literacy test and low voter turnout, several consequences followed. Literacy tests in the covered jurisdictions—all in the South—were suspended and, at the discretion of the attorney general, federal "examiners" and observers were sent to monitor elections.[11]

In addition, section 5 stopped all "covered" states and counties (those identified by section 4's statistical trigger) from instituting any new voting procedure without prior federal "preclearance."[12] Only changes that were shown to be nondiscriminatory could be approved—that is, "precleared." State and local laws are usually presumed valid until found otherwise by a court. But whenever a covered jurisdiction altered a rule or practice affecting enfranchisement, guilt was presumed. The submitting jurisdiction (the defendant) carried the burden of proving its innocence, which meant proving a negative—the absence of discrimination. It was a constitutionally extraordinary demand. In the context of the time, however, it was clear that only such a punitive, burden-shifting measure had any hope of forcing the South to let blacks vote.

The point of preclearance, then, was to reinforce the suspension of the literacy tests. Section 4 banned such tests in the covered jurisdictions—those southern states identified for emergency intervention. Section 5, by requiring prior approval of every change in the method of election in covered states, made sure the effect of that ban stuck. Anticipating southern resistance, the provision was a prophylactic measure—a means of guarding against new efforts to stop blacks from registering and voting.

Attorney General Nicholas Katzenbach briefly explained the need for such a harsh provision at the U.S. House of Representative hearings prior to the passage of the act. "Our experience in the areas that would be covered by this bill," he said, "has been such as to indicate frequently on the part of state legislatures a desire in a sense to outguess the courts of the United States or even to outguess the Congress of the United States."[13] Southern segregationists weren't expected to surrender without a fight.

But for changes in voting procedure to be rejected, Katzenbach noted, they would have to have the effect of denying the rights guaranteed by the Fifteenth Amendment.[14] Numerous witnesses at the hearings reassured their audience that those rights were expected to be narrowly defined. Thus, Roy Wilkins, executive director of the National Association for the Advancement of Colored People (NAACP), referred to the need to protect the citizen only "from the beginning of the registration process until his vote has been cast and counted."[15] New York representative Jonathan Bingham urged legislation that would reach "every essential activity affecting the vote"—political party meetings, councils, conventions, and referenda, as well as primaries and general elections.[16] But never during the hearings was "every essential activity affecting the vote" defined to include political decisions regarding redistricting, annexations, or the replacement of single-member districts with at-large voting. At the time, no one could imagine the scrutiny to which such changes would be subjected under section 5 in the future.

The Voting Rights Act would not have survived constitutional scrutiny had its scope been greater or its trigger less accurate—had it hit states outside the South and allowed federal intrusion into traditional state prerogatives to set electoral procedure where there was no evidence of appalling Fifteenth Amendment violations. As Chief Justice Earl Warren noted a year later in upholding the constitutionality of the act, the emergency provisions were passed in the context of "unremitting and ingenious defiance of the Constitution."[17] Those special provisions were legitimate only in the context of the time, in other words, and, given their unique design, were expected to sunset in 1970.

Even with the five-year limit, the constitutional doubts of the great liberal justice Hugo Black were not assuaged. The preclearance provision, he said, by providing that some of the States cannot pass State laws or adopt State constitutional amendments without first being compelled to beg federal authorities to approve their policies, so distorts our constitutional structure of government as to render any distinction drawn in the Constitution between State and Federal power almost meaningless.[18]

Justice Black (who was from Alabama) might have had a persuasive point if the South had not come to the argument with such dirty hands. All attempts to secure Fifteenth Amendment rights by more orthodox means had failed. Today, Black's discomfort is worth remembering as we think about the use of federal power—greatly enhanced since 1965—in the context of dramatic racial change in the South. His constitutionally serious point, however, was soon all but forgotten.

The act gave preclearance power to either the District Court for the District of Columbia or the attorney general of the United States. For good reason, it was only in the D.C. District Court that jurisdictions could file for a declaratory judgment that a proposed change in electoral procedure was not discriminatory. Southern lower court judges could not be trusted in 1965. The statute specified that special three-judge panels (composed of two district court judges and one from the U.S. Court of Appeals for the District of Columbia) would hear section 5 cases, with appeals from the court's judgment going directly to the Supreme Court.[19] Alternatively, at the DOJ, the assistant attorney general for civil rights (acting on behalf of the attorney general) was given the authority to make preclearance decisions. In fact, however, career attorneys in the voting section of the Civil Rights Division have been the first to scrutinize changes in voting procedure submitted for review, and they have usually had the first and last word. The political appointees to whom they report have seldom overturned their assessments.

The option of seeking administrative preclearance (DOJ approval) was provided as an alternative to litigation to permit the expeditious handling of submissions. Unexpectedly, however, the use of the D.C. court quickly became the rare exception for two reasons: time and money. It was faster and cheaper to go to the Justice Department, where the process was more collaborative than adversarial. Letters, telephone conversations, and negotiation could replace litigation. But a DOJ decision to approve or object to a proposed change could not be appealed. If preclearance were refused and the state or county wanted to fight on, its only option was to begin anew in the D.C. court—to start the process all over again, with no weight given to the administrative ruling, and with the United States (as defendant) ready and able to mount a vigorous defense.

In any case, seeking preclearance from the D.C. court was, as UCLA law professor Daniel Hays Lowenstein has said, an "utterly impracticable" option when the question was the legitimacy of new districting lines—a frequently submitted change in voting procedure. In the wake of a decennial census, there is no time to spare; elections must go forward. The jurisdiction might end up with a map at odds with its own (often legitimate) priorities, but at least the process of negotiation with the Justice Department was limited to sixty days, after which legislators would know what sort of plan would receive federal approval.[20]

Redistricting is, however, a complex and laborious process, and a plan that is rejected has been a waste of considerable political effort. More important, when the Justice Department interposes an objection, for all intents and purposes it assumes a legislative function normally assigned to the states. Thus, the option to take the fast administrative route has put basic decisions about the structure of elections in the hands of a small number of federal bureaucrats with very limited knowledge of race and politics in particular jurisdictions. Even worse, much of the work of assessing submissions is delegated to unpaid college interns, who do the initial reviews and much of the investigative work. The department allows undergraduate volunteers, who generally still see themselves as soldiers in the war against racism, to substitute their judgment for that of state elected officials, many of whom, by now, are black.[21]

The Emergence of Section 5

In retrospect, it is the inattention to section 5 in the 1965 congressional debates on the proposed act that seems most startling. Section 4, with its ban on literacy tests, along with section 3, which provided for federal registrars where needed, were viewed as the main tools to combat historic disfranchisement. Thus, the Senate committee report failed even to mention preclearance in its summary of the bill's key provisions, and the House report gave it only a cursory and less than illuminating glance. And yet, within five years, it became the statute's central provision.

The new prominence of section 5 was, in part, due to the speed with which southern resistance to black registration collapsed. For more than a decade after *Brown v. Board of Education*, schools in the Deep South remained segregated, but the Voting Rights Act had more immediate results. In Alabama, an estimated 19.3 percent of voting-age blacks were registered as of March 1965; the figure rose to 51.6 percent by September 1967. Mississippi took off from a low point of 6.7 percent; two years later it had the highest percentage of black registered voters (59.8 percent) anywhere in the South.[22] The ban on literacy tests and the availability of federal registrars had worked their magic, leaving government attorneys and civil rights groups free to focus on disfranchisement questions more subtle than access to the polling place.

That shift in focus, however, could not have occurred without a Supreme Court decision that redefined the meaning of voting practices and procedures in the preclearance provision. *Allen v. State Board of Elections*, handed down on March 3, 1969, expanded the reach of section 5 to include devices that "diluted" the impact of the black vote.[23] Until *Allen*, it was assumed that, in the covered states, changes in voting registration procedures, absentee ballot rules, the format of ballots, and other such obvious disfranchising devices would need to be precleared. Basic enfranchisement was the point of the act. But with *Allen*, quite suddenly, the Justice Department acquired the power to review newly instituted at-large voting, switches from elected to appointed offices, and, down the road, redistricting, annexations, and other changes potentially affecting minority voting strength.[24] The decision (on which chapter 2 will dwell at some length) rewrote the legislation, altering its core purpose.

Thus, the Voting Rights Act was structured to deal with one kind of question, but after 1969 quite another kind was raised. Preclearance, a barely noticed provision in 1965, permitted the Justice Department to halt renewed efforts to limit the exercise of basic Fifteenth Amendment rights, allowing swift administrative relief for obvious constitutional violations.[25] Before 1969, attorneys in the Civil Rights Division were expected to confront a straightforward question: Would the proposed change in voting procedure keep blacks from the polls? *Allen*, however, opened the door to a much broader inquiry: Had the method of election been restructured to weaken black power?

The decision led in time to denials of preclearance on the ground that "better" districting plans or other methods of voting could have been adopted to ensure racial representation that was more nearly proportional to the black population. A law initially designed simply to open the doors of electoral opportunity was transformed into an effort to protect minorities from any measure that might weaken their electoral strength—and then into one requiring proactive efforts to maximize their political power. At the time *Allen* was decided, however, the issue was simply southern racist efforts to reduce the power of newly enfranchised black voters.

The decision consolidated four cases, the most important of which involved a 1966 amendment to Mississippi law that allowed counties to replace single-member districts (some of which would have been majority-black) with at-large voting in the election of country supervisors.

In expanding the list of potentially disfranchising devices to include countywide voting, the Court did not reinvent the meaning of electoral equality. Already in 1964, in *Reynolds v. Sims*, it had held that the power to elect representatives must be evenly distributed among voters—one person, one vote.[26] Districts with unequal population numbers give voters unequal electoral power.[27] In *Allen* the Court adopted—in the context of minority voting rights—the concern with the *weight* of the individual ballots cast that was at the heart of *Reynolds* and other Fourteenth Amendment equal-population decisions.

"Each and every citizen has an inalienable right to full and effective participation. . . an equally effective voice," the majority contended in *Reynolds*.[28] But, as Justice John Marshall Harlan pointed out, equally populated districts did not necessarily result in equal representation. Beyond the individual were interest groups, which were the building blocks of political life—a dimension that mathematical parity overlooked.[29] This was the dimension that the Court began to explore in *Allen*, and that Congress, lower courts, and the Justice Department subsequently took up.

There is a further, related point, to which the introduction has already alluded. Even without racist efforts in Mississippi and elsewhere to curtail the impact of the Voting Rights Act, before long the Court would surely have added its voice to that of civil rights activists who were skeptical that votes alone could shake the pillars of the southern status quo. Those who went to Mississippi in the summer of 1964 to participate in a dangerous voter registration drive saw themselves as working toward a much larger goal: true racial equality. In much of the South, black enfranchisement would not, by itself, bring black electoral power. And yet, holding public office came to be viewed as critical to the larger aim: ending, once and for all, white supremacy.

This conviction had a clear impact on the high Court's decision in *Allen*, which referred to changes in the method of election that might "nullify" the ability of black voters "to elect the candidate of their choice just as would prohibiting some of them from voting."[30] Here is the start of that slippery slope to which the introduction referred. The Court had taken a big step beyond stopping efforts to pull blacks back from gains they had made with the passage of the Voting Rights Act—gains that included the likely election of black candidates in naturally occurring majority-black, single-member districts. After *Allen*, protection from attempts to deprive blacks of the electoral power that enfranchisement promised was no longer the entire point of preclearance. Minority voters, the Court implied, had a right to elect the candidates of their choice. Those candidates were elected to what were, in effect, reserved legislative seats. But in 1969 in the South, the alternative was a perpetuation of political power as a white entitlement. As I argued in the introduction, safe black and Hispanic seats were a remedy demanded by the wrongs of the time.

The Amendments of 1970

Allen was followed within just a few months by congressional hearings on the reauthorization of the special temporary provisions of the Voting Rights Act—too quickly for the decision's import to have registered on participants in those proceedings. And, indeed, compared to the amendments of 1975 and 1982, the 1970 revisions were superficially minor—but only superficially.

Those first amendments extended the emergency provisions for another five years, banned literacy tests *nationwide* during that period, and expanded coverage to include states and counties that had previously employed such tests and had had a voter turnout in the 1968 presidential election of less than 50 percent.[31] Thus, every state lost its traditional freedom to set literacy qualifications for voting—not just those in the South, with its history of Fifteenth Amendment violations. The use of the 1968 turnout figures to determine which jurisdictions were subject to preclearance also extended the geographical reach of federal authority, giving the act a more national cast. Jurisdictions covered in 1965 (using voter participation figures for 1964) were still covered, but additional counties caught by the revised trigger joined them.

In 1965, the authors of the Voting Rights Act knew which states they wanted to cover, and they designed a statistical test to target them precisely. Applying the benchmark of 50 percent turnout to the 1968 figures had a haphazard result, however. In the presidential contest between Richard M. Nixon and Hubert Humphrey, turnout had been low across the country, and counties in which it had dropped below the 50 percent mark were in such disparate states as Wyoming, Arizona, California, and Massachusetts, none of which had a history of black disfranchisement. While all had made eligibility to register dependent on passing a literacy test, outside the South these tests were not instituted to keep blacks from the polls. Moreover, literacy tests were far more discriminatory in the South because they were given to citizens who had been educated in segregated school systems that provided clearly inadequate educational opportunities.

Thus, under the revised act, three counties in New York City were arbitrarily covered, even though black New Yorkers had been freely voting since the enactment of the Fifteenth Amendment in 1870, and for fifty years had held municipal offices. The city had not changed; the doors of political opportunity had not suddenly been closed to minority voters. But in the 1968 presidential election, reflecting the national trend, a few more residents than before had stayed home.

In 1965, the statistical trigger for section 5 coverage was crafted to catch only those states known to have *intentionally* barred blacks from the polls. It was reasonable to assume that, deprived of the opportunity to use literacy tests for purposes of disfranchisement, they would deliberately search for other means to accomplish that same end; hence, the demand that suspect states institute no voting practice or procedure without prior federal approval, requiring the jurisdiction to prove itself above suspicion. But there was no cause to distrust those places that were brought under coverage in 1970, all of which were outside the South and none of which had a record of official hostility to black political participation. In 1969, the Supreme Court had read the existing statutory language in an unanticipated way, but judicial decisions are open to further modification. The alteration of the statute itself in 1970 was effectively written in stone; Congress was highly unlikely to rethink the change. The beautiful design of 1965 had lost its elegance.

Amended Again in 1975

Allen stopped covered states from substituting at-large voting for single-member districting plans that would have given newly enfranchised African Americans seats on county and other governing bodies. County- or citywide voting was an old and legitimate means of conducting elections, but Mississippi and other southern states were showing their racist colors in their sudden enthusiasm for such voting. Their racially motivated action showed that literacy tests and racist registrars were not the only barriers to black political equality that the statute had to combat. Hence, the decision in *Allen*.

That case, however, combined with the 1970 amendments, was the beginning of radical statutory change, and once the process started, the propriety of further change—whether by Congress, the courts, or the Department of Justice—became increasingly hard to judge. The acquired legitimacy of one change obscured the questionable legitimacy of another. Once the Supreme Court had blurred the distinction between electoral arrangements that stopped blacks from voting and those that could "nullify" their ability "to elect the candidate of their choice," it was inevitable that federal authorities would, in time, insist on districting maps drawn to maximize black officeholding. And once minorities in three New York boroughs qualified for protection originally intended for vulnerable blacks in the South, there was no logical place to stop.

Thus, in 1972, the Department of Justice used its preclearance power to object to a Brooklyn districting plan that contained a state senate district whose population was an allegedly insufficient 61 percent black. The DOJ decided that the district had to be 65 percent African American for it to be considered "safe"—certain to elect a black representative.[32] (DOJ administrators arrived at the 65 percent mark in the belief that compensating for low black turnout was a federal obligation.) And yet why was an absolutely secure black legislative seat in a northern state in which blacks had long been political players an entitlement? And, if section 5 demanded districts that were 65 percent black in Brooklyn, what about the adjacent borough of Queens, which was not covered?

In 1975, when the emergency provisions were again up for renewal, Congress confronted another variation of the why-not-Queens question: If the act applied to blacks (never specifically named but clearly the sole concern in 1965), then why not to Hispanics and other minority groups, also said to suffer from discrimination? And if section 5 covered Georgia, then why not Texas, with its high concentration of Mexican-Americans? In 1975, that provision was rewritten to extend federal preclearance power to Texas, Arizona, and Alaska in their entirety and to scattered counties in South Dakota, Michigan, Florida, and California.

This further extension of the geographical reach of section 5 was accomplished by changing both elements in the formula for coverage. Turnout in the 1972 presidential election was added to the trigger based on that of 1964 and 1968; low participation levels in any one of those three elections made the state or county racially suspect and changes in its method of voting subject to federal preclearance. In addition, the literacy test acquired a new definition. The traditional test had been banned in 1970, and that ban was made permanent in 1975—but it did not apply to states such as Texas, for instance, which had never screened registrants for their ability to read. Texas did, however, provide ballots (and related literature) printed only in English, and the 1975 amendments labeled that English-only election material as a "literacy test," no different from the barriers to black political participation erected in the Jim Crow South.

States and counties that had been covered by the 1965 statistical trigger (and its updated version in 1970) remained subject to federal preclearance. The 1975 amendments expanded the list of covered jurisdictions to include those in which more than 5 percent of the voting-age citizenry were members of a single "language-minority" group and registrants were expected to read English in casting ballots. Only four groups qualified as "language minorities": Asian Americans, American Indians, persons of Spanish heritage, and Alaskan

Natives. A California county with a 7 percent Hispanic population and elections in English, therefore, was thenceforth required to submit for federal review municipal annexations, redistricting, and all other changes in electoral procedure. The county would conduct its electoral affairs under a cloud of suspicion, carrying the burden of proof to demonstrate an absence of discrimination, even though it had never deliberately disfranchised minority voters.

Equating fraudulent southern tests that had barred blacks from the polls with English-only election materials was indefensible. Moreover, if English-only ballots were "disfranchising," mandating the provision of bilingual election materials should have solved the problem.[33] The 1965 act had permitted an inference of *intentional* disfranchisement from the combination of literacy tests and low levels of voter participation. Now, however, the act permitted a similar inference where voting fell short of the 50 percent mark and where no bilingual ballots were provided for a language minority exceeding 5 percent of a state's or county's population.

An Imaginative Solution to a Problem

The 1975 amendments contorted beyond recognition the formula for section 5 coverage. But the redefinition of literacy tests was the imaginative solution to a particular problem: how to bring the benefits of preclearance to Texas. The Justice Department had been using the preclearance provision to insist that covered jurisdictions employ methods of election that maximized black officeholding. The Mexican-American Legal Defense and Education Fund (MALDEF) wanted the same extraordinary privilege for its constituents— a structural advantage in their efforts to elect the candidates of their choice.

The fact that literacy tests, the chief means used to disfranchise blacks in the South, had never been employed in Texas was only one of several difficulties MALDEF faced in bringing the state under the aegis of the act's special provisions. The Fifteenth Amendment protected citizens against denial or abridgment of the right to vote only on account of "race or color." The 1965 statute had given life to the clear constitutional command that the franchise was not to be restricted by virtue of the irrelevant, ascribed characteristic of race. But (with the single exception of 1930) the Census Bureau had historically classified Mexican Americans as white, reflecting the way in which a substantial number of Hispanics thought of themselves. To stretch Fifteenth Amendment rights to cover groups that had not been protected by the amendment was, well, a stretch—hence, the new category that avoided any reference to race: "language minorities." The four designated groups had Fourteenth Amendment (equal protection) rights, rather than Fifteenth Amendment voting rights.

Changing the definition of a literacy test, inventing a minority group whose members suffered from "language" discrimination, and enlarging the base of the statute to include the Fourteenth Amendment—all of these solved technical problems created by the desire to extend the benefits of preclearance to Hispanics in Texas and elsewhere. But they left unanswered a fundamental question: Was it legitimate to equate the history of Hispanics with that of southern blacks prior to 1965?

Prior to the passage of the Voting Rights Act, the overwhelming majority of blacks in the Deep South could not register and vote. It is impossible to argue that Hispanics had suffered equivalent disfranchisement. As a representative of MALDEF later admitted, "We were able to produce those horror stories" needed to suggest obstacles to voting. "But," he went on, "not many of them. . . . We really did it by the skin of our teeth."[34] Those who wrote the 1965 legislation had had an abundance of evidence of widespread disfranchisement throughout the Deep South—the extensive litigation experience of the Justice Department. There was no matching record of suits against Texas registrars and other officials.[35] Even the assistant attorney general for civil rights, J. Stanley Pottinger, was forced to acknowledge that the Justice Department had "concluded that the evidence does not require expansion [of coverage] based on the record currently before us. In other words, that record is not compelling."[36]

In 1965, the authors of the Voting Rights Act feared that merely suspending literacy tests might not be enough to ensure black enfranchisement. Southern states had a record of evading federal desegregation efforts with ingenious ploys; hence, the preclearance requirement was created as a prophylactic measure—a means to stop mischief before it started. But it was precisely the historical commitment of these states to keeping blacks from the polls that made section 5 necessary. No equivalent discriminatory commitment had been shown to lie behind the absence of bilingual election materials in the Southwest, California, or elsewhere.

Nevertheless, a majority on the House Judiciary Committee decided that the case for extending protection to "language minorities" was "overwhelming," a judgment in which their Senate colleagues concurred.[37] Having weighed the evidence before it, the Senate report found a "systematic pattern of voting discrimination and exclusion."[38]

Buried in the House report, however, was the real point. The "central problem documented," it said, "is that of dilution of the vote—arrangements by which the votes of minority electors are made to count less than the votes of the majority."[39]

"Are made to count less": In that deliberately woolly language, the implication was clear. Whites had intentionally devised methods of election—such as districts in which voting was at large rather than in wards—that wasted Hispanic votes. Hispanic ballots fully counted only if they were cast within majority-minority districts that were designed to elect members of the group. The stated rationale for the statutory revision—protection against "language" discrimination—was never serious and thus quickly ignored.

By 1975, when the Hispanic question was debated, a "systematic pattern of . . . exclusion" and "dilution of the vote" had become one and the same. "Beatings and gerrymanderings," California senator John V. Tunney said, both "keep people from registering and voting."[40] He was not alone in equating the evils of blacks barred from the polls with the harm arising from casting ballots in majority-white districts. Civil rights attorney Frank Parker likened the results of election-related violence in Mississippi in 1964 to those that flowed from the retention of an at-large electoral system in the state capital ten years later.[41] And, looking back to the bloody days of Selma, Alabama, Arthur Flemming of the U.S. Commission on Civil Rights saw disfranchisement in 1965 as only more "spectacular" than that which was still occurring a decade later.[42]

Beneath the hyperbolic rhetoric lay a partial truth that clearly applied to blacks, although much less plainly to Hispanics. Without continuing protection against the substitution of at-large voting for single-member districts (the action that prompted the Supreme Court's decision in *Allen*), the value of the vote for blacks could be severely diminished. Moreover, the disproportionately low number of southern blacks in office was clearly a holdover from the era of total black exclusion.

But the Mexican-American experience was not the same, as the congressional hearings revealed. Factors other than racism played a significant role in keeping Mexican-American officeholding disproportionately low.[43] Nevertheless, Democrats on the committees handling the revision of the statute's temporary provisions were committed to passing the bill—whatever the record showed—long before any witnesses testified. They were determined to give courts and Justice Department attorneys the power to attack at-large voting, districting plans, and other aspects of the electoral environment with the same extraordinary force they had used against outright denials of the right to vote, whenever their use might adversely affect the electoral prospects of Hispanic candidates, as well as those who were black.

The advocates of renewal and amendment in 1975 believed that the right to vote included the right to representation; that minority representation could be measured by the number of minority officeholders; that justice demanded a national commitment to protecting black candidates from white competition; and that black ballots were meaningless in the absence of black electoral success. Moreover, they viewed these principles as applying to Hispanics and other "language-minority" groups as well. And, with a minimum of debate, Congress went along.

Section 2 Rewritten

The 1975 amendments renewed the life of section 5 for seven years and extended its geographical reach to Texas, Arizona, Alaska, and scattered counties in California and elsewhere. But the point of preclearance was no longer to provide prophylactic protection against either new efforts to stop blacks from voting or racist manipulations of the method of voting to maintain white political power. Section 5 had become a means by which the Justice Department and federal courts could insist on single-member districts drawn to reserve legislative seats for blacks and Hispanics. The renewed temporary provisions of the act were extended for seven, rather than five, years so they would not expire until after the redistricting following the 1980 census—making that redistricting subject to federal approval.

In making the case for amending the law to provide preclearance protection for "language-minority" voters, witnesses at the hearings confused two issues: the widespread, well-established use of at-large elections in Texas, on the one hand, and annexations, redistricting, and newly introduced at-large voting, on the other. "The at-large structure, with accompanying variations of the majority run-off numbered place system, is used extensively among the 40 largest cities in Texas. And under state statute, the countless school districts in Texas elect at-large," the House Judiciary Committee reported in May 1975.[44] As those in Congress surely knew, however, such voting would rarely be vulnerable to attack under the preclearance provision, which was concerned solely with *changes* in electoral arrangements whose purpose or effect suggested a desire to disfranchise blacks anew—to circumvent the enfranchisement the act otherwise ensured. The longstanding at-large systems that were so familiar in Texas could only be challenged in constitutional suits in which plaintiffs claimed that such methods of voting denied their right to "an equally effective voice."[45]

A series of such constitutional suits were, in fact, decided in the 1970s. They asked: Did minorities defined by race or ethnicity have equal electoral power when, for instance, they cast their ballots in multimember districts in which whites were the majority? Did it matter whether Hispanics in a particular setting had, as one decision put it, a history of discrimination that "at times touched" on electoral participation?[46] Were alleged cultural barriers important in assessing voting rights violations?[47] The Supreme Court was not willing to declare all such districts unconstitutional, and yet there were no obvious criteria by which to judge the legitimacy of a challenged practice—a subject to which I will return in chapter 3. Incoherent decisions were the consequence.

That constitutional incoherence might have had little impact on the larger picture of minority voting rights enforcement had not section 2—a previously dormant preamble to the statute—been rewritten in 1982. Two years earlier, the entire line of Fourteenth Amendment cases decided in the 1970s had come to an end with the Supreme Court's decision in *City of Mobile v. Bolden*, which held that the equal protection clause required the same showing of discriminatory intent in voting rights cases as it had in employment, school segregation, and other contexts.[48] But in 1982, in amending section 2, Congress rescued from the trash those constitutional standards that *Bolden* had, in effect, discarded, and wrote them into the statute itself. Plaintiffs in Fourteenth Amendment cases—including those involving alleged electoral inequality between minorities and whites—could not prevail without evidence of discriminatory purpose. But the 1982 amendment to section 2 gave them the right to challenge methods of voting on the basis of a "results" test—the same test, voting rights advocates argued, that had governed constitutional decisions prior to 1980 and thus already had the Court's imprimatur.

No method of voting, the new section 2 read, shall be "imposed or applied . . . in a manner which results in a denial or abridgement of the right . . . to vote on account of race or color." A violation is established if, "based on the totality of circumstances," it is shown that members of minority groups "have less opportunity than other members of the electorate to participate in the political process and to elect representatives of their choice."[49]

The language was a civil rights lawyer's dream: a disparate impact test for discrimination wrapped in the rhetoric of opportunity. Who can possibly support policies that compromise opportunity? But a legitimate method of election might nevertheless produce disproportionately low minority office-holding in some cases. Public policy—the Social Security Act, for instance—often has a statistically disproportionate impact on certain groups, for reasons unrelated to racism. Nevertheless, civil rights advocates had long argued that impact, not intent, should be the standard for discrimination. A clever rewriting of section 2, making disparate racial result and unequal opportunity one and the same, gave them what they wanted.[50]

As chapter 3 will make clear, the amendment of section 2 turned out to be more significant than any previous statutory change. Section 5 directed federal authorities to look at the "effect" of electoral changes on the weight of black ballots, but (until the amendments of 1970 and 1975) only in jurisdictions already known to have been engaged in persistent, systematic Fifteenth Amendment violations. In such communities—historically committed to disfranchisement—the discriminatory impact of a new districting scheme was likely to indicate invidious purpose.

Unlike section 5, the new section 2 enabled plaintiffs to challenge long-standing methods of voting—at-large voting, for instance, that dated back to the good-government reforms of the Progressive Era—on the grounds that they had a discriminatory result, regardless of intent.[51] Moreover, the section 2 results test applied nationwide, and thus to places in which minorities had never been disfranchised and had long held public office. That power to challenge voting methods was constrained only by the fact that—again, in contrast to the preclearance provision—jurisdictions were presumed innocent until proved guilty, and thus a method of voting could be implemented without prior federal approval. In addition, the burden of proof was on the plaintiffs, who could bring suit in any local federal district court.

The amended section 2 is a permanent powerhouse that has been used since its passage in 1982 essentially to eliminate almost all at-large voting and multimember districts in the nation, even though neither method of election is intrinsically incompatible with democratic government. Voting rights advocates were right that, where racism was rampant and whites were in the majority, blacks were likely to be shut out of electoral office unless single-member districts were drawn to protect their candidates. But the crucial distinction between racist and nonracist localities—heavily stressed in the hearings on the passage of the amendment—was soon lost.

As Justice Sandra Day O'Connor pointed out, the new statutory language, which promised minorities an equal opportunity "to elect representatives of their choice" could only mean one thing: "a right to usual, roughly proportional representation on the part of sizable, compact, cohesive minority groups."[52] That right was not confined, it should be clear, to the South; section 2 reached every jurisdiction in which districting maps favorable to minority candidates could be drawn. Moreover, if the members of a minority group were not residentially concentrated, districts could be drastically gerrymandered to create majority-minority constituencies.

Combating Southern Racism: The Forgotten Goal

Blacks and Hispanics had acquired a right to reserved legislative seats, as both sections 2 and 5 had come to be understood in the 1970s. Safe seats ensure direct representation for blacks and Hispanics—that is, representation by a member of the group. I argued in the introduction that the presence of blacks on school boards, county councils, in state legislatures, and in Congress was both symbolically and substantively important in the South as long as blacks were still political outsiders. But the North was not the South (another distinction that was forgotten), and while white bloc voting against black candidates could be found in every region, the bar for proving racial exclusion in section 2 cases should have been higher than it turned out to be.

The highly questionable definition of white bloc voting most commonly used—whites and blacks consistently preferring different candidates—meant that the Justice Department and courts could find it wherever black candidates ran campaigns that were unlikely to attract a majority of whites. By definition, then, all districts in which the majority of voters were Republican were racially polarized. Thus, it became the exceptional section 5 submission or section 2 case in which there was no finding of suspected or real electoral discrimination. If blacks and whites voted differently, and that difference usually defeated the minority group's preferred candidates, the failure to draw majority-minority districts (where possible) was a statutory violation. This was the logic that made proportional representation a right. But while race-based districts did bring black faces into public office, they also carried high costs, I suggested in the introduction; by now, they may be impeding the further integration of American politics. This is a subject to which I will return.

The focus on remedies for racism that was lost in the enforcement of section 2 disappeared with the first extension and amendment of section 5 in 1970, as well. In theory, a concern with remedies for racism animated every provision of the Voting Rights Act. Prior to 1965, Deep South racism disfranchised blacks. Section 5 was designed to stop racist changes in voting before they were implemented. But how did the amendments to that provision square with the rest of the act?

How did banning literacy tests nationwide further the aim of combating racism? Outside of the South, their use was not motivated by racial animus. And why rest preclearance coverage on turnout data from the 1968 presidential election, in addition to those from 1964? In 1965, those who wrote the statute knew which states they wanted to cover and designed the section 4 statistical test to single them out. An important element in that test was a jurisdiction's use of a literacy test, which correlated perfectly with voter turnout below 50 percent—the other element. The 1965 trigger captured precisely the states that genuinely needed federal supervision; subsequent revisions to the act lost that logic and precision.

Using the 1968 voter participation figures, for instance, meant that three boroughs in New York City fell under the coverage of section 5. Those boroughs had been using a literacy test, but not one that was fraudulent or ever used to keep blacks from the polls. Even the *New York Times* objected strongly to the imposition of preclearance on the city. As the mayor pointed out, "the need in New York [was] for educative and organizational efforts" to get out the vote; there was no discrimination at the polls.[53] The city did not regard its literacy tests as discriminatory; in its view, the polls were open, and blacks did not show up in high numbers. New York representative Emanuel Celler, a staunch liberal, compared the attack on literacy tests in his and other northern states to "trying to stem a flood in Mississippi by building a dam in Idaho or Wyoming."[54]

The use of turnout figures for 1972 and the redefinition of a literacy test in the 1975 revision of sections 4 and 5 was another giant step away from combating racist exclusion from political participation—the sole aim of the 1965 act. The experience of Hispanics in Texas was not analogous to that of blacks in the Jim Crow South, and the state had never employed a literacy test to stop "unwanted" voters from registering.

The Voting Rights Act gave federal authorities overwhelming power to intrude into state and local electoral affairs; that power was constitutional only in the context of a long history of intentional Fifteenth Amendment violations. The Supreme Court's 1969 decision in *Allen* clearly met the constitutional test. But subsequent amendments to the trigger (section 4) and to section 5 (preclearance) did not.

The section 4 trigger has not been updated since 1975. Section 5 coverage still depends on the turnout figures for 1972—one of numerous arbitrary elements now built into the statute. But section 5 was renewed and amended again in 2006, extending its life to 2031. Thus, the emergency of black disfranchisement is now treated as a near-permanent condition, despite decades of extraordinary racial progress; moreover, that extended emergency is assumed to apply equally to Hispanics. If section 5 expires as currently scheduled, it will have been in place for sixty-one years, maintaining close federal oversight over all districting decisions, as well as polling place relocations and other election-related changes.

Preclearance has come to be used to protect white, as well as black, Democrats. Whether preclearance remains constitutional is a question before the Supreme Court as I write. The answer will not only profoundly affect the prospects for further political integration, but also the partisan landscape. This is another topic to which I will return.

2

Interpreting Section 5:
The Mess the Courts Have Made

Never before or since has a state or local jurisdiction needed permission from the federal government to put its own laws into effect.

—Richard L. Hasen, professor of law, Loyola Law School[1]

Section 5's preclearance provision started life as an extraordinary, although minor, element of the Voting Rights Act. As the previous chapter noted, it was barely mentioned in the congressional hearings that preceded passage of the statute in 1965. But a decade later it was declared to be, as the chairman of the U.S. Commission on Civil Rights said, "the centerpiece of the statute."[2] Civil rights attorney Frank Parker thought it was "possibly . . . the most effective provision ever enacted by Congress for blocking and deterring racial discrimination affecting the right to vote."[3]

Parker's statement was an eloquent tribute to the success of the act. Ten years earlier, most southern blacks could not even register to vote. But it was section 4, banning literacy tests where their use was suspect, that had solved the primary problem. By 1971–72, the difference between black and white registration rates in the South was so extraordinarily small that, three years later, the assistant attorney general for civil rights in the Department of Justice could assure members of Congress that "enforcement of §5 is the highest priority of the Voting Section."[4] His staff could concentrate on reviewing submissions for preclearance because basic access to the ballot had so rapidly and substantially become a problem of the past.

Congress, the courts, and (through its far-reaching interpretations of the act) the Department of Justice have all amended the Voting Rights Act. And they continue to do so, with Congress having altered the statute as recently as 2006 and, as I write, the Supreme Court is expected soon to decide on the constitutionality of section 5. Both the congressional action and the Court's rulings will change Justice Department enforcement, as well.

Four decades after its passage, section 5 is not only out of date; it is increasingly an unjustified intrusion on electoral decisions that are best made by states and localities unless an emergency dictates otherwise. Political bargaining over districting maps is integral to self-government. The point is not just theoretical. To proceed expeditiously toward elections, redistricting committees often need to turn the drawing of legislative maps over to federal bureaucrats remote from the immediate scene. And yet only local and state actors know race and politics in their jurisdictions and can properly weigh competing considerations and interests. Moreover, that bargaining determines the partisan balance on legislative bodies, large and small, and both Republicans and Democrats have viewed preclearance as a means to advance party ends. And within particular districts, who runs and who wins are often very much determined by the precise configuration of the lines. Thus, indirectly, preclearance decisions determine public policies at every level of government.

The problem of state and local authorities being at the mercy of federal power in exercising one of their core functions has been compounded by the conflicting and often murky legal standards that govern the enforcement of section 5. The standards governing municipal annexations (a voting change) simply make no sense. With respect to districting decisions, no covered jurisdiction can know with certainty what is permissible. As Justice Sandra Day O'Connor, writing for a majority of the Court in a 2003 section 5 decision, wistfully noted: "The ability of minority voters to elect a candidate of their choice is important but often complex in practice to determine."[5]

As the previous chapter noted, only rarely are changes in electoral procedure submitted to the D.C. District Court, from which appeals go directly to the Supreme Court. In theory, at least, the Justice Department is a surrogate court; the legal standards articulated in judicial opinions are supposed to determine administrative decisions. The reality is quite different, but that is the subject of chapter 4. Here, I focus solely on the cases in which jurisdictions sought from the judiciary a declaratory judgment that a new method of election was free of discrimination—the cases whose outcomes should have determined all Justice Department rulings.

Allen v. State Board of Elections

Section 5's preclearance provision requires federal approval of any "voting qualification or prerequisite to voting, or standard, practice, or procedure with respect to voting different from that in force or effect on November 1, 1964." Changes in election procedures after that date were eligible for preclearance only if they did "not have the purpose and [would] not have the effect of denying or abridging the right to vote on account of race or color."

Originally, that language seemed quite straightforward, as chapter 1 noted. It provided protection from discrimination at the ballot box. For example, New York congressman Jonathan Bingham, testifying at the 1965 House hearings on the bill, urged legislation that would reach "every essential activity affecting the vote"—political party meetings, councils, conventions, and referenda, as well as primaries and general elections.[6] There was clearly no expectation that this list would be expanded to include redistricting, annexations, or changes to at-large voting. At the time, no one could have imagined the scrutiny to which such changes would be subjected under section 5 after *Allen*.

Allen, decided in 1969, involved amendments to state laws, replacing single-member districts with countywide voting in the election of local supervisors (the officials known as commissioners in other states). The revised laws were clearly intended to stop blacks from being elected to local office from majority-black constituencies. Where whites were a majority of voters in a county as a whole, at-large voting ensured the election of the candidates they preferred. The question was, were such amendments to laws in Mississippi and elsewhere voting "practices" or "procedures" and, as such, subject to the preclearance requirement of section 5? Faced with such a clear attempt to prevent blacks from exercising their newfound political power, the Court felt compelled to agree that they were.

"The Voting Rights Act was aimed at the subtle, as well as the obvious, state regulations which would have the effect of denying citizens their right to vote because of race," Chief Justice Warren wrote for the Court.[7] The historical record suggested otherwise, but the Court was inclined to see the act's powers in expansive terms. In the 1965 hearings the assistant attorney general for civil rights had said unequivocally, "The problem that the bill was aimed at was the problem of registration."[8] In Warren's view, however, other testimony at the hearings was more important. "There are an awful lot of things that could be started for purposes of evading the 15th amendment if there is a desire to do so," the attorney general had stated.[9] The reference to an "awful lot of things," the chief justice argued, was incompatible with a narrow definition of voting practices and procedures. It was clear, he went on, "that the right to vote can be affected by a *dilution* of voting power as well as by an absolute prohibition on casting a ballot."[10]

A majority-white county that switches from single-member districts, one or more of which are majority-black, to countywide elections has diluted black voting power. The point could have been put more simply: In Mississippi in 1969, such a switch meant no blacks would be elected to the county board of supervisors, and no elected white was likely to represent the interests of black voters.

Chief Justice Warren's reading of legislative history showed considerable ingenuity; the congressional record of hearings betrayed no discernible concern with changes that affected the *weight* of the ballots cast, rather than mere access to the ballot itself. And yet, Warren's central point was right—in the context of that time and place. The entire statute was built on distrust of the South—distrust that was well earned. Every voting initiative in Mississippi (the state with under 7 percent of voting-age blacks registered in 1964) was rightly viewed with the deepest suspicion. Moreover, the state had tried to deny enfranchised African Americans the political power they would have in counties that elected supervisors from single-member districts. In so doing, it had clearly violated the spirit of section 5, included in the statute to guard against racist mischief.

Nonetheless, *Allen* was a radical decision. The Voting Rights Act was written to enforce basic Fifteenth Amendment rights. After 1969, those who enforced it were compelled to struggle with theoretical political questions. As Justice Clarence Thomas later wrote, the Court had "converted the Act into a device for regulating, rationing, and apportioning political power among racial and ethnic groups." It had read the law, he went on, "essentially as a grant of authority to the federal judiciary to develop theories on basic principles of representative government."[11]

In an eloquent opinion that concurred in part and dissented in part, Justice Harlan in *Allen* argued that section 5 could only be interpreted to reach Mississippi's blatantly biased behavior if sections 4 and 5 were viewed as independent provisions. Enfranchisement, the majority opinion implied, had one meaning in one section, another in the other. Yet the two were inextricably linked by the fact that section 4 contained the statistical formula that determined section 5 coverage: Where turnout in the presidential election of 1964 was below 50 percent, it banned literacy tests and similar qualifications that kept blacks from the polls. That was section 4 in its entirety; it did not bar procedures that "diluted" the black vote. Yet after *Allen*, section 5 permitted federal authorities to prohibit the introduction of new methods of voting (such as countywide elections), even though those same methods were not considered disfranchising by the definition contained in section 4.

The two provisions, Justice Harlan wrote, were "clearly designed to march in lock-step." The purpose of preclearance (section 5) was not "to implement new substantive policies but . . . to assure the effectiveness of the dramatic step that Congress had taken in § 4." The purpose of section 4 was to enforce Fifteenth Amendment rights; section 5 reinforced those enfranchising steps. Enforcement and reinforcement were the clear, inseparable goals of the two interlocked provisions. Thus, when section 4 expired (in 1970, according to the original statute), its ban on literacy tests would be lifted, and the protection provided by section 5 would also end. "As soon as a State regains the right to apply a literacy test or similar 'device' under § 4, it also escapes the commands of § 5," declared Harlan.[12]

His basic point was incontrovertible: As a result of *Allen*, these two provisions, envisioned as inseparable, were now separated by distinct definitions of enfranchisement. Moreover, implicitly section 5 made no distinction between electoral changes that had a discriminatory "purpose" and those that had an unacceptable "effect." In the southern context in 1965, new methods of voting that disfranchised black voters, it was fair to assume, were instituted with that purpose in mind. But in expanding the list of election-related changes to include at-large voting, districting, the format of ballots, rules governing special-election dates, referenda requirements, and the like, *Allen* turned intent and effect into separate questions.

Municipal annexations illustrate particularly well the new separation between intent and effect. If annexations added proportionally more whites to a city, they diminished black electoral power, and, thus, by 1971 they were considered changes in the method of voting, requiring preclearance.[13] Most boundary changes, however, are driven by a desire to expand the municipal tax base, not by racial animus. The effect of an annexation, in other words, provided no evidence as to its intent. Treating the enlargement of a city as a voting change was an important change. Once impact alone constituted evidence of discrimination, then the likelihood of disproportionately low minority officeholding as a consequence of a voting change could, in itself, condemn it. It was the big step toward assuming that only proportional racial representation is racially fair—and, having taken that step, there was no going back.[14]

In districting cases, as this chapter will make clear, the Supreme Court refused to make proportional legislative seats the measure of racial equity. But the annexation cases were quite a different story. Moreover, as chapter 4 will argue, the D.C. District Court was far more receptive to the idea, and so was the Justice Department.

Disparate impact was an especially troubling concept in the context of section 5, since merely *suspected* discriminatory effect condemned a voting change. If a polling place change arguably might have an impact on black turnout, or an annexation of almost empty territory might attract an influx of white residents (changing the racial balance in the city), then a section 5 objection could be lodged.

But—again, in the context of the time and place—the *Allen* decision was on solid ground. It squared with section 5, as originally conceived, as later disparate impact decisions would not. Mississippi had deliberately tried to prevent the transfer of political power from whites to blacks after the 1965 statute was passed. The state's intention was clear, even if the decision was framed in discriminatory impact terms. Within a very few years, in annexation cases, the reasoning in *Allen* would turn into an argument for racial balance on legislative bodies and, thus, for single-member districts designed to create quotas for blacks and Hispanics. It would also affect the courts' interpretation of section 2. But in 1969, the Court was focused narrowly on the attempt to undermine voting rights in the most racist of all racist states.

Discrimination Redefined

Ostensibly, *Allen* only involved the question of coverage—what kind of changes qualified as alterations in voting "practice or procedure." But, in fact, it also posed a new problem: how to identify those situations in which the method of voting had unacceptably diluted the voting power of blacks.

After *Allen*, a few cases addressed coverage issues, but most section 5 decisions struggled with defining discrimination for preclearance purposes.[15] The purpose of preclearance, Justice Harlan had argued in his *Allen* dissent, was not "to implement new substantive policies."[16] In fact, however, nothing short of a substantive policy would answer the questions posed by annexations, redistricting, and other proposed changes submitted for federal review after 1969.

Federal authorities could not simply veto new districting lines without suggesting what sort of map might be approved. If the D.C. District Court or the attorney general objected to the plan, the jurisdiction did not have the option of reinstating the old districts; over the decade they would undoubtedly have become malapportioned, violating the one-person, one-vote mandate. A new plan was needed; and yet, without a definition of racial equity, how could a jurisdiction redraw the lines, confident that federal authorities would not suspect possible discrimination in some form or another—when mere suspicion was sufficient to condemn a plan?

The point applied to annexations, as well. As mentioned previously, annexations are typically undertaken to expand a city's tax base. If the decision is litigated, it can take years to resolve the case, and, in any case, insisting on a return to the status quo ante would likely reduce the economic vitality of the municipality and wreak political havoc. If there was no going back to the old boundaries, to what sort of remedy were black voters entitled if their proportion of the population had been reduced—even slightly?

Courts have given only inconsistent and unsatisfactory answers to these questions—at sea in their effort to define racially fair representation, a question more suited to the legislature and the academy. In fact, the Supreme Court's legal standards have differed from one context to another, and, perhaps partly as a consequence, neither lower courts nor the Justice Department have felt particularly obligated to follow its lead, leaving jurisdictions in the dark as they try to comply with the law.

The Annexation Cases

One can identify many points at which the understanding, interpretation, and enforcement of the Voting Rights Act went off the rails. What was Congress doing in twice "updating" its originally perfect trigger for section 5 coverage, which combined low voter turnout and the use of a literacy test to target precisely those parts of the country with a long history of disfranchising blacks? The entire states of Texas and Arizona, as well as an arbitrary list of counties in New York, California, Florida, New Hampshire, and elsewhere, became subject to preclearance as a result of the 1975 amendments, although none of these places had a history of denying Fifteenth Amendment rights comparable to that of the South. The 2006 House Judiciary Committee report supporting a very questionable extension and revision of section 5 claimed, "The expiring provisions of the Voting Rights Act only apply to jurisdictions that have the most extensive histories of discrimination and segregation."[17] It was pure nonsense, but hardly uniquely so.

Congress had much company in rewriting the Voting Rights Act in ways that undermined its logic and legitimacy. The courts played an important role, and the annexation cases are a prime example. Municipal annexations are extremely common. Cities deciding to expand their boundaries do so for economic reasons; I do not know of a case in which that was not the motivation. In labeling annexations "voting" changes, courts focus on the demographic change that might occur as a consequence of the city's acquisition of new territory. In a racially mixed setting, the percentage of black residents (and thus voters) might increase or decrease as a result of the annexation. But no cities are demographically stagnant; their populations grow and shrink for a variety of reasons. The Voting Rights Act was designed to deal with the methods of voting corrupted by racism. Annexations simply don't fall into that category. They should never have been on the list of changes that require preclearance.[18]

An annexation was the issue in *City of Petersburg, Virginia v. United States*, the first of the post-*Allen* cases to explore the definition of a discriminatory change. In 1966, a black city council member in Petersburg, Virginia, believing the city would benefit economically, had introduced an annexation ordinance that was unanimously adopted. Racial animus could not have played a role in this black-initiated action, but the annexation did change the city's racial balance, lowering the black population from 56 percent to 47 percent.

The plan was submitted for preclearance to the Justice Department, which lodged an objection. With the addition of a large number of white residents, the proportional voting strength of blacks had been reduced, it said, and "in re-adopting the at-large election system in the context of [this] significant change of population . . . the potential for an adverse and discriminatory voting effect [had] been written into the Petersburg election law."[19] In fact, Petersburg had not "re-adopted" its at-large system; it had simply retained it. Elections for municipal government within both the old and new boundaries were citywide. Moreover, in the mid-1960s, when the city was still overwhelmingly white, two blacks had been elected at large to the five-member city council—compelling evidence that at-large elections in Petersburg did not exclude blacks from the political process.

Nevertheless, the city had no better luck with the D.C. District Court, where it sought relief from Justice's objections.[20] The persistence of at-large elections would reduce the "weight, strength and power" of black votes in the city, the court held, and it ordered the municipality to institute single-member districts.[21] Ward voting, it said, "will most certainly result in a present increase in black representation on the City Council that has every prospect of being permanent. Thus, the force of black voting strength will be increased over the results [blacks] have been able presently to achieve even with a majority of the voters."[22]

Here we have the real point: The court believed that the act had created an entitlement to electoral arrangements that would be most favorable for minority officeholding. The annexation, the three-judge panel found, impaired the "ability of blacks to elect candidates of their choice and to have their ideas on political matters afforded the recognition to which they are entitled on their merits and by virtue of their individual citizenship and their numerical strength in the community."[23]

The political views of African Americans in the city are entitled to recognition—that is, representation—in proportion to their "numerical strength" in the city, the court had declared. Proportional racial representation, in its view, had become a right under the Voting Rights Act. The original statute was designed to protect against the disfranchisement of individual black citizens in the South. *Allen* had expanded the definition of voting rights violations. But *Petersburg* changed the focus of the act from the rights of individual voters to the equitable representation of groups, redefining the core purpose of the law, at least with respect to annexations.

The decision also provided a means of evading a constraint at the heart of section 5. While the civil rights community viewed longstanding at-large and other methods of voting as discriminatory, per se, they could not be attacked using the preclearance mechanism as it had been understood before *Petersburg*. The preclearance provision had been designed to prevent attempts to undermine the act—that is, *new* disfranchising efforts. But after *Petersburg*, if a municipality chose to expand its boundaries to increase its tax base and economic vitality, its citywide voting could not survive.

The Petersburg district court holding was followed five years later by the Supreme Court's first annexation decision, *City of Richmond, Virginia v. United States*. In 1970, Richmond had decided to enlarge its boundaries, with the result that the black population dropped from 52 percent to 42 percent. There was strong evidence that Richmond's elections were racially inclusive. Even though blacks had never constituted a majority of registered voters in the city, candidates endorsed by Richmond's leading black organization had won three of the nine seats on the city council in at-large elections both before and immediately after the annexation. Nevertheless, hoping to avoid federal objection to the boundary change, and concerned that such evidence of black electoral participation would not suffice, the city preemptively instituted the *Petersburg* remedy and adopted single-member districts.[24]

Nevertheless, the district court in 1974 denied the city's application for a declaratory judgment that would have cleared the annexation of suspected discriminatory purpose or effect. Different facts, the court ruled, made this a different case. Without the annexation, black voters might soon have become the majority, at which point at-large voting would have been to their advantage—an interesting argument given the otherwise consistent opposition of civil rights groups to citywide elections as, per se, discriminatory.[25]

In any case, the court said, the institution of the ward plan was itself suspect:

> Since substantial doubt exists that the dilution of the black vote caused by the annexation was eliminated by the adoption of the ward plan, it appears that the white political leadership presently in control of Richmond adopted the ward system for the purpose of doing what they could to maintain the dilution of the black vote produced by the annexation.[26]

It was curious reasoning: A could not be shown to have eliminated B; therefore, A had been adopted to promote B. Thus, not only the annexation but also the single-member districts were found to have the purpose of abridging the right to vote—although there was no evidence of racial animus driving any of these decisions.

If racism had motivated either the boundary change or the subsequent ward plan, the obvious remedy was deannexation. But since the expansion was already four years old, such a contraction would have expelled residents of several years' standing. Moreover, there was evidence (relegated to a footnote in the ruling) that the annexation had some black support.[27] The court offered an alternative remedy: "When the purpose of the annexation is specifically to dilute the vote of black citizens, an extra burden rests on that city to *purge* itself of discriminatory taint."[28] The city could do so only by structuring elections so that blacks were likely to win the number of legislative seats they *might* have had when blacks were a slight majority of the population.

"Political power in Richmond turns on controlling five majority seats on the City Council," the district court wrote.[29] The city had created four safe black seats, but had drawn its ward plan "without reference to the racial living plans" in the city. It had placed misguided emphasis on such factors as "'compactness,' 'physical boundaries,' and 'likeness of area.'" A racially gerrymandered plan would have been better, the court suggested.[30]

This was a bit much for a slim majority of five on the Supreme Court, which overturned the decision. The ward plan developed by the city would do, Justice White announced.[31] The section 5 standard has been met, the Court said, if the system "fairly reflects the strength of the Negro community as it exists after the annexation."[32] The Court could not approve the "requirement that the city allocate to the Negro community in the larger city the voting power or the seats on the city council in *excess* of its proportion in the new community and thus permanently to underrepresent other elements in the community."[33]

Beer v. United States

The high Court in *Richmond* rejected the district court's extraordinary vision of section 5; annexations could be precleared, it said, if a single-member districting plan was adopted that promised proportional racial representation. A decade after the passage of the original act, the Court had slid all the way down that slippery slope from access to legislative quotas. The danger inherent in *Allen* had been quickly realized in the annexation cases. Perhaps, however, a majority on the Court was not entirely comfortable with where it had landed; just one year later, in its first section 5 districting decision, it pulled back, abandoning its commitment to proportional officeholding as the standard by which to assess the discriminatory effect of an election-related change submitted for preclearance.

Beer v. United States involved the drawing of new districting lines for the election of councilmen in New Orleans.[34] Roughly one-third of the city's registered voting population was black. The Crescent City had redrawn its districting map after the 1970 census, and that map was the issue. Under the new plan, two seats on the city council were elected at large, five from wards. Only one of the five newly drawn wards contained a majority of registered voters who were black. When the plan was submitted for preclearance, the attorney general found it objectionable. The right of blacks to vote had been abridged, he said, by drawing district lines in such a way as to put them in the minority in every district except one. Only "compelling governmental need"—a compelling reason to adopt the proposed lines—could relieve the city of its obligation to adopt an alternative plan that would likely give blacks more seats.[35] The DOJ assumed, following the courts' lead in the annexation cases, that only a districting map containing a maximum number of safe minority seats should be precleared.

The D.C. court, to which the city next turned, had much the same view. The "inexorable consequence of the plan," it held, would "be a drastic reduction in the voting strength of the black minority."[36] But a reduction relative to what? Not to the previous ward plan, which contained no safe black seats. Under "historically unsuppressed conditions," the district court continued, registration figures indicated that New Orleans blacks had a "natural potential" of 2.42 seats.[37] The key word here is obviously "natural," with its implication that, in the absence of racism, proportional representation in all areas—employment, contracting, schools, and officeholding—comes naturally. It clearly doesn't, a point to which I will return.

The original point of section 5 had been to freeze southern electoral arrangements pending federal approval of any proposed change; in the 1970s, the D.C. court and the Justice Department viewed the southern political landscape as frozen and used section 5 to thaw it. It was only one of the many ways in which courts and the process of administrative review came increasingly to ignore racial reality and distort the statute to serve an agenda quite different from that which had been articulated by Congress.

The Justice Department and the courts assumed that race relations in New Orleans were basically unchanged and unlikely to change ("No Negro candidate will win in any district in which his race is in the minority," the court concluded—despite evidence to the contrary), so they relied on the simplest measure of political inclusion: the number of legislative seats that minorities held.[38] Similarly, their insistence on realizing the "natural potential" for black officeholding rested on assumptions of an enduring majority-white city and a permanently racially charged electorate. In fact, blacks were already on the political move, and in 1978, four years after the district court's decision, the city elected Ernest N. Dutch Morial as its first black mayor—running at large, of course.

The district court's reasoning in *Beer* was perfectly consistent with that of the Supreme Court in *Richmond*; nevertheless, the high Court vacated the lower court's judgment. Whether the city could have devised a plan likely to result in more black councilmen was not the question, Justice Potter Stewart wrote for a majority of five. Courts should ask instead whether the "ability of minority groups to participate in the political process and to elect their choices to office [had been] augmented, diminished, or not affected by the change in voting."[39] How could a change that improved the position of minorities—as the New Orleans plan did—be called discriminatory? The purpose of section 5 had been to bar changes that would result in a "retrogression in the position of racial minorities with respect to their effective exercise of the electoral franchise."[40] Since new district lines had actually increased the likelihood of a victorious black candidate, it could hardly be termed "retrogressive."

Beer allowed jurisdictions to maintain the status quo, even when that meant sticking with two majority-minority districts where, in fact, four could be drawn. Or zero, where at least one could be drawn. As a result, Justice Thurgood Marshall wrote in dissent, the Court had approved "a blatantly discriminatory districting plan for the city of New Orleans."[41] But the Court's interpretation of section 5 squared with the structure of the Voting Rights Act, and delegated to actors remote from the scene—the D.C. court and Department of Justice—a limited, and thus manageable, task: stopping the institution of electoral arrangements that undermined the force of the 1965 law. Courts and federal attorneys could be expected to ascertain a relative loss of electoral power as a consequence of new election-related rules; fairly judging allegations of racial inequity, in some absolute sense, was a much more difficult task.

There was an obvious problem, however. When a city changed its internal districting lines—rather than its external boundaries—why were minorities entitled only to the representational strength that they had previously possessed? A newly enlarged city was required to abandon at-large voting (widespread in the covered jurisdictions of the South and Southwest) and draw single-member districts that would elect blacks roughly in proportion to the black population. And yet, if blacks had two safe seats on a city's governing council, but three could be created, section 5 required only that the existing two be maintained, the Court said.

Beer committed the Court to a double standard that could not be sustained. Retrogression was the test in *Beer*; proportional representation in *Richmond*. Both standards were perfectly clear—as of 1976. But the two cases were simply incompatible, and, over time, *Richmond's* standard prevailed. In its *Brief for the United States* in *Beer*, the attorney general had argued unsuccessfully that since alternative maps could contain more majority-black districts, the New Orleans plan should not be precleared.[42] In subsequent years, both the DOJ and the D.C. District Court continued to insist on "fairly drawn" districting plans, ignoring the majority holding in *Beer*.[43] The Justice Department also used section 2 and a freewheeling definition of discriminatory intent to circumvent the retrogression test. In so doing, they had the support of four justices on the Supreme Court who joined the civil rights community in remaining convinced that "the Court was mistaken in *Beer*."[44] The decision had only the most tenuous hold on voting rights enforcement.

Bossier I

It is difficult to separate entirely the story of judicial interpretations of section 5 from that of Justice Department enforcement—the subject of chapter 4. The two are deeply intertwined. In fact, section 5 has become entangled as well with another provision in the Voting Rights Act—section 2.

As previously noted, in 1982 Congress rewrote an innocuous preamble to the act, confusingly called section 2 despite the fact that there was no section 1. As revised, the provision provided plaintiffs with a powerful tool to attack pre-1965 methods of election anywhere in the nation that had the "result" of denying the right to vote on account of race or color. Section 5 kicked in only when jurisdictions altered some aspect of electoral procedure. But section 2 could be used to attack the status quo. It allowed a finding that voting rights had been violated if "the totality of circumstances" showed that the "political processes . . . [were] not equally open" to blacks and Hispanics. The provision defined a "not equally open" process as one in which minority group members had "less opportunity than other members of the electorate to participate in the political process and to elect representatives of their choice."

The term discriminatory "result" in section 2 was chosen to make clear the difference between that provision and section 5, which protected against methods of voting that had a discriminatory "effect." "Effect" in section 5, the Supreme Court had said, meant "retrogression"—although only with respect to assessing redistricting plans, not annexations, it will be recalled.

Determining retrogression in redistricting cases required a before-and-after comparison: Had the proposed change in the method of voting left minority voters worse off, *relative* to their previous electoral strength? A plan that contained two majority-black districts when previously there had been three would not be precleared. On the other hand, a new map that created two safe African-American seats would suffice, even if drawing a third were possible.

Assessing the "result" of a change in election procedure under section 2, though, demanded a complicated assessment of the electoral environment—the setting in which voting took place. It asked whether minority voters had been denied an equal electoral "opportunity" in some *absolute* sense. In the section 2 context, opportunity and results were one and the same. Thus, if that third majority-minority district could be drawn, it was an obligation. Maximizing the number of safe black districts would make for elections with racially fair results. But *Beer*, with its emphasis on backsliding, had closed the door on that interpretive option.

In theory, then, the two provisions were very different and attacked different forms of discrimination; but already in January 1985, when new procedures for the administration of section 5 were proposed, it was clear that the assistant attorney general for civil rights would be resting objections to voting changes submitted for preclearance on the unprecedented ground that they violated section 2's prohibition on discriminatory results.[45] Nothing in the congressional record preceding the revision of section 2 sanctioned his decision; in rewriting section 2, Congress had made no mention of a consequent revision of the preclearance standard. Moreover, in 1982, Congress not only amended section 2; it renewed section 5, and it did so, the Supreme Court noted in 1997, "without changing its applicable standard."[46]

Reno v. Bossier Parish School Board (*Bossier I*), that 1997 decision, was the first of two successive cases that dealt with school board redistricting in Bossier Parish, Louisiana.[47] (A "parish" in the Pelican State is the equivalent of a county elsewhere.) After the 1990 census, the school board had redrawn its twelve single-member districts, adopting a plan that the Justice Department had already precleared for use in electing members of the "jury"—the chief governing board in the parish. The two plans were thus identical, with neither containing any majority-black districts. School authorities naturally assumed that the same map drawn to elect a different body would be approved.

They were wrong. The plan violated the section 2 results test, the attorney general decided. And if it offended section 2, it also clashed with section 5, he informed the parish. The section 2 standards had been incorporated into section 5—an obvious attempt to circumvent the constraint imposed by the Court when it had held that retrogression was the sole question the Justice Department should consider in reviewing districting plans. The new map the parish had drawn was clearly not retrogressive; black political power was not diminished in any way, since the new map had replaced a districting plan with the same number of safe black districts—that is, zero. But an alternative plan offered by the NAACP contained two majority-minority districts, and, thus, the Justice Department objected to the proposal submitted for preclearance. That proposed districting map diluted black voting strength, the parish was informed.[48] It could have drawn more majority-black districts, and, in failing to do so, it had not met its burden of proving an absence of discrimination.

It was a reading of section 5 that could not be squared with *Beer*, and the school board turned to the D.C. District Court, which sided with the parish. A failure to satisfy the racial equity standards in section 2, the court said, does not constitute an independent reason to deny preclearance, and, on appeal, the Supreme Court agreed. Sections 5 and 2 "combat different evils" and thus "impose very different duties upon the States," Justice O'Connor (writing for a majority of five) concluded. Were the Court to hold otherwise, she went on, "compliance with § 5 [would become] contingent upon compliance with § 2."[49] The standards for section 2 would replace those of section 5. The position of the district court would "shift the focus of § 5 from nonretrogression to vote dilution, and . . . change the § 5 benchmark from a jurisdiction's existing plan to a hypothetical, undiluted plan."[50]

Of course, inescapably, the hypothetical would be a plan ensuring minority officeholding in proportion to the black population—a point O'Connor did not mention. But Justice Stephen Breyer in his dissent explicitly acknowledged the inevitability of proportionality as the benchmark.[51] What other measure of a clearly "undiluted" vote could there be? Anything short of proportionality would suggest at least *partial* dilution.

Bossier II

Justice O'Connor's 1997 opinion in what came to be known as *Bossier I* was not the Court's last word on school board redistricting in that Louisiana parish. The case went back to the lower court and then returned to the high Court, which decided *Bossier II* in 2000.[52] This time, however, it was Justice Antonin Scalia who wrote for a majority of five.

The district court (on remand) had failed to answer a question that, surprisingly, had never been raised in the decades since *Beer* had been decided. The preclearance provision referred to both discriminatory intent and effect. Did the retrogression test for discrimination govern the question of unacceptable effect alone, or was it equally applicable to assessments of invidious purpose?[53] If a districting plan was suspected of racial animus, although its "effect" did not leave black voters worse off than they had been before, should it be precleared? In enforcing section 5, was there one legal standard or two quite separate ones?

On the surface, the question might seem a tad ridiculous. Could the Court really argue that intentionally discriminatory districting maps did not violate section 5 if they were not retrogressive? It could and should, Justice Scalia argued for the Court. Appellants would recast section 5's phrase "'does not have the purpose and will not have the effect of x' to read 'does not have the purpose of y and will not have the effect of x,'" he wrote.[54] They "refuse to accept the limited meaning that we have said preclearance has in the vote-dilution context," he went on. That limited meaning

> does not represent approval of the voting change; it is nothing more than a determination that the voting change is no more dilutive than what it replaces, and therefore cannot be stopped in advance under the extraordinary burden-shifting procedure of §5, but must be attacked through the normal means of a §2 action.[55]

In other words, remember how abnormal section 5 is. It allows the Justice Department to stop a state or locality from even provisionally implementing districting and other decisions that are the products of democratic politics, and it shifts the burden of proof, normally on plaintiffs, to the defendant jurisdictions. Those jurisdictions must convince the attorney general that the proposed changes are beyond suspicion. Civil rights advocates often suggest that only the powers of preclearance, generously interpreted, stand between political exclusion and inclusion for minority voters. But, in fact, if plaintiffs believe the exclusive focus on retrogression has left discriminatory methods of election in place, they have not run out of legal options. As Justice Scalia noted, they can bring a suit under section 2—or under the Fourteenth Amendment, he could have added. Those options, however, would require plaintiffs to carry the burden of proving their charge of purposeful discrimination in a federal court; they could not prevail on the basis of suspected illegality alone.

The civil rights community regarded *Bossier II* as a devastating blow to the enforcement of section 5. In applying the backsliding test to questions of both discriminatory purpose and effect, the Court had "fundamentally redefined—and weakened—the purpose requirement," civil rights advocates argued. ACLU voting rights attorney Laughlin McDonald called the decision "a parody of what the VRA stands for."[57]

The open-ended definition of "purpose," to which the plaintiffs' bar and DOJ voting section attorneys were deeply committed, provided a level of interpretive freedom that the much narrower focus on retrogression did not. It allowed objections even to new districting maps supported by black legislators (if it were possible to draw a map with more majority-minority districts), or to an annexation that added only a total of two whites to the town's population.[58] Indeed, as chapter 4 will make clear, in the 1980s and, especially, in the 1990s, the DOJ took full advantage of that freedom, resting its objections most often on a finding of discriminatory intent.[59]

The annexation decisions had established a right to single-member districts drawn to provide a rough approximation of proportional racial representation. With its first redistricting case, the Court appeared to have had second thoughts about proportionality as the measure of electoral discrimination, and replaced it with retrogression—a reduction in the electoral power of black voters relative to that which they had previously enjoyed. The point of section 5, the Court made clear in *Beer*, was to stop jurisdictions from altering electoral procedure such that black voters would be robbed of the gains that enfranchisement promised. It was not to create a perfect political world in which blacks and whites were equal players; the larger and much more complicated questions of electoral inequality were addressed only in full-scale trials enforcing section 2 or the Fourteenth and Fifteenth Amendments. Swift and cursory administrative preclearance was no substitute for a judicial proceeding with a thorough examination of the factual record, expert witnesses, depositions, and a full exploration of the issues through the opposing arguments of attorneys for both sides.

The annexation decisions turned out to be outliers—totally misguided ones, I have suggested. The literature on voting rights most often simply ignores them. And yet the civil rights community, the D.C. court, and the Justice Department were totally committed to proportionality as the correct legal standard by which to assess section 5 violations. They were at war with *Beer* from the outset. And since judicial decisions interpreting section 5 were few and far between, the Justice Department was, for the most part, in the driver's seat, a story that chapter 4 will explore. The Supreme Court periodically insisted that *Beer* remained good law, but it had a weak hand, particularly because four members of that Court never agreed with the majority's view.

In *Bossier I* and *Bossier II*, the Court tried to put brakes on the imaginative ways in which the Justice Department was interpreting section 5 to circumvent the retrogression test, and, indeed, for a few years those decisions did have an impact. But in 2006, Congress overturned the more important of the two—*Bossier II*—and restored intent as a question separate from the retrogression effects test. Neither congressional action nor these judicial decisions addressed a growing problem that was first confronted in 2003 in *Georgia v. Ashcroft*: Wasn't the whole notion that blacks needed safe legislative seats becoming out of date? Didn't the profound racial change in America, even in once-terrible Mississippi, suggest that perhaps the question of black representation was now much more complicated than it was in 1965?

Ashcroft

Who counts as a black representative? The answer was long overdue by the time the Supreme Court finally took up the question in 2003. By then, the Court could no longer avoid the issue; black legislators were raising it themselves. And while Republicans had benefited from racially gerry-mandered districts in the 1980s and 1990s, the Democrats now began to see that spreading the black vote around a bit would actually help the party. In fact, if every district in which African Americans were a crucial constituency could be labeled "black" for section 5 retrogression purposes, the statute could, in effect, be used as a Democratic Protection Act. Plans would receive preclearance if the jurisdiction could show that the proposed redistricting plan had not reduced the number of black coalition and influence districts. "Coalition" districts were those under 50 percent black in which black voters could nevertheless elect their candidates of choice by forming reliable coalitions with members of other racial and ethnic groups.[60] An "influence" district was one in which minority voters "may not be able to elect a candidate of choice but can play a substantial, if not decisive, role in the electoral process," thereby ensuring attention to their interests.[61] Those districts, which were likely to elect Democrats and were thus assumed to protect black interests, had become untouchable when jurisdictions redrew the lines on the districting map.

As mentioned previously, with *Bossier II* in 2000, the Court brought an abrupt end to the interpretive liberty that the D.C. District Court and the Justice Department had enjoyed for the better part of two decades. *Georgia v. Ashcroft,*[62] decided three years later, sanctioned a different sort of definitional license in enforcing the section 5 retrogression test. This decision, however, received a decidedly mixed reception from the established civil rights bar.[63]

Ashcroft reviewed a districting plan for the Georgia State Senate. The plan was not one that could be described as "max-black"; indeed, almost all black legislators felt perfectly comfortable drawing districts with lower-than-usual African-American concentrations. They felt they could spread black voters around a bit more, improving the prospects for Democratic candidates in those districts, while still carrying their own. They were black Democrats, but both identities were important, in their eyes. They believed they could help themselves by helping white liberals. The racial ground had shifted, and they were responding—something that prominent civil rights groups typically resisted. Thus, Representative John Lewis, defending Georgia's decision to create some coalitional districts, rather than safe black-majority districts, testified that Georgia

is not the same state it was. It's not the same state that it was in
1965 or in 1975 or even in 1980 or 1990. We have changed.
We've come a long distance. It's not just in Georgia, but in the
American South. I think people are preparing to lay down the
burden of race.[64]

The state had sought a declaratory judgment from the D.C. District
Court that its new plan was not discriminatory in either intent or effect.[65] A
three-judge panel had refused to preclear it, even though ten out of eleven
black state senators had supported the submitted map, along with thirty-
three out of thirty-four black representatives in the Georgia House. The
Supreme Court vacated the judgment and remanded the case for further
consideration consistent with a fresh analysis of the retrogression standard.[66]

The plan that the lower court had refused to preclear had lowered the
percentage of black voters in some districts (although not below 50 percent),
while increasing the number of districts certain to elect white Democrats.
The Court explained the logic: "The goal of the Democratic leadership—
black and white—was to maintain the number of majority-minority districts and also increase the number of Democratic Senate seats."[67] More
Democratic seats would mean more black representation: "No party contests
that a substantial majority of black voters in Georgia vote Democratic."[68]
Congressman John Lewis (as well as the black leadership in the state) had
signed on to the plan, since, as Lewis put it, he believed it was "in the
best interest of African American voters . . . to have a continued Democratic-
controlled legislature in Georgia."[69]

Not for the first time, Justice O'Connor, writing for the Court, had become
concerned that a maximum number of safe black districts did not necessarily
maximize black representation, and that, indeed, minority "representation"
was not so easy to define.[70] White Democrats elected in both "coalition" and
"influence" districts could be considered "representative" of minority voters,
the Court held.[71] In judging the level of black representation, other factors
were to be weighed, such as the leadership positions held by white incumbents who had been supported by black voters, O'Connor argued.

The Court had never "determined the meaning of 'effective exercise of
the electoral franchise,'" Justice O'Connor acknowledged.[72] It was a remarkable admission. Section 5 protected minority voters from schemes that

robbed them of acquired power—but how was that power to be defined? Beginning with *Allen* in 1969, definitional questions with unsettled and inconsistent answers had plagued voting rights enforcement, with annexation and redistricting decisions providing very different answers.

"The power to influence the electoral process is not limited to winning elections," O'Connor continued.[73] Section 5 gives states the flexibility to choose substantive over descriptive representation. It allows districting plans designed to increase the number of white Democrats, although the cost might be a reduction in the number of seats that were totally safe for black incumbents.[74] It was a risk that the black majority leader of the Democratic-controlled state senate and the black chairman of the redistricting subcommittee had been willing to take.[75] About a third of the Democratic legislators were black, as was the state attorney general who defended the plan in court. The logic behind the support of these powerful black politicians was clear. They were worried that Georgia was tipping Republican, as, indeed, it began to do with the election in 2002 of its first Republican governor since 1868, followed in 2004 with the victory of both GOP candidates for the U.S. Senate. A greater dispersion of black voters could help elect more white Democrats, they believed.[76]

"*Georgia v. Ashcroft* may be a dubious piece of jurisprudence," Robert Bauer, a Democratic Party operative, wrote on a blog devoted to commentary on regulating the political process. "But there is something there worth taking seriously, which is respect for politics—for 'horse-trading' and the like by those elected to do precisely that and to answer for it."[77] Bauer had made an important point. *Ashcroft*, despite its obvious flaws, made good political sense. The Court had recognized that the normal districting process involves a complicated weighing of numerous political objectives.[78] As Daniel Lowenstein has noted, "Districting is part of the woof and warp of [a] state's politics and political culture."[79]

The Court in *Ashcroft* had said, in effect, let legislators be legislators. And let black legislators make the deals they see as politically beneficial to their constituents. It's not 1965 any more, and blacks are well represented in these legislatures; it is time once again to presume that the normal political processes will produce reasonable results. If black legislators agree to a plan that protects white Democrats, they are politicians, not "Uncle Toms." In 1965, politics as usual in a state like Georgia could not be trusted, but the entire black establishment had been a partner in the state's post-2000 redistricting process.

There was a fundamental problem with the Court's message, however: It was at odds with the core of the Voting Rights Act, the whole point of which had been to deny covered jurisdictions the privilege of running their own political shops. Distrust of the South was the foundation upon which the temporary, emergency provisions in the 1965 act had been built. And, almost forty years later, that distrust still ran very deep among civil rights advocates.

As discussed above, the decision also threatened to make preclearance dependent upon a showing that the districting benefited Democrats, since that was the party to which African Americans generally belonged. Coalition and influence districts were synonymous with safe Democratic constituencies. The decision turned federal authorities into protectors of the interests of one political party—a disturbing distortion of a statute whose only constitutionally legitimate purpose was protection against racism.

Finally, if a federal law guaranteeing minority voters "the ability to elect the candidates of their choice" was still essential in 2003, *Ashcroft* was no guide. It provided no coherent legal standards to govern an inevitably limited administrative preclearance process. It tried to solve one definitional problem (the unsettled meaning of the "effective exercise of the electoral franchise") only to create others. When was an "influence" district influential?[80] When did a white incumbent hold committee or other legislative power that was truly invaluable to black constituents? With *Ashcroft*, Justice Potter Stewart's famous definition of pornography applied equally to the question of equitable minority representation: Judges and DOJ attorneys were expected to know it when they saw it.[81]

Unresolved Issues

What a legal mess the courts had made—one that was compounded by careless congressional amendments and by the Justice Department's creative lawmaking in its role as a surrogate for the D.C. District Court, as chapter 4 will argue. The legal standards governing annexations suspected of violating the voting rights of minorities were clear but indefensible. Those arrived at in districting cases were logical and manageable, but only if the retrogression standard was adhered to strictly—which it was not, when cases were in the Justice Department's hands. And when, in 2003, the Supreme Court finally decided it was time to update the definitions of electoral power and minority representation to reflect the political and racial realities of the twenty-first century, the result was a decision indifferent to the limited capacity of DOJ attorneys to sort out complicated questions involving racial equity in the electoral process, as well as one laced with definitional problems.

As New York University law professor Samuel Issacharoff has written,

> In moving section 5 from a bright-line rule under *Beer* to an assessment of the competing political considerations in securing effective black representation, the Court introduced for the first time to section 5 the fine grained calculus of trade-offs of political influence versus descriptive representation. . . . So long as the preclearance requirement is limited to mechanical inquiries, and so long as the ability to provide an "equal or fair opportunity" for minority electoral success is not a factor in the preclearance equation, the *Beer* standard could work well as a matter of administrative law. As soon as effectiveness of representation and totality of circumstances are added to the mix, however, the simple regulatory regime begins to break down.[82]

In other words, a before-and-after comparison involving a simple count of the number of safe minority seats not only squared with the original notion of section 5 as a prophylactic measure to stop racist moves that would erode black political gains; it was also a manageable task for DOJ staff given sixty days to accept or reject a new districting map. As argued above, the larger questions of racial equity could only be properly addressed in local federal district courts.

Although the Court in *Bossier I* had tried to draw a bright line between sections 5 and 2, in *Ashcroft* once again the distinction between racial equity and retrogression had been lost. The decision underscored the questionable legitimacy of preclearance almost forty years after the passage of the Voting Rights Act. Once the Court had admitted that minority political power can take many forms and that no simple formula can identify proper representation, the extraordinarily intrusive political power given to federal attorneys to override state and local districting decisions on the basis of crude formulas could not be justified.

That power was legitimate only as long as straightforward racism was the evil to be combated. Correctly assessing race and politics in a more complex setting—deciding whether blacks were better off with a white incumbent than with a black representative, for instance—was a matter that belonged in the hands of democratically elected decision-makers. In 1966, it may be recalled, Justice Black had argued that the preclearance provision had "compelled" states "to beg federal authorities to approve their policies," and thus "so distorts our constitutional structure of government as to render any distinction drawn in the Constitution between State and Federal power almost meaningless."[83] By 2003, his concerns had become important to remember. Southern states deserved the status of supplicants in 1965; they do not today.

Political scientist Bernard Grofman has called *Ashcroft* "arguably the most dramatic single change ever made in Section 5 statutory interpretation."[84] But either that decision or section 5 could survive—not both. In the end, it was *Ashcroft* that did not stand; Congress, in renewing the emergency provisions in 2006, superseded the Court's 2003 decision. The issues it raised cannot be ignored for long, however; they are fundamental to any serious inquiry into race and democratic representation.

3

Interpreting Section 2: Judges Lost in a Political Thicket

The Voting Rights Act is a statute in search of a theory.

—Lani Guinier, professor of law, Harvard University[1]

In 1965 the theoretical assumptions underlying section 5 and, indeed, the entire Voting Rights Act, were clear enough: The Fifteenth Amendment protected against disfranchisement on the basis of race or color, and gave Congress the power to enforce that protection. The statute was thus pure antidiscrimination legislation—in keeping with the temper of the time. Its aim was to stop southern racists from barring blacks from the polls.

But tinkering by Congress, the courts, and the Justice Department—along with racial progress taking place at a speed no one imagined in 1965—destroyed the theoretical coherence of the original Voting Rights Act. The 1970 change in the statistical trigger for preclearance coverage contained in section 4 was mindless, and that which Congress adopted in 1975 was, at best, questionable. The Supreme Court's first important ruling interpreting section 5—*Allen v. State Board of Elections*—was a legitimate effort to stop southern attempts to deny blacks political power, but the annexation decisions wrote an entitlement to proportional racial representation into the statute—a change that never could have gotten through Congress, and which violated basic American principles of democratic representation. The *Beer* test governing preclearance assessments for redistricting, though true to the statute, was abhorred by a minority of four on the Supreme Court, the majority on the D.C. circuit court, the Justice Department, and the civil rights groups. Its survival was touch and go.

As a consequence, by 1982, the Voting Rights Act was, indeed, a statute in search of a theory. The murky language of the rewritten section 2, conflating opportunity and results, reflected a zeitgeist greatly altered since the heyday of the civil rights movement. Access to the ballot was no longer seen as sufficient. If blacks could vote but could not—or did not—elect blacks to public office, then they remained disfranchised.

The evolution of the school desegregation provisions of the 1964 Civil Rights Act tells a parallel story that may help to place the voting rights story in context. "'Desegregation,'" the earlier statute read, "means the assignment of students to public schools and within such schools without regard to their race, color, religion, or national origin, but 'desegregation' shall not mean the assignment of students to public schools in order to overcome racial imbalance." Within a few years, however, the Supreme Court, in decisions resting on the Fourteenth Amendment, was ordering *precisely* what the Civil Rights Act had originally forbidden: race-based school assignments to create racial balance.[2] The Court did acknowledge the problem of the statutory language, but creatively rewrote the legislative history. In employment law, as well, the focus switched from the equal treatment of individuals, regardless of race, to race-conscious remedies for the underrepresentation of groups in the workforce.[3]

Voting rights advocates, in keeping with the time, also wanted racially fair outcomes, which meant racial balance on legislative bodies, as well. The freedom of individuals to register and vote had come to be seen as securing formal, but not substantive, equality. And in 1982 they successfully persuaded Congress to rewrite section 2 to allow plaintiffs to sue any jurisdiction in which, arguably, minority voters had been denied an equal opportunity to secure equal electoral "results"—that is, to elect the representatives of their choice.

Assessing Racial Equality

The amendment of section 2 was one of several major turning points in the evolution of the Voting Rights Act. The section 5 annexation decisions created a right to single-member districts drawn to create proportional representation on municipal governing bodies, to the greatest extent feasible. But new districting lines drawn to meet the one-person, one-vote mandate were somehow different. Ours is not to reason why. New districts did not violate section 5 as long as the revised map was not retrogressive—as long as it did not reduce black electoral power. And in *Bossier I* and *Bossier II*, the Court tried to stop the use of allegations of discriminatory intent and section 2 violations to get around the retrogression standard. Supreme Court voting rights decisions are few and far between; interpretation and enforcement are mostly a Justice Department story (which will be told in the next chapter). But the Court's intermittent guidance was the law, and after its 1975 decision in *Richmond*, it was clear that the antidiscrimination language of section 5 promised nothing more than protection from racist efforts to undermine the force of the statute.

The civil rights community was frustrated; its allies in the Justice Department were frustrated; and so were those on the bench who believed that a society free of racism would have a perfect correspondence between the percentage of blacks in a particular jurisdiction and the number of African Americans elected to legislative positions. If the high Court did not buy that reasoning, the statute needed revision. The innocuous section 2 was the obvious vehicle.

The story of the 1982 amendment of section 2 actually starts with a series of constitutional cases—a line of voting rights decisions entirely separate from those that rested on the statute. In 1971, the Supreme Court held, for the first time, that a method of voting had diluted the votes of blacks and Hispanics in violation of the equal protection clause.[4] (In the same year, the Court approved "bus transportation as one tool of school desegregation" and took the first step toward requiring employers to hire on the basis of race.)[5] The Fourteenth Amendment, as the basis of a voting rights suit, had an obvious advantage over the Voting Rights Act: It applied to every jurisdiction in the country and to methods of election that long predated the statute and were thus not subject to preclearance.

Like *Allen v. Board of Elections*, this series of voting rights decisions picked up from where the one-person, one-vote cases left off; but, unlike *Allen*, which dealt only with the reach of section 5, the constitutional cases grappled with a core substantive issue: the meaning of equal electoral opportunity. Until the revision of section 2 in 1982, that question was directly addressed only in these Fourteenth Amendment decisions, whose language was lifted by those who drafted the new section 2.

Justice Harlan, dissenting in *Reynolds v. Sims*, had presciently anticipated the problem of group rights to representation that was ignored in the one-person, one-vote decisions, as chapter 1 indicated. He had argued that creating equally populated districts—mathematical parity—did not necessarily result in equal representation.[6] Such a stripped-down version of the American system of representation was open to challenge. There were bound to be questions about the rights of groups left by the wayside— interest groups that found themselves without the "equally effective voice" the Court had promised. The power to elect representatives, Chief Justice Warren had said, must be evenly distributed among voters. What, beyond equal population districts, did that mean? Did minorities defined by race or ethnicity have equal electoral power, for instance, when their votes were submerged in multimember districts in which whites were the majority?

As Harlan had predicted, questions about the constitutionality of multi-member districts, at-large voting, majority-vote requirements, and other electoral practices that arguably diluted minority group strength were soon raised. And, in a new line of cases beginning in 1971 and ending in 1980, minority plaintiffs challenged long-standing procedures by which elections had been run in both the North and the South, often since early in the century. Blacks and whites were on unequal electoral footing, they charged.

The contrast with section 5 should be clear. Preclearance affected only new election practices in the racially suspect covered jurisdictions, all of which were located in the South in 1965. At least with respect to redistricting, section 5 was solely concerned with efforts to rob black ballots of their expected weight after the passage of the statute. Federal bureaucrats, with limited time and information with which to work, could easily count blacks in office and calculate retrogression. But the constitutional cases were quite different. They could be brought anywhere, and in the South the methods of voting under attack had often long predated black enfranchise-ment. Most important, they addressed a fundamental and very large question: the meaning of equal protection in the context of elections. Courts had to tackle the question of how to assess racial equality in the political sphere—or, rather, how to assess the inevitably imperfect equality that the Constitution protects.[7] It wasn't a question suitable for swift and cursory administrative review.

Whitcomb v. Chavis

The first in this series of Fourteenth Amendment cases was *Whitcomb v. Chavis*, decided by the Supreme Court in 1971.[8] It involved Indiana's state legislative apportionment—specifically, the creation of one multimember district for all of Marion County, from which eight state senators and fifteen assemblymen would be elected. The plan, plaintiffs had charged, unconstitutionally minimized the voting power of the county's blacks, who were largely concentrated in Indianapolis's "Center Township Ghetto."

The district court was convinced.[9] It drew a picture of two separate societies—one with power, the other without—that closely resembled the description of America in the 1968 Kerner Commission Report.[10] This was no coincidence; the *Whitcomb* decision had been written by Otto Kerner himself, who had become a judge on the Seventh Circuit and, in this capacity, had been appointed to a special three-judge panel to try the case.

Judge Kerner looked at the distinctiveness of Indianapolis ghetto life—at the degree of residential concentration and the relative poverty of the black population, as well as at the lack of legislators elected from the "Center Township Ghetto"—and concluded that the voting strength of inner-city blacks had been impermissibly diluted. The number of black legislators was disproportionately low. Residentially clustered groups with distinctive interests, he suggested, were without the political influence to which they were entitled as long as their votes were submerged in a multimember district.

Judge Kerner did not explore the possibility that the primary explanation for disproportionately low black officeholding might not be race. Electoral defeat, he seemed to assume, had a meaning different for African Americans than for whites: White candidates lose for partisan and personal reasons, but blacks for only one—color. In fact, blacks in Marion County had been active participants in Indianapolis political life. The Democratic Party routinely slated black candidates, chosen by black districts, and, in general elections, those candidates fared no worse (and no better) than whites. The stumbling block was the repeated defeat of the entire Democratic slate. This was a Republican county, and Democrats (whatever their race) seldom won.

Reviewing the district court's decision, the Supreme Court took a second look at the status of Indianapolis blacks and found nothing abnormal in the way of political isolation or unequal access. It was not exclusion, but the process of party competition and the principle of majority rule that denied blacks the representation they sought. Since blacks were Democrats in a largely Republican county, the dilution of their voting strength was, in the Court's words, a "mere euphemism for political defeat."[11] Faced with a choice between white Democrats and black Republicans, voters in the ghetto chose whites. Disproportionately low black officeholding, the Court concluded, was not evidence of invidious discrimination, "absent findings that ghetto residents had less opportunity than did other Marion County residents to participate in the political processes and to elect legislators of their choice."[12]

The task that Judge Kerner imposed upon the courts had been relatively straightforward: identifying groups with seemingly distinct interests and disproportionately low representation. But the Supreme Court asked courts to judge the setting in which the voting took place and to distinguish those situations in which minority candidates lost as a result of unequal opportunity from those in which blacks either did not run or did not win for reasons *other than race*. It was the right standard—but it made the process of judging racial equity much more difficult. Distinguishing racial attitudes and political views was seldom easy, and while it was safe in the 1970s to make assumptions about southern white attitudes, generalizations about northern politics were much more dangerous.

White **and** Zimmer

Whitcomb had raised doubt that minority plaintiffs outside the South could successfully challenge a method of election on constitutional grounds. More than ten years passed before another attempt was made to persuade a court that minorities in a northern city had less opportunity than whites "to participate in the political process and to elect legislators of their choice."

Thus, a southern state—Texas—was the setting in the next case. Black and Mexican-American plaintiffs challenged the 1970 reapportionment plan for the Texas House of Representatives, and, in *White v. Regester*, decided in 1973, the Supreme Court held that the multimember districts used in Bexar and Dallas counties violated the Fourteenth Amendment guarantee of equal protection.[13]

Two leading civil rights attorneys described the Court's findings in *White* as "difficult to catalogue."[14] The decision referred to low registration rates in Bexar County, but not in Dallas. Only in Dallas, however, did it find that whites controlled the process of candidate selection. It casually used vague terms such as "cultural incompatibility" to describe elements in a picture of discrimination against Hispanics, but failed to mention the election and repeated reelection of Henry Gonzalez to Congress, starting in 1961. The opinion was laden with "factual findings" that consisted of unexplained assertions of indeterminate weight. Nevertheless, the language of the decision was transferred directly to section 2 when that provision was rewritten in 1982. For that reason, the decision remains to this day extremely important. Its unintelligible reasoning became a statutory problem, as well.

Three months after *White v. Regester*, the Fifth Circuit attempted unsuccessfully to clarify the Supreme Court's perplexing decision by providing that missing catalogue of findings relevant to a determination that black voters had been denied the equal protection of the law, in violation of the Fourteenth Amendment. The case, *Zimmer v. McKeithen*, involved at-large voting for the school board and the policy jury (the equivalent of a county council) in a tiny rural Louisiana parish that was 58.7 percent black.[15]

The equal protection clause has been violated, the Fifth Circuit said, when minority plaintiffs can show a lack of minority access to the slating of candidates; the "unresponsiveness of legislators to their particularized interests"; a "'tenuous' [backed by neither tradition nor persuasive reason] state policy underlying the preference for multi-member or at-large districting"; or a history of past discrimination that "precludes . . . effective participation in the election system." The significance of any of these factors is "enhanced by a showing of the existence of large districts, majority-vote requirements, antisingle shot voting provisions and the lack of provision for at-large candidates running from particular geographical subdistricts," such that all candidates running at large can reside in one neighborhood—perhaps affluent and white.[16] Conspicuously absent from the list was what would later become central to section 2 litigation: "racial bloc voting"—the consistent preference of minority and majority voters for different candidates.

Zimmer propounded a simple solution to the apparently intractable problem of how to detect situations in which the inequality between minority and white voters demanded a new method of voting. The constitutional

cases, more often than not, took weeks to try. The factual record was volu-
minous. But courts now had a checklist that they could—and did—use.
From 1973 to 1980, vote "dilution" claims were routinely tested by the
Zimmer criteria.

But *White* and *Zimmer* solved only the rhetorical, not the substantive,
problem. While providing a vocabulary upon which courts could draw,
these decisions left unsettled the basic question of why the particular factors
listed had been selected. The *Zimmer* list looked systematic; in fact, it
was no less arbitrary than *White's*. But criteria that measure an undefined
phenomenon are necessarily arbitrary. The primary issues had not been
addressed: When is the right to vote assured? When is the election process
one in which all citizens can choose to partake? What does a democracy look
like in practice? The slating of candidates, an annual registration requirement,
linguistic barriers, a history of inequality, a majority-vote requirement, a
paucity of minority officeholders—the significance of each element depends
on how it fits in a broader framework, a vision of the political and constitutional whole.[17]

White and *Zimmer* offered "a laundry list of factors, but . . . never
[oriented] the inquiry," James Blumstein, professor of law at Vanderbilt
University, has written. The decisions demanded "a balance" but provided
"no scale."[18] Left without a "scale" and deprived of bearings, judges weighed
facts and arguments on a purely intuitive basis; the orientation became
their own. With the *Zimmer* criteria in place, "the judicial investigation
into dilution assume[d] an orderliness and rationality that disguise[d] the
subjectivity of the enterprise," political scientist Timothy O'Rourke testified at
1982 Senate hearings on amending the Voting Rights Act.[19] In subsequent
years, that problem was conspicuously evident in the implementation of the
revised section 2, which, as noted earlier, pulled the confusing, inadequate
constitutional standards into the Voting Rights Act itself.

Bolden and the 1982 Amendments to Section 2

The *Whitcomb*, *White*, and *Zimmer* line of Fourteenth Amendment cases
ended in 1980 with the Supreme Court's decision in *City of Mobile v. Bolden*.[20]
The right to vote meant the entitlement of citizens to cast their ballots in an

electoral system uncontaminated by racial purpose, the *Bolden* Court held. Plaintiffs must show invidious *intent* in the adoption or maintenance of the challenged voting procedure in order to prevail. It was not a unique demand, although it had not been made in the voting rights context before. In 1976, in an employment discrimination case, the Court held that "a law or official act" is never "unconstitutional *solely* because it has a racially disproportionate impact. . . . The invidious quality of a law claimed to be racially discriminatory must ultimately be traced to a racially discriminatory purpose."[21] The point was equally applicable to Fourteenth Amendment voting rights claims, the Court concluded.

It was another decision that did not sit well with the civil rights community, which regarded the demand for a showing of discriminatory purpose as almost impossible to meet (although in subsequent years it applauded when the DOJ relied heavily on findings of intent to strike down new electoral practices on section 5 grounds).[22] In response, it quickly persuaded Congress to take the opportunity presented by the 1982 expiration of sections 4 and 5 to reword section 2 as a means of pulling the pre-*Bolden* constitutional standards into the Voting Rights Act itself.[23]

As written in 1965, section 2 was a slightly wordy restatement of the Fifteenth Amendment:

> No voting qualification or prerequisite to voting, or standard, practice, or procedure shall be imposed or applied by any State or political subdivision to deny or abridge the right of any citizen of the United States to vote on account of race or color.

After the 1982 amendments, the radically altered language read:

> No voting qualification or prerequisite to voting, or standard, practice, or procedure shall be imposed or applied . . . in a manner which results in a denial or abridgement of the right . . . to vote on account of race or color. A violation . . . is established if, based on the totality of circumstances, it is shown that the political processes leading to nomination or election in the State or political division are not equally open to participation by members of a [protected] class of citizens . . . in that its members have

less opportunity than other members of the electorate to participate in the political process and to elect representatives of their
choice. The extent to which members of a protected group have
been elected . . . is one circumstance which may be considered:
Provided, That nothing in this section establishes a right to have
members of a protected class elected in numbers equal to their
proportion of the population.

The final sentence is known as the "Dole compromise." Kansas senator
Robert Dole was known to have presidential aspirations and thus wanted to
sign this civil rights legislation. He managed to get the "compromise" tacked
on at the last minute to respond to Republicans' concern that racially fair
electoral "results" could only mean one thing: racial quotas.[24]

Civil rights spokesmen argued that the amended language would not
actually alter section 2; the constitutional standards and those inherent in
section 2 were considered one and the same prior to the *Bolden* decision,
they said—even though, in fact, neither *Whitcomb* nor *White* mentioned
section 2. The *Bolden* Court did refer to the provision, only to say it added
nothing to the appellees' claim.[25] Nevertheless, the point of the amendment
was only to clarify—not alter—the provision, they contended.[26]

In actuality, the aim of the civil rights groups, which in 1980 began
to organize a massive lobbying effort to revise section 2, went far beyond
clarifying the preamble and writing *White v. Regester* into the statute. Those
who participated in the disciplined and determined campaign genuinely
believed, as Jesse Jackson said, that if "South Carolina's population is 30 percent black, [then] . . . 30 percent of the [state] senate should be black."[27]
They hoped that section 2 would, at a minimum, eliminate at-large voting
from the nation's repertoire of legitimate methods of election, and would
create as many safe black districts as could be drawn.[28]

Undoubtedly, disproportionately low officeholding in the South in the
early 1980s was mainly a holdover effect of past black disfranchisement.
There was considerable merit to the notion that, whatever share of political
power was "fair," blacks did not have it, particularly in the South. But that
region had a distinctive history, and citywide voting was not, per se,
discriminatory. In any case, perfect proportionality was the wrong
standard—in schools, in places of employment, and on legislative bodies.

Statistical disparities are a sign of possible discrimination, but they should never be more than the beginning of an investigation.

And, in fact, voting rights advocates, at least on paper, had gotten less than they wanted. The new section 2 gave blacks not their statistically "fair share" of political offices, but only a "fair shake"—a chance to play the electoral game by fair rules.[29] There was, in theory, no entitlement to legislative seats reserved for black officeholders. Moreover, the phrase "representatives of their choice" plainly suggested a definition of representation broader than would have been conveyed had the wording been "*minority* representatives of their choice."

It was only in racist settings that minority voters were denied their fair shake—the electoral opportunities with which the amended section 2 was concerned—the 1982 Senate Judiciary Committee report concluded. Blacks lacked an equal chance to elect representatives of their choice in cases where race had left them politically isolated, without potential allies in electoral contests. The report listed "factors" to which courts were instructed to refer in judging the merits of a vote dilution suit.[30] It was another unsatisfactory checklist, but it did rule out disparate impact as the test for electoral discrimination.

Racism was the test, the list implied. Judges were instructed to identify those situations in which either a history of discrimination or ongoing racism left minority voters at a distinct disadvantage in the electoral process. A South Carolina district court decision was cited as a faithful application of the allegedly familiar "results" test. The plaintiffs had prevailed in that decision because black candidates, the court found, lost elections "not on their merits but solely because of their race."[31] The report issued by the Senate Subcommittee on the Constitution expressed concern that precisely that distinction would be lost.[32] Not so, retorted the full committee's own report. In "*most*" jurisdictions, white voters would support black candidates. But, "unfortunately," the report noted, "there still are some communities . . . where racial politics do dominate the electoral process."[33]

Just a few lingering holdouts—"some" racist communities—remained in which well-established methods of voting escaped preclearance review: That was also the case made for section 2 by a key civil rights advocate who testified at the hearings. Armand Derfner and others made a substantial effort to reassure those who, like Utah senator Orrin Hatch, believed that a "results" test for methods of election would alter the American electoral landscape,

instituting racial gerrymandering wherever minority office-holding was disproportionately low.[34] Derfner contended that single-member districts had no
"precisely correct racial mix." The entitlement was not to districts that were,
say, two-thirds black and one-third white—districts designed to protect minority candidates from white competition. Section 2 only promised an electoral
process that was *fluid*—open to racial change—not "frozen." Would minority
voters have "some influence"? courts were expected to ask. Claims of dilution
would rest, Derfner said, on "evidence that voters of a racial minority [were]
isolated within a political system . . . 'shut out,' i.e. denied access . . . [without]
the opportunity to participate in the electoral process."[35]

When were minorities "frozen" out? Neither Derfner nor any other
witness offered a definition of that total electoral exclusion against which
the act protected, except to say that the test had been met when a group had
"really been unfairly throttled"—unfairly throttled by racism, the Senate
report, as well as the entire history of the statute, seemed to make clear. The
entire point of the Voting Rights Act had been protection from racism—
effective enforcement of Fifteenth Amendment rights. Only that 1870 constitutional amendment legitimized the extraordinary power that the statute
conferred on federal authorities, and political exclusion on the basis of race
was its indisputable concern.

That was not the basis on which courts interpreted the amended provision, however. The fears of Senator Hatch and others who testified in 1982
in opposition to a "results" test for electoral discrimination proved prescient,
although they were ignored at the time. They understood perfectly what was
on the horizon: section 2 cases decided by a formulaic accounting of whites
voting for black-preferred candidates and blacks holding office. Reliance
on numbers would provide a norm against which to measure evidence of
discrimination, and it would reduce judicial discretion. But once Congress
had voted, of course, the concerns of Hatch and others became irrelevant
history—as did the soothing rhetoric of Derfner and his colleagues.

Thornburg v. Gingles: The Court Weighs In

Inevitably, once the amended section 2 became law, the provision took on a
life of its own, as the civil rights groups undoubtedly had expected and

hoped it would. They viewed the focus on racism as too confining, but the constitutional cases upon which those who rewrote section 2 also relied permitted what one court called "almost unbridled discretion."[37]

The "results test of section 2 was a return to the standard of *White v. Regester*," voting rights advocates agreed.[38] But recall James Blumstein's description of *White* and *Zimmer* as offering "a laundry list of factors" that never orients the inquiry. University of South Carolina law professor Katharine Butler chose another metaphor, that of a "Chinese menu."[39] Any combination of items from a list that included, for example, a history of discrimination and a majority-vote requirement could be selected at random and used to prove discrimination.[40] In the Supreme Court's first interpretation of the amended section 2, which remains its most important, Justice William Brennan, writing for a patched-together majority, concocted a new "Chinese menu."

The case was *Thornburg v. Gingles*, decided in 1986, which involved North Carolina's state senate and house redistricting plan.[41] At issue were five multimember districts that plaintiffs challenged as impairing the opportunity of black voters "to participate in the political process and to elect representatives of their choice," although, as the district court found, black candidates had enjoyed a high degree of success in the state.[42]

The Court was badly split, with different parts of Brennan's opinion joined by different justices, and three additional separate opinions either concurring in part or concurring and dissenting in part. The riot of opinions delivered a clear message: The amendment of section 2 had solved none of the definitional and normative problems so evident in the Fourteenth Amendment cases decided between 1971 and 1980. All pretense of a focus on racism had disappeared, and the meaning of equal electoral opportunity was as unsettled as ever.

"A court must assess the impact of the contested structure or practice on minority electoral opportunities 'on the basis of objective factors,'" Justice Brennan wrote.[43] Among the "objective factors" were those listed in the Senate report, but that list was "neither comprehensive nor exclusive," Brennan said. A resolution in section 2 cases demanded "a searching practical evaluation of the 'past and present reality'"—of that "totality of circumstances" that results in "unequal access to the electoral process."[44]

What that meant was anybody's guess. "What precisely does the Court ask itself after it has looked at the totality of circumstances?" Senator Orrin Hatch had wondered at the 1982 hearings, clearly worrying that a lack of precision in the statutory language itself would spell trouble down the road, whatever the Senate report said. "Look at the results," Maryland Senator Charles Mathias had replied.[45] "What is the judicial inquiry?" Hatch had asked Steve Suitts, the executive director of the Southern Regional Council. "I think a judge would be bound . . . to look at whether or not the scheme of circumstances created by the jurisdiction creates a discriminatory scheme," Suitts had responded.[46]

Such answers were, of course, useless, and so the *Gingles* Court forged ahead, exercising considerable creative license. To prevail in a section 2 suit, Brennan said, plaintiffs must demonstrate the presence of three "preconditions." The minority group must be able to show that it is sufficiently large and geographically compact to constitute a majority in a single-member district; it must demonstrate its political cohesiveness; and it must have evidence that the white majority votes as a bloc, so as to enable it usually to defeat the minority group's preferred candidates.[47]

Justice Brennan called the last precondition, racial bloc voting, a "key element of a vote dilution claim," but he eliminated from racially driven choices the logically essential element of racism: white resistance to black candidacies. "The reasons black and white voters vote differently have no relevance to the central inquiry of § 2," he concluded. "It is the difference between the choices made by blacks and whites—not the reasons for that difference—that results in blacks having less opportunity than whites to elect their preferred representatives."[48] So, if 52 percent of blacks vote for the Democratic candidate but only 48 percent of whites do so, racially polarized voting exists. It was an implicit repudiation of *Whitcomb*, with its holding that political affiliation, not racism, explained white Republican victories in Marion County, Indiana. And yet *Whitcomb* was one of the cases upon which section 2 was built, and only three justices joined Brennan on this point.

The rest of Brennan's opinion was a hodgepodge of woolly points meant to clarify the opaque language of section 2. "The essence of a § 2 claim is that a certain electoral law, practice, or structure interacts with social and historical conditions to cause an inequality in the opportunities enjoyed by black and white voters to elect their preferred representatives," he said.[49] It wasn't exactly helpful language for courts looking for concrete guidance.

What was the logic, in any case? Brennan referred to blacks having less education, menial jobs, and lower incomes, as well as low rates of home and car ownership. Echoing the 1982 Senate report, he noted that members of minority groups "bear the effects of discrimination in such areas as education, employment, and health." All undoubtedly true, but why was the remedy for housing, educational, and other inequalities race-based districting? If there were health disparities, surely health programs would be the answer. And if there were "vestigial effects" of a history of housing discrimination and the need to compensate for them by creating safe black districts, as Brennan asserted, then every American community with a minority population was vulnerable to a section 2 suit.[50] By Brennan's vague standard, a history of discrimination in some form could always be found, and jurisdictions, in trying to defend themselves, faced very heavy odds.

O'Connor's Concurrence

Justice Sandra Day O'Connor wrote a concurring opinion in *Thornburg v. Gingles* that reads like a dissent. "Amended § 2," she wrote, "is intended to codify the 'results' test employed in *Whitcomb v. Chavis* and *White v. Regester*," but "the vote dilution analysis adopted by the Court today clearly bears little resemblance to the 'results' test that emerged in *Whitcomb* and *White*."[51] When section 2 was revised, the legal definitions of "minority voting strength" and "racial bloc voting" had been left largely unaddressed, she went on. "The Court resolves the first question summarily: minority voting strength is to be assessed solely in terms of the minority group's ability to elect candidates it prefers."[52] And it uses the level of minority electoral success to assess significant white bloc voting, as well. If the candidates preferred by minority voters have lost, then whites must have voted to defeat them.[53]

In the 1982 Senate Judiciary Committee report on the bill to amend section 2, the level of minority officeholding was only one criterion by which electoral exclusion was supposed to be measured.[54] But the emphasis on electoral success in Brennan's opinion, O'Connor observed, simply ignored that report's emphasis on racism as distorting the political process, and left "vote dilution" still undefined.[55] "How should undiluted minority voting strength be measured?" she asked. "In order to decide whether an electoral system has made it harder for minority voters to elect the candidates they prefer, a court must have an idea in mind of how hard it 'should' be for minority voters to elect their preferred candidates under an acceptable system."[56]

O'Connor's concern was a variation on the central point in Justice Felix Frankfurter's famous dissent twenty-four years earlier in *Baker v. Carr*, the first of the one-person, one-vote constitutional decisions. Courts were being asked, Frankfurter had said, "to choose among competing theories of political philosophy" to define the nature of equitable representation—a task that should not have been theirs.[57] Dissenting in *Allen v. State Board of Elections*, Justice Harlan had made essentially the same point:

> It is not clear to me how a court would go about deciding whether an at-large system is to be preferred over a district system. Under one system, Negroes have some influence in the election of all officers; under the other, minority groups have more influence in the selection of fewer officers. If courts cannot intelligently compare such alternatives, it should not be readily inferred that Congress has required them to undertake the task.[58]

Nevertheless, Justice O'Connor noted, Brennan had a "simple and invariable" answer to the question of a norm against which to measure dilution:

> A court should calculate minority voting strength by assuming that the minority group is concentrated in a single-member district in which it constitutes a voting majority. . . . The representatives that it could elect in the hypothetical district or districts in which it constitutes a majority will serve as the measure of its undiluted voting strength.[59]

It was the measure of electoral inclusion Brennan had unsuccessfully urged in his dissent in *Richmond v. United States*; the majority, in his view, had not gone far enough in insisting on race-conscious, single-member districts drawn to elect black councilmen. It was thus no surprise that, in writing for the majority in *Gingles*, he had created what O'Connor correctly called a right to usual, roughly proportional representation on the part of sizable, compact, cohesive minority groups. If, under a particular multimember or single-member district plan, qualified minority groups usually cannot elect the representatives they would be likely to elect under the most favorable single-member districting plan, then § 2 is violated.[60]

That was not, however, what Congress intended. In fact, recall that section 2 explicitly rejected the idea of a right to proportional racial and ethnic representation with a disclaimer that read, "Nothing in this section establishes a right to have members of a protected class elected in numbers equal to their proportion in the population." But a number of witnesses at the 1982 Senate hearings warned that proportionality was nevertheless the inevitable standard. "You are proving deviation from a norm—what can the norm possibly be except racially based entitlements?" James Blumstein had asked. Without a definition of a voting rights violation, there would be "an inexorable trend towards using an easy standard, the numbers standard."[61] Donald Horowitz, professor of law at Duke, pointed to the obvious difference between sections 5 and 2. The preclearance provision, aimed only at revisions in electoral law, allowed a before-and-after comparison, while section 2 applied not merely to changes but to existing electoral law. "The only way to judge the effect," Horowitz noted, "will be to see whether minority voters have representatives in proportion to their population in that jurisdiction. By what other standard could one possibly judge dilution under section 2?"[62]

There was, in fact, no other logical standard; in any case, it was the one to which voting rights advocates were committed, although it was politically impossible to admit as much at the 1982 hearings. A nonracist society, they were convinced, would elect minorities to public office in proportion to their population.[63]

Three Preconditions

Gingles compounded the already daunting problem of deciphering minority voting rights under the 1965 statute and made even more confusing a bewildering provision that was intended to resurrect the perplexing legal standards in *Whitcomb v. Chavis* and other Fourteenth Amendment decisions. It left the lower courts and the Supreme Court in subsequent cases to struggle with making sense of two layers of complexity: the statute itself and the Court's interpretation of it in its 1986 decision, with its implicit (yet legally impermissible) entitlement to proportional racial and ethnic representation.

Even *Gingles'* three preconditions—the threshold questions—left important matters unresolved. When was a "minority group . . . sufficiently large and geographically compact to constitute a majority in a single-member district"? As it turned out, neither "large" nor "compact" had an obvious definition. Neither did political cohesion. If blacks were Democrats in a Republican-dominated jurisdiction, were they "cohesive" for section 2 purposes—potentially entitled to special protection?

Superficially, the first precondition seemed clear enough. Clearly, majority-minority, single-member districts were the expected remedy for a section 2 violation, and there was no point in insisting they be drawn if the black population was too small and geographically scattered to allow their creation.[64]

But when was the minority population "sufficiently large"? In redrawing district lines to meet the one-person, one-vote constitutional mandate, total population numbers—irrespective of eligibility to vote—are used.[65] In calculating minority electoral "opportunity," the most frequent measure of electoral strength is voting-age population. But in some settings where turnout is usually low, a majority-minority district has been defined as one with a 65 percent (or higher) black or Hispanic population.[66] In the case of Hispanics, many residents could be noncitizens, a fact that legislators routinely take into account.[67]

Probable turnout is not the only factor courts consider in assessing potential minority voting strength in a single-member district drawn to provide greater electoral opportunity for black and Hispanic voters. Litigation in the early 1990s over congressional districts in Texas illustrates this point vividly. Eddie Bernice Johnson, an African American, was at that time a state legislator with the power to design a congressional district from which she would be sure to be elected to the U.S. House of Representatives. She searched, she testified, for "performing" black voters. She did not, for instance, want neighborhoods where felons, who could not vote, were concentrated. Because renters were too residentially mobile to depend on, she wanted homeowners.[68] A seemingly safe black district wasn't safe (its minority population "sufficiently large") if too few of its residents were eligible and reliable voters.

The first *Gingles* precondition had another component besides the size of the minority group in a district: A district had to be geographically "compact." It quickly became apparent, however, that courts were prepared to ignore the plain meaning of the term. For instance, in a 1988 decision involving at-large voting for an Alabama county board of education, the district court said it was "apparent from the *Thornburg* [v. *Gingles*] opinion that compactness is a relative term . . . The term is a 'practical' or 'functional' concept. . . . A district is sufficiently geographically compact if it allows for effective representation."[69] In other words, a "compact" district was one that elected minority candidates—whatever its shape. The only demand was contiguity—an insistence that the scattered residential enclaves touch at some point on the map.[70]

There was good reason for voting rights advocates to stress a "functional" concept of compactness, liberating the term from geographical constraints. It permitted those who drew the maps to create more majority-black districts,[71] and it allowed the district lines to adjust to demographic change. Thus, Congresswoman Johnson explained the shape of Texas Congressional District 30 "including the various 'finger'-like extensions . . . as a conscious effort to pick up African-American voters who had dispersed from the core [Dallas] area."[72]

But as minority families continue to move up into the middle class and from city to suburb, the legitimacy of wandering district lines chasing after these mobile residents to maintain safe black legislative constituencies is likely to become increasingly questionable.[73] Black and Hispanic families who leave central cities don't necessarily identify with their old neighborhoods. Their sense of socioeconomic status may alter. They acquire new neighbors with interests tied to the schools and other institutions and organizations in the immediate area. In different parts of a far-flung district, different media markets may operate, weakening their connection to candidates.[74] And yet, these families often remain politically linked to their old neighbors in noncompact "compact" districts.

Minority political cohesion was the second *Gingles* threshold question, but near-universal black loyalty to the Democratic Party (or to party surrogates in local nonpartisan races) made their political solidarity a foregone conclusion. The core concern in section 2 was with racial groups whose distinctive interests were thwarted by hostile whites; but if "a significant number of minority group members *usually* vote[d] for the same candidates," the test for cohesion, as Brennan had defined it in *Gingles*, had been met.[75] Plaintiffs could satisfy one of the three preconditions to a section 2 suit if they simply pointed to "usual" minority voter support for Democratic candidates, and they would prevail if the challenged district was majority-Republican and could be redrawn as majority-Democratic.

If that was the correct reading of the law, however, the statute had become a Democratic Protection Act. It was a danger the Court recognized in the 2006 Texas congressional districting case when it concluded that Representative Martin Frost's convoluted district had been "drawn for an Anglo Democrat." Since it was not designed to elect a minority, it had no privileged Voting Rights Act status and need not be preserved, the Court held.[76]

The problem of defining "cohesion" raised another question. Did Justice Brennan mean to imply that lower courts could sometimes regard blacks and Hispanics as a single, cohesive minority group? If so, he was ignoring the reality that, as a Texas district court noted in 1994 with respect to Dallas County, "there is little evidence of coalition voting between blacks and Hispanics." To combine groups, one witness testified at trial, "would be the 'worst scenario' because 'they will vote for members of their own ethnic group, making it more likely that a nonminority candidate will win.'"[77] The point did not apply to Texas alone; black and Hispanic tension is well documented in cities like Los Angeles, for instance.

Black and Hispanic coalitions are often "ephemeral political alliances having little or no necessary connection to discrimination," Judge Patrick E. Higginbotham had noted, dissenting in an earlier Texas case. Such ephemeral political alliances must be distinguished from "cohesive political units joined by a common disability of chronic bigotry."[78] There was no voting rights violation without a showing of that "disability." "A coalition based on a similar political agenda . . . is not one for which Section 2 should provide protection," Katharine I. Butler and Richard Murray have argued. "Were the rule otherwise, then any coalition could seek Section 2 relief, so long as some number of its members were 'protected' minorities."[79]

The wording of the provision itself suggested that two groups could not be treated as one. As the Sixth Circuit observed in a 1996 decision, "Even the most cursory examination reveals that §2 of the Voting Rights Act does not mention minority coalitions, either expressly or conceptually." Moreover, the court continued, a group must show that "*its* members have less opportunity than other members of the electorate." The statutory language does not refer to groups, plural, who must demonstrate that "*their* members have less opportunity."[80]

A finding that white bloc voting usually defeated minority-preferred candidates was the third precondition to finding a section 2 violation. But, once again, *Gingles* left a host of questions in its wake. When were whites a "bloc" whose power usually defeated the preferred candidates of minority voters? Brennan had used the level of minority electoral success to assess significant white bloc voting, O'Connor had pointed out in her concurrence. But many factors—party affiliation, as well as low name recognition or a poorly run campaign, for example—could defeat black candidates.[81] Racial animus was only one possibility. And, if the white vote were split, at what point did it cease to be "bloc"?

The *Gingles* decision had "brought the racially polarized voting inquiry into the undisputed and unchallenged center of the Voting Rights Act," Samuel Issacharoff has written.[82] It was a problematic "center." Neither *White* nor *Zimmer*, in their laundry lists of factors to be considered in assessing unequal electoral opportunity, had mentioned racially polarized voting.[83] The term simply does not appear in the Fourteenth Amendment cases from which section 2 took its language. Moreover, in 1982 Congress had written into the statute an explicit statement rejecting proportional racial representation as a right. And yet that entitlement was implicit in the notion of a likely section 2 violation whenever, for instance, white Republicans and black Democrats in a majority-white district generally supported different candidates and Republicans (white or black) won in contested elections.

Justice Byron White illustrated the absurdity of the Brennan definition of polarized voting—a definition to which only four members of the *Gingles* Court had signed on:

> Suppose an eight-member multimember district that is 60%
> white and 40% black, the blacks being geographically located so

that two safe black single-member districts could be drawn. Suppose further that there are six white and two black Democrats running against six white and two black Republicans. Under JUSTICE BRENNAN'S test, there would be polarized voting and a likely [section] 2 violation if all the Republicans, including the two blacks, are elected, and 80% of the blacks in the predominantly black areas vote Democratic. I take it that there would also be a violation in a single-member district that is 60% black, but enough of the blacks vote with the whites to elect a black candidate who is not the choice of the majority of black voters. This is interest-group politics rather than a rule hedging against racial discrimination.[84]

Justice White's second hypothetic closely resembles the context in which Representative John Lewis would first get elected to Congress later that year: He won only a minority of the black vote running in the Democratic primary against Julian Bond, but a majority of whites supported him. Most blacks had voted for Bond, most whites for Lewis. By Brennan's definition, voting in that Democratic district was racially polarized. Black electoral success, Brennan had written in *Gingles*, "does not necessarily prove that the district did not experience polarized voting in that election." Special circumstances might have accounted for the result.[85] The election of minority candidates "does not foreclose a §2 claim."[86] Had there been electoral exclusion in Georgia's Fifth Congressional District, which Lewis has been representing ever since that 1986 election?

A number of lower court judges (along with a majority on the high Court) rejected Brennan's definition of racially polarized voting. "When racial antagonism is not the cause of an electoral defeat suffered by a minority candidate, the defeat does not prove a lack of electoral opportunity but a lack of whatever else it takes to be successful in politics," Judge Bruce M. Selya of the First Circuit argued in 1995, rejecting the vote dilution claims of Hispanic voters in Holyoke, Massachusetts.[87]

Judge Higginbotham, writing for the Fifth Circuit in a 1993 case involving the election of Texas state trial judges, explored the point at length.[88] As he observed, disagreement among judges with Brennan's definition of white bloc voting cut "deep, reflecting quite different visions of voting rights and their statutory treatment."[89] He resurrected *Whitcomb v. Chavis*, the central point of which had been mostly airbrushed out of section 2 decisions. Courts could distort the statute; they could not alter the text of section 2 itself, which refers to voting rights abridged or denied "on account of race or color." The lower court, he wrote, "in holding that the failure of minority-preferred candidates to receive support from a majority of whites on a regular basis . . . sufficed to prove legally significant racial bloc voting . . . [had] loosed § 2 from its racial tether and fused illegal vote dilution and political defeat."[90]

In 1982, the Senate report accompanying the amendment of section 2 had described its congressional concern as confined to elections in indisputably racist settings—settings in which (as Drew Days, former assistant attorney general for civil rights, put it) "a combination of public activity and private discrimination have joined to make it *virtually impossible* for minorities to play a meaningful role in the electoral process."[91] Judge Higginbotham returned to both *Whitcomb* and that history, reminding district court judges that the Senate (where the debate on section 2 took place) had chosen to retain *Whitcomb*'s sharp distinction between "built-in bias" and "political defeat at the polls." Racial bloc voting was evident, he argued, only when race was found to be "the predominant determinant of political preference."[92] Where there is no racial animosity, overlapping interests—common ground between white and minority voters—make victorious interracial coalitions possible.[93]

A year after Higginbotham's opinion in *LULAC v. Clements*, the Eleventh Circuit reiterated the importance of finding evidence that the "voting community is driven by racial bias."[94] The case involved the election of Florida judges, and Judge Gerald B. Tjoflat, writing for an en banc court, also went back to the legislative history and concluded that "the language of section 2 as amended . . . explicitly retains racial bias as the gravamen of a vote dilution claim."[95]

Taking racial bias out of the test for section 2 violations carried the danger that Justice O'Connor had identified in *Gingles* in 1986: If the reasons whites voted as they did were unimportant, then only the bottom line—election results—counted. Had a proper number of black candidates won? The standard against which to measure those results was inevitably office-holding in proportion to the minority population; anything less suggested compromised representation. It was a point picked up by Judge Selya in his 1995 Holyoke, Massachusetts, decision: Dismissing nonracial reasons when blacks lost elections was "a back-door approach to proportional representation," he wrote.[96]

The bias toward single-member districting that promised roughly proportional minority officeholding was also the result of a quandary in which legislators found themselves. As Daniel Polsby and Robert Popper have pointed out,

> State legislatures that wish to follow the precept of the plurality [in *Gingles*] can realistically conclude that they have a duty to alter any electoral system in which racial bloc voting has *prevented* proportional representation. A cause of action appears to exist whenever a plaintiff can argue that proportional representation could have been achieved, but was not. The possibility of proportional racial representation, in other words, establishes the *necessity* of proportional racial representation.[97]

Most state legislators drawing districting maps and many judges accepted "the necessity of proportional racial representation." The legislators were responding to political pressure from blacks, but also steering the safest course of action, protecting themselves from the threat of section 2 lawsuits. As UCLA law professor Daniel H. Lowenstein has explained,

> Much is at stake for politicians and the interests they represent in a districting plan, and enacting a plan is typically a difficult and contentious process. Once they strike a deal, they want it to stay struck, and therefore they tend to be risk-averse with respect to possible legal vulnerabilities in a plan.[98]

The three "preconditions" to finding a section 2 violation left important matters unresolved, I have argued. Judges could not even agree on the weight to be given those threshold questions. How much more did plaintiffs need to show, once a court had become convinced that at least one majority-minority district could be drawn, that blacks or Hispanics were politically cohesive, and that whites were bloc-voting against the candidates whom minority voters preferred?[99] Brennan in *Gingles* had called for "a searching practical evaluation of the 'past and present reality'"—of that "totality of circumstances" that results in "unequal access to the electoral process." But, in most cases, both the three preconditions and the list of factors the courts were expected to go through in assessing that "totality" were cavalierly checked off.[100]

Taking their cue from *Gingles*, the courts administered what Samuel Issacharoff has called "a simplified test to determine whether white voters as a group had frustrated the electoral aspirations of a cohesive set of minority voters and, if so, whether an alteration of electoral practices could relieve the diminution of minority electoral opportunity."[101] But minority voters were always "a cohesive set," given their overwhelming loyalty to the Democratic Party. Brennan's definition had made racial bloc voting close to ubiquitous. It could be found whenever, for partisan or other reasons, candidates supported by minority voters failed to get a sufficient number of white votes to win election.

The Totality of Circumstances

Gingles instructed lower courts to look beyond the three preconditions and also assess the "totality of circumstances" that might be frustrating "the electoral aspirations of a cohesive set of minority voters." Armed with the assumption that every contemporary racial disparity was the consequence of past injustices, most judges easily found the "effects" of historic discrimination in education, employment, and other spheres. In addition, with few exceptions, the number of minority candidates elected to office was found to be predictably less than it theoretically could have been.

A number of dangers lurked in such a simplification, aside from its tension with statutory history and its implicit partisan tilt.[102] *Gingles* had involved a mid-1980s southern setting in which white racism was on the wane but undoubtedly still operating to depress black representation. The disproportionately low number of blacks in elected office was a legitimate source of concern. But with the passage of time and the large number of section 2 suits brought in multiethnic jurisdictions outside the South, easy assumptions about white hostility and minority electoral opportunity no longer held. To equate Hispanics in, say, Holyoke, Massachusetts in 1995 with southern blacks thirty years earlier turned the statute into one indifferent to reality—in keeping with much civil rights rhetoric and the enforcement of other civil rights laws.[103]

Section 2 cases can be brought in any jurisdiction in which it is remotely plausible to argue that different districting lines or other changes in the method of voting would benefit minority voters. But race and politics in subtle ways differ from one place to another. The three-preconditions checklist (even assuming a resolution of the definitional problems) as an aid to establishing a voting rights violation is of only limited use in the contemporary racial and ethnic environment. As Judge Selya wrote in the Holyoke case, "The resolution of [section 2] claims demands a careful sifting of imbricated, highly ramified fact patterns."[104]

The diversity of the racial and political landscape had been apparent to the Supreme Court as early as 1973; assessments of electoral exclusion, it had said in *White v. Regester*, required an "intensely local appraisal."[105] More recently, racial change has greatly magnified the point. The Eleventh Circuit described the proper process of assessing vote dilution in particularly arrest- ing language. "Like a Seurat painting," the court said, judges create

> a portrait of the challenged scheme. . . . Only by looking at all of the dots on the canvas is a district court able to determine whether vote dilution has occurred. A court should not exclude certain types of relevant evidence—certain colors on the canvas— from its examination if doing so would leave an incomplete view of the circumstantial evidence picture.[106]

The danger of ignoring some "colors on the canvas"—of reducing the section 2 question to that of black and white voting patterns—is, of course, a misguided finding of vote dilution or its absence.

Racial and ethnic change has accentuated a host of other questions that were either unnoticed or barely apparent in 1986 when *Gingles* was decid- ed. "'The power to influence the political process is not limited to winning elections,'" Justice O'Connor had said in her concurrence, quoting *Davis v. Bandemer*, a 1986 partisan gerrymandering case.[107] If that statement had been made in 1965 and with reference to black electoral power in the South, it would have been heard as callously dismissive of the importance of descriptive representation—of seeing black faces in office—after so many decades of total exclusion. Two decades later, however, it expressed legitimate concern that ignoring racial progress and continuing to insist on drawing a maximum number of majority-black constituencies could waste black votes.

It seems safe to say that in 1982, when section 2 was amended, no one was worried about plaintiffs seeking to improve upon a districting plan that *already* provided majority-minority districts roughly in proportion to the black population; the level of black officeholding was still very low. But just a dozen years later the picture had changed, and that question actually was put to the Supreme Court. It was not necessary to go beyond proportionality, the Court held in 1994 in *Johnson v. De Grandy*. "One may suspect vote dilution from political famine, but one is not entitled to suspect (much less infer) dilution from mere failure to guarantee a political feast," Justice David Souter wrote. "However prejudiced a society might be, it would be absurd to suggest that the failure of a districting scheme to provide a minority group with effective political power 75 percent above its numerical strength indicates a denial of equal participation in the political process. Failure to maximize cannot be the measure of § 2."[108]

Souter's opinion in *De Grandy* contained another important acknowledgment of an altered racial climate—and one in which the minority population included both blacks and Hispanics, which was an additional complexity absent from the North Carolina setting in *Gingles*. "There are communities in which minority citizens are able to form coalitions with voters from other racial and ethnic groups, having no need to be a majority within a single district in order to elect candidates of their choice," he said. "Those candidates may not represent perfection to every minority voter, but minority voters are not immune from the obligation to pull, haul, and trade to find common political ground, the virtue of which is not to be slighted in applying a statute meant to hasten the waning of racism in American politics."[109]

By 1994, even one of the most liberal members of the Court had come close to the point of describing blacks and Hispanics as members of normal political interest groups. Moreover, Souter had distanced himself from the much-quoted aphorism of Justice Harry Blackmun in the 1978 *Bakke* case: "In order to get beyond racism, we must first take account of race."[110] We will get beyond racism, Souter had implied, by expecting minority voters to "pull, haul, and trade to find common political ground," as every other group must do. It was a remarkable statement, given the continuing entitlement of minority voters to a unique privileged status—with their candidates of choice protected from electoral defeat—decades down the road of racial change.

LULAC v. Perry

The Supreme Court in *De Grandy* and other, more recent, decisions— including *Georgia v. Ashcroft* in 2003, with its radical rewriting of the legal standards under section 5—was clearly flirting with abandoning some of the core assumptions upon which courts and the Justice Department had traditionally based their decisions.[111] But the limits to the Court's willingness to abandon familiar ground were apparent in its 2006 decision in *League of United Latin American Citizens [LULAC] v. Perry*.[112]

The case involved redistricting for Texas congressional seats, regarded by Democrats as "one of the most notorious partisan power grabs in our history."[113] There had been a 2001 map already in place, drawn by a court when the state legislature was deadlocked, but Republicans who had become the political majority since then viewed the court's lines as giving unfair advantage to Democrats. And, thus, in 2003, following a colorful political brawl in which the Republicans prevailed, the legislature drew new districting lines.[114]

The section 2 challenge to the revised map centered primarily on three congressional districts (CDs): 23, 24, and 25. CDs 23 and 25 had been redrawn in such a way as to deprive Hispanic voters of their opportunity to elect the candidates of their choice, appellants from adverse district court decisions argued. The two districts were, in effect, a package. Henry Bonilla, a Republican, represented CD 23, but he was losing ground politically. The number of Hispanic citizens of voting age in the district was growing, and they generally voted Democratic. In reconfiguring the district lines in 2003, Republican legislators reduced the Hispanic electorate from 57.5 percent to 46.0 percent, hoping the reduction would protect Bonilla. The drop in Hispanic numbers was arguably a violation of section 5, however, so a new, overwhelmingly Hispanic (and Democratic) CD 25 was drawn to compensate for the "retrogression."

District 24 was a different story. Since 1978 it had continuously elected Democrat Martin Frost, who had become dean of the Texas congressional delegation. But the new plan "cracked" the old CD 24, with the result that Frost's former constituents were now scattered in five districts, none of which was likely to elect a Democrat. With the new District 24 inhospitable territory for Frost, he decided to run in another district altogether and lost. *LULAC* appellants argued that the destruction of Frost's district was a violation of section 2. Although the congressman was white, he had been black voters' "candidate of choice," they claimed. His district could not be reconfigured; it was a minority entitlement.

Justice Anthony Kennedy wrote for the Court. Four of his colleagues signed on to one part or another, while another four dissented, although not in one voice, making for a cacophony of discordant perspectives on section 2.[115]

District 23 (Bonilla's) was the focus of much of the Court's argument. Its new lines violated section 2, Kennedy concluded. It was no longer the Latino "opportunity-to-elect" district that it previously had been. "District 23's Latino voters were poised to elect their candidate of choice. They were becoming more politically active, with a marked and continuous rise in Spanish-surnamed voter registration. . . . In successive elections Latinos were voting against Bonilla in greater numbers, and in 2002 they almost ousted him," Kennedy wrote. Thus, the state legislature had taken away "the Latinos' opportunity because Latinos were about to exercise it."[116]

In redrawing District 23, Republican state legislators had reduced the Latino voting-age population to a slim majority (50.9 percent), hoping that would be sufficient to protect the district against a section 2 suit. The action was unconstitutional, Nina Perales, an attorney from the Mexican American Legal Defense and Education Fund, stated in oral argument: "Texas violated the Equal Protection Clause by making excessive use of race in its changes to district 23. After removing 100,000 Latinos from district 23, the State used race to craft a razor-thin Latino majority."[117]

The point occasioned a near-comic exchange between Chief Justice John Roberts and Perales, as the chief justice plumbed the Goldilocks formula of racial gerrymandering. If a slim majority is insufficient, what number of minority voters is enough for a district to be counted as "Hispanic-opportunity"? he asked Perales seven times, in several different ways. Where is the line between looks good and actually good? "I'm just trying to get the number," he said in evident frustration.[118]

"That number would be the number that shows Latinos have the opportunity to elect their candidate of choice," was the best answer she could give. Minority voters, she believed, were entitled to a maximum number of "opportunity-to-elect" districts, which had, in fact, nothing to do with "opportunity" and everything to do with the right racial, ethnic—and partisan—results. That right result, in this case, was the election of a Hispanic Democrat.

Texas had argued that, in altering the boundaries of Representative Bonilla's district, it nevertheless met its obligations under the Voting Rights Act by creating CD 25, an additional majority-Hispanic district. But the Court didn't like its looks. The district was not compact; it was a long bacon strip. Looks were not the real problem, however—and could not be, since a number of other Texas CDs appeared much less compact. Hispanics were clustered hundreds of miles apart in "different communities of interest" and yet were grouped together for purposes of representation, Kennedy noted.[119] "Latino communities at the opposite ends of District 25 have divergent 'needs and interests,' owing to 'differences in socio-economic status, education, employment, health, and other characteristics.'"[120] In a district containing two such disparate communities, "one or both groups will be unable to achieve their political goals."[121] (Kennedy's acknowledgment of these complexities was uncharacteristic of previous civil rights decisions, although *Miller v. Georgia* in 1995 had also contained a brief but welcome recognition that not all members of a minority group are necessarily alike).

Finally, even with a Hispanic population of close to 70 percent in the new District 25, the Court argued, the number of majority-minority districts fell short of proportionality. Looking at the statewide numbers, "the five reasonably compact Latino opportunity districts amount to roughly 16% of the total, while Latinos make up 22% of Texas' citizen voting-age population. . . . Latinos are, therefore, two districts shy of proportional representation."[122]

Chief Justice John Roberts and Justice Samuel Alito rejected the majority's entire argument, running through it point for point. "What is blushingly ironic is that the district preferred by the majority—former District 23—suffers from the same 'flaw' the majority ascribes to District 25, except to a greater degree," Roberts and Alito noted. "Old District 23 runs 'from El Paso, *over 500 miles*, into San Antonio and down into Laredo. It covers a much longer distance than . . . the 300 miles from Travis to McAllen [in District 25]'. . . . So much for the significance of 'enormous geographical distance.'"[123]

The majority had asserted that the old 23 was a cohesive Latino "opportunity-to-elect" district, whereas the new 25 was not—or not to the same degree.[124] The chief justice was baffled. Although the districts drawn in 2003 had "*better* prospects for the success of minority-preferred candidates than an alternative plan," the majority nevertheless had found a denial of equal electoral opportunity "simply because one of the State's districts combines different minority communities, which, in any event, are likely to vote as a controlling bloc."[125] Hispanic voters in both Travis and Hidalgo counties (three hundred miles apart) were likely to prefer the same candidates, and thus enjoyed full "opportunity" to elect them.

"Latinos are . . . two districts shy of proportional representation," the Court had found. But in drawing that conclusion, Justice Kennedy had looked at statewide numbers, which was not the standard the Court had established in *De Grandy*.[126] Latino districts in south and west Texas were the sole issue, and in those relevant areas Latinos controlled five out of seven congressional seats, which made "their effective political power 46% above their numerical strength."[127]

As for the shape of CD 25, "'bacon strip' districts are inevitable, given the geography and demography of that area of the State," the lower court had explained.[128] In any case, Chief Justice Roberts noted, "States retain broad discretion in drawing districts to comply with the mandate of § 2."[129] And, further on: "Section 2 is, after all, part of the Voting Rights Act, not the Compactness Rights Act." The word "compactness" appears nowhere in section 2, the chief justice pointed out—not even in the "agreed-upon legislative history."[130] Recall that in *Gingles*, the potential to draw a compact majority-minority, single-member district was only a "precondition"—one part of the test for the availability of a remedy, should a section 2 violation be found. But compact districts were not an entitlement, Roberts was reminding the majority.

In reducing the Hispanic population in CD 23 and attempting to compensate for that reduction by creating CD 25, the state had deprived Latinos of an "opportunity-to-elect" district, a majority on the Court had found. But on the question of Martin Frost's entitlement to District 24, Justices Kennedy and Stevens were joined by the chief justice and Justice Alito.

District 24 had been only one-quarter black (in voting-age population) before it was redrawn, but that black minority had voted consistently for Frost. Moreover, black votes constituted 64 percent in the decisive Democratic primary. Thus, "an African-American minority effectively controlled District 24" and "§ 2 entitles them to this district," appellants claimed.[131] But CD 24 could not be called a district in which blacks could elect the candidate of their choice; Frost had never had a black opponent in the Democratic primary whom black voters might have preferred, the Court pointed out.[132] Indeed, the district had been drawn specifically to elect a white.[133] "That African-Americans had influence in the district . . . does not suffice to state a § 2 claim in these cases," Kennedy wrote:

> The opportunity "to elect representatives of their choice," requires more than the ability to influence the outcome between some candidates, none of whom is their candidate of choice . . . The fact that African-Americans preferred Frost to some others does not . . . make him their candidate of choice. Accordingly, the ability to aid in Frost's election does not make the old District 24 an African-American opportunity district for purposes of § 2.[134]

Justice Scalia, joined by Justice Thomas, turned their gaze to an entirely separate question, and one that the majority did not address: the constitutionality of District 23. Had the state, in moving Hispanics out of the district, violated the equal protection clause? Establishing a conflict with the Fourteenth Amendment required a showing of discriminatory purpose and the absence of a compelling state interest to justify the race-conscious policy. But the lower court had found no invidious racial intent behind the district's reconfiguration, and that finding could only be overturned if it was clearly in error—which it was not, Scalia concluded.[135]

The constitutional questions were the only ones addressed at any length in Scalia's opinion for a simple reason: His main statutory point had been made exhaustively by Justice Thomas, concurring a dozen years earlier in *Holder v. Hall*, a section 2 case in which the Court held that counties could elect to be governed by a single commissioner without violating minority voting rights.[136]

A brief allusion to that opinion was all that was required in *LULAC*. "I would dismiss appellants' vote-dilution claims premised on § 2 of the Voting Rights Act of 1965 for failure to state a claim, for the reasons set forth in Justice Thomas's opinion, which I joined, in *Holder v. Hall*," Scalia wrote.[137] There could be no legitimate section 2 claim, Thomas had argued in *Holder*, because "districting systems and electoral mechanisms that may affect the 'weight' given to a ballot duly cast and counted [are] simply beyond the purview of the Act."[138] There was no point in running through the section 2 issues in *LULAC* one by one when the core allegation lacked all legitimacy, in other words.

To this day, Justice Thomas's concurrence in *Holder* stands as a unique moment in the history of section 2 case law. It was the only time an attempt had been made to address the issues left unresolved, first by *White v. Register* and subsequent Fourteenth Amendment decisions, and then by the revision of section 2 built on the pre-1982 equal protection rulings: When are Fifteenth Amendment rights secure? What does it mean to say citizens are entitled to equal electoral opportunity? What is the measure of undiluted minority electoral strength? Who counts as a "minority" representative?

Section 2 cases raise these questions, Thomas argued in *Holder*, but the Court need not answer them—indeed, *cannot* answer them. "The matters the Court has set out to resolve in vote dilution cases are questions of political philosophy, not questions of law," he wrote. "As such, they are not readily subjected to any judicially manageable standards that can guide courts in attempting to select between competing theories."[139]

This was the view Scalia imported into *LULAC*. The contrast with the other conservatives on the bench was striking. Roberts and Alito engaged in a lengthy, point-by-point debate with Justice Kennedy and the liberal bloc of the Court. They argued about the length of the new District 25 in contrast to the old District 23, and whether CD 25 was more or less likely to elect a Latino. They quarreled about how to measure proportional representation and the definition of "compactness." And, on a number of central issues, there was a consensus across the ideological spectrum that only Scalia and Thomas did not join.

Those on left and right who debated the questions that swirled around Latino districts 23 and 25 agreed, most importantly, that section 2 entitled minority voters to "opportunity-to-elect" districts roughly in proportion to their population numbers, counted one way or another. Roberts and Alito accepted the *Gingles* framework and confined their disagreement with those who joined Kennedy's majority opinion to interpretive matters within that accepted framework. In this important respect, on questions involving minority voting rights, the real split on the Court was between Thomas and Scalia, on one side, and the other seven members of the Court, on the other. Only Thomas and Scalia dissented from the belief that section 2 permanently conferred upon blacks and Hispanics a level of protection from electoral competition that members of no other groups enjoyed.

The views of Thomas and Scalia are not likely to be adopted as those of the majority in the foreseeable future. That would require throwing aside all precedent interpreting section 2. Nevertheless, it is conceivable that the Court will chip away at the notion that proportional racial representation remains the measure of electoral equality at a time when minority groups are themselves becoming increasingly diverse and when black legislators are questioning the costs of max-black districting maps. White racism did create a black "community" in which all members shared the common experience of being second-class citizens, separate and unequal. That notion of a community that has no representation except by members of the group—with proportional racial representation as the corollary—is a holdover from a fading time. Today, it perpetuates stereotypical notions of black identity and works against black political integration—against a true fulfillment of the aim of the Voting Rights Act, in other words.

A Statute in Search of a Theory

What a mess—that is a mantra that runs through this book. A statute in search of a theory, Harvard law professor Lani Guinier once called the Voting Rights Act.[140] It wasn't true in 1965, but by 1982, when section 2 was rewritten, a revised civil rights vision had redefined disfranchisement and reshaped the remedies to which successful plaintiffs were entitled.

The result was not only the elimination of multimember districts and at-large voting, but an insistence that single-member districting plans be redrawn if different boundaries would create more "opportunity-to-elect" constituencies. Section 2 suits and anticipated suits changed the electoral landscape, particularly in the South, much more dramatically than the power of preclearance had been able to do. The proliferation of successful suits brought by civil rights groups put other jurisdictions on notice. Better safe than sorry, elected officials usually concluded.[141] If black officeholding proportionate to the black population had become a right, it was only prudent to redraw legislative maps before civil rights groups and the plaintiffs they found prevailed in a court of law and undid the laborious work of redistricting committees.

The new section 2 was the product of an era in which civil rights advocates had become concerned with processes and institutions that had a racially disparate impact, as well as those that were the obvious product of intentional racism—hence, the provision's ban on methods of election that were discriminatory in "result." But it gave protection as well against voting procedures that provided minority voters with "less opportunity [than whites] . . . to participate in the political process and to elect representatives of their choice." As earlier noted, the two concepts—opportunity and results—were very different, and yet the provision mashed them together, creating an indecipherable entitlement. The resulting confusion was, in great part, an inheritance from a line of Fourteenth Amendment cases that left in its wake a series of unanswered questions.

Section 5 provided a remedy for vote dilution *relative* to the electoral strength that blacks and Hispanics had enjoyed before a jurisdiction changed the rules that governed voting. Section 2, in contrast, guaranteed electoral equality in some absolute sense—undefined and undefinable. To this day, no court has found anything near consensus on how to assess such absolute equality. The fractured Court in *Gingles*, the Supreme Court's first attempt at making sense of section 2, was a flop by any minimum standard of clarity in sorting through the tough questions. It needs to be revisited.

The most basic issues remained unresolved. When were black and white voters on equal electoral footing? When did inequality between minority and white voters demand a new method of voting? Did defeat have a different meaning for minority candidates than for those who were white? How should the terms in the three *Gingles* threshold questions—"compact," "large," "cohesive," and so forth—be defined? The Court in *Gingles*, as Justice O'Connor pointed out, had implicitly endorsed a right to roughly proportional representation. But that right assumed—against all evidence to the contrary—that in a nonracist society minority officeholders and, indeed, minorities in all occupations would be present in proportion to the black and Hispanic population numbers. On what basis could that assumption be justified?

These questions were inherent in section 2 from the outset, but others have been raised by continuing racial progress, as I have suggested above. By now we might ask, just for starters, don't black candidates clearly lose elections—in the South, as well as the North—for reasons unrelated or marginally related to race?[142] In the 2008 presidential election, Barack Obama took North Carolina and Florida (neither in the Deep South, of course), but the majority of whites in the South vote Republican. They would not be likely to vote for a Democrat, black or white, in any election.

Is that because white southerners are racists, as many in the academy and the media would have us believe? As University of Virginia politics professor Gerard Alexander has pointed out, "The GOP finally became the region's dominant party in the least racist phase of the South's entire history, and it got that way by attracting most of its votes from the region's growing and confident communities—not its declining and fearful ones." That is, the GOP's southern base in recent decades has not, according to Alexander, been

> rural, nativist, less educated, afraid of change, or concentrated in the most stagnant parts of the Deep South. It [has become] disproportionately suburban, middle-class, educated, younger, non-native-Southern, and concentrated in the growth-points that were, so to speak, the least "Southern" parts of the South.[143]

The notion that the Republican Party today wins southern whites because those voters are racists ignores much evidence to the contrary.

Section 2 suits charging inadequate electoral opportunity and discriminatory results can be brought against jurisdictions anywhere in the nation. By now, even in the South, race cannot be assumed to be driving political choices. White voters in, say, Alabama rural counties may have quite a different profile than more upscale residents in suburban areas. The need for courts to engage in those "intensely local appraisals" to which *White v. Regester* referred has thus increased. What are judges to look for in making such appraisals? The same question obviously applies to the Justice Department's initiation of section 2 suits challenging practices it believes to be discriminatory in "result." *Zimmer* and the 1982 Senate report had provided checklists. And yet criteria that measure an undefined phenomenon are necessarily arbitrary, I argued earlier. Is there a way to stop rampant judicial subjectivity, the danger of which has increased with the growing complexity and subtlety of the racial landscape?

Racial change has made increasingly apparent, in Justice Souter's words, "the obligation [of blacks and Hispanics] to pull, haul, and trade to find common political ground" to engage in normal politics to gain office.[144] If blacks and Hispanics now need less protection from white competition, how much less? What is the ongoing justification for *any* such protection?

And, finally, perhaps it is a sign of racial progress that, in 2006, Justice Kennedy objected to the new District 25 on the ground that different Hispanic communities of interest had been grouped together for purposes of representation. The communities had "divergent 'needs and interests,' owing to 'differences in socio-economic status, education, employment, health, and other characteristics,'" Kennedy said, and he worried that "one or both groups will be unable to achieve their political goals."[145]

The implications were not spelled out. Did the Court mean to suggest that poor Hispanics (on the Mexican border) and those who were more affluent (in and around Austin) should each get their own districts? If so, Justice Kennedy had signed on to the novel—and welcome—notion that not all Hispanics are alike, as I suggested above. Perhaps down the road, the Court will come to believe that blacks aren't all alike, either. At that point, much of the structure of Voting Rights Act enforcement will likely come tumbling down. As a discussion in chapter 5 of recent Fourteenth Amendment cases will make clear, the Court has worried about racial stereotyping in the equal protection context. But it did not suggest before *LULAC* that, for statutory purposes, members of minority groups are not fungible.

Divvying Up

I have argued that in *LULAC v. Perry*, Justices Roberts and Alito were as bogged down in debating the fine details of the Texas redistricting map as Kennedy and company were. Only Justices Scalia and Thomas were willing to restate the big questions, with their reference to Thomas's concurrence in

Holder. The Roberts opinion, however, did contain one small hint of possible concurrence with Thomas and Scalia in a future section 2 decision. "It's a sordid business, this divvying us up by race," the chief justice wrote.[146] But racial sorting is obviously what the Voting Rights Act is all about—as Thomas had pointed out, arguing that the Court had "collaborated in what may aptly be termed the racial 'balkanization' of the Nation."[147]

To question the "divvying us up"—combined with Kennedy's suggestion that members of minority groups are not necessarily fungible—was to attack the very foundation of section 2 as it has been understood since 1986. To take the two points seriously is to start down a very different road from the one on which the courts and the Justice Department have been traveling, and to force what Justice Thomas demanded in *Holder*: "a systematic reexamination" of the Court's interpretation of the Voting Rights Act.[148]

4

Section 5 Enforcement:
The Mischief That Government
Bureaucrats Can Make

This plan does not come close to the criteria outlined by the Attorney General last summer, when he specifically told the states covered by the Act that wherever possible, you must draw majority black districts, wherever possible.

—Georgia state representative Tyrone Brooks[1]

The litigation over the 1991 Georgia congressional map is a remarkable story of a lawless Republican Department of Justice that forced a state to accept a plan drawn by the American Civil Liberties Union in its capacity as advocate for the black caucus of the state's general assembly, of which state representative Tyrone Brooks, quoted above, was a leading member. The enforcement of the Voting Rights Act has long made for strange bedfellows—although only superficially. In the Georgia case, John Dunne, the assistant attorney general for civil rights from 1990 to 1993, was an unambivalent champion of race-based districting to maximize minority officeholding. His alliance with the ACLU and the state black caucus served the Republican Party's interests, as well: What the ACLU called a "max-black" plan was also "max-white"—more black voters in some districts meant fewer in others, and, in the South particularly, districts that had been "bleached" were fertile ground for Republican political aspirations.[2]

Of course, redistricting is not the only area in which Republican opposition to what Chief Justice John Roberts called the "sordid business . . . [of]

divvying us up by race" has been shown to be pure myth. It is the rare Republican in elected office (or elsewhere) who has been willing to object publicly to racial sorting. But seldom is the magnitude of the gap between alleged principle and a quite different reality so fully on display as it has been in some of the redistricting cases.

Republican complicity in reshaping the Voting Rights Act to become the means by which "racially fair" methods of election have been imposed upon states and counties by the U.S. Department of Justice is one part of the story that runs through this chapter. A second part concerns the power of federal bureaucrats operating below the radar screen of public scrutiny to, in effect, rewrite federal legislation. They had considerable help from the courts in this endeavor, as previous chapters have suggested. But behind closed doors they also read ambiguous statutory language and inconsistent and carelessly written judicial decisions as an invitation to reshape the act to reflect the priorities of voting rights advocates who believed in proportional racial representation.

Those priorities were never publicly debated. Race-based districting is a form of racial preference; majority-minority districts confer upon members of two groups—African Americans and Hispanics—a uniquely privileged status in the American political system.[3] The candidates of their choice are generally protected from defeat. Such racial preferences have not been popular with the majority of Americans, but their values were simply of no interest to these self-appointed reformers on a moral mission. And they had a free hand, since few Americans paid attention to the decisions they made.

The Roadblocks Ahead

The Georgia House and Senate redistricting committees, when they began the map-drawing process following the 1990 census, had no idea of the roadblocks that lay ahead.[4] They drew one map and then another, both of them raising the number of majority black districts in Georgia from one to two. In considering these plans it is important to remember the Supreme Court's 1976 holding in *Beer v. United States*: Jurisdictions had no obligation to improve on the status quo—no obligation to draw districting lines that gave minorities the greater electoral power they might have had under what voting rights advocates considered a "better" plan.[5] The point of preclearance had been to prevent racially suspect states from depriving blacks of the political gains that basic enfranchisement promised—not to ensure a "fair" number of legislative seats. Georgia had clearly met the demands of the law.

Nevertheless, the Justice Department—indifferent to the law—found both maps in violation of section 5. John Dunne informed the state that it had not adequately explained its failure to create a *third* majority-minority district.[6] "No legitimate reason has been suggested to explain the exclusion of the second largest concentration of blacks in the state from a majority black Congressional District," a March 20, 1992, letter of objection read.[7]

Dunne wanted, among other changes, more black voters added to the Eleventh District, while some of the district's existing residents would be moved to a newly created Congressional District 2. But the reconfiguration would create an Eleventh District that connected black neighborhoods in metropolitan Atlanta and poor black residents on the coast, 260 miles away and "worlds apart in culture," as the Supreme Court put it in its 1995 decision in *Miller v. Johnson*. "In short," the Court continued, "the social, political and economic makeup of the Eleventh District [told] a tale of disparity, not community."[8] Dunne's insistence on heavy-handed racial gerrymandering forced candidates to run in four major media markets, while leaving CD 2 still only minority-black.[9]

Dunne's communications were entirely guided by ACLU attorney Kathleen Wilde, who had drawn up a "max-black" plan. As the district court noted, "Throughout the preclearance process, from this first objection letter to the final submission, [the Department of Justice] relied on versions of the max-black plan to argue that three majority-minority districts could indeed be squeezed out of the Georgia countryside. Ms. Wilde's triumph of demographic manipulation became DOJ's guiding light."[10] In fact, the Georgia legislators and staff who met with Justice Department attorneys in Washington were "told to subordinate their economic and political concerns to the quest for racial percentages."[11]

These legislators on the redistricting committee, many of whom were veteran mapmakers, were essentially cut out of the districting process by the Justice Department. Excluding them raised grave constitutional questions. As the Supreme Court stated in its 1995 decision rejecting the "max-black" plan as unconstitutional, "Electoral districting is a most difficult subject for legislatures, and so the States must have discretion to exercise the political judgment necessary to balance competing interests." Plainly, judicial or Justice Department review "represents a serious intrusion on the most vital of local functions."[12]

To make matters worse, DOJ attorneys had cultivated "informants" within the state legislature; "'whistleblowers' became 'secret agents,'" the district court found.[13] One of these informants described one black state senator who had not toed the line as a "quintessential Uncle Tom" and "the worst friend of blacks in Georgia."[14] By contrast, attorneys from the ACLU and the voting section of the DOJ's Civil Rights Division were characterized as "peers working together." They discussed the smallest details of the Wilde plan and its revisions, with the result that "there were countless communications, including notes, maps, and charts, by phone, mail and facsimile." In fact, the lower court found, the "DOJ was more accessible—and amenable—to the opinions of the ACLU than to those of the Attorney General of the State of Georgia."[15] The DOJ's March 1992 objection letter, quoted above, actually arrived at the state attorney general's office *after* members of the Georgia black caucus were already discussing it with the press, since the Justice Department attorneys had told the ACLU lawyers of their decision before informing any state official.[16] The court found this "informal and familiar" relationship between federal attorneys and an advocacy group "disturbing" and an "embarrassment."[17]

A Law Office Working for Minority Plaintiffs

The preclearance process was not supposed to work as it did in Georgia in the early 1990s, as well as in countless other jurisdictions, large and small, at that time. Officially, preclearance decisions are the responsibility of the attorney general, but as a practical matter, the power to decide has been delegated to the assistant attorney general for civil rights, as chapter 2 indicated.[18] In the 1965 statute, administrative preclearance was clearly a substitute for the D.C. District Court, and, by implication, DOJ decisions were expected to conform to the legal standards developed on the bench. The Civil Rights Division was thus envisioned as a more accessible court, although jurisdictions relinquished the benefit of a full-scale trial in which facts and arguments are aired in a public courtroom, with the burden of proof on the plaintiff and the possibility of appeal from an adverse ruling. By 1991, however, when the Justice Department reviewed the Georgia plan, this initial vision of the preclearance process had completely broken down. The voting section of the Civil Rights Division was operating as a law office for minority plaintiffs, working as partners with civil rights advocacy groups.

Considerations of time and money had made the Justice Department the preferred route for most jurisdictions seeking to obtain preclearance. Georgia needed to hold elections in 1992. Even when it found itself at loggerheads with the voting section, it could not afford to begin anew in the D.C. court, risking months of litigation. In a trial, the burden would have been on the state to prove an *absence* of wrongdoing; its lawyers would have had to contend with the full weight of the Justice Department in opposition; and an unfavorable outcome might have meant the imposition of a temporary court-drawn map.[19] Thus, the state sought preclearance from the DOJ.

The legal standards governing the assessment of Georgia's new districting plan should have been those developed in *Beer v. United States.* In 1983, the Supreme Court had reaffirmed the retrogression test in *Beer*; yet for purposes of administrative preclearance that decision was soon wiped from the books by Justice Department lawyers.[20] The New Orleans districting plan approved by *Beer* in 1976 would not later have passed administrative review; what the high Court had precleared, the Justice Department would not.

Nevertheless, *Beer* remains good law to this day, recognized as such in subsequent Supreme Court decisions and in the debates over the reauthorization of section 5 in 2006.[21] The decision not only squared with the original conception of section 5 as a prophylactic device to stop the institution of new disfranchising devices; it had delegated to DOJ attorneys, equal opportunity specialists, and other staff (including student volunteers and temporary employees) the limited, and thus relatively manageable, task of identifying jurisdictions that were attempting to pull blacks back from already realized gains.

A limited number of manageable questions would seem essential in the preclearance process. The DOJ is not, in fact, a good substitute for a trial court. Attorneys, who have only sixty days in which to make a decision, make site visits only on the rarest of occasions, and know relatively little about many of the places—often relatively small cities or counties—whose districting lines (or other changes in electoral procedure) require pre-clearance.[22] Equal opportunity specialists initially screen submissions, relying in part on information from a self-selected group of contacts. Every interested citizen is invited to lobby the DOJ staff. The whole process, as one scholar has described it, is "permeable"—although those who get a hearing are almost always civil rights activists.[23] Trial court judges, on the other hand, not only hear testimony from plaintiffs, defendants, and their expert witnesses, but also have at their disposal a rich documentary record depicting race and politics in the locality.

There is another DOJ problem: Those whose judgment generally carries the most weight bring to the task of analyzing jurisdictions a predisposition to suspect discrimination. Voting section attorneys—the career staff—have tended to start and end every assessment with the assumption that electoral changes in covered jurisdictions, particularly in the South, are driven by racism. And while political appointees (who have the last word) come and go, the career staff tends to remain for the reason they frequently chose to work in the Civil Rights Division to begin with: They see themselves as valiant defenders of civil rights holding the line against pressures from opponents of race-based districting and other race-conscious politics.[24] In addition, political appointees have little information other than that obtained from the career staff, and the sheer volume of section 5 submissions elevates the power of these civil servants and the importance of bureaucratic rules of thumb in responding to submissions. The number of electoral changes requiring pre-clearance started to rise precipitously with the decision in *Allen v. State Board of Elections* in 1969, going from 358 in 1970 to over 22,000 at the high-water mark of 1992.[25]

Throughout the presidency of George W. Bush, considerable tension between the career voting section staff and the political appointees was widely reported.[26] But in the 1980s and 1990s, throughout both Republican and Democratic administrations, the views of the section's line attorneys and those to whom they reported were generally the same. Two Republican and one Democratic assistant attorneys general for civil rights—William Bradford Reynolds, John Dunne, and Deval Patrick——all saw their jobs as making sure that jurisdictions had racially "fair" methods of election; "fair" meant proportional representation.

No Discernible Standards

If the Georgia redistricting story were unique, it would be of minor interest. But as the appellees complained in their Supreme Court brief in *Miller v. Johnson*, the 1995 Georgia case, the voting section had "no established fact-finding procedures, no administrative hearing and no discernible standards for evaluating information."[27] The Justice Department did issue guidelines to guide jurisdictions in the submission process; those guidelines were of very little use, as the discussion below suggests. Redistricting is a delicate, politically charged process, with much at stake; in covered jurisdictions, those entrusted with the task are both pressured by politics and uncertain as to what the law will permit. Federal intrusion on constitutionally sanctioned local prerogatives should be of special concern when the legal boundaries are not clear and decisions are seemingly made on the basis of administrative whim.

The complaint of the appellees in *Miller* was shared by a number of scholars. "Courts, covered jurisdictions, interested citizens, and even the Department of Justice lack guidance in determining how a particular covered change should be decided under section 5," Hiroshi Motomura wrote in an 1983 article reviewing voting section policy. "Objection letters," he went on, "do not cite other objection letters or make any apparent effort to create an independent body of section 5 law based on precedent."[28] Another study described the preclearance process as "transpiring in the absence of specified decision criteria that are well known in advance to those who have the obligation to comply with Section 5."[29] But while it was true that Georgia and other covered states and counties were never officially told they should create every possible majority-minority district, whatever the political cost, their unstated marching orders were clear. They had to know, from the record of objections in the 1980s (discussed below), that drawing a "max-black" map would protect them from a DOJ objection and allow them to conduct elections unimpeded.

In 1971, the department had, in fact, published guidelines to help states understand the process.[30] They listed the type of electoral changes covered by section 5, the address to which submissions should be sent, the required contents of those submissions, the right of private individuals to comment on proposed changes, and the speed with which the department was expected to act.

Jurisdictions were additionally informed that the burden of proving an absence of discriminatory purpose or effect was on the jurisdiction; that a submission to the attorney general did not affect the right of the jurisdiction to bring suit in the D.C. court; that no administrative or legislative changes in electoral procedure could be implemented without prior federal approval (although those changes could not be reviewed prior to their actual enactment); and that submissions were expected to include relevant material of a demographic, geographic, or historical nature. Furthermore, they were told, any individual or group could forward relevant information to the attorney general concerning the proposed voting procedure and could request confidentiality, although the department would maintain a registry of interested individuals and groups. After an objection, a jurisdiction could request reconsideration in light of new information.

For all this seeming comprehensiveness, the guidelines were mute on the most important questions. There was no mention of the criteria used in judging submissions. Localities were told only that these standards would not differ from those employed by the D.C. court.[31] The district court, which frequently fashioned its own law, should not have been the decisive authority, however. "In light of the limited number of section 5 cases, the Attorney General can only 'guess' what the [D.C.] court would do with any particular case," one scholar noted.[32] Supreme Court decisions were few and far between, and the legal standards governing districting and annexation cases, discussed in chapter 3, were inconsistent; with four members of the Court convinced that the standards relied upon in the annexation cases should have governed redistricting as well, the Justice Department was, in effect, encouraged to ignore *Beer*.

In addition, since the burden fell on the jurisdiction to prove an absence of wrongdoing, the Justice Department had considerable freedom to use extremely vague language in denying preclearance. The legal basis for a refusal to preclear a revised method of election was often not clear. The DOJ's letter of objection would refer to electoral processes that raised "concern," or state its inability to conclude that a method of election would not "occasion an abridgement of minority voting rights" while providing no evidence of actual discrimination.[33]

In May 1985, the Justice Department finally sent new guidelines out for comment. While they were not officially adopted until January 1987, for the first time the department outlined its criteria in assessing preclearance submissions. It would be considering the following:

- The existence of a reasonable and legitimate justification for a submitted change

- The extent to which the jurisdiction afforded members of racial and language-minority groups an opportunity to participate in the decision to make the change and took their concerns into account

- Departures from objective guidelines and fair and conventional procedures in adopting the change

- Clear and compelling evidence of a violation of section 2, consisting of unreasonable fragmentation of minority voter concentrations, submergence of minority voter concentrations, or denial of access to the political process

- Evidence of discriminatory purpose

- A pattern of racial bloc voting

- Unnecessary concentrations of minority voters

- A refusal to consider alternative plans that would reduce minority voting strength less than the submitted plan did

- The extent to which minorities had been denied an equal opportunity to participate in political activities

- The extent to which minorities had been denied an equal opportunity to influence election outcomes and decision-making

- The extent to which continuing effects of past discrimination had resulted in lower voter registration and election participation rates for minority group members than for other persons

- The extent to which district lines departed needlessly from objective redistricting criteria.[34]

It was an outrageous, yet uncontroversial, list—uncontroversial because almost no one was willing to question policies packaged as promoting civil rights. But if *Beer's* retrogression standard was supposed to guide DOJ decisions, most of these considerations were completely irrelevant. Why was the department looking at the opportunity of minority voters to participate in the decision-making process, possible section 2 violations, racial bloc voting patterns, the potential to draw alternative plans, and so forth?

The line between sections 5 and 2 had been almost erased, and the Civil Rights Division of the DOJ had been empowered to answer questions very different from those posed by section 5—questions about electoral equality, the answers to which required what First Circuit Judge Bruce Selya had called "a careful sifting of imbricated, highly ramified fact patterns."[35]

Many of the terms in the list were undefined—and open to a wide variety of interpretations. What were "reasonable and legitimate" reasons for a submitted change in voting procedure? When did minority groups have a sufficient "opportunity to participate" in the decision to make that change? What was the measure of excessive minority-voter concentration? If jurisdictions decided to pack black voters into newly drawn districts that were, say, 80 percent African American, those "unnecessary" concentrations would waste African-American ballots—but what was the right percentage in drawing a max-black plan? When was the power to "influence" elections and "decision-making" inadequate? All of the familiar, unresolved questions about racially fair electoral processes ran through the new guidelines.

As political scientist Timothy O'Rourke aptly remarked, the new guidelines read like a criminal statute that states, "Among the things you may be arrested for are. . . ." In other words, the proposed guidelines provided no guidance.[36] But they did make clear the means that the Department of Justice had developed to circumvent the Supreme Court's retrogression standard as articulated in *Beer*—and just how far the department had wandered from the limited before-and-after comparison that was, in theory, at the heart of section 5.

The 1980s: Detours around Retrogression

Much of the literature on the history of section 5 enforcement draws a bright line between the story of an out-of-control, outside-the-law Justice

Department in the 1990s and that of law-abiding federal administrators in previous decades.[37] It is only a partial truth, as should already be apparent. The provisional DOJ guidelines discussed above, which basically brushed *Beer* aside, were sent out for comment in 1985. And by the early 1980s, scholars were already noting that the grounds for refusing to preclear changes were unclear in objection letters—as, indeed, they were.

William Bradford Reynolds was the assistant attorney general for civil rights throughout most of the decade. Briefs and letters signed by him were too often indifferent to voting rights law. For instance, an existing districting plan would be labeled an inappropriate benchmark against which to measure retrogression in a newly proposed plan if lines in place at some earlier date could be said to be the true point of comparison. The implicit argument was that the current plan had been erroneously precleared, that blacks had been better off at some earlier date.[38]

If the Justice Department was determined to object to a submitted districting plan but could not redefine the appropriate benchmark, altering the meaning of retrogression itself was another option. A plan that was not "fairly drawn" was "retrogressive," the DOJ frequently argued. "Fairly drawn" plans were those that gave blacks "safe" seats in proportion to the black population—to the greatest degree possible.

As the voting section staff explained to Reynolds in a 1981 memo on county council districts for Barbour County, Alabama, calculating what was "fair" was simple:

> Since blacks constitute 40.5 percent of the voting age population, they would be entitled to 2.8 districts, that is two viable districts plus a third district in which their interests must be taken into account even though they cannot control the election.[39]

"Viable," or "electable," meant districts that had a black concentration of 65 percent or perhaps slightly higher, compensating for low black turnout.[40] Thus, when Reynolds, as a novice, questioned his staff as to why the plan submitted by Barbour County did not meet the test of proportionality, the answer was that only one out of seven districts was, in fact, "viable."

The voting section itself drew up a plan for Barbour County, demonstrating that, in fact, "a seven-member plan could be drawn which afforded blacks an opportunity to elect three of the seven members [of the county council] (42%) which is roughly equal to the black percentage of the county's population (44%)."[41] Such calculations became a routine part of the preclearance process. School board districts for Sumter County, Georgia, were redrawn after the 1980 census and required preclearance. The file on the submission contained the following comment from Reynolds:

> I agree that an objection is required. The submitted plan provides for but two black-majority districts out of the 7 proposed. In view of the fact that the black population of Sumter County commands 43.4% of the total population, and a fairly drawn plan can be— and indeed was—drawn giving blacks three majority districts, the submission cannot survive Section 5 scrutiny without full explanation from the County.

Districts that were not "fairly drawn" and not "viable" could not expect Justice Department approval. Reynolds objected to maps for North Carolina's senate and congressional districts, the New York City Council, and the board of supervisors in Adams County, Mississippi, among others, for not "fairly reflect[ing] black voting strength." Other districting plans were said to "needlessly pack" or "needlessly fragment" black population concentrations. For instance, needless "packing" tainted congressional districts in Texas and those for the Virginia House of Delegates. But a commissioner precinct plan for Uvalde County, Texas, "unnecessarily fragment[ed]" the Mexican-American community, and thus had the "inevitable effect" of diluting minority voting strength. Fragmentation was likewise the problem with Texas state legislative districts in two counties.[42] In all such preclearance reviews, the DOJ invariably assumed that race defined a community of interest.

Discriminatory effect was one question; purpose was another. Yet one searches through voting section memos from this period in vain for a clear discussion of what constituted evidence of discriminatory intent. Files contain such illuminating statements as, "While it is not possible to conclude that the change was made with the proscribed racial purpose, the totality of the facts indicate that race may have been a purpose."[43]

In the case of school board districts in Sumter County, Georgia, the Department of Justice had proposed a map, which the local authorities had rejected; according to the voting section, that rejection, in itself, was evidence that the county's plan was discriminatory in both purpose and effect.[44] Letters from the Justice Department routinely objected to submitted plans on both grounds.[45] A jurisdiction had no way of knowing what sort of evidence contributed to which finding.

Ironically—given the militant opposition of the civil rights groups to any purpose test in the 1982 congressional hearings—both minority spokesmen and the Justice Department seemed to assume that effect and purpose were interchangeable concepts. Moreover, intent was remarkably easy to prove. The NAACP's brief in a South Carolina State Senate districting case implied that any jurisdiction that failed to implement redistricting suggestions made by that organization was guilty of deliberately obstructing black voting rights.[46] Could any minority organization (not just the NAACP) with a plan of its own thus veto that of the state? If so, the carefully constructed detours around *Beer* were superfluous, since the effects test was barely needed as a means by which to condemn proposed redistricting schemes.

The Department of Justice moved perilously close to this position, frequently suggesting that jurisdictions refusing to implement an alternative, more racially "fair," plan were engaging in deliberate discrimination.[47] And, with recourse to that option, *Beer* could be safely ignored. Sumter County, Georgia, might complain that section 5 demanded only a relative test for discriminatory impact—that slippage, or "retrogression," not statistical parity, was the proper question. But the Department of Justice could simply counter by shifting the ground of its objection to that of racially tainted intent.

Or it could throw in everything but the kitchen sink. A 1984 Justice Department memorandum submitted to the district court in the South Carolina Senate districting case cited above is a good example of this tactic:

> The State seeks a judgment "on the issue of effect under Section 5," a judgment that in our view is broader than the issue of whether Act 257 is retrogressive. Relevant to the Section 5 issue of the racially discriminatory "effect" of Act 257 is the issue of the potential effect of a plan intentionally drawn to minimize black voting strength or one that has a discriminatory "result" in violation of Section 2.[48]

The reasoning here is impenetrable. Given that proof of discriminatory intent alone was sufficient to condemn a plan, why was the court obligated to decide whether that intent had an actual effect? And why was the question of a violation of section 2 raised? The memo reveals the use of the new section 2 "results" test in assessing section 5 submissions a year before the 1985 revised guidelines were made public.

Which of the available arguments would be made under what circumstances? The standard changed, depending on the facts. A legal standard should be a method of judging particular facts; in reviewing redistricting submissions, the voting section let the facts dictate the appropriate standard. Almost invariably, the unstated but determining question was, by what method (or methods) of reasoning would black officeholding be maximized? *Beer* had allowed jurisdictions to draw maps that contained only two majority-minority districts if two was the previous number. It was legally irrelevant that an alternative plan might contain a third safe black or Hispanic seat, the Court held. But voting rights activists had never liked the retrogression test, as chapter 3 noted. They wanted the proportional representation standard for racial fairness that the Court had embraced in the annexation decisions to apply to districting cases as well. And so in the 1980s, attorneys in the Justice Department, on an interpretive path of their own, quietly, covertly, extended the logic of the annexation cases to redistricting plans.

The 1990s: A Lawless Civil Rights Division

By 1990 the basic elements of a thoroughly revised section 5 were in place. Without a settled definition of what constituted "before," the requisite before-and-after comparison was often a sham. In any case, a finding of discriminatory intent frequently substituted for the retrogression test, and that finding could rest on nothing more than a failure to adopt the alternative "max-black" map drawn by voting section attorneys or an advocacy group. The demand that districting plans be "fairly drawn" shifted the section 5 inquiry from assessing relative electoral power to evaluating racial equity, making safe minority seats in proportion to the population an entitlement—openly acknowledged as such in voting section memos. In order to take account of generally lower black and Hispanic turnout, a safe seat was defined as having at least a 65 percent minority voting-age population, as noted earlier. And, finally, an alleged violation of section 2 quietly became an additional reason for objecting to a plan on section 5 grounds.

In the 1990s, the DOJ's voting rights enforcement differed from that of the previous decade only in the degree to which its general indifference to sanctioned legal standards increased. In objecting to districting plans, it was more openly dedicated to insisting on ones that contained a maximum number of majority-minority districts, the consequence of which was the transparently race-driven districts that prompted a series of Fourteenth Amendment equal protection suits. The 1991–92 Georgia congressional redistricting story had the highest profile of any to come out of the decade, simply because the district court explored the history in unusual detail, but it was certainly not unique. In fact, the corrupted preclearance process affected the drawing of new districts at all levels of government, from school boards to county councils and on up the legislative ladder.

Take, for example, the 1996 district court decision in *Smith v. Beasley*. The issue was a new map for the South Carolina House and Senate, not congressional districts.[49] As in Georgia, the black legislative caucus, along with the ACLU, the NAACP, and other allies had maintained constant contact with the DOJ's Civil Rights Division, which had dropped all pretense of serving as a surrogate court. These voting rights activists argued that African Americans were entitled to proportional representation. "One-third of our state's population should have no difficulty garnering at least one-third of the seats in the general assembly. Any other alternative is unacceptable," stated Joe Brown, chairman of the South Carolina Legislative Black Caucus. Deval Patrick, the assistant attorney general for civil rights in 1994 (and now governor of Massachusetts), took the same position when the house map was under review.[50]

Deval Patrick didn't know how to read the law, the district court made clear. "The Department of Justice in the present case, as it had done in *Miller* [*v. Johnson*], misunderstood its role under the preclearance provisions of the Voting Rights Act," the court found. "Here, Department of Justice attorneys became advocates for the coalition that was seeking to maximize the number of majority BVAP [black voting-age population] districts in an effort to achieve proportionality."[51] And yet, the court continued, "the purpose of section 5 review has been explained above and it does not require maximization; it is intended to prevent retrogression."[52]

In his letter of objection to the first plan drawn by the general assembly, Patrick "went into great detail in explaining the areas in which additional majority-black districts could be created," the district court wrote.[53] His plan was essentially the "dream plan" that had been drawn and pushed by the black caucus and other advocates. The court held that, in providing such coercive advice, the Justice Department had clearly crossed the line between finding a plan suspect and dictating to the state what its map should look like.[54]

Advisory opinions like that offered by the assistant attorney general were no more legally legitimate coming from the Justice Department than they would have been if offered by a court. But, to be fair, Patrick was only continuing a practice started by his Republican predecessor. In the Sumter County case discussed above, a staff attorney had taken the unusual step of making a local visit. Before departing, he had drawn a map, saving local officials the trouble of reading Justice Department tea leaves to discern what an acceptable plan might look like. "I allowed Mr. ___ to keep the map which I had marked with the understanding that it not be publicized as a Department of Justice proposal so as to avoid any public misperception that the Department was wedded to a particular plan," he subsequently reported.[55] It would not have been a "misperception"; the department was, obviously, wedded to a particular plan—as it would be in the case of South Carolina more than a decade later. That such coercion substituted administrative fiat for fundamental democratic processes was evidently of no concern in either case.

Two district court opinions dealing with the constitutionality of Louisiana's congressional districting after the 1990 census provide further evidence that, as Judge Jacques L. Wiener noted, the office of the assistant attorney general for civil rights "arrogated the power to use Section 5 preclearance as a sword to implement forcibly its own redistricting policies, rather than as a shield to prevent lamentable historical abuses."[56] Once again, the Justice Department assumed legislative powers, providing a blueprint that the state could follow in creating two majority-black districts, rather than the one the state had proposed, even though the single safe black seat satisfied the retrogression standard. And, once again, even though nothing in the law mandated a two-district plan, "the Legislature uniformly believed that they needed to create such a redistricting plan to secure preclearance."[57] Given the Justice Department's deliberately dishonest message, it could hardly have concluded otherwise.

The Civil Rights Division was working with a "perverted syllogism," Judge Wiener wrote when the case came back to the court. The assistant attorney general would "preclear a redistricting plan only if it included two majority-minority districts out of seven; the Legislature must obtain timely preclearance; ergo, the Legislature must adopt a plan containing at least two majority-minority districts."[58] In his first opinion, Judge Wiener had noted that "neither Section 2, nor Section 5 of the Voting Rights Act justifies the AGO's [Attorney General's Office] insistence upon two black districts."[59] The unconstitutional gerrymander was not forced upon the state by the statute. No matter. The court required the state to draw a new map, and when that revised plan was submitted for preclearance, the DOJ once again informed legislators "that the Voting Rights Act requires the state to devise a congressional districting plan with two black-majority districts."[60]

These Louisiana decisions, like that in *Beasley*, were based on the Fourteenth Amendment. I discuss them here because they provide such a clear picture of a coercive Civil Rights Division indifferent to the legal standards the Supreme Court had set for the enforcement of section 5. But since the focus in the decisions was on the unconstitutionality of such race-conscious districting, the Court's opinions contain almost no discussion of the precise statutory grounds upon which the attorney general had refused to preclear the submitted districting plans. There is no doubt, however, that in the 1990s the Civil Rights Division increased its reliance on groundless findings of discriminatory intent, as well as on alleged section 2 violations, in objecting to newly drawn maps. In addition, new computer software allowed mapmakers to capture with unprecedented precision data on small pockets of minority voters, producing racially gerrymandered districts that occasioned some very colorful metaphors. One post-1990 Texas district looked like "a microscopic view of a new strain of disease," while a majority-black North Carolina district resembled a "Rorschach ink-blot test" or a "bug splattered on a windshield," federal courts declared.[61]

John Dunne's Section 5

Maurice Cunningham, in his carefully researched account of the Voting Rights Act in the 1990s, was particularly struck by the increased reliance in

DOJ letters of objection on findings of suspected discriminatory intent. "Proponents of maximization and [Civil Rights] Division attorneys came to focus upon Section Five's prohibition against purposeful discrimination," he wrote.

> Though the term connotes some act taken with the intention to impair minority participation, the CRD came to accept another interpretation . . . a reading whereby a failure to adopt a maximization plan if one had been presented to the state would raise a presumption of discriminatory purpose.[62]

The emphasis on the presumption of intent had a distinct advantage. *Beer* had held retrogression to be the standard only in judging discriminatory "effect." The Court's exclusive focus on the definition of "effect" in that decision—its silence on the meaning of "intent"—left DOJ attorneys free to strip from charges of purposeful discrimination the notion of deliberate, conscious action to deprive minority voters of their "ability . . . to participate in the political process and to elect their choices to office."[63] They could find purposeful discrimination lurking in every districting plan they didn't like.

State legislators in covered jurisdictions always want to know what they have to do to obtain Justice Department approval of a new districting plan. Prolonged uncertainty can be devastating to potential candidates. In a 1991 speech, John Dunne provided the needed information. "A discriminatory purpose," the assistant attorney general for civil rights explained, "means a design or desire to restrict a minority group's voting strength, that is, the ability of that group to elect candidates of its choice, below the level that minority might otherwise have enjoyed." A plan that provides less, he went on, needs "to be explained in a Section Five submission so that we can be sure that the state has satisfied its burden of proving the absence of racially discriminatory purpose."[64] In other words, draw every last majority-minority district that you can, or else you will be in trouble.

"The Civil Rights Division recognizes that there may be many legitimate reasons for not creating additional minority districts," Dunne wrote in 1993. "But a jurisdiction's desire to preserve the status quo is not one of them, when doing so means perpetuating underrepresentation of minority voters."[65]

"Underrepresentation" was, of course, a euphemism for a level of officehold-ing below that of proportional representation.

Dunne had another interesting argument. North Carolina's egregious racially gerrymandered congressional districts had prompted the first of the Fourteenth Amendment cases challenging race-driven plans on equal protec-tion grounds.[66] The case was unusual in that the legislative black caucus had supported the state's districting plan, which contained only one majority-black district. The caucus, in other words, had split with its allies in other cases: the Republican Party, the ACLU, and other advocacy groups. The leg-islature's refusal to adopt a map with two black districts that had been drawn by the GOP constituted evidence of discriminatory purpose, the Republican-led Justice Department argued—even though the black caucus supported the one-seat map.[67] "Minority legislators," Dunne explained,

> may have a host of reasons for going along with a redistricting plan, even if the plan is not optimal for minority voters outside their districts. Those legislators may have been promised choice committee assignments or leadership positions, or they may be acting out of party loyalty.

"On the other hand," he went on, "close attention is paid to the positions of such advocacy groups as MALDEF, ACLU, LULAC, and the NAACP."[68] The motives of such groups were evidently pure, unlike those of elected black legislators who, in this case, had "sold out," as Dunne's confidante, ACLU attorney Kathleen Wilde, put it.[69]

It is important to remember that Dunne could rest objections on pure speculation—"minority legislators *may* have a host of reasons . . . those legislators *may* have been promised"—because there was no actual need to prove discrimination. Suspected wrongdoing was sufficient to sink a sub-mitted plan; the burden was on the jurisdiction to provide evidence of its innocence. Thus, the North Carolina objection letter charged that the state was "well aware" of alternative plans, and that the alter-native was rejected "for what appears to be pretextual reasons." Like John Dunne's 1993 remarks, letters from the Justice Department were often sprinkled with such words as "appears," "seems," and "alleged," without indicating the sources upon which its suspicion rested or the credibility of those sources.[70]

The extreme views and general lawlessness of the career lawyers in the Voting Section and the Civil Rights Division in general were demonstrated by the fact that from 1993 to 2000, the Division was forced to pay over $4.1 million in attorneys' fees and costs awarded against DOJ for filing frivolous and unwarranted discrimination claims in ten lawsuits.[71] These included Section 2 lawsuits like *U.S. v. Jones*, filed against county officials in Dallas County, Alabama, in 1993.

In affirming the district court's dismissal of the lawsuit, the Eleventh Circuit Court of Appeals concluded that "a properly conducted investigation would have quickly revealed that there was no basis for the claim that the Defendants were guilty of purposeful discrimination against black voters. . . . The filing of an action charging a person with depriving a fellow citizen of a fundamental constitutional right without conducting a proper investigation of its truth is unconscionable. . . . Hopefully, we will not again be faced with reviewing a case as carelessly instigated as this one."[72]

Merging Sections 5 and 2

The original vision of preclearance—of section 5 in its entirety—had been that of a means to prevent a "particular set of invidious practices which had the effect of 'undoing or defeating the rights recently won by nonwhite voters.'"[73] Clearly, a refusal to draw the maximum possible number of majority-minority districts could not be construed as an effort to undo recent gains in black electoral power, and yet only that prophylactic function could justify the extraordinary intrusion on federalism, which is so integral to the American constitutional structure.

It was a fundamental point that the Justice Department ignored in the 1980s and 1990s, until the Supreme Court in 2000 temporarily curtailed the interpretive freedom voting section attorneys had been exercising.[74] In the 1990s, particularly, the prohibition on voting changes suspected of discriminatory intent became the main means by which the beautifully designed, logically tight law was circumvented. But there were other routes around the law, as well. Resting objections on section 2 also avoided the retrogression test, it may be recalled. In fact, the proposed and final guidelines for use in understanding section 5 that were issued in 1985 and 1987, respectively, only sanctioned officially the reliance on section 2 that had already become quiet practice.

The incorporation of section 2 into the legal standards that governed the enforcement of section 5 gave the DOJ an additional, potentially useful, but limited tool to employ in objecting to changes in the method of election. It allowed the voting section to determine that a new method of voting had a discriminatory "result" without having to prove its case in the adversarial setting of a full-scale trial. On the other hand, the Civil Rights Division could not write letters of objection full of vague phrases such as "it appears" and "some have alleged." In section 2, the burden of proof was on those who charged discrimination, and that burden did not shift when the results test was used in the context of section 5. Mere suspicion of wrongdoing would not do.

Thus, while DOJ letters charging suspected discriminatory intent could suggest a whiff of unlawful motive in the air, the DOJ had to bring real facts to the table in relying on section 2. For that reason, the provisional 1985 guidelines referred to the need to show "clear and convincing evidence of . . . a [section 2] violation that remains unrebutted by the submitting authority." The final 1987 document altered the language slightly, but the burden was basically unchanged. "Where the facts available to the Attorney General clearly demonstrate that implementation of the submitted change will result in a Section 2 violation, an objection will be entered," the revised guidelines stated. "Clearly demonstrate" was a much tougher standard to meet than the process of section 5 review normally demanded.

William Bradford Reynolds, as assistant attorney general for civil rights, was responsible for the decision to incorporate section 2 standards into the preclearance process. But after the 1985 guidelines were released for public comment, he ran into significant opposition from those who saw a sharp and important distinction between the two provisions and feared more DOJ mischief in interpreting section 5. In late August 1986, at an American Political Science Association panel on the Voting Rights Act (which I chaired), Reynolds buckled under pressure and suddenly announced he had changed his mind.[75] In assessing electoral changes in the covered jurisdictions, the Civil Rights Division would stick to the language of section 5; those who wished to challenge a method of voting on the quite different section 2 grounds could litigate the matter in a local federal district court.

Once again, however, he found himself facing determined opposition—although from a different political corner. His about-face instantly triggered a well-organized campaign by civil rights activists, which led to congressional hearings and a House subcommittee report supporting the consideration of section 2 standards in reviewing submitted voting changes under section 5. The civil rights community welcomed any and all additional tools to force jurisdictions to draw race-conscious maps, even if the use of a results test was limited in the preclearance context. The campaign succeeded: When the 1987 guidelines were issued, Reynolds flip-flopped again; section 2 was back in the preclearance picture.[76]

It is worth noting that no statutory language had sanctioned such a revision of section 5. The advocacy groups and their friends in Congress who had pressured Reynolds had only a footnote in the Senate Judiciary Committee report to go on. That footnote, written by the same group of advocates, had been dropped surreptitiously into the report at the last minute.[77] Had an alteration in standards used in judging preclearance submissions been included in the revised statute itself, it would surely have been regarded as meriting debate by those who were altogether opposed to the amendment of section 2. As it was, it was never even mentioned in the course of the 1982 congressional hearings.

From 1987 to 1997, the Justice Department was able to deny preclearance on section 2 grounds. Civil rights advocates had regarded that addition to the section 5 toolbox as potentially very valuable—which was precisely what worried those who were already concerned about the potential effect of the revised section 2. As it turned out, advocates for resting preclearance objections on section 2 got less than they hoped for. In 1997, the Supreme Court decided in *Bossier I* that sections 5 and 2 should not be confused, but the decision did not have much practical effect. In the 1980s and 1990s, only between 1 and 2 percent of all objections rested on violations of section 2, undoubtedly due to the more difficult evidentiary demands made by the provision.[78] By way of contrast, a quarter of all objections in the 1980s were based on suspected discriminatory intent, and that figure rose to 43 percent in the 1990s. The impact of *Bossier II*, limiting the meaning of discriminatory purpose, was substantial, three voting rights scholars have concluded, while that of *Bossier I* was "inconsequential."[79]

Detailed Data and Sophisticated Software

Neither the Justice Department's use of suspected discriminatory purpose nor its reliance on section 2 was a new development in the 1990s. But one real change early in the decade had unmistakably large consequences: New redistricting technology, along with much more detailed census data, transformed the process of drawing legislative districts.[80] The extent of that transformation was vividly described in the 1994 district court opinion in *Shaw v. Hunt*, scrutinizing North Carolina's congressional districting lines:

> The critical redistricting data—total population, voting-age population by race or national origin, voter registration by party and race—was now made available by the Census Bureau and state legislative staff not only down to townships and precincts, but even further down to the level of the "census block," a geographical unit usually smaller than precincts. Incorporated into a newly acquired computer software program along with digital map files, these allowed the rapid call-up and visual display on computer terminals of critical demographic and statistical data down to the census block level, along with geographic features—highways, streets, rivers, railroads—and political boundaries. . . . The capability thus provided to call up demographic and statistical data and on its basis to make district line adjustments at this geographic level had therefore significantly increased the flexibility of the redistricting process, freeing up the planners from their former confinement to existing political boundaries.[81]

The district court in *Shaw v. Hunt* was reviewing the history of congressional redistricting in North Carolina after the Supreme Court, in *Shaw v. Reno* in 1993, had looked at the outlandish lines the state had drawn and found "unsettling how closely the North Carolina plan resemble[d] the most egregious racial gerrymanders of the past."[82] In the 1870s, Reconstruction opponents in Mississippi "concentrated the bulk of the black population in a 'shoestring' Congressional district running the length of the Mississippi River, leaving five others with white majorities."[83] Racial gerrymandering was an old and dishonorable practice—once practiced by white supremacists, but a century later imposed by the federal government, allegedly in the service of black interests. Ironically, civil rights advocates today support practices once favored by the Ku Klux Klan.

Leaving aside the ugly history of racial gerrymanders, the Court was "unsettled" by the North Carolina congressional map for good reason. Here is how Justice O'Connor described the second majority-black district that the Justice Department had forced the state to draw:

> It is approximately 160 miles long and, for much of its length, no wider than the I-85 corridor. It winds in snakelike fashion through tobacco country, financial centers, and manufacturing areas "until it gobbles in enough enclaves of black neighborhoods." Northbound and southbound drivers on I-85 sometimes find themselves in separate districts in one county, only to "trade" districts when they enter the next county. Of the 10 counties through which District 12 passes, 5 are cut into 3 different districts; even towns are divided. At one point the district remains contiguous only because it intersects at a single point with two other districts before crossing over them. One state legislator has remarked that "'if you drove down the interstate with both car doors open, you'd kill most of the people in the district.'"[84]

The art of gerrymandering reached a new height of precision in the 1990s. The final products were the work of many participants. As already noted, the Republican Party had a stake in race-conscious districting, and it made its sophisticated districting software available to civil rights organizations and other interested parties at no cost and with no strings attached.[85] Indeed, with the new software and the detailed census information, anyone could easily come up with a variety of maps from which to choose.

The early 1990s was a heady time for the civil rights groups as they acquired unprecedented technological power to create elaborate, convoluted majority-minority districts that maximized minority officeholding. Armed with "dream" maps and closely allied with Department of Justice voting section attorneys, they were able to convince state legislators and others in charge of mapmaking that they held the key to preclearance—which they did. The result, as we have seen, was the creation of numerous race-driven districts at all levels of government in the years immediately following the 1990 census.

The Justice Department Memo

The drive to maximize the number of majority-minority districts affected section 2 litigation (and threatened litigation), as well as the enforcement of the preclearance provision. Section 5 provided for federal oversight only in covered jurisdictions, but section 2 suits could, of course, be brought wherever a sufficient concentration of black or Hispanic voters made it possible to argue that an alternative method of voting would yield less discriminatory "results."

In addition, while preclearance kicked in only when the method of election had been changed, section 2 could be used to attack both new and old practices. The Court's 1986 reading of the provision in *Thornburg v. Gingles* (discussed in chapter 3) had bestowed a right on minority groups to roughly proportional representation, Justice O'Connor had pointed out. That right was taken seriously by the Justice Department, which had the power to initiate section 2 suits. Justice embarked on an active search for localities where disproportionately low minority officeholding suggested legal vulnerability. Thus, the commitment to a maximum number of "max-black" (or max-Hispanic) districts affected map-drawing nationwide. The tentacles of federal voting rights enforcement power reached into every nook and cranny of the country.

A series of Fourteenth Amendment decisions beginning in 1993 put some brakes on the most egregious racial gerrymandering, but their bark was worse than their bite. As the chapter 6 will argue, the effect of these decisions was only to curb slightly the districting that was most brazenly race-conscious. The Supreme Court's *Bossier II* decision, which narrowed the definition of discriminatory intent in section 5, did have an important effect on the letters of objection issued by the Justice Department. The Civil Rights Division had been stopped from using the charge of suspected discriminatory purpose with the same freedom as it did in the 1980s and 1990s. But in 2006, Congress superseded *Bossier II* in the renewal of the Voting Rights Act, restoring the DOJ's power to use a freewheeling definition of discriminatory intent. How that new power will be used after the next round of redistricting after the 2010 census has yet to be seen, of course.

After the 2003 decision in *Georgia v. Ashcroft* (until it, too, was superseded by Congress three years later) the DOJ could insist on maps containing "opportunity-to-elect" districts designed to maximize the election of *all* candidates—minority or white—who were arguably the choice of minority voters.[86] Justice O'Connor, it may be recalled, had noted that since blacks vote for Democrats, any increase in the number of Democratic officeholders—even if they were white—would boost the representation of minority interests. But if Democrats counted as minority representatives, then perhaps all existing Democratic districts were untouchable; altering the lines in ways that would make them more Republican could be called retrogressive and a violation of section 5. *Ashcroft* threatened to turn the Voting Rights Act into a statute to protect safe seats for white Democrats who appeared to be the choice of black and Hispanic voters.

But which Democrats were those? As chapter 2 noted, in *Ashcroft* O'Connor had admitted that "the ability of minority voters to elect a candidate of their choice is important but often complex in practice to determine."[87] In calculating the level of "minority representation," the Court had held, there were factors to be weighed even beyond whether a white incumbent was "sympathetic to the interests of minority voters." For instance, did he or she hold an important committee post? But Justice Souter, writing in dissent, saw "trouble ahead." How could the Court measure influence that was less than decisive? "Would it be enough for a State to show that an incumbent had previously promised to consider minority interests before voting on legislative measures?" he asked.[88]

By the time *Ashcroft* was decided, most post-2000 maps were in place, limiting its immediate impact; the congressional districting plan for Texas was a notable exception. A leaked internal Justice Department memo on the legality of that plan provides a fascinating window on just how useful *Ashcroft* promised to be, permitting, as it did, preclearance objections on the basis of a new set of ill-defined grounds.

The Texas map was the issue in *LULAC v. Perry*, a section 2 case discussed in chapter 3.[89] Prior to the litigation, the challenged map had been submitted for section 5 preclearance to the Justice Department. The career staff didn't like the revised lines, and in a seventy-three-page internal memo argued that "the state of Texas has not met its burden in showing that the proposed congressional redistricting plan does not have a discriminatory effect."[90]

Nevertheless, the attorney general approved the plan, which infuriated the five lawyers and two analysts who had recommended that he find a violation of section 5. Two years later, on the eve of the argument in *LULAC* before the Supreme Court, and at a time of growing tension between political appointees at the DOJ and the career staff, the document was leaked to the *Washington Post*.[91] But a second memorandum, which was not leaked, had been prepared by three other lawyers in the Civil Rights Division, who saw factual and legal inaccuracies, mistakes, and misrepresentations in the first, and recommended preclearance.[92]

The lengthy, rambling, barely coherent memo originally prepared by the staff used *Ashcroft* as its framework in analyzing the legality of the Texas map. Both Texas and the Justice Department staff agreed that a new plan must not reduce the number of districts that sent blacks or Hispanics to Congress. But as the second memorandum pointed out, the first mistakenly concluded that there were eleven majority-minority districts that had to be preserved in Texas, not eight. It reached this conclusion by characterizing Representative Martin Frost, a white Democrat, as also "responsive" to minority interests. In addition, Frost was a political powerhouse, which the Court in *Ashcroft* had declared highly relevant. Never mind that his district was only a quarter black, as chapter 3 noted and the second memorandum also pointed out; the staffers argued that blacks were able to control the outcome of the Democratic primaries, since a high percentage of whites voted Republican. It was a black "opportunity-to-elect" district. The effect of dispersing its residents, as Texas had done, was retrogressive—discriminatory in effect.

The importance of preserving what was once Congressional District 25, which sent Representative Chris Bell to Congress, was another key point in the memo. (An entirely new CD 25 had been created and the old district redrawn as CD 9.) Like Martin Frost, Bell was white and had defeated a black candidate in the Democratic primary in 2002 when he was first elected in an open-seat race. He won despite the fact that the losing black candidate had received a majority of the black vote; thus, as the second memorandum correctly pointed out under the applicable legal precedent, Bell was obviously not the "candidate of choice" of black voters. Yet the original, leaked memo described Bell as "responsive" to black and Hispanic interests. Altering his district thus violated section 5, the memo argued, even though the Texas mapmakers believed CD 9 would be more likely to elect a black than the old

CD 25 had been. They turned out to be right: In the 2004 election, Al Green won and became a third black congressman in the Texas delegation. Throughout the memo, the career staffers attempted to read various political tea leaves, predicting the race or political sympathies of candidates to be elected from the various Texas districts under the new plan. It was a practice invited by Justice O'Connor's opinion, but, sitting in Washington, the staffers were not very good at it, as the example of District 9 suggests.

Still another district, CD 29, had been represented by Gene Green, a white whom Hispanics overwhelming supported and who had been described by a Houston city councilman as "basically Hispanic." It was an interesting description. In the Jim Crow South, white civil rights workers were often depicted as "black." And some blacks have been slandered by their political enemies as being basically "white." In the staffers' view, some whites were, well, not really white.

On the other hand, there was the problem of Representative Henry Bonilla, who had been raised in a Latino neighborhood on the south side of San Antonio and whose ethnic identity was unmistakable. The original staff memo argued that CD 23 should be counted as safely Hispanic, but not as safe for Bonilla who, as a Republican, was not the "candidate of choice" for Hispanic voters. Only his incumbency had kept him in office. Texas tried to protect Bonilla by removing a substantial number of Hispanics and adding whites (likely to be Republican) to his district, but the effort was a violation of section 5, staffers concluded. It was irrelevant that the new map contained an entirely new, compensating CD 25, which was sure to elect a Hispanic and thus should have satisfied DOJ staffers. The second memorandum pointed out that CD 25 was a perfectly acceptable substitute Hispanic district that satisfied the requirements of the retrogression standard of section 5.

As the leaked memo indicated, a war was going on in 2003 between the political appointees on the one hand and the career staff who had written it on the other. It was a war that led the career attorneys to take the most unprofessional action of giving an internal, privileged memorandum to the media. Prior to 2001, the division had a reputation for hiring only liberals—career people who could easily have come from the ACLU or the NAACP, and often returned to such activist organizations. That was perfectly legal; while civil servants could not be chosen on the basis of party affiliation, there was nothing wrong with taking into account their views on civil rights issues.[93]

That history, however, sheds important light on the preclearance enforcement decisions in the 1980s and 1990s (under Democrats and Republicans) that I have found so troubling.[94]

The war between left and right within the Civil Rights Division when the two memos were written in 2003, and one was leaked two years later, was in part a consequence of the appointment of a small number of conservative attorneys in the Bush administration. But in part it reflected the increasing complexity of voting rights issues as white racism even in the South was waning, and descriptive representation no longer seemed—even to liberals—to be the acid test for minority inclusion. Who counted as a representative of black or Hispanic interests? Those who wrote the memo believed Martin Frost, Chris Bell, and Gene Green all qualified, although all three were white. As the second memorandum pointed out, however, they conveniently ignored a prior federal court decision that had specifically found only eight majority-minority districts in Texas, and none of the districts represented by Frost, Bell, or Green had qualified.[95] Stretching preclearance and ignoring a federal court decision to defend the districts these men represented raised the specter of new DOJ power to make decisions with serious partisan implications.

The Fog

A confusing Supreme Court opinion cannot be held entirely responsible for the ideologically driven work of career staff in the Justice Department, but attorneys and voting rights analysts did have permission, in effect, from the *Ashcroft* Court to place districts represented by white legislators in the category of those permanently protected by section 5. These had become "minority" districts even though they did not elect black or Hispanic representatives. In the next redistricting round, the lines of those that had elected Frost, Bell, and Green—all Democrats—would have to be preserved. A new map that served Republican interests in that Republican state would be seen as retrogressive.

In chapter 2, I argued that *Ashcroft* was both a blow for common sense and a deeply flawed decision. The gloss given it by DOJ career staff turned the decision into one more novel means of imposing racially "fair" districting on jurisdictions—though with the definition of fairness altered to include districts that would not previously have counted as providing minority "opportunity." On the other hand, by 2003, when the DOJ initial memo on Texas congressional redistricting was written, the original notion of the provision as protection against renewed disfranchisement had long since disappeared into an ever-thickening fog that obscured the original notion of section 5 as a prophylactic measure to protect minority voters from new disfranchising efforts.

That fog did not roll in overnight, this chapter has argued. Already, by 1985, when the Justice Department proposed revised guidelines for the enforcement of section 5, *Beer's* substantial constraint on the DOJ's freedom to impose "racially fair" districts had, in effect, been overturned by staff attorneys in the Civil Rights Division. "Racially fair," of course, meant districts that ensured (to the degree that geographically based districting can) proportional racial representation. It was a definition that Democrats, Republicans, and the civil rights community actively promoted. In the 1980s, the voting section of the Justice Department became, in effect, a law firm working for minority plaintiffs, in partnership with civil rights advocates. Not all black legislators agreed that "max-black" districts always served minority interests, but their views were dismissed by the assistant attorney general for civil rights as less important than those of the ACLU and other advocacy groups.

The 1990s added more flourishes to the architecturally imaginative statutory reconstruction project in which the Justice Department had already engaged in the previous decade. On paper, retrogression was still the test for discriminatory effect, but the DOJ's definitional games stripped away the core notion of racist actions designed to deny blacks their hard-won political gains. Other definitional strategies also played havoc with any common-sense notion of discriminatory purpose; if the NAACP, for instance, had a "better" districting plan than that drawn by a jurisdiction, a failure to embrace the proposed alternative was, in itself, evidence of racist intent.

In the 1990s, preclearance objections typically rested on either suspicion of discriminatory purpose or allegations of section 2 violations. In addition, new redistricting software (shared by civil rights groups and Republicans) transformed the process of drawing districts and made possible the intricate racial gerrymandering that would prompt a series of Fourteenth Amendment challenges to racial sorting. That gerrymandering was, in great part, responsible for the wave of new black legislators elected in 1992. On the other hand, it also aided the growth of the Republican Party in the South.

This story of federal bureaucrats distorting a federal statute unimpeded by public scrutiny is not exceptional. Title VII of the Civil Rights Act of 1964 outlawed employment discrimination—the intentionally disparate treatment of individuals in the workplace. If anyone could find "any language which provides that an employer will have to hire on the basis of percentage or quota related to color, race, religion, or national origin," the chief sponsor of the act, Senator Hubert H. Humphrey, had said, "I will start eating the pages one after another, because it is not in there."[96]

But almost immediately, the Equal Employment Opportunity Commission (EEOC), which did not initiate lawsuits but in all other ways enforced Title VII, began to rewrite the legal standards that governed findings of discrimination. The agency's first compliance chief, Alfred W. Blumrosen, believed in what he later called "creative administration."[97] He wanted the statute's provisions to be construed "liberally" rather than literally—to be read "as charters of equality."[98] That meant using the act as an instrument to maximize the hiring of members of a group. Over time, the disparate treatment standard, which required evidence of intent to discriminate, was replaced by a disparate impact or results standard, in which discrimination was redefined so that mere statistical imbalance, with no evidence of intent or disparate treatment, was enough to make an employer liable. Blumrosen himself admitted a problem with his interpretation of the law—namely, that it "required a reading of the statute contrary to the plain meaning."[99] But no one in Congress objected.

Advocates for policies that would lead to racially "fair" results were deeply involved, early on, in the enforcement of both the 1964 Civil Rights Act and the 1965 Voting Rights Act. Though they became a lobby both outside and within the government, it was their unprecedented status as insiders that was particularly important. As Hugh Davis Graham has written, "The arcane, technical nature of the modern administrative state yielded enormous advantages to the new social regulators." The public is unlikely to get exercised over a regulation buried in the *Federal Register* implementing an executive order or statutory provision, Graham said, "yet students of public policy and public administration are increasingly aware that out of such bureaucratic boilerplate . . . can come fundamental shifts in public policy."[100]

As this chapter has argued, in the 1980s and 1990s an important shift in the definition of fair representation—going far beyond that which was occurring more openly in Congress and the courts—was buried in the written and unwritten regulatory rules and regulations that governed the enforcement of section 5 of the Voting Rights Act. Political appointees, career attorneys, and nonlegal staff in the Justice Department became self-appointed, out-of-sight arbiters deciding questions fundamental to democratic government in a multiracial, multiethnic nation. It was not a role sanctioned by the statute, nor one that could be regarded as legitimate by anyone concerned about the democratic health of the nation.

5

The Fourteenth Amendment Cases: Trafficking in Racial Stereotyping

A reapportionment plan that includes in one district individuals who belong to the same race, but who are otherwise widely separated by geographical and political boundaries, and who may have little in common with one another but the color of their skin, bears an uncomfortable resemblance to political apartheid. It reinforces the perception that members of the same racial group—regardless of their age, education, economic status, or the community in which they live—think alike, share the same political interests, and will prefer the same candidates at the polls.

—Justice Sandra Day O'Connor, *Shaw v. Reno* (1993)[1]

The Fourteenth Amendment is the liberals' best friend—except when it's not. It brought us *Brown v. Board of Education*, busing to desegregate school districts, *Roe v. Wade*, and *Reynolds v. Sims*. But it has also been read to allow the internment of Japanese Americans during World War II, to stop cross-district busing, to uphold a federal ban on partial birth abortions, and to subject racial preferences to "strict" constitutional scrutiny. In the area of minority voting rights, too, it has been a source of both satisfaction and alarm for the political left.

As we have already seen, the Supreme Court picked up where the one-person, one-vote cases left off, and it found in the Fourteenth Amendment a right to equally weighted votes of a different sort. In a line of decisions that began in 1971, it took a hard look at at-large voting and other electoral arrangements that allegedly diluted the power of the black and

Hispanic vote and deprived minority voters of an equal opportunity to participate in the political process and elect the legislators of their choice. The Fourteenth Amendment thus became a means of insisting on majority-minority, single-member districts across the nation, much to the delight of civil rights advocates.

Much to their dismay, however, that line of decisions ended in 1980 with *City of Mobile v. Bolden*.[2] The Court in *Bolden* insisted on a showing of invidious intent—tainted racial purpose—in the adoption or preservation of a challenged voting procedure, and in so doing brought its voting rights decisions in line with others resting on the Fourteenth Amendment. But Congress quickly came to the rescue, amending the Voting Rights Act in 1982 to incorporate into the statute itself the protections against vote dilution developed in the constitutional cases. That section 2 story has been told in previous chapters. In this chapter, we return to the Fourteenth Amendment, picking up that broken thread and exploring a quite different line of decisions in which, from the outset, the civil rights community believed the Court was deeply misguided.

Shaw v. Reno

By the early 1990s, as the previous chapter discussed, the Department of Justice had distorted the preclearance provision beyond recognition. The question of discriminatory effect, defined as retrogression, was simply ignored. A freewheeling definition of discriminatory intent and, intermittently, an indefensible reliance on section 2 were both used to strike down districting plans that failed to provide for a maximum number of safe minority districts. Jurisdictions were, in effect, forced to adopt racially "just" maps, even when black legislators had played a decisive role in the condemned state redistricting process.

The voting section of the Civil Rights Division is responsible for enforcing section 2, as well as section 5. The former is enforced not only through suits brought by private individuals and groups, but also by litigation initiated solely by the Justice Department. With its aggressive use of both provisions to maximize minority officeholding, the Justice Department had, in effect, been provoking the Court, and in 1993 a majority of justices responded. In the creation of new districting maps, some race-driven configurations crossed a constitutional line, the Court held in *Shaw v. Reno*, one of three voting rights cases decided in its 1992–93 term.[3]

The issue was congressional districting in North Carolina, briefly discussed in chapter 4. Recall that, following the 1990 decennial census, the state had drawn a plan that provided for one majority-black district; that plan was thrown out by the Justice Department. One safe black district would not suffice if two could be drawn, the DOJ had said, although the Supreme Court had explicitly rejected precisely such reasoning in *Beer v. United States*.[4]

Although the contours of this second congressional district were substantially determined by the need to find black voters to meet the demands of the DOJ's voting section, Democratic state legislators also had partisan aims. Whatever the exact mix of race and politics in their motivations, the result (as noted in chapter 4) was a long, exceedingly thin district that stretched approximately 160 miles along an interstate highway; indeed, much of it served only to connect quite separate black residential areas and was no wider than the highway itself. By conventional districting standards, the lines of CD 12 were ludicrous. Moreover, those of District 1— the first of the majority-black constituencies—were not much better.[5]

Five North Carolina residents filed suit, alleging that the state had created an unconstitutional racial gerrymander. In using race as the basis upon which to sort citizens into legislative districts, it had violated the principle of equal treatment that was at the heart of the Fourteenth Amendment. The ground had been laid for such a claim by the Court's prior equal protection decisions. It had found some race-driven policies to be out of constitutional bounds, for instance, in *Regents of the University of California v. Bakke* and *City of Richmond v. J. A. Croson Co.*[6] "The race of those burdened or benefited by a particular classification" was irrelevant to equal protection violations, Justice O'Connor had announced in *Croson*.[7] Moreover, plaintiffs did not need to identify any particular individuals who had suffered harm as a consequence of a plan involving racial preferences. It was the racial classification of voters, in and of itself, that violated the Fourteenth Amendment.

Although the intellectual foundation for this argument had been laid in other contexts, in suits charging electoral inequality, this was a new idea, analytically unrelated to the earlier Fourteenth Amendment voting rights cases involving the weight of the ballots cast. Vote dilution was the question at the core of *Whitcomb v. Chavis, White v. Regester*, and other equal protection decisions that had picked up where *Reynolds v. Sims* had left off.[8] Plaintiffs in *Shaw* did not argue that North Carolina's congressional districts had minimized the electoral power of blacks; instead, they contended that the racial agenda driving the districting violated the equal protection clause. It was a plan with a racial purpose and, thus, constitutionally suspect and open to challenge on Fourteenth Amendment grounds—regardless of whether it served minority voters well or ill.[9]

In *Shaw*, however, the question before the Court was simply one of justiciability: Had the plaintiffs stated a legitimate Fourteenth Amendment claim? Writing for a majority of five, Justice Sandra Day O'Connor found the districting plan to be so "highly irregular . . . on its face" as to constitute "an effort to 'segregate . . . voters' on the basis of race."[10] The plaintiffs, the Court concluded, were thus on firm legal ground in filing an equal protection suit.

O'Connor was quick to say the Court had never held that "race-conscious state decision-making is impermissible in all circumstances."[11] The plaintiffs had alleged that the North Carolina districts were a violation of their constitutional right to participate in a colorblind electoral process. That, however, was a right the Court did not recognize; it had long held that racial classifications were not, per se, discriminatory, but were subject to strict scrutiny.[12] They were presumed unconstitutional unless narrowly tailored to serve a compelling state interest.[13] Racial classifications, O'Connor noted in *Shaw*, "are by their very nature odious to a free people."[14] And, for this reason, "redistricting legislation that is so bizarre . . . demands the same close scrutiny that we give other state laws that classify citizens by race."[15]

"We believe," O'Connor continued, "that reapportionment is one area in which appearances do matter."[16] A districting map that segregates voters threatens "to stigmatize individuals by reason of their membership in a racial group" and to "balkanize us into competing racial factions . . . [carrying] us further from the goal of a political system in which race no longer matters—a goal that the Fourteenth and Fifteenth Amendments embody, and to which the Nation continues to aspire."[17]

Racially gerrymandered districts also send a pernicious message to elected representatives, argued O'Connor. "When a district obviously is created solely to effectuate the perceived common interests of one racial group, elected officials are more likely to believe that their primary obligation is to represent only the members of that group, rather than their constituency as a whole. This is altogether antithetical to our system of representative democracy," she concluded.[18]

O'Connor implied that districts that look bad are bad. Indeed, they bear "an uncomfortable resemblance to political apartheid," she said.[19] But what qualified as a "looks-bad" district? Did geographically "bizarre" contours constitute reliable circumstantial evidence of race-driven motive? And how bizarre did they have to be? If the district was more or less compact— no extraordinarily tortured lines—but the legislative history suggested a focus on race, could the charge of segregating voters nevertheless stick? The Court left these and other questions that were raised by numerous critics for another day.

Justice Byron White, joined by Justices Harry Blackmun and John Paul Stevens, dissented. (Justice David Souter wrote separately.) "The grounds for my disagreement with the majority are simply stated," White wrote. "Appellants have not presented a cognizable claim, because they have not alleged a cognizable injury." An injury involving voting rights consists either of an outright deprivation of the right to vote or a practice that diminishes the influence of a group on the political process.[20]

The definition of an equal protection injury has been so circumscribed, White continued, because districting is a unique context; race-consciousness is inevitable. "Legislators routinely engage in the business of making electoral predictions based on group characteristics—racial, ethnic, and the like."[21] The question, then, is not the use of race, per se, but its impact on electoral strength. In the case of North Carolina, "members of the white majority could not plausibly argue that their influence over the political process had been unfairly canceled."[22] Indeed, if a districting plan did not attempt to "minimize or eliminate the political strength" of a group, but was designed to "provide a rough sort of proportional representation," surely that could not be constitutionally illegitimate, White argued.[23]

The shape of the districts was of no relevance, in his view. "Given two districts drawn on similar, race-based grounds, the one does not become more injurious than the other simply by virtue of being snakelike, at least so far as the Constitution is concerned and absent any evidence of differential racial impact."[24] North Carolina had done no more than respond to the attorney general's objection to the map it had drawn.[25] White assumed that such an objection established a voting rights violation; the state's remedy was nothing more than a laudable "attempt to equalize treatment, and to provide minority voters with an effective voice in the political process."[26] Plaintiffs were not entitled to relief.

The majority and minority on the Court were obviously far apart. The four dissenters asked what the injury was, and argued that race-conscious districting positively helped black voters. The harm, O'Connor answered, was the racial classification in itself. Making distinctions among people on the basis of the color of their skin inevitably involved trafficking in invidious racial stereotyping. She could have strengthened her point by noting that the stigmatic harm that came from racial sorting had been at the core of the Court's decision in *Brown v. Board of Education*.[27]

Miller

The *Shaw* Court only settled the question of whether the plaintiffs had stated a claim under the equal protection clause; it did not resolve the substantive question of when "highly irregular" districting lines that appeared race-driven could be rationally explained on other grounds. The case was remanded to the D.C. District Court. Could CD 12 meet the demands of strict scrutiny to which all racial sorting was subject? Had the district been narrowly tailored to meet the compelling state interest that the Fourteenth Amendment demanded? The lower court, taking a second look, found it could survive strict scrutiny, but by the time the case reached the Supreme Court in 1996, the high Court's own post-*Shaw* decision in *Miller v. Johnson* had put additional meat on the bare constitutional bones in *Shaw*, and the lower court's holding was reversed.[28]

In the wake of the 1993 decision in *Shaw*, lawsuits challenging race-conscious districting started to burst out all over. *Miller*, which involved Georgia's CD 11 and was discussed at some length in the previous chapter, reached the high Court in 1995. The district court's opinion in the case vividly illustrated just how far outside the law the Justice Department had wandered in its misguided enforcement of section 5. Voting section attorneys and the ACLU were on the coziest of terms, and John Dunne, the assistant attorney general for civil rights, had embraced the organization's "max-black" plan as the only option that would satisfy the state's obligation to comply with section 5.

Georgia believed it was compelled to adopt the ACLU's plan if it wanted its districts precleared in compliance with section 5. Was the state's interest in getting its map approved by the Justice Department sufficiently compelling to meet the Fourteenth Amendment test for permissible racial classifications? The statute had not compelled "abject surrender to [Dunne's] maximization agenda," the district court concluded.[29] Indeed, the "informal and familiar" relationship between federal attorneys and an advocacy group was an "embarrassment."[30] Justice Anthony Kennedy, writing for a majority of five, concurred:

> Compliance with federal antidiscrimination laws cannot justify race-based districting where the challenged district was not reasonably necessary under a constitutional reading and application of those laws. . . . In utilizing § 5 to require States to create majority-minority districts wherever possible, the Department of Justice expanded its authority under the statute beyond what Congress intended and we have upheld.[31]

The Justice Department had willfully misread the statute.

It was perfectly obvious that the "max-black" plan (by definition) was race-driven. In fact, by the measure of looks alone, Georgia's Eleventh Congressional District was racially gerrymandered. Its contours were "bizarre"—the term used in *Shaw* to describe North Carolina's District 12.[32] But, surely, as Justice White's dissent in *Shaw* argued, segregating voters by race could also be the aim behind some more compact, more "normal" districts.[33] The Court could not paint itself into a corner in which the legal question hinged on "pretty" or "ugly."

The *Miller* Court recognized Justice White's point. Appearance was not the standard, Justice Kennedy replied:

> Our observation in *Shaw* of the consequences of racial stereo-typing was not meant to suggest that a district must be bizarre on

its face before there is a constitutional violation. . . . Shape is relevant . . . because it may be persuasive circumstantial evidence that race for its own sake, and not other districting principles, was the legislature's dominant and controlling rationale in drawing its district lines.[34]

But parties may rely on other evidence to establish reliance on racial stereotypes in legislative mapmaking, Kennedy wrote:

The plaintiff's burden is to show, either through circumstantial evidence of a district's shape and demographics or more direct evidence going to legislative purpose, that race was the predominant factor motivating the legislature's decision to place a significant number of voters within or without a particular district. To make this showing, a plaintiff must prove that the legislature subordinated traditional race neutral districting principles, including but not limited to compactness, contiguity, respect for political subdivisions or communities defined by actual shared interests, to racial considerations.[35]

A coercive Justice Department had handed the *Miller* plaintiffs a perfect case. There was no need to produce circumstantial evidence; it was clear from the record that John Dunne would have accepted nothing less than a plan in which a maximum number of majority-black districts had been drawn. At the insistence of the assistant attorney general for civil rights, racial considerations had obviously taken precedence over race-neutral districting criteria. The department ended up agreeing to pay almost $600,000 to settle plaintiffs' claims for attorneys' fees, expenses, and costs.[36]

But the Justice Department was more careful in the future. It never again left such tracks in the wake of a preclearance decision—such a rich record indicating unmistakably "that the legislature [had] subordinated traditional race neutral districting principles" in drawing districting maps. *Miller* had told the Justice Department, in effect, *Whisper, don't shout*, when telling jurisdictions to draw maps that would maximize black officeholding. It could easily do so. But there was not another districting round until after the 2000 census, and by that time the Court itself had decided that if racial considerations had not been clearly more important than political ones in fashioning a district like CD 12, then the seemingly gerrymandered lines were constitutional.

Post-*Miller*

Most districting decisions are influenced by a variety of political considerations. After *Miller*, could plaintiffs prevail where legislators had balanced competing interests in drawing lines on a map—where "race for its own sake" was not so obviously the legislature's "dominant and controlling rationale" in fashioning revised districts?

"The distinction between being aware of racial considerations and being motivated by them may be difficult to make," the *Miller* Court noted. Redistricting is sensitive, legislative judgments are owed considerable deference, and courts must therefore "exercise extraordinary caution in adjudicating claims that a state has drawn district lines on the basis of race."[37] It was a warning: In the absence of evidence that the Justice Department had engaged in a "subversion of the redistricting process," the Court would be reluctant to conclude that racial considerations drove the mapmaking process.[38]

Miller was followed by other Supreme Court decisions involving the constitutionality of racially gerrymandered district lines, some of which were discussed in the previous chapter. *Shaw v. Hunt* (*Shaw II*) and *Bush v. Vera* were both decided in 1996. In *Shaw II*, as noted above, the Court rejected North Carolina's Twelfth Congressional District as race-driven, and in *Bush* it likewise declared three Texas congressional districts in violation of the Fourteenth Amendment.[39] That same year, a lower court struck down Louisiana's congressional districts.[40] The court stated that "the Justice Department impermissibly encouraged—nay, mandated—racial gerrymandering" and that "the Legislature succumbed to the illegitimate preclearance demands of the Justice Department."[41]

A year later, in *Abrams v. Johnson*, the Court approved a court-drawn map for Georgia that contained only one majority-black congressional district; it replaced the plan containing three black districts that the Court had struck down in *Miller*.[42] Finally, in 1999 and 2001, the Court returned to those problematic North Carolina congressional districts that had first been found constitutionally questionable in *Shaw v. Reno*; in *Hunt v. Cromartie* (*Cromartie I*) and *Easley v. Cromartie* (*Cromartie II*) no Fourteenth Amendment violation was found.[43] O'Connor had switched sides, which was the difference that made all the difference. All the Court's decisions finding unconstitutional "segregation" had been five to four; losing O'Connor's vote meant, as it turned out, the end of this particular line of Supreme Court decisions—or so it appears, as of this writing.

Cromartie I dealt with the question of whether the appellees challenging the plan as unconstitutional were entitled to summary judgment, and the Court reversed a district court judgment that had granted their request. The more important decision was *Cromartie II*, which examined the relative importance of race and politics in the mapmaking process in North Carolina. Recall that in the early 1990s the state legislature, with the support of the legislative black caucus, had created a second safe black congressional seat only because the Justice Department had refused to preclear a plan without it. But that two-seat map had been struck down as unconstitutional race-based districting. In response, the legislature did not return to its obviously legitimate first plan, containing only one majority-black district, but instead modified the lines of the second seat—District 12—to meet the Court's Fourteenth Amendment demands. As *Cromartie I* noted, it had remained "a 100-mile-long, snake-like agglomeration" that ran roughly parallel to an interstate highway. However, when the Court looked at it for the *fourth* time in 2001, in *Cromartie II*, it chose to ignore the history of federal coercion that had forced North Carolina to give top priority to maximizing black officeholding.[44]

Thus, with the stroke of a judicial pen, CD 12 was transformed from an unconstitutional, race-driven district imposed upon the state by a lawless Justice Department to one whose shape was perhaps determined more by politics than race, although it had retained "its basic 'snakelike' shape and continue[d] to track Interstate-85."[45] In *Cromartie I*, ruling on those same North Carolina congressional districts, the Court had described the appellees as having offered only circumstantial evidence supporting their claim that the legislature had subordinated traditional race-neutral districting principles to racial considerations. Two years later, in *Cromartie II*, Justice Stephen Breyer for a majority of five stressed the degree to which "racial identification is highly correlated with political affiliation." He concluded: "The attacking party has not successfully shown that race, rather than politics, predominantly accounts for the result."[46]

Miller had, in effect, given notice that a decision like that of *Cromartie II* was in the offing. The decision underscored the weight of the burden on future plaintiffs who would seek to show that racial considerations predominated over political ones in the districting process. As Ohio State University professor of law Daniel P. Tokaji has said,

> With a wink and a nod, the Court . . . signaled that it will allow race to be considered in drawing districts . . . so long as there is a colorable argument that "politics" rather than race is the real reason for the districts. Because voters' race so often correlates with political affiliation, it will be easy to sneak racial considerations into the districting process under the table.[47]

Moreover, the burden on plaintiffs to prove pernicious racial sorting in the districting process had become considerably heavier after the Court, in the two *Bossier* decisions in 1997 and 2000, significantly curtailed the power of the Justice Department to force states (and other jurisdictions) to maximize the number of majority-minority districts. Those decisions, it may be recalled, stopped the use of section 2 and a freewheeling definition of discriminatory intent in judging changes in election-related practices submitted for preclearance. *Bossier II* was superseded by Congress when section 5 was renewed and amended in 2006, but the two decisions clipped the wings of the Justice Department, curtailing its creative lawmaking through the post-2000 redistricting round. As noted above, after the turn-of-the-century census, the DOJ was careful to leave no record of race-driven maps forced upon the states. It did not make the *Miller* mistake again. In addition, the *Shaw* "looks-bad" test for districts that violated the Fourteenth Amendment had already been abandoned in *Miller*, and, after *Cromartie II*, even geographically bizarre lines were constitutionally permissible as long as they were (by some unspecified standards) driven by political and not racial goals.

Misguided Hyperbole

In less than a decade, the Fourteenth Amendment voting rights decisions that began with *Shaw v. Reno* came and went. In 1993, Justice O'Connor had written an emotional, arresting opinion for the Court. Race-based districting, she had said, "segregates" voters; conveys the terrible perception that members of the same racial or ethnic group think alike; stigmatizes individuals "by reason of their membership in a racial group"; balkanizes us into "competing racial factions"; and suggests that the primary obligation of elected representatives is to represent their racial constituencies. It was tough stuff—only she wouldn't stand by her own argument and, in *Cromartie II* in 2001, she beat a retreat, joining justices who had been deeply critical of her reasoning just eight years earlier. Her sudden discovery that both politics and race had shaped the districting decisions was implausible; as a former politician herself, she surely knew that politics had always been an ingredient in districting.

Had O'Connor's retreat been driven by the cacophony of criticism prompted by *Shaw*? We will probably never know. Her opinion in the 1993 decision prompted an avalanche of hyperbolic rhetoric. In his swearing-in ceremony as assistant attorney general for civil rights in March 1994, Deval Patrick promised "to restore the great moral imperative that civil rights is finally all about," with the enforcement of voting rights as one of his priorities.[48] That "moral imperative" evidently included renewing the commitment to race-driven districting that O'Connor had questioned. In a speech before the NAACP National Convention in July 1994, Patrick called *Shaw* "an alternately naïve and venal decision," and accused the Court of starting down the path of "an exclusion of Black and other minority representatives from positions of power."[49] That November, he suggested that the 1993 decision and the lower court rulings that followed in its wake were reminiscent of 1901, when the last black Reconstruction congressman from North Carolina left Washington.[50]

Patrick's reaction was not unique. *Shaw* came down in late June, and, in September, U.S. Representatives John Lewis and Cynthia McKinney joined thirty black elected officials from Georgia in an emergency meeting to discuss its impact. "This ruling is the greatest threat to the Voting Rights Act since it was signed on August 6, 1965," Congressman Lewis said. Georgia representative Tyrone Brooks called it "a racist political attack on minority voting rights," while Congresswoman McKinney (a little wobbly on her history) predicted a "second Reconstruction—when blacks will once again be expelled from Congress because of their color."[51] Brenda Wright of the Lawyers' Committee for Civil Rights Under the Law termed the decision "an excuse for leaving black voters out of the political calculus."[52] And, two years later, awaiting decisions on the constitutionality of racially gerrymandered districts in post-*Shaw* cases, Ted Shaw of the NAACP's Legal Defense and Educational Fund warned: "If we lose these cases, the Congressional Black Caucus will be meeting in the back seat of a taxicab."[53] Representative Mel Watt took the point another step further. "Without these districts," he said, "you're not going to have minority representation in Congress. It's just that simple."[54]

In the view of these civil rights advocates, blacks are always on the verge of disfranchisement—or at least they depict them as such, which is a good fundraising and political mobilization strategy. As it turned out, these predictions of doom were entirely misplaced: Black candidates did very well in the states in which Fourteenth Amendment suits had been brought. Neither the district court's final decision regarding the constitutionality of the North Carolina districts nor subsequent decisions striking down racially gerrymandered districts in Georgia, Louisiana, Texas, and elsewhere halted the impressive growth in the number of black elected officials. Civil rights spokesmen argued that these candidates had the advantage of incumbency (an argument they had not made prior to the elections); in fact, they were not incumbents in the newly reconfigured districts.

The Fourteenth Amendment decisions did not slow the growth of black officeholding, as predicted by the civil rights groups. In the 1990s the number of southern black members of Congress tripled. By 2004, 18 percent of the congressmen from the racially suspect southern states originally covered by the preclearance provision were black, while blacks were 25 percent of the voting-age population in that region. Add in Texas and Florida (only partly subject to section 5), and the percentage of blacks elected to Congress rose to near proportionality.[55] In addition, every congressional district that was at least 40 percent black sent a Democrat to Congress.[56] Black voters had become indispensable to the party's fortunes.

The View from the Academy

Civil rights activists, as noted above, were not alone in their dismay at *Shaw* and its progeny. The decision did not have many fans among voting rights scholars, either, although the tone of academic writing was quite different from the pronouncements of Deval Patrick, Cynthia McKinney, and other peddlers of preposterous alarm. Moreover, some scholarly comment took the form of using the Fourteenth Amendment decisions to look at the problems posed by race-conscious districts other than those identified by Justice O'Connor, without, however, rejecting the goal of ensuring minority representation.

It is important to note that O'Connor had friends as well as foes in the academy, and that not every scholar who wrote on the decisions fit neatly into one camp or the other. Among her supporters, the most prominent was University of South Carolina law professor Katharine Butler. "*Miller* and *Shaw* are cases about the state's use of race. They are only incidentally about minority representation," Butler wrote. "The Voting Rights Act comes into play only when offered as a justification for the state's use of race, which the Court has consistently subjected to heightened judicial scrutiny." They are thus "unremarkable decisions"—perfectly consistent with the whole line of cases that had treated policy decisions made on the basis of race as highly suspect.[57]

While Stanford law professor Pamela Karlan and others claimed that no harm flowed from race-conscious districting, Butler, echoing O'Connor and using the school desegregation cases as an analogy, argued that the racial classification itself—the "racial sorting . . . designed to serve a racial purpose"—was the "evil."[58] Racially gerrymandered districts sort citizens by race in the same way that school busing plans substitute race for the ordinary bases upon which school assignments are made.[59] "Just as segregated schools cannot be supported by showing that education is equal for all, or that no stigma is perceived because of the one-race character of the school, supplanting standard districting criteria with racial ones is inherently harmful. No further injury need be demonstrated."[60]

Butler had a strong argument that the racial gerrymandering cases should be seen as a variation on a familiar theme. The equal protection decisions in general were a bewildering mess, however. Critics of *Shaw* have expressed considerable impatience with O'Connor's initial notion that ugly districts are constitutionally suspect, since the "looks-bad" standard is more or less that which has been applied in cases involving, for instance, university admissions. In 2003, the Court struck down preferential admissions to the University of Michigan undergraduate college, while permitting them for the U-M law school. The difference between the two cases, as Justice Ruth Bader Ginsburg noted, was the willingness of the law school to engage in "winks, nods, and disguises" to make its actually more blatant racial preferences look *prettier* than those used by the college.[61] If *Shaw* and the other Fourteenth Amendment voting rights cases were a muddle, it was equally true of almost all decisions involving race-based public policies. What principle separated acceptable from unacceptable racial classification? The Court has had no answer to that question—in voting rights cases, or in those involving education, employment, or contracting.

Advocates who believed that the benefits of race-based public policies outweighed any possible harm dismissed O'Connor and Katharine Butler. Critics of the racial gerrymandering decisions saw the majority-minority districts as analogous to preferential policies in employment, contracting, and education—the only sure means of providing protection against persistent white racism that threatened to eradicate or greatly diminish black progress. While the majority on the *Shaw* Court had looked at the North Carolina congressional districts and thought something was amiss, a majority of law review authors looked at *Shaw* and registered their conviction that the flaw lay in the Court's reasoning, not the district lines.

Since the 1970s, professors T. Alexander Aleinikoff and Samuel Issacharoff have written, race-conscious measures have been adopted to "ameliorate the exclusion of African Americans and others from important economic and educational opportunities."[62] Safe black and Hispanic districts are essential to the "full integration" of American politics, a cause for which "hundreds of thousands of Americans marched, and some even died," Karlan argued.[63]

Race-based districts, such proponents suggested, serve the compelling state interest of enhanced representation—a level of minority officeholding that political jockeying as usual will not bring. Black candidates, in their view, were entirely dependent on black votes to win public office; black legislators who thought otherwise in Georgia and elsewhere could not be trusted; and black voters who were concentrated in racially defined, rather than geographically based, districts paid no political price.

The districts were needed, these critics held, and the decisions condemning them were incoherent. "Bizarreness is a subjective, 'I know it when I see it' standard, [giving] trial courts a roving warrant to strictly scrutinize districts they do not like," Karlan wrote.[64] Aleinikoff and Issacharoff echoed her view. The Court did not demand compact districts, they said, and, without such a requirement, "there is a strong risk that *Shaw* will be nothing more than an invitation to ad hoc judicial review of redistricting decisions."[65] The Court announced no clear and decisive norm by which to judge districts, they continued. "The result is an unhappy one for lower courts and litigators looking for guidance in this complex and charged area of law located at the core of American political life."[66]

The *Miller* Court had announced a "predominant factor" test for when racial considerations played too large a role in drawing district lines. But what did "predominant" mean? "It is virtually impossible that race or any other single consideration could be the sole cause of a district's configuration, especially if the districting plan is enacted through a political process," UCLA law professor Daniel Hays Lowenstein rightly noted. And "if a plan only partially explainable by race can be unconstitutional and yet race-conscious districting is not always unconstitutional, how can a line be drawn?" he asked.

In any case, "to ask whether one factor 'predominates' over others is to imply that the districting process consists of a weighing or balancing of factors," as Lowenstein said,

> but that is not what occurs with race in redistricting. Under the VRA, race is not a "factor" at all, but a prior requirement in a lexical ordering. . . . A consideration that is lexically prior is a privileged consideration. It is a necessary precondition of what comes afterward, and aside from that, there is little that can be said about how it is "weighted" against the rest.[67]

The Court, in its Fourteenth Amendment cases, had another crucial point wrong, Lowenstein argued. References to respect for "traditional districting principles such as compactness, contiguity, and respect for political subdivisions" ran through *Shaw*, *Miller*, and others. But districting is not "a matter governed by principles . . . Districting is a matter of competition and negotiation. . . . The only 'principle' that guides the process as a whole is that the outcome should fairly reflect the competition and negotiation that occurred."[68]

The racially gerrymandered districts to which the Court objected, however, did not reflect a process of "competition and negotiation." As Lowenstein himself pointed out, that process had been relegated to second place by an overzealous Justice Department, which did believe in racial quotas as a matter of principle. Blacks here, whites there, in just the right numbers to ensure the election of blacks to public office roughly in proportion to their population numbers—that was what racial fairness demanded, in the view of the Civil Rights Division of the DOJ. As I have argued at a number of points earlier in this book, the standard of proportionality rests on a profound misconception of the "natural" distribution of racial and ethnic groups across the residential, occupational, and other aspects of the social landscape. Jews, for instance, are under 2 percent of the American population, but they hold approximately 13 percent of the seats in Congress. Should federal power be used to correct that imbalance? Given the history of racism in America, it has certainly been legitimate to provide remedies when racist exclusion seems the likely explanation for a paucity of black office-holders. But racist exclusion, not statistical imbalance, is the proper question.

Race-Districts: A Defective Hybrid

Some academic criticism of the wrongful-districting cases reframed (or partly reframed) the issues raised by racial gerrymandering. Aleinikoff and Issacharoff, for instance, were struck by the limited ability of race-conscious districting to ensure racial equality. The remedy, in their view, had not gone far enough. "To the extent that districting under the Voting Rights Act is intended to be the path to inclusion of minority interests, it has been under-inclusive of the full community that needs to be served," they wrote.[69]

The basic problem, as they saw it, was the Court's reluctance to question geographical districting—that is, with "first past the post," winner-take-all districts. "Geographically based districts assume that political identity will primarily correlate with geography," they have written. "However, the focus on geographic proximity in districting developed in a time when communities were smaller and transportation was more difficult. Today, no geographically based lines can necessarily properly capture 'political communities of interest.'"[70] *Shaw*, they speculated, "could bring renewed attention to nondistricted concepts of representation, both as remedial tools in voting-rights litigation and as a potentially more substantively fair mechanism for running elections."[71] They found particularly appealing modified proportional representation systems that created a closer match between the percentage of votes received by candidates identified with particular interest groups and the number of legislative seats assigned to them.[72]

While proportional representation (even in modified form) is traditionally out of political bounds in the American context, it is the role of scholars such as Aleinikoff and Issacharoff to flirt with unconventional ideas. And yet, as should be clear from previous chapters, the Voting Rights Act brought notions of proportionality into the nation's political system through the back door. "Voting-rights controversies today arise from two alternative conceptions of representative government colliding like tectonic plates," Richard H. Pildes and Richard G. Niemi have written.

> On one side is the long-standing Anglo-American commitment to organizing political representation around geography. As embodied in election districts, physical territory is the basis on which we ascribe linked identities to citizens and on which we forge ties between representatives and constituents. On the other side is the increasing power of the Voting Rights Act of 1965 (VRA), which organizes political representation around the concept of interest. . . . Whenever these two plates of territory and interest collide, surface disturbances in voting-rights policy erupt.[73]

"Alternative" and incompatible, Pildes and Niemi should have said. Single-member districts and interest-group representation are mutually exclusive electoral systems. Methods of election designed to ensure proportional racial representation are not conceptually based on the traditional

American notion that, for purposes of representation, geography defines a constituency. They rest on a quite different assumption: that shared racial identity creates a distinctive interest group, and that race therefore defines a political community that is entitled to representation. Indeed, given the history of blacks in America, the argument for that entitlement is much stronger than for other groups that voters have voluntarily formed as free citizens.

It was upon that assumption that, in enforcing the Voting Rights Act, federal actors built into the statute a commitment to districts drawn to ensure (to the extent possible) proportional representation for blacks and Hispanics—and for them alone. Anything less than proportionality suggested compromised representation for voters victimized by persistent discrimination.

And yet, as Daniel D. Polsby and Robert D. Popper have argued, "The system created under the VRA is neither fish nor fowl. It is not single-member-district plurality-voting; a 'fix' has been added that increases the probability that racial minorities, if they are large enough, will be proportionately represented."[74] Nor is it a true system of proportional representation, which would allow the unregulated proliferation of parties based on feminism, environmentalism, black nationalism—whatever issue turns voters on in sufficient numbers to command at least one legislative seat. Those parties would be the product of choices that voters have made to coalesce around issues of intense interest to them. A Black Panther Party in a true proportional representation system would have an agenda that individual voters had freely chosen to embrace. But majority-minority districts are composed of voters whom the federal government has designated as belonging together—quite a different matter.

Polsby and Popper called such federally created designer districts "defective hybrids." Candidates are not pushed toward the political center as they are in geographically based, single-member districts, which contain voters with a multiplicity of agendas.[75] Instead, black candidates, who face competition only from other blacks, have every incentive to run as the most racially committed—the most "authentically" black. That is, they have every incentive to run at the political margins rather than as mainstream candidates eager to build a broad base of support by appealing to a diversity of voters who live close to one another but may have little else in common.

Of course, there is some political diversity within black caucuses in Congress and in state legislatures. Playing the authentically black card has not always worked to secure victory in black-on-black contests. Nevertheless every member of the Congressional Black Caucus is a Democrat and has a composite liberal voting score (as assigned by the *National Journal*) above the congressional average; only Sanford Bishop of Georgia, with a score of 54.8, has a record close to the mean, while half of the members score above 80.[76] The result, arguably, has been too many black officeholders who have been less influential than they might have been had their politics been more centrist. In addition, their clustering on the left within the Democratic Party would seem to support Justice O'Connor's point: Racially gerrymandered districts work to reinforce "the perception that members of the same racial group—regardless of their age, education, economic status, or the community in which they live—think alike, share the same political interests, and will prefer the same candidates at the polls."[77]

Expressive Harms

Race-based districts also deliver normative messages about the importance of racial identity, the role of race in American society and institutions, and the definition of representative government. Pildes and Niemi are certainly not the first to touch on that point; I, myself, made it many years ago.[78] But their formulation has received unprecedented attention. Perceptions were what *Shaw* was all about, they argued in their much-cited article, "Expressive Harms," to which I have referred above.

"*Shaw* must be understood to rest on a distinctive conception of the kinds of harms against which the Constitution protects . . . expressive harms, as opposed to more familiar, material harms," they wrote.[79] Racially distorted districts express a message that the policymaking process has been tainted by an excessive focus on race:

> In the Court's view, the process of designing election districts violates the Constitution not when race-conscious lines are drawn, but when race consciousness dominates the process too extensively. . . . Under *Shaw*, race is not an impermissible factor

that corrupts the districting process—as long as it is one among many factors that policymakers use.[80]

Public officials must maintain a commitment to "value pluralism," they argued. Too great a stress on the single value of racial representation violates "constitutionally unwritten" public norms.[81] Legitimacy depends on perception. "The meaning of a governmental action is just as important as what that action does."[82] Expressive harms occur when the public's understanding of a proper balance among values is violated. In the case of districting, the proper balance struck must be between geographically defined interests and those tied to race:

> When physical geography is stretched too thin, when it is twisted, turned, and tortured—all in the apparent pursuit of fair and effective minority representation—at some point, too much becomes too much. That appears to be the judicial impulse that accounts for *Shaw*: in the conflict of territory and interest, the Constitution requires policymakers somehow to hold the line and accommodate both.[83]

Aleinikoff and Issacharoff have made a related argument. The Court in *Shaw* had referred to the pernicious message that all blacks think alike; but, as they pointed out, white stereotyping should have been of equal concern. "Race essentialism" is unacceptable, whatever the color of members of the group. In a 1977 voting rights decision, it was assumed that Hasidic Jews in Brooklyn, New York, were fully represented by Manhattan's Upper East Side whites, who had little in common with the Hasidim, a discrete and insular minority with its own culture.[84] That decision, like *Shaw* and subsequently, *Miller*, involved a racial gerrymander that flashed the message "RACE, RACE, RACE," as Aleinikoff and Issacharoff put it. Compact districts honoring geographically natural boundaries never sent that message. "A bizarrely shaped district bespeaks a willful manipulation of the districting system to force an electoral outcome upon a disinclined electorate."[85]

A "willful manipulation" of districting lines . . . by whom? Aleinikoff and Issacharoff did not say, but the answer was obvious—and should be obvious to readers of this book by now. These were districts forced upon states by both Democratic and Republican Justice Departments indifferent to the law, typically working in close collaboration with civil rights groups but sometimes (as in the case of the North Carolina) willing to act against the wishes of a state's own legislative black caucus. As Daniel Lowenstein noted, "State legislatures, acting on their own, do not carry race-based districting to excess. Racial and ethnic groups, like other groups, will be accommodated, but none will be privileged."[86] When politics, not race, drives the districting process, the nonracial electoral agendas of parties, incumbents, and candidates are not so recklessly dismissed.

Racial sorting has created advantaged and disadvantaged categories—groups that are privileged and groups that are subordinate, Aleinikoff and Issacharoff argued.[87] The majority-minority districts upon which the DOJ insisted have become safe for black or Hispanic candidates, as intended, but they have also turned white voters into what these two scholars called "filler people."[88] Whites have become irrelevant to the outcome of the elections in districts designed to elect minorities, unless they serve as the swing vote in a black-on-black contest. They have been included in such districts only to make sure that the black population does not become so concentrated as to make some black ballots superfluous and, therefore, wasted. They have not been "expected to compete in any genuine sense for electoral representation . . . lest they undo the preference given to the specified minority group."[89] It's an arrangement that would seem at odds with the pursuit of political equality that was supposed to be the core purpose of the Voting Rights Act.

A Rorschach Test

Justice O'Connor in *Shaw* described North Carolina's congressional district as a "Rorschach ink-blot test."[90] But the racial gerrymandering decisions were themselves a Rorschach test; academic scholars who struggled to make sense of them had widely varying interpretations of the case law. Something is clearly wrong with the Court's reasoning when serious voting rights scholars are forced to embark on an imaginative search for explanations that will lend coherence to otherwise bewildering decisions.

The Fourteenth Amendment decisions that began with *Shaw* in 1993 amounted, in the end, to a brief constitutional episode, lasting only eight years. When, in 2001, O'Connor switched sides in *Cromartie II*, joining the four justices who had dissented in *Shaw*, it might be said that the liberals on the Court had had the last word. No new Fourteenth Amendment cases were filed as a consequence of the post-2000 round of redistricting. But the end of this complicated line of cases, Lowenstein has suggested, was not really a defeat for conservatism. The Court's rejection of the definition of racial fairness embedded in the federal imposition of race-driven districts had been music to conservative ears. Those on the right had enthusiastically embraced O'Connor's eloquent attack on the racial stereotyping encouraged by the creation of districts designed to ensure that the allegedly different political voice of blacks was heard. And yet, Lowenstein argued, in important respects the racial gerrymandering decisions were not conservative.[91] Liberals disliked them, but conservatives should have, as well.

They violated bedrock conservative principles, Lowenstein contended. The Court had found state districting decisions unconstitutional even though the states had acted only as they were compelled to do by a lawless Justice Department. In 1965, the Voting Rights Act had substantially reduced the constitutional authority of southern states to fashion their own systems of representation—for excellent reasons at the time. After 1970, the reach of section 5 extended to scattered counties, and after 1975 to some entire states outside the South. The 1982 amendment of section 2 made districting decisions across the nation vulnerable to federal interference, with often questionable justification; and in the 1990s, the wrongful-districting cases (as they are sometimes called) further eroded state power over their own electoral arrangements.

These decisions placed states in an impossible bind. Race-conscious districting was the precondition for preclearance; at the same time, legislatures could not engage in the type of racial sorting that a court might find constitutionally offensive—by erratic and impenetrable standards. These were not decisions that advocates for judicial restraint should have celebrated. As Lowenstein put the point:

> The decisions offend conservative conceptions of federalism. A constitutional doctrine that permits the federal government to strictly regulate functions central to the self-government of the states—and then, on the theory that it is unconstitutional for the states to comply with such regulation, takes additional important

powers away from the states—is not a doctrine that is friendly to state government.[92]

The racial gerrymandering cases, in Lowenstein's view, not only treated states with contempt. They were also at odds with the emphasis conservatives have long placed on equal opportunity for members of racial groups. The Voting Rights Act, as it had come to be interpreted, mandated districting plans that ensured racially "fair" results. The Court never questioned the constitutionality of that mandate; its quarrel was solely with its implementation—the *excessive* emphasis placed on the racial identity of voters in the drawing of racially determined district lines.

Genuinely conservative justices, Lowenstein argued, would have insisted that black and Hispanic legislators have the opportunity to compete within the political system for the kinds of districts they believed were in their own or their constituents' best interests—with no guaranteed results.[93] The record in *Shaw* itself indicated that North Carolina's legislative black caucus had supported the state's plan, which contained only one majority-black district; caucus members had hoped that the Justice Department would respect their political priorities and the districting agreement they had negotiated. But the DOJ voting section rejected the option of ethnic politics within a democratic system responsive to politically strategic choices made by minority legislators.

Rather than targeting states that drew the districts as the DOJ demanded, a genuinely conservative Court, in Lowenstein's view, would have rejected a reading of the Voting Rights Act as mandating racial quotas—proportional racial representation. The Court, in other words, would have exercised its authority to read the statute and control the DOJ's interpretation of it: "A decent regard for the role of the states and for the free functioning of democratic politics demands at least that the federal government confine its intrusions into districting to the minimum necessary to achieve racial justice."[94]

By now, it should be apparent that I agree. What constituted the "minimum necessary," however? Surely the answer depends on whether we are talking about 1965 or 1993 (the date of *Shaw*)—or some date in between. And it depends on one's assessment of the level of ongoing white racism and its potential to affect electoral outcomes. These are questions with which I grapple in chapter 6 and the conclusion.

6

The Serbonian Bog

In 1965, Congress enacted the Voting Rights Act. Three decades later, the legislation remains a Serbonian bog in which plaintiffs and defendants, pundits and policymakers, judges and justices find themselves bemired.

—Judge Bruce M. Selya, U.S. Court of Appeals
for the First Circuit[1]

At its inception, the Voting Rights Act stood on very firm constitutional ground; it was pure antidiscrimination legislation designed to enforce basic Fifteenth Amendment rights. A clear principle justified its original enactment: Citizens should not be judged by the color of their skin when states determine eligibility to vote. That clarity could not be sustained over time. As a result, more than four decades later, the law has become what Judge Bruce Selya so vividly described in 1995 as a "Serbonian bog." The legal land looks solid but is, in fact, a quagmire, into which "plaintiffs and defendants, pundits and policymakers, judges and justices" have sunk.

Extrication will not be easy. As previous chapters have recounted, the bog was created by cumulative congressional, judicial, and Justice Department decisions that span the history of the statute. The Supreme Court has never "determined the meaning of 'effective exercise of the electoral franchise,'" Justice Sandra Day O'Connor wrote in 2003.[2] The problem was apparent when the Court, in 1969, first blurred the distinction between electoral arrangements that stopped blacks from voting and those that could "nullify" their ability "to elect the candidate of their choice."[3] It continues to this day. Political equality is still the aim of the statute, but the definition of racially fair elections remains elusive. In fact, as the act came to be reshaped, blacks became entitled to political *inequality*. Their preferred candidates of choice acquired unique protection from white competition.

The questions of equitable representation with which the Supreme Court has struggled involve basic democratic norms that are beyond the capacity of courts to sort out. It is no wonder that the Court's legal standards have often been conflicting, arbitrary, and murky, differing from one context to another. But the result has been that neither lower courts nor the Justice Department have felt particularly obligated to follow its lead, and jurisdictions have been left in the dark as they try to comply with the law.

The aim of the statute remained eliminating racism from the electoral sphere. The distinction, however, between racist and nonracist localities was lost over time. The 1970 amendments extended preclearance to three New York boroughs and other counties with no history of disfranchisement; the problem was exacerbated in 1975 when Hispanics in Texas and elsewhere came under preclearance protection, although Hispanics had never experienced racist exclusion in a form comparable to that which kept blacks disfranchised in the Jim Crow South. And yet providing a remedy for disfranchisement was the entire justification for the constitutionally radical statute.

The Department of Justice was a large player in undermining the solid constitutional terrain on which the original statute stood. The problem was not only the confusing legal standards set by the courts; the DOJ engaged in much creative lawmaking of its own. Voting section attorneys (along with most judges on the D.C. District Court and a minority on the Supreme Court) never liked the retrogression test for discriminatory effect and charted numerous detours around it, regularly traveled until the high Court intervened (with only temporary effectiveness) in 1997 and 2000. The retrogression test—backsliding from the status quo—was discarded in favor of judging electoral equality by the absolute standard contained in section 2, and redefining discriminatory intent so that it meant anything and everything.

These detours gave the Justice Department the freedom to insist on racially gerrymandered districts—which ultimately prompted a series of Fourteenth Amendment decisions that curtailed the DOJ's power to insist on what are sometimes called "bug-splat" districts. Those race-driven districts involved the unconstitutional sorting of voters, the Court held. In 1993

Justice O'Connor described a North Carolina congressional district as a "Rorschach ink-blot test" but the racial gerrymandering decisions themselves elicited a wide variety of interpretations, and in 2001 the Court abandoned its effort to set clear legal standards.[4] Race-driven lines were also determined by partisan considerations, and the two came to be seen as too difficult to disentangle.

I began this chapter by saying that extrication from the bog created by all parties who participated in the remaking of the Voting Rights Act will be hard. Congress acted to update the statute as recently as 2006 and, incredibly, strengthened federal antidiscrimination powers in the face of racial progress on a scale almost unimaginable. Unless forced to do so by the Supreme Court, it will not revisit those amendments, which are described below. The Justice Department in the Obama administration, closely tied to the civil rights groups, is not likely to abandon a core conviction that has been driving all problematic voting rights enforcement: that in a nonracist society, minorities would be elected to political office in numbers proportional to the black and Hispanic populations.

That core conviction is willfully blind to the complexity of a multiracial, multiethnic society. In fact, in whatever ways individuals define themselves, the groups to which they choose to belong are not likely to be proportionally represented in most walks of life. It was reasonable in the years following the passage of the Voting Rights Act to look at the paucity of minority officeholders, particularly in the South where blacks had been disfranchised for so long, and to say, *too few*. The absence of elected blacks was evidence of a historic wrong that required a remedy. But it was a big leap from there to a belief in proportional racial representation as part of the natural order—what should be expected across the political, social, and professional landscape in a racially fair society.

In a case currently on its docket, the Supreme Court will have the opportunity to reject the standard of proportional representation as the measure of racial equality, turn its back on racial sorting, and reiterate Chief Justice John Roberts's concern that the statute has engaged the nation in the "sordid business . . . of divvying us up by race."[5] Plaintiffs are challenging the constitutionality of section 5, more than forty years after its enactment as an emergency provision. I will return below to a discussion of this case and the Court's options.

Competing Principles

The question of proportionality as the measure of racial equality is not unique to voting rights. The Supreme Court has addressed the issue in other contexts—and repeatedly rejected a simple test of statistical parity in judging discrimination. For instance, in an important 1989 employment law case, *Wards Cove Packing Company v. Atonio*, Justice Byron White argued that looking at the numbers—simply counting the minority and nonminority employees in skilled and nonskilled jobs in an Alaskan salmon cannery—was not very revealing. Alaskan Natives and Filipinos were under-represented among the skilled labor jobs—but how many minorities in the state had the education and skills needed for those jobs? And among those who did, how many had actually applied for a job with the company? To ignore those questions would be to make every employer with a racially imbalanced segment of his workforce vulnerable to expensive and time-consuming litigation, White argued. "The only practicable option for many employers [would] be to adopt racial quotas," which Title VII of the 1964 Civil Rights Act "expressly rejected."[6]

In a decision that same year involving minority set-asides in public contracts issued by Richmond, Virginia, Justice O'Connor referred to racial classifications as "strictly reserved for remedial settings."[7] It was "sheer speculation how many minority firms there would be in Richmond absent past societal discrimination," she said.[8] The assumption that blacks would be proportionally represented in the municipal contracting program had no empirical basis. The imposition of racial quotas could not be constitutionally ordered without "direct evidence" of discrimination.[9]

Without such "direct evidence," the case for racial set-asides rested on statistical evidence of disparities between the number of prime contracts awarded to whites and those awarded to "minority business enterprises." A statistical imbalance, however, did not justify color-conscious policies. Nor did findings of "various forms of past societal discrimination," which Justice Lewis F. Powell in 1978 had called "an amorphous concept of injury that may be ageless in its reach into the past."[10] Any other conclusion invited quotas with no end in sight—no logical stopping point. Statistical imbalances are ubiquitous and part of the normal social order. And, as Powell implied, a history of past societal discrimination can be found wherever blacks reside. These are not criteria that can distinguish a legitimate adoption of fundamentally suspect racial classifications from an illegitimate one.

The Powell quotation was from the first important decision involving racial preferences in higher education. In the classroom, the workplace, and government contracting, most people would like to see some racial diversity—a sign that doors are open in the land of opportunity. But the majority of Americans reject racial preferences or quotas as a matter of principle.[11] They do not believe in judging Americans by the color of their skin, and when the issue is providing special protection from white competition for blacks and Hispanics hoping for admission to a selective college or a promotion to a better job, the argument for standing on that high moral ground is very strong.

I, too, have long rejected racial preferences on precisely the moral ground that troubles most Americans: Racial double standards are demeaning and patronizing to their alleged beneficiaries. But race-conscious policies in the voting rights context are somewhat different from those in other settings. It is relatively easy to take an uncompromising, principled stance against racial classifications in higher education, for instance. It is much less so when the issue is districting lines drawn to increase black officeholding.

The differences are important. Racial double standards in student admissions, for instance, throw meritocratic principles to the wind, an action that is in itself morally troubling. Furthermore, proponents of racial preferences see the importance of black faces in the Alabama state legislature and that of black faces in a University of Michigan classroom as analogous. But the alternative to preferences in education is not anything like all-white schools; William G. Bowen and Derek Bok, in their well-known 1998 book, *The Shape of the River*, calculated that approximately half the black students in the selective schools they studied needed no distinctive treatment to gain admission.[12] And, despite a 1996 amendment to the California State Constitution that banned the use of race in the admissions processes in public colleges and universities, non-Asian minority students are as well represented in the University of California system as they had been prior to the constitutional amendment.[13]

Finally, there is strong evidence that racial preferences in higher education don't even work as advertised; a recent study by UCLA law professor Richard Sander, for instance, has shown that black students preferentially admitted to law schools have disproportionately low rates in passing the bar exam. They are less likely to end up as attorneys than are African Americans who choose to attend law schools where the academic credentials of the average student match theirs.[14]

The contrast with the realm of politics is marked. There are no objective qualifications for office—the equivalent of a college or professional degree, a minimum score on the LSATs, a certain grade-point average, or relevant work experience. The districting process has always been political—and, consequently, subjective. And race-based districts work precisely as advertised: They elect blacks and Hispanics to legislative seats. In the South such descriptive representation had an importance far greater than increasing the number of black and Hispanic students at, say, Duke University.

The election of blacks to political office was the single most important sign that the Jim Crow order had truly collapsed; indeed, it was a prerequisite to the final destruction of the system of white supremacy and black subordination. And yet, when the Voting Rights Act was passed in 1965, it quickly became clear that only a federal sledgehammer could break open a southern political system barricaded against black entrance. In the early years, without an insistence on race-conscious methods of election to prevent ongoing racist subordination, the number of blacks elected to public office in Mississippi, Georgia, Louisiana, and South Carolina, as well as a good many counties in North Carolina and elsewhere, would likely have been a morally sobering close-to-nil.

Voting rights enforcement has, therefore, required a difficult assessment of the balance between two principles. People should not be judged by the color of their skin: That was the classic position of the civil rights movement in its heyday and should never be lightly abandoned. On the other hand, the problem of all-white politics in those parts of the South in which blacks had not even been allowed to register to vote prior to 1965 demanded a degree of race consciousness if the principle of racial equality in electoral politics were to be realized.

When did the region turn a racial corner? For how long did it remain legitimate to give substantial weight to statistical evidence of disproportionately low minority officeholding and to fashion race-conscious districts accordingly? There is no clear answer to that question. A 2008 Supreme Court decision refers to the 1980s as the period in which Alabama's "transition from a blatantly discriminatory regime was underway."[15] Others would argue that the race-conscious districts drawn following the 1990 census, which greatly increased the number of blacks elected to Congress from the South, were vital to the integration of politics.

My own view should be clear. Wherever one draws the line, by now, the force of the second principle—that equality may demand race-conscious policies when the alternative is a sector of American society basically reserved for whites—has finally faded. America has increasingly opened its doors to black aspirations in politics and the full panoply of public and private pursuits. In a society that is genuinely open to black opportunity, colorblind principles have no moral competition.

The 2006 Voting Rights Act

My views are not those of the civil rights community, which has continued to see much racial exclusion in American society. The need for extraordinary federal oversight over electoral arrangement has not faded, voting rights advocates insist, and they brought their perspective to the congressional debates in the summer of 2006 over the extension and amendment of the preclearance provision, due to expire for the fourth time a year later.

By 2006, forty-one years had passed since the enactment of the Voting Rights Act, with its extraordinary powers responding to the national emergency of southern black disfranchisement. In 1966, the statute had been found constitutional only because "voluminous legislative history" convinced Congress that it was "confronted by an insidious and pervasive evil which had been perpetuated in certain parts of our country through unremitting and ingenious defiance of the Constitution."[16] The civil rights community that mobilized in 2005 and 2006 was determined to create that same "voluminous legislative history." In its absence, would section 5 still stand up to constitutional scrutiny?

In the face of racial change on a scale unimaginable in 1965, House Judiciary Committee hearings on the 2006 Fannie Lou Hamer, Rosa Parks, and Coretta Scott King Voting Rights Act Reauthorization and Amendments Act offered a blizzard of anecdotes as evidence of ongoing voting discrimination and inadequate electoral opportunity in America today. The nearly three-hundred-page collection of stories was accompanied by some statistics on voter participation, minority officeholding, and the DOJ preclearance record, but those data did not demonstrate clear differences between the covered and noncovered jurisdictions. More important, the individual stories told by witnesses fell far short of painting a picture of widespread and egregious discrimination even vaguely reminiscent of the kind that was common in the Jim Crow era.

Anecdotal accounts included changes in the location of polling places "often on short notice"; voters "forced to cast votes outside of the voting booth . . . because there was no room available"; "white poll workers treat[ing] African American voters very different from the respectful, helpful way in which they treated white voters"; and Alaskan ballot initiatives that resulted in "elders" marking ballots "wrong" because the language was "confusing."[17] The gravity of the charges contained in the anecdotal material varied, but their weight was impossible to assess; they were splattered across the pages of testimony as if they spoke for themselves. How frequently did black voters experience "disrespect"? Was there no room in the polling place because an unprecedented number of voters showed up, and, if so, how common had that problem been? What elected official was responsible for overseeing that election?

Was the experience of voters in, say, Alabama notably different today from that of voters in Ohio? Were the stories of discrimination qualitatively different from those that were heard following the 2000 elections in Florida counties that were not covered by section 5? As Roger Clegg, president of the Center for Equal Opportunity, has pointed out, the few comparisons between covered and noncovered jurisdictions offered at the hearings mostly undermined the case for the bill. For instance, the statement by Charles D. Walton of the National Commission on the Voting Rights Act concluded that "discrimination in voting and in election processes in the northeastern states is a significant problem" and there would be "a great benefit to having more of the country covered by the preclearance provisions of section 5." A letter submitted by Representative William Lacy Clay complained mostly about Florida and Missouri, while Representative Gwen Moore complained about Milwaukee.[18] In short, where was the evidence of systematic and distinctive discrimination in the covered jurisdictions that justified continuing to single them out for federal oversight?

Some of the charges involved racially polarized voting, but here and elsewhere definitional problems plagued the account. VRARA proponents assumed the validity of Brennan's 1986 definition of such voting in *Thornburg v. Gingles*, which ignored the complexity of blacks' and whites' preferences for different candidates for partisan reasons.[19] Their arguments implied that a majority of the Court had accepted Brennan's definition, when, in fact, only a plurality joined his view that bloc voting depriving minority voters of their equal opportunity to participate in the electoral process occurred whenever black and white voters consistently voted differently—for whatever reason.

"Substantial progress has been made over the last 40 years," the 2006 House Judiciary Committee report admitted. "Despite these successes, the Committee finds that the temporary provisions of the VRA are still needed. Discrimination today is more subtle than the visible methods used in 1965. However, the effects and results are the same."[20] Surely, rarely in the rich annals of congressional deceit and self-deception have more false and foolish words been uttered. No meaningful evidence supports such an extraordinary claim. It is a disservice to the nation to refuse to recognize the remarkable revolution in race relations that occurred in the second half of the twentieth century.

Reauthorization of the Voting Rights Act in 2006 was a foregone conclusion; there was no chance Congress would let the emergency provisions lapse or that the George W. Bush White House would raise questions, although even a number of distinguished voting rights scholars who were on the political left agreed it was time for fresh thinking, a story to which I will return below.[21] It quickly became apparent, as well, that updating section 5—altering the trigger for preclearance coverage, for instance, to reflect contemporary reality—was inconceivable. The only politically safe course of action was to strengthen the statute further, on the assumption that today's more "subtle" forms of white racism required even more aggressive countermeasures.

The VRARA statutory language itself alleged that "vestiges of discrimination" remained, and concluded that "without the continuation of the Voting Rights Act of 1965 protections, racial and language minority citizens [would] be deprived of the opportunity to exercise their right to vote, or will have their votes diluted, undermining the significant gains made by minorities in the last 40 years."[22] It was fear-mongering nonsense. Blacks might tomorrow be once again "deprived . . . of the right to vote"? Such alarmist rhetoric was positively dangerous, suggesting that white supremacists were waiting for the opportunity to resume control of southern politics. Conspiracy theories about AIDS, drugs, and the deliberate persecution of black officials by the government were already rife in the black community, and they reached across the lines of social class.[23] Such rhetoric in the 2006 statute reinforced convictions that fed deeply worrisome black alienation and thus undermined integration.

The 1965 protections must be continued, the amended statute stated. The Supreme Court had "significantly weakened" the act's effectiveness. The point was clear: Section 5, as it was understood before the 2000 and 2003 decisions in *Bossier Parish II* and *Georgia v. Ashcroft*, had to be restored. Rewriting the statute to respond to those two decisions was, in fact, the central aim of the 2006 amendments.[24]

Bossier II, it will be recalled, had held that the two halves of section 5—discriminatory intent and discriminatory effect—were a whole. Together, they protected only against new methods of voting that left minority voters worse off than they had previously been. The sign of a racially suspicious change in election procedure was not the failure to create a method of voting that maximized black officeholding, but one that took from blacks the gains they expected to make when the literacy test and other barriers to registration and voting came down.

Thus, preclearance, Justice Scalia argued for the Court, "does not represent approval of the voting change; it is nothing more than a determination that the voting change is no more dilutive than what it replaces, and therefore cannot be stopped in advance under the extraordinary burden-shifting procedure of §5, but must be attacked through the normal means of a §2 action."[25] In other words, if minority voters believe they have been victims of deliberate discrimination, they can bring a section 2 complaint in the local federal court, where the burden of proof will be on them. Preclearance was only intended to stop efforts to undermine the enfranchising impact of the 1965 statute.

The 2000 *Bossier II* decision had been an attempt to rein in the Justice Department which, without any judicial sanction, had been refusing to preclear new methods of voting on suspicion of discriminatory intent—having defined intent so broadly as to be almost devoid of meaning.[26] Every electoral change could be called possibly suspicious, and that possibility (real or imagined) sufficed to deny preclearance. Scalia's precise definition of intent not only squared with the provision's prophylactic purpose; it made administrative review a manageable process. A before-and-after comparison could be accomplished in the requisite sixty days; exploring the much larger question of discriminatory purpose behind a proposed voting change, on the other hand, demanded a full-scale trial, with depositions, evidence, and opposing arguments—which section 2 provides.

In 1965, the section 5 language said that no voting change could be precleared unless the D.C. court or the Justice Department had found it did not "have the purpose and will not have the effect of denying or abridging the right to vote on account of race or color." The "and" had united the two terms, implying they should be read together, which meant that the standard governing "effect" (retrogression) also governed intent. All of section 5 protected against retrogression—slippage from gains promised by the basic enfranchisement ensured by section 4. But the 2006 VRARA separated the two terms, permitting a definition of intent independent from that effect. Under the revised statute, jurisdictions had the burden of proving that voting changes would have "neither" the purpose "nor" the effect of denying or abridging voting rights.

The VRARA thus allowed the Justice Department once again to regard discriminatory "intent" as a stand-alone question, and to consider the failure to draw a maximum number of majority-minority districts suspicious. Or it could find that a jurisdiction had not met its burden of proving there had been no discriminatory intent if it failed to show an absence of circumstantial evidence that might indicate invidious purpose. In adopting the voting change, had there had been no deviation from normal practices, no historical background that might indicate invidious purpose, no sequence of events that might suggest anything suspicious, and no dubious legislative or administrative history?[27] If, indeed, that was the new post-VRARA standard, obtaining preclearance had become immeasurably harder.

As suggested above, President Obama's Justice Department will undoubtedly have very close ties to the civil rights community. If, as seems likely, the department reverts to using questionable allegations of discriminatory purpose to impose "bug-splat" districts in the post-2010 round of map drawing, it may once again set the Voting Rights Act on a collision course with the Fourteenth Amendment—inviting a new round of *Shaw*-like suits alleging the creation by states of unconstitutional racial gerrymanders.[28]

The VRARA also added new language addressing the problem that civil rights groups had with *Georgia v. Ashcroft*. In its 2003 decision, the Court had responded to the problem of a statute that was still being used to insist on a maximum number of black legislative seats despite the concerns on the part of some black legislators that such districting reduced African-American political power. If black voters were dispersed a bit, more white Democrats might be elected, these black legislators had argued.

The risk of endangering some totally safe black seats was one that black state officials had been willing to take, but not one of which Congress approved. No method of voting could be precleared that had the purpose or effect "of diminishing the ability of any citizen of the United States on account of race or color . . . to elect their preferred candidates of choice," the VRARA stated. *Ashcroft* had created a "vague and open-ended 'totality of circumstances' test [that] opened the door to allow all manner of undefined considerations to trump the minority's choice of candidate," the House Judiciary Committee report charged. The Court, it continued, had encouraged "states to spread minority voters under the guise of 'influence' and would effectively shut minority voters out of the political process." It had allowed states to "turn black and other minority voters into second class voters who [could] influence elections of white candidates, but who [could not] elect their preferred candidates, including candidates of their own race."[29]

The precise impact of the VRARA will remain unknown until a new record of section 5 enforcement has been created. The House report described Congress as only "partly" rejecting *Ashcroft*, which suggested the decision survived in some unspecified respects. But in what respects? This much seems clear: In effect, the Court had tried in *Ashcroft* to ease the burden section 5 placed on jurisdictions by loosening the ropes that bound them to max-black plans if they hoped to have new districts approved. Coalition and influence districts could offset a reduction in the number of absolutely safe black constituencies, Justice O'Connor had said. After the *Ashcroft* decision, DOJ staff attorneys used that case, as chapter 4 discussed, to write a memo urging the department to count, for instance, Martin Frost's 25 percent black district in its preclearance decision. That district should be in the "opportunity-to-elect" column, staff wrote. They did not win that argument in 2003, when the memo was written, but Congress accepted a variation of that reasoning in adopting the VRARA.

Jurisdictions, the 2006 amendments seem to imply, are still obligated to draw majority-minority constituencies wherever they can, but section 5 demands the retention of coalition and influence districts, as well. Those districts apparently are still relevant in assessing the potential for minority representation, but, while *Ashcroft* had tried to give jurisdictions new freedom, the VRARA amounted to a new straitjacket. Jurisdictions now seem to be under a dual obligation: creating both majority-minority districts and maintaining those in which minority representation is increased by the potential for creating political coalitions in which black or Hispanic voters are a political force.

If this interpretation is correct, the Justice Department cannot allow jurisdictions to substitute influence or coalition districts for majority-minority constituencies in reviewing maps for preclearance. But if blacks claim a district as their own, that is what it is. Martin Frost's Texas district, for example, had been only 25 percent African American, but blacks had been the swing vote in the decisive Democratic Party primary, and they had wanted it preserved. The rewritten language of the VRARA suggested the district in the future would count as one whose lines could not be redrawn.

The state could not deliberately create such an influence district if there were a better alternative. On the other hand, no asserted state interest in altering the configuration of an existing district could outweigh the section 5 demand to preserve it, lest black electoral power end up "diminished," it seemed. Indeed, the revised statute implied that a district that had been, say, 55 percent minority and had become 55 percent white as a consequence of demographic change was still a minority entitlement. The language was a Democratic Party dream. Minorities were Democrats; all districts in which they played a role in electing Democrats (white or black) would likely be considered sacrosanct.

Dueling House and Senate Reports

Democrats and Republicans voted nearly unanimously for the VRARA in July 2006, but they differed on the substance of what they had wrought.

Consensus was staged—a joint effort to avoid open argument over a civil rights matter. Disagreement, always lurking just below the surface, broke out after the bill had already passed and the media had moved on to other topics. Once the conflict was out of public earshot, it became politically safe to disagree again.[30]

Thus, in the final Senate Judiciary Committee report, the Republicans broke with Democrats who had wanted a statement of "Joint Views" that would mirror the House report's finding of pervasive "subtle" electoral discrimination. (The report was written after that near-unanimous vote, which was highly unusual; in part, the timing was a consequence of the haste with which the bill was passed.) The House and Senate reports thus read quite differently, even on the question of discriminatory purpose. "A voting rule change motivated by any discriminatory purpose . . . cannot be precleared," the House report stated.[31] It provided no further information to clarify the House's definition of discriminatory purpose. Senate Republicans were not willing to risk such vague language. Using the testimony of well-known voting rights advocates (who were undoubtedly crafting their message in hopes of getting solid bipartisan support), the Senate report confined the definition of discriminatory purpose to that which the Court had found to be implicitly contained in the Fourteenth and Fifteenth Amendments, upon which the statute rested.

"This is familiar language," that report read. "It is the language of cases such as *City of Mobile v. Bolden*"—fighting words, since that decision was abhorred by the civil rights community.[32] A change in voting practices submitted for preclearance should be precleared unless "purposefully taken . . . to lock out racial and language minorities from political power," it went on.[33]

> Courts and the Justice Department should ask whether the decision not to create a black-majority district departed from ordinary districting rules. If a state has a large minority population concentrated in a particular area, ordinary rules of districting—following political and geographic borders and keeping districts as compact as possible—would recommend that those voters be given a majority-minority district. If the State went out of its way to avoid creating such a majority-minority—one that would be created under ordinary rules—that is unconstitutional racial discrimination.[34]

A finding of illicit purpose thus had to rest on a determination that the state had gone "out of its way" to avoid drawing a majority-minority constituency. Such an interpretation of the new statutory language was clearly a far cry from what the civil rights community would ever endorse. But Republican senators hoped to bar the return of the old DOJ habits. "This amendment," the report stated, "also has the effect of preventing the recurrence of some Justice Department policies." Forcing states "to maximize majority-minority districts at any cost" with race-driven "maps gerrymandered beyond recognition" remained unacceptable.[35]

The Senate report also discussed *Ashcroft* at some length. The amendments protected only "naturally occurring geographically compact majority-minority districts," it explained. That focus would ensure "that minority voters will not be forced to trade away solidly majority-minority districts for ones defined by ambiguous concepts like 'influence' or 'coalitional'"— districts that would be more accurately described as Democratic Party gerrymanders:[36]

> This legislation definitively is not intended to preserve or ensure the successful election of candidates of any political party, even if that party's candidates generally are supported by members of minority groups. The Voting Rights Act was intended to enhance voting power, not to serve as a one-way ratchet in favor of partisan interests.[37]

Republicans were clearly trying to minimize the damage done by the statutory language for which they had felt compelled to vote. While their interpretation might have influenced a Justice Department in a new Republican administration, the Obama Justice Department will certainly reject it outright. What the courts will do is a separate matter.[38] Considerable weight might be given to the legislative history, as it was in *Thornburg v. Gingles*, in which the Court relied on the 1982 Senate report in "effectuat[ing] the intent of Congress."[39]

The Senate report tried to quash Democratic hopes that the statute could be shaped to serve partisan interests while advancing the agenda of civil rights advocacy organizations. But in voting for the amended statute, Republicans had relinquished the opportunity to use the report as an occasion on which to ask fundamental questions about the continuing need for emergency provisions that had been fashioned to respond to a crisis of black disfranchisement four decades earlier. They could interpret the statute's vague phrases to their liking, but they could not attack the record of continuing electoral discrimination that they had already accepted as valid.

There was one point on which the House and Senate reports did agree: The new statute restored the legal standards articulated by *Beer* in 1976.[40] But what standards were those? The *Beer* Court's decision had held that section 5 only protected against backsliding; if a districting plan provided fewer safe black seats than the previous plan, it was retrogressive and could not be precleared. On the other hand, the Justice Department in the 1980s and 1990s had paid, at best, lip service to that narrow definition of the scope of section 5. Were the reports endorsing *Beer* as it had evolved, or as the Court had interpreted it almost thirty years earlier?

The evolution of section 5 is an unfinished story. Will the civil rights community continue to oppose distributing minority voters over more districts, rather than concentrating them in those in which they are a majority of voters? Perceptions about race will continue to change, and those perceptions will likely influence the enforcement of the statute in ways we cannot know today. Meanwhile, however, the Supreme Court may be forced to clarify, once again, what *Beer* meant and means in the decision expected at the end of the 2008–9 term.

Bartlett v. Strickland: Revisiting Section 2

The 2006 VRARA superseded the Supreme Court's 2003 decision in *Georgia v. Ashcroft*, stating clearly that minority voters were entitled "to elect their preferred candidates of choice." Influence districts were no substitute for those that were totally safe for black candidates. *Ashcroft* had been a section 5 case and therefore did not settle a closely related section 2 question: If a majority-black district could not be drawn, did the act compel jurisdictions to draw the most advantageous *minority*-black district it could?

That is the question the Court very recently addressed in *Bartlett v. Strickland*.[41] At issue was North Carolina's House District 18, which was only 39 percent black. With white crossover voting, other such minority-black districts had been electing black state legislators for quite some time. As the NAACP brief in the case stated,

> Today, there are seven African Americans in the North Carolina Senate. While all of them represent districts with significant black populations, none of them serves a district that has a black majority in voting-age population. And eleven African-American members of the North Carolina state house represent districts that range from 39.36 to 49.97% black in voting-age population.[42]

In the belief that section 2 required it to maintain District 18 as a black "opportunity-to-elect" district, where reliable white support for black candidates would likely continue to ensure the election of a black representative, the state's general assembly had drawn the district's lines so that they split Pender County. The county and five of its commissioners sued, alleging that the plan violated the state constitution's "Whole County Provision," which stipulated that counties could not be divided in the design of state legislative districts.[43] North Carolina officials, in response, pointed to the Voting Rights Act. As they read the statute, if the state *could* draw such a district, it was obligated to do so. A district respecting county lines would have left the state vulnerable to a section 2 vote dilution suit.

North Carolina's highest court sided with the county, concluding that the state could have adhered to its own constitution, with its Whole County Provision, without running afoul of the Voting Rights Act.[44] In 1986, the *Gingles* Court had explicitly held that a minority group had to be "sufficiently large and geographically compact to constitute [a majority in] a single-member district" before a court could proceed to judge a section 2 claim.[45] If a majority-minority district could not be drawn, there was no remedy for the wrong of vote dilution—for black voters deprived of the power to elect the candidates of their choice because those candidates were not the choice of whites. In the case of District 18, North Carolina had been unable to meet that first *Gingles* requirement. It could not draw a reasonably compact district that was over 50 percent black. Even if a wrong could be alleged, there was no remedy, as *Gingles* had read the law.

The civil rights community, however, regarded District 18, with its 39 percent African-American population, as serving black interests and, thus, a section 2 entitlement. The twenty-year-old *Gingles* rule was out of date, the NAACP brief argued. In the organization's view, remarkably, the waning of white racism—the greater willingness of white voters to support black candidates—compelled an expansion of federal power under section 2. Enforcing that provision now required the state to draw *minority*-minority districts wherever reliable white votes gave blacks the opportunity to elect candidates of their choice. This position, if adopted by the Court, would have completed the transformation of the Voting Rights Act from a law designed to protect blacks from racial animus in politics—providing equal political opportunity—to one intended simply to maximize African-American political power by whatever means, while augmenting Democratic Party power as well.

"It is time to scrap once and for all a rule that imposes an arbitrary threshold of 50% before a minority group can be protected against vote dilution under Section 2 of the Voting Rights Act," argued J. Gerald Hebert, former voting section attorney in the DOJ Civil Rights Division.[46] It was an interesting assertion, given how hard the civil rights community worked to overturn *Ashcroft* when Congress was amending section 5 in 2006. Georgia had actually retained the 50 percent rule, while marginally reducing the African-American percentage in some districts, but the Court's action in sanctioning that action had deeply alarmed voting rights advocates.

The argument had much in common with that made in *LULAC v. Perry* by Texas representative Martin Frost, who had been elected from a 24 percent black district until the state scattered his voters.[47] Frost was white, but he had won in the decisive Democratic primaries due to black support. He was the candidate preferred by black voters, and, as such, his district was protected from retrogression by section 5, he claimed; its lines could not be altered. The district court, however, found that Frost's district had been deliberately designed to be majority-white, and whites did control it. The high Court, in reviewing the decision, could find no clear error with that reasoning.[48]

Martin Frost had insisted his black constituents had elected the candidate of their choice. North Carolina also argued that blacks in District 18 could elect their preferred candidates; it was a reliable crossover district. In response, Pender County officials pointed to the actual language of section 2. The provision protected the right of minority voters "to elect representatives of their choice." It did "not purport to protect the right 'to help elect' or 'to form a coalition to help elect' a representative."[49]

In addition, if the state were to prevail, "the courts could be in an endless morass of litigation," the county warned. "The threat of Voting Rights Act litigation would hang precariously over the states when any population of minorities—regardless of size—alleges that it is unable to elect its candidate of choice," provided it could do so if the minority percentage were adjusted.[50] In other words, if African-American voters in a 32 percent black constituency could successfully argue that just five more percentage points would give them an "opportunity-to-elect" district, the courts would be flooded with section 2 suits demanding "better" *minority*-minority districts. The problem of overloaded courts trying to decide cases without consistent and intelligible legal standards might actually be worse than the county envisioned. Suppose the district were only 25 percent African American and additional blacks were in short supply; why couldn't minority plaintiffs demand a constituency with more white Democrats and fewer Republicans? If those Democrats were reliable crossover voters (Martin Frost's constituents), why wouldn't such a district be a minority entitlement? Were the courts in section 2 suits paying sufficient attention to the lines that could be drawn to increase the number of heavily white Democratic districts that might serve the interests of black constituents?

Those who argued for updating the *Gingles* test for the availability of a vote dilution remedy saw a new era in which whites would vote for black candidates, and they asserted, in effect, that racial progress only underscored the need for extending the scope of the Voting Rights Act and its authority over the districting process. Rather than being a sign that the extraordinary political privileges provided by the act were no longer needed, these advocates saw it as a new opening to protect more districts from revision in the course of redistricting cycles.

"The Voting Rights Act should be interpreted in such a way as to encourage a transition to a society where race no longer matters," North Carolina's solicitor general, Christopher G. Browning Jr., stated in his opening argument before the Supreme Court. "In North Carolina, coalition districts have been crucial in moving towards Congress's ultimate goal. Coalition districts bring races together by fostering political alliances across racial lines."[51] But Chief Justice John G. Roberts Jr. was quick to ask the obvious question:

"How can you say that this brings us closer to a situation where race will not matter when it expands the number of situations in which redistricting authorities have to consider race?"[52]

Bartlett was decided in March 2009, and the Court's majority opinion, written by Justice Anthony Kennedy, made precisely that point. "If §2 were interpreted to require crossover districts throughout the Nation," he wrote, "it would unnecessarily infuse race into virtually every redistricting, raising serious constitutional concerns."[53] The Court rejected North Carolina's arguments across the board. Both section 2 and *Gingles* meant just what they said: The provision did not impose a duty to draw the best possible crossover district, and a jurisdiction's ability to draw a majority-minority district was still the threshold requirement for plaintiffs who would seek a remedy for vote dilution.[54] If whites were supporting black candidates in a majority-white setting, surely they were not bloc-voting to defeat the choices of minority voters.[55] North Carolina had been asking the Court to throw its own 1986 decision to the winds.

Kennedy also agreed with the county's "endless morass" point:

> Determining whether potential districts could function as crossover districts . . . would place courts in the untenable position of predicting many political variables and tying them to race-based assumptions. The judiciary would be directed to make predictions or adopt premises that even experienced polling analysts and political experts could not assess with certainty, particularly over the long term.[56]

The majority-minority rule was an objective numerical test. In districts in which blacks and Hispanics were a minority, members of those groups had "the same opportunity to elect their candidate as any other political group with the same relative voting strength."[57]

The civil rights groups had wanted to expand "the number of situations in which redistricting authorities [had] to consider race," as the chief justice had charged in oral argument. These additional race-conscious and protected districts would all be Democratic, a point to which Justice Kennedy only indirectly alluded.[58] The Supreme Court had refused to wade into the turbulent waters of partisan gerrymandering—districting maps drawn to the advantage of one political party or the other. But through the back door, civil rights groups had tried to get the Court to force states to increase the number of safe Democratic districts. *Bartlett* was really a partisan case masquerading as one involving race. As Michael Carvin testified at the 2006 Senate hearings, "The 'influence' district theory seeks to convert the Voting Rights Act's mandate of equal opportunity for minority voters into a statutory mandate for partisan preferences."[59] At that point, what constitutional legitimacy would the Voting Rights Act still have?

Waiting for *NAMUDNO*: Section 5 in Jeopardy

The constitutional legitimacy of section 5 is the question in a case before the Supreme Court as I write. In the summer of 2006, Congress lacked the courage even to debate seriously the continuing need for the temporary, emergency provisions of the Voting Rights Act, forty years after the statute's passage. The case now awaiting decision, *Northwest Austin Municipal Utility District Number One v. Holder (NAMUDNO)*, will force the Justices to tread where Congress dared not go.[60]

NAMUDNO, filed in the D.C. District Court in 2006 immediately after the passage of the VRARA, involves a tiny utility district just outside of Austin, Texas, that was formed in 1987 mainly to provide water to unincorporated areas. The utility district, its complaint stated, had "always supported full and open voting rights for all residents," and yet, because the 1965 statute treated all Texas localities as racially suspect, the Justice Department had to "preclear" its decision to move a polling place out of a residential garage and into a public school—a move "calculated to increase public access to the ballot."[61] The federal requirement, in the plaintiff's view, had been an irrational and "burdensome imposition" on its "sovereign rights" to manage its own electoral affairs.[62] Not only had the district had no history of electoral discrimination; it didn't even exist in 1975 when the Voting Rights Act was amended to bring Texas under its purview.

The case had now come to the Supreme Court on appeal from a three-judge panel that had rejected the plaintiff's claim that section 5 was no longer constitutional, given today's high level of black political participation.[63] Alternatively, the utility district had asked the lower court to force the Justice

Department to allow it to "bail out" from section 5 coverage, as section 4(b) of the act allows. The statute, however, is generally understood to provide for bailout only by whole counties or other political subdivisions that have the power to register voters, which the water district did not have. (Voter registration is by Travis County, in which the district is located.)

If the D.C. court had allowed the utility district to bail out from pre-clearance coverage, it would not have needed to evaluate the issue of section 5's constitutionality. It was the obvious solution to the absurdity of federal oversight over polling place relocations in a tiny, special-purpose govern-ment unit. But Judge David S. Tatel read the statutory language to easily dispose of the bailout claim. In any case, the real aim of the plaintiff's suit was a finding that the emergency provisions—the most important of which was section 5—had lasted long beyond the end of the emergency that had justified them in 1965. The Texas utility district had never disfranchised a single citizen in its short history. It wanted the whole preclearance provision to be declared unconstitutional, given the transformation in the level of political opportunity open to minorities four decades after the passage of the original act.

The D.C. District Court rejected the constitutional argument in its entirety. Judge David S. Tatel wrote for a three-judge panel:

> Applying the standard set forth by the Supreme Court in *South Carolina v. Katzenbach*, we conclude that given the extensive legislative record documenting contemporary racial discrimina-tion in voting in covered jurisdictions, Congress's decision to extend section 5 for another twenty-five years was rational and therefore constitutional.[64]

In *Katzenbach* in 1966, an almost unanimous Court had found, as pre-viously noted, a "voluminous legislative history . . . [revealing] unremitting and ingenious defiance of the Constitution."[65] The statute's "constitutional propriety," Chief Justice Earl Warren had stressed, "must be judged with ref-erence to the historical experience which it reflects."[66] Context matters, in other words. "Congress felt itself confronted by an insidious and pervasive evil," Warren continued.[67] The Court did not deny that "Congress had exercised its authority under the Fifteenth Amendment in an inventive manner."[68] But, "as against the reserved powers of the States, Congress may use any rational means to effectuate the constitutional prohibitions against racial discrimination in voting."[69]

Did *NAMUDNO* fit the *Katzenbach* framework, however? The 1965 context to which the chief justice had given such importance did not remotely resemble that in 2006, and while the rational-basis test in judging policies enforcing the Fourteenth and Fifteenth Amendments worked in 1966, arguably it did not forty years later. The policies whose constitutionality was questioned were entirely different. Here is how the chief justice had described the point of section 5 in *Katzenbach*: Congress knew that some of the covered states

> had resorted to the extraordinary stratagem of contriving new rules of various kinds for the sole purpose of perpetuating voting discrimination in the face of adverse federal court decrees. Congress had reason to suppose that these States might try similar maneuvers in the future in order to evade the remedies for voting discrimination contained in the Act itself.[70]

The "new rules" to which Warren had referred were renewed efforts to "perpetuat[e] voting discrimination" of the sort that the Voting Rights Act was initially enacted to combat: fraudulent literacy tests and other rudimentary barriers to the exercise of Fifteenth Amendment rights. Section 5, designed to stop racist "maneuvers," passed the lenient "rational" test for constitutionality. By 2006, however, when Judge Tatel was writing, pre-clearance had become something quite different—a means to impose race-conscious districting upon covered jurisdictions to promote black officeholding.

What, then, is the proper legal standard by which to assess the transformed section 5? The question was raised by several legal scholars when the VRARA was being debated prior to its passage in July 2006.[71] Race-conscious districting classifies voters by race, and racial classifications are assessed by legal standards quite different from those used to judge the legitimacy of removing racist barriers to casting ballots. They are constitutionally questionable, although not impermissible. They must meet be narrowly tailored to meet a compelling state interest—that is, they are subject to heightened judicial skepticism and detailed scrutiny.[72] If that is, indeed, the standard by which the constitutionality of the revised section 5 will be judged, it may not survive Supreme Court scrutiny.

Judge Tatel accepted evidence of widespread wrongdoing, drawing upon the 2006 House Judiciary Committee records. A number of voting rights experts who supported an extension of section 5 but were concerned about its ability to withstand a constitutional challenge found the case made by the House committee worrisomely weak. Mark Posner, for instance, a voting rights advocate and independent consultant who spent more than a decade in the Civil Rights Division of the Justice Department, argued in June 2006 that there were "good reasons for ramping down the current reauthorization proposal." Minority voters, he noted, "in the covered areas are in a much stronger position today than in 1982."[73] In a similar vein, New York University law professor Samuel Issacharoff wrote, "Much of the debate is about what to conclude from the basic *absence* of a record of willful exclusion of the sort that could easily be marshaled in 1965 and even 1982."[74]

Such a record could not be so easily marshaled now, given the altered racial landscape. Even advocates admit that the historical record raises questions about the constitutional viability of section 5 today. As Ellen Katz, professor of law at the University of Michigan, wrote,

> The record Congress amassed to support the 2006 reauthorization of section 5 does not appear to document the type of widespread unconstitutional conduct the Justices have said must underlie the passage of new civil rights legislation. Insufficient evidence of rampant unconstitutional conduct led the Court to toss out six federal statutes over the last decade, statutes that sought to do things like promote religious freedom and remedy gender-motivated violence.[75]

The Supreme Court's 2000 decision in *Bossier Parish II* had deprived the Justice Department of the freedom to find suspicious racial intent behind every electoral change it didn't much like. As noted above, in the section 5 context, discriminatory purpose referred to changes in the method of election that were designed to have a retrogressive impact, the *Bossier II* Court held. That definition of discriminatory intent at least somewhat protected section 5 against challenges that it was unconstitutional by increasing the odds that the Supreme Court would find the provision narrowly tailored—which would meet half the constitutional test.

The congressional amendments of 2006, however, restored the pre-*Bossier* intent standard; once again, section 5 contains what the *Miller* Court called an "implicit command that States may engage in presumptively unconstitutional race-based districting."[76] The likelihood has thus increased that the Court in *NAMUDNO* might once again find that preclearance, as enforced by the Justice Department, is in conflict with the Fourteenth Amendment. I cannot predict, of course, what the Court will do with the case; I will spell out my own hopes in the conclusion.

How Much Has the South Changed?

The 2006 amendments, I have argued, increased the odds that the Court would view section 5 as no longer meeting the Fourteenth Amendment strict scrutiny test, if that is, indeed, the test that the Court finds appropriate. As noted above, that test had two components: narrow tailoring and compelling state interest. The logic was well stated by Justice John Paul Stevens in 1980: "Racial classifications are simply too pernicious to permit any but the most exact connection between justification and classification."[77] If there are race-neutral alternatives to a race-conscious policy, that policy has not been narrowly tailored to serve the state's important objective.

With the return to the pre-*Bossier II* definition of discriminatory intent, the provision could not be described as narrowly tailored. But what about the question of compelling state interest behind the policy—in this case, the race-conscious districting that section 5 had come to mandate? Section 5 prevents states from acting to exercise traditional constitutional prerogatives without prior federal permission; it is unique in American law. Do contemporary voting problems still justify extraordinary Justice Department and judicial control over politically sensitive districting and other election-related decisions?

The question of persistent racism runs explicitly or implicitly through all discussions of minority voting rights—indeed, of civil rights more broadly. The 2006 House Judiciary Committee concluded that America was still plagued by widespread and persistent electoral discrimination little different from that which existed in the Deep South in 1965, and Judge Tatel had embraced every word in the record and pulled much of it into his district court opinion in *NAMUDNO*.

The picture that Congress and Judge Tatel accepted of an America still spinning its wheels in the racist muck of its Jim Crow past doesn't pass the laugh test. Recall that in 1965 the average black registration rate in the original covered states was only 29.3 percent.[78] The figure for Alabama was just 18.5 percent, for Georgia 27.4 percent, and for Mississippi a dismal 6.7 percent.[79] It was, of course, the distinctiveness of low southern registration and turnout rates (along with the use of literacy tests) that justified section 5 coverage. This was a region of the country with distinctive—and constitutionally impermissible—barriers to free elections.

That justification is gone. As early as 1976, registration rates in covered jurisdictions had reached the national average. By this measure, the goal of the Voting Rights Act was thus accomplished decades ago. A stunning 68.2 percent of the black population in original section 5 states was registered to vote for the presidential election of 2004, a rate a few points *higher* than that in the rest of the country.[80] Even the voter participation data in the Congressional Record in 2006 revealed striking racial change. In summarizing the data, the Senate Judiciary Committee report—breaking ranks with the Democrats after the measure had already passed—stated: "Covered jurisdictions have demonstrated equal or higher voter registration rates among black voters as non-covered jurisdictions since the mid-1970s."[81] It had been more than three decades since the last meaningful structural barriers to the enfranchisement of African-American voters had been eliminated.

Black turnout rates, as well, have been impressive. In the 2004 election, 60 percent of blacks cast votes in both covered and noncovered jurisdictions. Alabama, for instance, had a turnout rate of almost 70 percent, Georgia 54.4 percent, Louisiana 62.1 percent, Mississippi 66.8 percent, South Carolina 59.5 percent, and Virginia 49.6 percent. In 2008 black turnout overall increased substantially over 2004; the total share of the national vote represented by black voters rose from 11 percent to 13 percent, according to exit polls. In six states, the increase in the black share of the statewide vote over the previous election was very large. Looking again at the

South, we see that in Alabama, the black voting-age population was 25 percent of the total electorate; the black share of the vote rose from 25 percent in 2004 to 29 percent in 2008. In Georgia, where blacks are 24.6 percent of the voting-age population, their share of the electorate was 30 percent. In Virginia and North Carolina, as well, blacks overvoted their share of eligible population in 2008.[82]

Whether candidates preferred by the group are able to win elections is another test of equal electoral opportunity. Statistical parity is not the definitive test, I have argued; nevertheless, numbers are not irrelevant in looking at black progress, and as the measure used by voting rights advocates they cannot, in any case, be ignored.

Answering the question of officeholding gains is more difficult than it might seem, however. A sizable minority group that leans strongly Republican, for example, will have less success in electing its preferred candidates in a state whose electorate is strongly tilted in favor of Democrats. With southern blacks, we have the reverse situation: an overwhelmingly Democratic minority group in a region that leans strongly Republican. Furthermore, it would be impractical to determine who was the preferred black candidate in every one of thousands of electoral contests.

With these caveats in mind, the record of electoral success of black candidates in recent decades is impressive. In 1964, only 5 African Americans held seats in the U.S. Congress. None was from any of the covered states, or indeed any other southern state. Just 94 blacks served in any of the fifty state legislatures, with only 16 coming from the southern states that held half of the nation's African-American population.[83]

By 2008, there were 41 members of the Congressional Black Caucus.[84] Almost 600 African Americans held seats in state legislatures, and another 8,800 were mayors, sheriffs, school board members, and the like. It is remarkable that 47 percent of these black public officials lived in the seven covered states, though those states contained only 30 percent of the nation's black population. Especially striking is that Mississippi, which once had a well-deserved reputation as the most white supremacist state in the union, now leads the nation in the number of blacks it elects to political office.[85]

Over the years between 1970 and 2002, the number of black elected officials in the country soared from 1,469 to 9,430, a rise of more than sixfold. Black political power grew by leaps and bounds. The gain in the seven covered states was even more rapid, a jump from 407 black elected officials to 4,404, almost double the overall rate of increase! In 1970, the covered states had just 28 percent of all black elected officials; by 2002 it was 47 percent. In the covered states, in short, African Americans made political gains at a dramatically higher rate than elsewhere in the country.[86] This may have been a reflection of how far those states had to go—but it is surely also an indication of how far they have come, in an absolute and meaningful sense.

More recent data are available to gauge the rate of black progress in winning election to state legislatures. In 2007, the proportion of seats in the Alabama House of Representatives held by blacks (24.8 percent) almost exactly mirrored their share of the state's voting-age population (24.7 percent).[87] In Mississippi, blacks had 12 percent fewer seats than their share of the voting-age population, and in Georgia, 13 percent less. It was lower still in other covered states, with an overall average of 19 percent short of parity. This is a huge advance over the complete lack of representation in state legislative bodies at the time the Voting Rights Act was passed, although it also indicates that there is room for further gains.

Before leaping to the conclusion that the covered states thus still need special supervision by federal officials, we should notice that the pattern in the six southern states that are not covered by section 5 is not significantly different. In these states, blacks had 16 percent fewer seats in the houses than their share of the voting-age population. In the covered states they were 19 percent below parity, hardly a large enough difference to support the claim that preclearance is needed for another generation.

In the six northern states with populations at least 10 percent black, African Americans did win almost exactly their proportional share of seats in the lower house, falling short by only two points. The most likely explanation is not that northern white voters are less afflicted by prejudice than their southern counterparts. It happens that this group of northern states (New York, New Jersey, Illinois, Michigan, Ohio, and Pennsylvania) tended to lean strongly Democratic, so candidates from a monolithically Democratic ethnic group would find it easier to attract votes from whites.

Elections to the state senates display a similar pattern. In fact, the record of the covered states is slightly *better* than that of the southern states that are not covered. In the covered states, blacks were 26 percent below parity in the share of senate seats they held in 2007; in the southern states not affected by the provisions of section 5, they were 29 percent below parity. It's important to note, as well, that lower houses are the entry rung in state-level politics. It takes time to move up; in a few years senate numbers are likely to improve as house members throw their hats into the more competitive races in the larger senate districts. It will be harder to reach parity in the upper chamber, however; there are fewer seats, and creating majority-minority constituencies is easier in the smaller districts.

In assessing the level of ongoing discrimination, preclearance data are also significant. In 2006, while the Department of Justice received 4,094 submissions for preclearance, it objected to only 0.002 percent of those submitted changes in the method of voting.[88] The small percentage of objections would seem to have a clear explanation: Most jurisdictions by that time understood what was required to obtain federal approval, and, needing to get on with elections, simply took the precaution of doing what they knew would be acceptable.

Black officeholders today have political power; in fact, black voters are the Democratic Party's most reliable constituency. Their unwavering loyalty makes them indispensable to the party's fortunes. Preliminary estimates of voter behavior in the presidential election of 2008 suggest the likelihood that black turnout (as a percentage of the population) actually exceeded that of whites.[89] A number of witnesses who testified on behalf of the 2006 amendments argued that section 5 had had a "deterrent effect"—suggesting that, without the threat of federal interference, southern state legislatures would feel free to engage in all sorts of disfranchising mischief.[90] It seems wildly improbable. Southern racists feared black ballots prior to 1965 because they knew the franchise would be the end of the old South; more than four decades later, the old South has become unimaginable for both blacks and whites born after roughly 1970. They feel no connection in their own contemporary lives to the terrible experiences of that time.[91] Not even Mississippi, the most racially brutal of the Jim Crow states, can peddle backward; it has over 900 black elected officials.

As a Clarksdale, Mississippi, newspaper editorial noted in June 2008, "There's probably less chance today of election discrimination against minorities occurring in Mississippi—given the high number of African-Americans in elected office, including as county election commissioners—than in many parts of the country not covered by the Voting Rights Act."

Black lawmakers in the state didn't have to rely on courts to stop the enactment of a voter ID law; they had the power to do so themselves. "Yet, Section 5 of the Voting Rights Act presumes that minorities are powerless to protect their own election interests in places where they actually have the most clout," the editorial concluded.[92]

Debate among Scholars

Evidence of continuing racial progress is all around us—impossible to miss unless one tries hard to ignore reality—but America's obsession with race as a subject endures. In a February 2009 speech before Justice Department staff, Attorney General Eric Holder called America "a nation of cowards." He wanted, he said, what we still do not have: a "frank" discussion of race.[93] There was an ironic, albeit unintentional, truth to the charge: The public discourse on racial matters in America does suffer from stifling political correctness—which inhibits any challenges to civil rights orthodoxy. The Democrats who controlled the judiciary committees in both houses of Congress in the summer of 2006 tried their best to silence opposition to the bill. And they succeeded, by and large.

But that summer, while Congress was busy stifling debate on the proposed amendment and extension of section 5, a number of distinguished voting rights scholars on the political left recognized the danger to the survival of the statute posed by the congressional decision to pretend that racial progress could be ignored. As I have noted above, if the record of continuing disfranchisement did not hold up, the case for the continuing constitutionality of the temporary, emergency provisions would be hard to make. I have already touched on the views of Samuel Issacharoff, one of these scholars; others as well wanted federal involvement in local and state elections to continue in some form, but broke with their usual allies among civil rights activists and in Congress by questioning the 2006 bill that became the VRARA.

In May 2006, Loyola Law School professor Richard Hasen noted the "good news" that "a vigorous debate is taking place over whether, and how, the relevant VRA provisions should be amended before they are renewed. The bad news," he continued, "is that this debate is taking place among academics, not among Members of Congress."[94] A month later, reacting to the proposal to extend preclearance for another twenty-five years, he wrote: "The bill . . . did not acknowledge that the state of minority voting rights in 2006 is not the same as the state of such rights in 1982 or in 1965." Those pushing the legislation, he went on, "act as though 2007 and 1982 are the same."[95] The renewal squandered "an opportunity for Congress to take a more serious look at how it can fix its voting laws to better protect minority voting rights in the Twenty-first Century."[96]

In retaining the act of 1965, Congress was abdicating its policymaking responsibilities, Richard Pildes of the New York University law school charged.[97] Samuel Issacharoff added that there are "important issues about the state of voting rights in the U.S. They [should force] a reexamination of the extent to which a model of racial exclusion continues to define the central defects in American elections."[98] These scholars have been willing to begin a new conversation on the extent of ongoing racial exclusion and the form appropriate voting rights legislation might take today.

The 2006 bill, Pildes argued at Senate hearings, would reauthorize a 1965 provision that had become a period piece. *Ashcroft* had been a sound decision, recognizing that there was "room in the statewide redistricting context for modest flexibility in Section 5, given the changes between today's circumstances and those in the 1970s and early 1980s"—and yet Congress was amending the statute to make clear its rejection of the decision's reasoning. The congressional record compiled by witnesses, in fact, undermined their case for the continuation of the extraordinary federal preclearance power, Pildes concluded. No "systematic differences . . . between the currently covered and non-covered jurisdictions" were found. Racially polarized voting (as the witnesses defined it) was ubiquitous. The 2000 and 2004 postelection legal disputes did not involve section 5.[99]

Both Pildes and Hasen urged voting rights legislation that matched the voting rights problems of today. "If Congress were designing legislation to help minority voters today, it likely wouldn't single out those jurisdictions covered by section 5 as the place where minorities need the most help," Hasen wrote.

> It might target Florida and Ohio. It certainly would target voter
> identification requirements that put financial burdens on poor

and minority voters. It might do something about the racially discriminatory impact of felon disenfranchisement laws. But it
wouldn't create an act so geographically limited, and it probably
wouldn't limit DOJ's scrutiny to changes in voting procedures.
Existing voting procedures can also be racially discriminatory.[100]

In other words, a statute that was serious about addressing contemporary
voting rights—and wrongs—would not even vaguely resemble that which
Congress passed in 2006.

The Voting Rights Act, Pildes wrote in a spring 2006 law review article,
had become "a model from earlier decades that [was] increasingly irrelevant
and not designed for the voting problems of today."[101] The selective targeting of the covered jurisdictions was no longer the best way to protect
minority voting rights. Pildes suggested, instead, radically different federal
legislation along the lines of the 2002 Help America Vote Act (HAVA), which
would establish uniform, national voting standards.[102]

The Voting Rights Act is indeed archaic. I have grave doubts about a
new HAVA-like statute as a replacement, however. Today's alleged voting
wrongs—felon voting, voter ID, provisional and absentee ballots, and the
like—are not equivalent to the massive disfranchisement of southern
blacks in 1965, which was the keystone of the whole structure of racial
oppression. But the Pildes proposal does have an important virtue: It would
restore the idea that voting rights legislation should focus on ensuring
opportunity, rather than results.

That should have remained the focus of the Voting Rights Act, even after
it became clear that the attainment of true electoral opportunity required
race-conscious measures to protect black candidates until the process of
political integration was clearly underway. It cannot be stressed too strongly:
The point of the 1965 statute was to create a political system in which blacks
participate as individuals, free to identify themselves as members of racial
and other groups, but only if they so choose. If we, as a nation, roughly
attain that goal, we will have achieved a politically integrated politics—the
above-and-beyond-race politics that many believed President Obama's
election promised.

Conclusion: Moving On

Here we are 45 years after the "I have a dream" speech. Forty years after the assassinations of Kennedy and King. And this party that I have been a part of for so long . . . is about to deliver the nomination for the nation's highest office to an African-American. How do you describe that? All those days in jail cells, wondering if anything you were doing was even going to have an impact.

—South Carolina representative James Clyburn, describing his emotions on the night of the last Democratic Party primary in 2008[1]

This is the America that Dr. King was talking about.

—Harold Ford Jr., contemplating the guests at a dinner meeting of black CEOs in New York[2]

On January 19, 2009, Martin Luther King Day, CNN released a survey showing that 69 percent of blacks believed King's "I Have a Dream" vision had been fulfilled.[3] One day later, Barack Obama was sworn in as the nation's first African-American president. King's dream was, of course, larger than a black president, but surely the dinner and the inauguration signaled a time far removed from Bloody Sunday in Selma and the passage of the Voting Rights Act.

Tony West is a black San Francisco lawyer in his early forties. West's parents grew up in the South, but he has led a very different life than theirs. "Their day-to-day life experience in dealing with discrimination, dealing with segregation, Jim Crow, is just something that at best I've read about or know the stories of as told to me," he told journalist Gwen Ifill. "It is not something that I have had to confront on a daily basis."[4]

For most ordinary Americans, the Jim Crow South is the stuff of history books. The extent of racial progress—of which I have made much in this book—is simply staggering. The change in politics is but one part of a larger picture. In 1964, only 18 percent of whites said they had black friends; the figure today is 87 percent. Raise the bar to "a fairly close personal friend" and the proportion jumps from a mere 9 percent in 1975 to 75 percent in 2005. The share of blacks with close white friends has soared from 21 percent to 82 percent over that same period.[5]

We don't have much in the way of historical data on interracial dating because, not so long ago, the figure would have been too low for pollsters to bother tabulating. But we do know that in 1963 only 10 percent of whites approved of it. In 2006, however, a *Washington Post*/Kaiser/Harvard poll found that 59 percent of black men and 41 percent of black women had dated someone who is white. And 41 percent of white women and 36 percent of white men had crossed the racial-dating divide. Today, the number of black–white marriages is up to almost half a million—still low, but a steep rise over the last forty years.[6]

The specter of contemporary residential "segregation" is a civil rights mantra. Here, too, the data tell a story of dramatic change. Half a century ago, only 20 percent of whites reported having black neighbors, while today the figure is above 81 percent. Blacks, on average, live in communities that are only half black—which is the percentage they believe is just about right, survey data reveal.[7]

The political picture is also very heartening. As mentioned in the previous chapter, political scientist David Bositis estimated in a preliminary analysis of the 2008 election that black turnout had jumped from 11 percent in 2004 to 13 percent. As a percentage of the black voting-age population, the turnout was 66.8 percent, which smashed all previous records. In fact, it is likely that black turnout—for the first time in history—surpassed that of whites in a presidential election.[8]

Obama's victory was only in part due to the surge in black voting. He received 43 percent of the white vote, two points above Democratic senator John Kerry's total in 2004. Moreover, as Bositis has pointed out, that national number does not even tell the whole story. In all states outside of the South, Obama received significantly more of the white vote than any Democratic nominee since Lyndon Johnson. He received an absolute majority of the white vote in sixteen states and the District of Columbia. In the rest of the states outside of the South (with the exception of the Republican candidates' home states of Alaska and Arizona, where Obama ran one point worse than Kerry had), Obama did better than the Democratic standard-bearer four years earlier. In the South, he won two states—North Carolina and Virginia.[9]

Columbia University law school professor Nathaniel Persily, one of the nation's experts on voting rights, contends that the picture is much less rosy. He argues from an analysis of voting patterns that "in 2008 race played a greater role in voter choice in the covered than in the noncovered jurisdictions."[10] His central finding is that Obama performed worse than John Kerry in the covered states than in the states not covered by section 5. The difference that so impresses him, however, is a mere six percentage points among white Democrats. This is hardly a dramatic gap, particularly in light of the dubious reliability of exit polls.[11]

A plausible alternative explanation is that white Democrats in the South gave slightly less support to Obama than to John Kerry because, as southerners, they would generally be more conservative and see Obama as considerably to the left of the 2004 candidate. In the eyes of many of these more conservative voters, Obama must have sounded weak on national defense, and far to the left on domestic policies such as health care. He talked openly about a redistribution of wealth. His emissions-trading proposal for global warming surely did not play well in areas of the South where coal-burning power plants are the primary source of energy, and his support for "card-check" could not have been appealing to workers in right-to-work states. In contrast, Kerry had been a decorated combat veteran; environmental issues were never prominent in his campaign; and he ran as the standard-bearer of a party that was generally not as far to the left as it had become by 2008. And Kerry had no equivalent to the Reverend Jeremiah Wright in his history—a figure surely more off-putting to southern whites than to, say, Massachusetts voters.

Reasons other than race, in other words, may well account for the Kerry–Obama gap in white support in the covered and noncovered jurisdictions. After all, Obama ran eleven points behind Kerry among gay voters;

are we to conclude that gays were motivated by racism in rejecting Obama? We need much more compelling evidence before we conclude that race played a decisive role in the choices that white voters made in 2008.

A Period Piece

In 1965, sections 4 and 5 of the Voting Rights Act were designed to deal with a world that by now has virtually disappeared. The statutory language itself makes clear just how dated they are. Registration and turnout are the trigger (contained in section 4) that determines the imposition of preclearance (section 5). But the last voter participation figures used to establish section 5 coverage are from 1972; the list of allegedly racially suspect jurisdictions that must submit all changes in voting procedure was compiled more than thirty years ago.[12] That is a long time, given the fast pace at which racial change has been occurring in recent decades.

In 1965, section 5 and other emergency provisions were designed to deal with the distinctive problems of a particular region. When the statute was passed, voter participation figures, combined with the use of a literacy test, accurately targeted states that were disfranchising blacks. The formula was perfect, built as it was by reverse engineering—knowing which states had to be covered and designing an accurate statistical trigger to do so.

The list of procedures subject to federal review came to include municipal annexations, polling place relocations, changes in the size of county councils, rules governing ballot format, ballot initiatives, special elections, candidate eligibility, campaign finance, absentee ballots, and provisional voting, as well as new districting maps.[13] Section 5 placed covered states and counties, in effect, in federal receivership. Changes in election-related rules and procedures could not be precleared unless a covered jurisdiction carried its burden of proving an *absence* of discrimination. They were assumed to be racist unless they themselves could prove otherwise— a perfectly good assumption about thoroughly discredited southern states in 1965.

Today, election-related decisions even in black-run cities such as Birmingham are still governed by federal authorities; and yet, not only in such black-dominated settings, but also throughout the region, African

Americans in politics have become a powerful presence. Black voters are the Democrats' most reliable constituency, and Republicans can ill afford to appear opposed to civil rights. As the last chapter noted, by 2002, 47 percent of the 9,400 black elected officials nationwide were from one of the seven covered states, although those states contained only 30 percent of the nation's black population. Many of these officials represented majority-minority constituencies, but would they lose their seats in the absence of federal oversight? Is their political power, in fact, so fragile?

What would be the sign that these states and localities could manage their political affairs without extraordinary federal protection? In renewing section 5 in 2006, Congress assumed that the states designated as suspect by voter turnout figures now more than thirty years old would remain untrustworthy for another quarter-century. Why another twenty-five years? The duration of the extension was arbitrary; the coverage had become arbitrary; and already, I argue below, the costs of continuing to freeze election arrangements pending federal approval outweigh its benefits.

Sections 4 and 5—designed to be temporary—are by now dated. Their survival into the twenty-first century in the face of massive racial change turned the Voting Rights Act, in important respects, into a period piece, raising questions about their constitutionality that the Supreme Court will address in *Northwest Austin Municipal Utility District Number One v. Holder* .[14]

From a Biracial to a Multiracial Polity

The constitutionality of the Voting Rights Act has become questionable for yet another reason. In the 1960s, America—and specifically the South—was a land of black and white; today, that world has been swept away, replaced by a much more diverse multiracial, multiethnic society. The central aim of the framers of the Voting Rights Act was to provide a remedy for black disfranchisement in a biracial world. In the Jim Crow South, virtually everyone was classified as white or black. Once the obstacles that prevented blacks from registering and voting were removed, the attainment of "descriptive representation"—black faces in public office—became the primary goal. Southern whites were not likely to relinquish voluntarily their monopoly on political power, and the law responded. Courts and the Justice Department came to insist on race-conscious, single-member districts that served to protect black candidates from white competition and ensure their election.

Such districts should have been a temporary fix, but once an entitlement, always an entitlement. The problem is that the drawing of majority-black districts to create reserved legislative seats for black candidates will likely become increasingly difficult. The nation has been demographically transformed. More than 30 million immigrants have entered the country in the decades since the statute was passed. That striking number is about 50 percent greater than the total black population in 1965.[15] Hispanics are now the largest minority group in the country. With the addition of Asians and American Indians, blacks are just 40 percent of the total minority population.[16] If there is a demand for yet another extension of section 5 in 2031, these nonblack minorities will outnumber African Americans by two to one, the U.S. Census projects.[17]

When the 1975 amendments extended coverage to four "language minorities"—citizens of Hispanic origin, Asian Americans, American Indians, and Alaskan Natives—these groups were viewed as similar to African Americans in their levels of residential concentration. Indeed, the law only affected jurisdictions in which one of these groups accounted for at least 5 percent of the population; the concern was with representation for minority "communities." Racial and ethnic clustering was expected to be the norm, making districts that advantaged one minority group relatively easy to draw—even if some did end up with contorted lines driven by both racial and partisan considerations. Few clashes among the interests of the residentially separated and distinct minority groups were expected, however. The great divide, and thus the potential source of tension, was between whites and nonwhites.

Since 1975, these "language-minority" groups have not only grown spectacularly; their members have burst out of their initial geographic concentrations, dispersing across the land. And they are increasingly sharing urban space with blacks, whites, and each other.[18] As a result, creating majority-minority districts will cease to be as straightforward a task as it has been. Already the current membership of the Congressional Black Caucus illustrates the problem. Of its forty-one members, seventeen have been elected from districts less than half black. In five of them, whites make up a majority of the population. These are Democratic strongholds in which blacks can count on crossover voting. In another dozen districts, no single racial group comprises a majority. But in five of them Latinos are a plurality. Charles Rangel represents New York's Congressional District 15; only 31 percent of his constituents are black, while 48 percent are Hispanic. California representative Maxine Waters is elected from a district that is 34 percent black, 47 percent Hispanic. In two other California districts that send blacks to Congress, Latinos outnumber blacks, and in a third a combination of Asians and Hispanics do. Of course, one major reason blacks represent areas with large Latino populations is the number of Hispanics who are not citizens and thus ineligible to vote; the raw voting-age-population figures thus exaggerate the Hispanic presence in minority-black constituencies that are nevertheless represented by blacks.

The 2006 House Judiciary Committee report successfully urged an amendment of section 5 intended to supersede *Ashcroft* and stop states from drawing districts that spread minority voters around. If the role of blacks and Hispanics, the report stated, were reduced to influencing the outcome of elections, or if they could only elect the candidates of their choice by joining coalitions, they would be turned into "second class voters."[19] But if influence and coalition districts relegate minority voters to "second class," there is a large problem looming on the horizon.

Minority voters, without any help from redistricting authorities, are increasingly spreading themselves around. Justice David Souter, dissenting in *Bartlett*, defined vote dilution as the distribution of "politically cohesive minority voters through voting districts in ways that reduce their potential strength."[20] Minority voters, by this definition, are diluting themselves. More black incumbents or aspiring black politicians will find themselves in districts in which African-American voters are only a plurality. The tradeoffs between majority-minority constituencies and influence or coalition districts can be debated as a matter of principle, legal precedent, or statutory construction. But such districts have been made inescapable by demographic change. Racial districting, in Justice Sandra Day O'Connor's words, threatened to "balkanize us into competing racial factions."[21] A movement away from race-conscious districting maps—forced by America's changing demography—would bring us closer to having a political system in which the role of racial identity is significantly diminished. At that point, however, what is the justification for keeping nine states (and many counties scattered elsewhere) under federal receivership? Would the statute still be a remedy for racial exclusion?

Demographic change, which will only accelerate, will make the quest for racially fair elections—arguably misguided by now—ever more elusive with each passing year.

Section 2: What Next?

Section 2 is a permanent provision of the Voting Rights Act and protected from congressional amendment as long as blacks remain such an important constituency in the Democratic Party, and the civil rights organizations can intimidate both Democrats and Republicans. Thus, the multitude of complicated questions that swirl around the enforcement of section 2 and its definition of the proper relationship between race and representation await resolution by the Supreme Court.

The *Bartlett* Court in March 2009 did tackle important section 2 issues, which were discussed in the previous chapter. The provision, it said, does not require the creation of crossover districts if they can be drawn. That does not mean, Justice Anthony Kennedy was careful to say, that jurisdictions cannot *choose* to draw *minority*-minority districts; they remain free to act on a belief that any sort of district—influence, coalition, or crossover—will "lead to less racial isolation, not more."[22] But courts, in their enforcement of section 2, are still obligated to regard *Thornburg v. Gingles* as good precedent; there is no remedy for the wrong of vote dilution without the ability to draw a single-member district in which the injured group will be a majority.

The Court was unwilling to reconsider the three *Gingles* preconditions for finding section 2 liability. But that 1986 decision should have been revisited in its entirety. It enshrined into law the standard of proportional racial representation as the measure of electoral equity, as Justice O'Connor noted in a concurrence.[23] Proportionality was the standard that civil rights organizations had believed in all along, which was why they saw retrogression as the wrong measure of discriminatory effect in the enforcement of section 5. All statistical disparities between white and minority officeholding had, in their view, one explanation: racism, past or present. But in 1982, when the provision was rewritten, Congress had rejected that assumption, and stressed the burden on section 2 plaintiffs to prove racist exclusion.[24]

Chapter 3 discussed at length the passage of the 1982 amendments, which radically altered section 2. A report by the Senate Subcommittee on the Constitution expressed concern that the distinction between black candidates losing elections for normal political reasons rather than racial ones would be lost in the revised section 2.[25] Not so, retorted the full committee's own report. In "*most*" jurisdictions, white voters would support black candidates. But, "unfortunately," the report noted, "there still are some communities . . . where racial politics do dominate the electoral process."[26] The problem was confined to just a few lingering holdouts—"some" racist communities—that were not covered by section 5, but in which the outcome of an election was predictable from the racial census. A key civil rights advocate who testified at the hearings also argued that section 2 only promised an electoral process that was *fluid*—open to racial change—not "frozen" by racism.[27]

The *Gingles* Court had veered off in a direction not sanctioned by this legislative history, as O'Connor observed.[28] In fact, the language of section 2 itself specifically prohibited any requirement of proportional representation— and thus, implicitly, the notion that jurisdictions must draw a maximum number of majority-minority districts. Moreover, in other decisions, the Court had been true to the original section 2. In *LULAC* it had stressed that the provision guaranteed "equality of opportunity, not . . . electoral success for minority-preferred candidates of whatever race."[29]

Proportional racial representation was thus both written into *Gingles* as an entitlement and strongly rejected in other important Supreme Court decisions—as it should have been. Statistical parity between the size of a minority population and the number of majority-minority districts is the wrong standard by which to measure equal electoral opportunity. Groups cluster in a variety of ways in American society; if there are "too few" Catholics at Harvard, are there "too many" Jews or Asians? Disproportionately low numbers of blacks in southern politics has long been telling, given the history of disfranchisement. But today Mississippi, the covered southern state with the worst history of exclusion, leads the nation in the number of black officials who hold elected office, as the previous chapter noted.[30] Although it still falls short of parity, that number has also kept growing apace.

The most frequent explanation for disproportionately low minority officeholding is the continuation of racial bloc voting, considered the most important sign of electoral exclusion. Such bloc voting is usually found wherever "black voters and white voters vote differently," although that is a definition not more than four justices on the *Gingles* Court accepted.[31] By this definition, polarized voting can thus be found virtually everywhere! If 95 percent of the blacks vote for a candidate but only 60 percent of the whites support that same candidate, there is racial bloc voting.

As New York University law professor Richard Pildes has noted, "the concept of polarized voting was developed in circumstances in which . . . a solid, hostile, bloc-voting white majority was overwhelmingly unified in its resistance to black candidates."[32] Perhaps such circumstances can still be found in pockets of the rural South, but elsewhere, surely, the reason blacks and whites have voted differently in a particular election is relevant— that reason usually being partisan preferences. "The VRA cannot be an entitlement to guarantee the Democratic Party as such a certain number of seats," Pildes has written.

> Yet that is close to what it would mean to say that if a majority of voters prefer Republicans, but a coalition of black and white voters prefer Democrats . . . the Act requires that districts be redesigned so that the white–black coalition be able to elect its candidates.[33]

There are no group rights to representation in America; minority voters are not entitled to elect their preferred candidates. If they reside in a majority-Republican district, they are no more disadvantaged than white Democrats. In enforcing section 2, courts can be guided by a few simple principles. The Constitution protects individual voters. Those voters belong to a variety of interest groups. If members share an interest in, say, the life of their local town and they would likely constitute the majority in a constituency whose contours are set by traditional districting rules, then residentially clustered voters who identify themselves as belonging to the black "community" are also entitled to districts with conventional boundaries. But districting decisions that arise out of normal political processes should not be overturned by courts unless the setting is one that is racially suspect, and the method of election dilutes the otherwise expected political power of black or Hispanic voters. That is, the Constitution and the 1965 statute entitle minority voters to equal—but not preferential—treatment.

Section 2's statutory language, as well as its legislative history, leaves much room for needed revision. The Court can undo some of its own misguided work by rereading the provision to stress the core concerns that drove the amendment in 1982 and that have animated some of its own decisions. Left on its current course, section 2 is an obstacle to black progress, a point to which I will return below.

Whither Section 5?

Section 5 is now badly outdated, I have argued. Civil rights groups—indeed, all Americans—should be celebrating a job well done. The original 1965 act was beautifully designed and, by transforming southern politics, it irrevocably changed the politics of the nation, as well. The preclearance provision was integral to its success. The Court will decide *NAMUDNO*, which has challenged the constitutionality of preclearance, before the end of the 2008–9 term.[34] The Obama administration has argued strongly against finding a violation of the Fourteenth and Fifteenth Amendments, claiming that the nation might revert to one in which racial- and language-minority citizens are deprived of the right to vote or find their votes have been diluted.[35] But every man or woman on a southern street knows that blacks are in no danger of being disfranchised once again. Nor will they or Hispanics be left out of a redistricting process in states in which they have become such a potent political force—Hispanic power is, in fact, growing in leaps and bounds, with the group already America's largest ethnic minority.[36]

Change is so ubiquitous that there is literally no chance blacks could be once again disfranchised or intentionally left vulnerable to electoral arrangements that reward white racism. What politician would even be tempted to risk the "R" charge? Equally important, how many Americans would even want to return to the days of old? With or without section 5, an army of activists, lawyers, and DOJ staff would continue to monitor American elections closely—and would have recourse to constitutional and statutory protections, including section 2 of the Voting Rights Act. The DOJ's criminal division prosecutes those who attempt to corrupt elections; it deals with such issues as ballot fraud, vote-buying, and ballot-stuffing. Moreover, since the election of 2000, the DOJ has greatly expanded the number of federal observers and monitors in federal elections. In 2004, it sent 1,463 observers and 533 monitors to possible trouble spots. In 2006, over 1,500 federal personnel served as monitors.

In addition, civil rights groups are well organized, vigilant, and powerful in their defense of voting rights; the days of the Student Nonviolent Coordinating Committee making a brave but near-hopeless effort to break the back of a regime deeply committed to black subjugation are long over. Is racism dead? Of course not—neither in America nor in any other country. But the level of clearly (or even allegedly) race-driven voting problems today does not justify keeping states and counties selected by a long-outdated statistical trigger under federal receivership.

In 2006, Congress strengthened section 5 not only in the face of the unmistakable and massive racial change, but also at a time when some black legislators, as well as important voices within the scholarly and civil rights communities, were expressing doubts—directly or indirectly—about a provision still designed to deal with yesterday's racism. These traditional voting rights advocates began to ask a question that few outside conservative circles had previously raised: In contemporary America, is having a maximum number of safe black constituencies really a civil rights strategy—a means of promoting racial equality and integration? In *LULAC*, the civil rights community argued that Martin Frost's 25 percent black congressional district in Texas should count as one that gave African Americans an "opportunity to elect." And in *Bartlett*, civil rights spokesmen urged the Supreme Court to include minority-minority districts with strong white crossover voting as a remedy for unequal electoral opportunity. These were section 2 cases, but the issues raised in the section 5 context often overlap.

Recall, as well, that Georgia representative John Lewis, testifying in the trial court hearing *Georgia v. Ashcroft*, argued for allowing the state legislature to lower the black percentages in minority-majority districts, placing more African Americans in majority-white settings where they could help elect white liberals.[37] Almost every African-American member of Georgia's state senate, including the majority leader, shared Lewis's belief that preserving very safe seats for black legislators and forfeiting greater potential power for white Democrats was a bad tradeoff.[38]

Nevertheless, Representative Lewis (along with the entire civil rights community) has argued strongly for the continuing constitutionality of section 5. In fact, only two Republican governors of covered states—Sonny Perdue of Georgia and Bob Riley of Alabama—have weighed in on the side of the utility district in *NAMUDNO*, a decision perhaps influenced by the fact that term limits prevent them from running for reelection in 2010.[39] Thus, the tiny district, which was forced to get federal approval to move its polling place to a more accessible location, is on its own save for the support of these two governors and the company of conservative groups such as the Pacific Legal Foundation and the Goldwater Institute. Travis County, in which the district sits, includes the city of Austin, the home of the University of Texas; it is strongly Democratic, and has submitted a supporting brief arguing that preclearance remains essential. For the same reasons that the 2006 VRARA passed with hardly a dissent, Mississippi, North Carolina, and New York, among others, have also chosen to side with the position depicted as pro–civil rights—arguing for the continued application of the act's emergency provisions to themselves. But they are standing on what feels like morally safe territory. For different reasons, Republicans and Democrats both see the Voting Rights Act with its mandate for race-conscious districting as beneficial to their parties' interests.

On the other hand, those who argue that section 5 is deeply intrusive on state prerogatives and is now unnecessary must explain a very complicated statute, stress out-of-fashion federalism concerns, and make the case that the law should not ignore the nation's remarkable racial progress. Even the last point—as obvious as it might seem—is not such an easy winner. Civil rights spokesmen argue, in response, that the Court owes deference to the factual findings of the trial court, and should not "take the extraordinary step of second-guessing the national legislature's judgment, given the fundamental nature of the right at issue."[40]

The racial progress to which the district points, they assert, would not have taken place without section 5—an argument that no data can settle one way or another. It is more than a little interesting, though, that these spokesmen have so little confidence in the ameliorative effects of preclearance over more than four decades that they think the provision is still indispensable to combating the "grave constitutional harm" of "purposeful discrimination in voting."[41] They see a preclearance provision that has extraordinary power to prompt change—but only superficial change; renewed disfranchisement evidently awaits only the disappearance of section 5. Also deeply troubling is the level of their pessimism about American racial attitudes, which is so high that they do not hesitate to argue that only a twenty-five year extension of preclearance powers prevents a repeat of the massive disfranchisement of the late nineteenth century. "The clock of progress has been turned back before in American history. This Court must not let it happen again," the Leadership Conference on Civil Rights stated in its *NAMUDNO* brief.[42] As I will suggest below, such historical ignorance and deliberate blindness to current reality actually endangers American racial progress.

Additionally, those who have lent their voices to that of the Justice Department claim that preclearance has become "painless and routine"; that section 5 helps protect jurisdictions against allegations of discrimination (Justice Department approval being a badge of racial health); that changes in the method of voting are no problem unless they are discriminatory; and so forth.[43]

The U.S. government's brief arguing for the continuing constitutional vitality of preclearance focused on how burdensome relying on section 2, rather than section 5, would be. The 1982 provision, it noted, was "purely an after-the-fact remedy, available only to challenge voting practices and procedures already in place." Cases can take years to litigate. "In some cases, an illegal voting practice must remain in effect for several election cycles before the plaintiff can gather enough evidence to demonstrate a discriminatory effect." In the meantime, elected officials enjoy the benefits of incumbency. It is far preferable "to ensure elections protect voting rights before they take place."[44]

Second, the Justice Department's brief argues that section 2, unlike section 5, places the burden of proof on minority plaintiffs to demonstrate discrimination. Jurisdictions are better positioned than individuals to amass the relevant information, a process that entails considerable expense, which local authorities have the resources to pay, while the plaintiffs often do not.[45] It is quite a remarkable argument. If section 2 litigation is too burdensome and expensive, with disputes often taking years to resolve, why not simply extend section 5 to cover the nation? The U.S. Commission on Civil Rights depicted counties in Florida that were not covered by section 5 as engaging in racial discrimination in the 2000 election.[46] Returns in Ohio in 2004 were also regarded as racially suspicious.[47] Pursuing such allegations of voting rights infringements in court, the brief seems to suggest, asks too much of potential plaintiffs. Of course, such suits in other contexts—education, employment, and contracting—carry all the burdens the solicitor general finds unacceptable in the voting rights context; somehow, however, they are different.

The utility district in *NAMUDNO* faces an uphill battle, but the Court is not limited to the two options of affirming or rejecting the lower court opinion. For instance, University of Michigan law professor Ellen D. Katz has suggested that five Justices might agree the amended section 5 is unconstitutional, but stay its order until Congress has time to revise the provision to meet the Court's objections.[48]

In substantial part, the outcome of the case will depend on the legal standard used to assess the constitutionality of the VRARA. Will it be judged by the deferential standard applied in *South Carolina v. Katzenbach*, which approved the original section 5 at a time when it was clearly a rational means to enforce basic Fifteenth Amendment rights? Or will the Court find that heightened ("strict") scrutiny is demanded in this case, as in all others than involve the inherently suspect classification of Americans on the basis of their race? Race-conscious districts as a section 5 remedy involve precisely such classifications; they sort voters out on the basis of their color. Is such districting still a narrowly tailored, carefully designed, minimally intrusive policy to meet the compelling state interest of protection against disfranchisement?

In theory, it would be possible for the Court to save section 5 by reducing its intrusiveness on the power of popularly elected officials to decide on districting and other matters at the heart of democratic politics. It could suggest that the continuing constitutionality of preclearance depends on taking seriously the retrogression standard that the 2006 amendments claimed to have preserved. The Court (or perhaps simply a concurring opinion by a fifth Justice) would have to issue, in effect, a warning that the VRARA could not survive strict scrutiny if enforced to impose upon jurisdictions the sort of race-driven districts that the Court had found constitutionally impermissible in the *Shaw* line of decisions. The 2006 statute had invited a return to the wide-ranging definition of discriminatory purpose used by the Justice Department prior to the 2000 decision in *Bossier II*. But embracing once again pre-2000 habits of enforcement would likely create what Justice Sandra Day O'Connor had called "political apartheid"— districting plans that so segregate voters as to violate the Fourteenth Amendment. The Court could well choose to remind the Justice Department of the constitutional dangers lurking in race-driven maps.

On the other hand, how long can even the retrogression test withstand the test of compelling state interest? That test demands the preservation of existing majority-minority districts, and yet that requirement may be on a collision course both with demographic reality and the self-interest of aspiring minority politicians. As residential integration increases and blacks, whites, and Hispanics become impossible to separate for political purposes, how are districts designed to create safe seats for only one group to be drawn? Moreover, minority candidates of the future may not find race-conscious districting politically to their liking; it has costs—the subject to which I will next turn. A crop of young black men and women have been appointed to important positions in the Obama administration; some may run for office in time themselves—joining the ranks of others who see opportunities not open to African Americans with the political profile of a Jesse Jackson or an Al Sharpton.[49] They will want to build biracial and multiracial coalitions, and they may want districts that help them do so.

Racial Progress Stymied

The 1965 Voting Rights Act is the crown jewel of federal civil rights laws. No one should doubt its importance in making America a very different nation from the one in which I grew up not so many years ago. While the 1964 Civil Rights Act was crucial in forcing southern whites to accept the blacks in their midst—in restaurants, hotels, theaters, places of employment, hospitals, schools, indeed, in the entire public sphere—that earlier statute had only minor and weak provisions guaranteeing the right to vote. And yet, black ballots were the levers of change that white supremacists most feared. Enfranchisement, they knew, would turn African Americans into true citizens. President Lyndon Johnson, in signing the act on August 6, called it "one of the most monumental laws in the entire history of American freedom," while John Lewis, a young leader in the civil rights movement at the time, saw the statute as "every bit as momentous and significant . . . as the Emancipation Proclamation."[50]

Black ballots alone turned out not to suffice. In Mississippi and elsewhere, whites in power were prepared to alter election processes to keep blacks out of public office—hence, the race-conscious districting as a temporary measure to give blacks what Daniel Lowenstein has called "a jumpstart in electoral politics." But Lowenstein makes a further, important point: "A jumpstart is one thing but the guy who comes and charges up your car when the battery's dead, he doesn't stay there trailing behind you with the cable stuck as you drive down the freeway. He lets it go."[51] It's time to let race-driven districting go the way of those jumper cables. America is better off with the increase in the number of black elected officials who gained office, in large part due to the deliberate drawing of majority-minority districts. But black politics has come of age, and black politicians can protect their turf, fight for their interests, and successfully compete even for the presidency, it turns out. It's a new world.

In today's America, the costs of continuing to insist on race-based electoral arrangements are very high. Had congressional committees in 2006 been willing to confront honestly the question of renewing and strengthening section 5, they would have acknowledged the constitutional problems at the core of a decision to extend further the emergency provision designed as a temporary measure to force the nation to live up to its constitutional promise. Special arrangements that provide privileged protection for black and Hispanic candidates are a serious distortion of a democratic system in which ethnic groups have no collective right to representation. Methods of voting based on the notion that individual citizens are indistinguishable members of a racial group and should be grouped accordingly are also deeply constitutionally suspect. The Fourteenth Amendment stops states from denying "the equal protection of the laws" to "any person"—not to "any group." Rights are individual in America; our liberty depends on that belief.

Congress in 2006, had it been willing to explore the status of American voting rights in the twenty-first century with some intellectual integrity, would also have acknowledged that maximizing the number of majority-minority districts impedes black progress in significant ways. The costs enumerated by Sandra Day O'Connor in *Shaw* cannot be empirically proved, but nevertheless seemed instinctively to have some validity. Such districts, she said, reinforce "the perception that members of the same racial group—regardless of their age, education, economic status, or the community in which they live—think alike"; they "threaten to stigmatize persons by reason of their membership in a racial group and to incite racial hostility"; they may "balkanize us into competing racial factions"; and they tell elected representatives that "their primary obligation is to represent only the members of that group, rather than their constituency as a whole."[52] Alex Aleinikoff and Samuel Issacharoff, it may be recalled, also argued that race-conscious districts not too surprisingly raise racial consciousness; they scream "RACE, RACE, RACE."[53]

And yet, increasingly, blacks may not see themselves as defined by racial identity, some recent polling suggests. In a 2007 national poll, 37 percent disagreed with the notion that blacks can "still be thought of as a single race," while 61 percent expressed their belief that, in recent years, "the values of middle class and poor blacks [have] become . . . more different."[54] Is America moving very slowly toward Harvard law professor Randall Kennedy's ideal of "all Negroes" being "voluntary Negroes"?[55] The luxury of racial identity is still quite new in America, and the deck is heavily stacked against such self-identification. It is hard to escape the world of boxes that demand that you check one to select your racial or ethnic group. But that is today, perhaps not tomorrow.

Hispanics are clearly not a united group, and if blacks as well are ceasing to see themselves as all belonging to one "community," the practice of drawing districting lines that chase after middle-class blacks who have chosen to move out of low-income neighborhoods has become truly offensive. For the courts and the Justice Department to insist that wherever you move, you still belong to a racially defined community reinforces stereotypical assumptions that all blacks are alike, and that race—never social class or residential location or identification with other interest groups—is still the characteristic that counts.

Blacks sit on legislative bodies ranging from elected school boards to the U.S. Congress, but many have acquired their seats by running in districts carefully designed to elect minority candidates. Reviewing data from 1992 to

2007 on the impact of race-conscious districting at the state and congressional levels, political scientist David Lublin and colleagues concluded, "The overwhelming number of minority legislators continue to represent majority-minority districts." As Lublin notes, in some of these districts the majority is composed of a black–Hispanic coalition, and where the minority population is less than 50 percent, it often controls the outcome of the decisive Democratic primary.[56] Of course, some minority-minority districts do elect black candidates with white crossover votes, as the civil rights community admitted in *Bartlett v. Strickland*, discussed in chapter 6.[57] But they are not the norm.

Majority-minority districts appear to reward political actors who consolidate the minority vote by making the sort of overt racial appeals that are the staple of invidious identity politics. Harvard law professor Cass Sunstein describes a larger phenomenon that is pertinent: People across the political spectrum end up with more extreme views than they would otherwise hold when they talk only to those who are similarly minded.[58] Districts drawn for the sole purpose of maximizing the voting power of a racial group surely encourage voters who live there to talk only to one another and lead candidates to focus on issues of immediate concern to their minority constituents. As a consequence, elected representatives seem to be left untutored in the skills necessary to win competitive contests in majority-white settings. It's a self-fulfilling prophecy: Very few black candidates risk running in majority-white constituencies; majority-minority districts thus become the settings in which blacks are most frequently elected.

In such settings, officeholders tend to be pulled to the left—or, in any case, are certainly under no pressure to run as centrists. Their left-leaning tendencies, along with a reluctance to risk elections in majority-white settings, perhaps explain why so few members of the Congressional Black Caucus have run for statewide office and none made a serious bid for the presidency before Barack Obama.[59] It is doubtful that anyone can imagine, for instance, South Carolina representative James Clyburn building a national campaign, despite the fact that he is a well-respected, long-serving political figure. Nevertheless, he's a *black* politician with a majority-*black* constituency. His race was his ticket to Congress. The contrast with Barack Obama's "postracial" campaign for the presidency is striking.

In 2000, Obama ran in the Democratic primary in Chicago for a U.S. House seat. "I've always thought," attorney Michael Carvin has said,

> the best thing that ever happened to Obama was [that] he ran for a heavily minority black congressional district in Chicago and lost. If he had won, he would have just become another mouthpiece for a group that is ghettoized in Congress and perceived as representing certain interest groups in the legislature.[60]

Obama did, however, win a seat in the U.S. Senate in 2004, and his status as a senator from a heavily white state enabled him to transcend that perception.

Blacks running in majority-minority districts, not acquiring the skills to venture into the world of competitive politics in majority-white settings—that is not the picture of political integration, equality, and the vibrant political culture that the Voting Rights Act should promote. By another measure, as well, equality may be compromised by race-conscious districting. The creation of these districts has not overcome the heritage of political apathy created by the long history of systematic disfranchisement; their residents are generally less politically engaged and mobilized, a number of scholars have concluded.[61] Vanderbilt University law professor Carol Swain found that turnout in black-majority congressional districts across the country was especially low. She noted, for example, that just 13 percent of eligible voters showed up at the polls in 1986 in Major Owens's 78 percent black district in New York City. If voters in Owens's district felt more empowered with a black man representing them in Washington, it certainly did not inspire many of them to bother to vote.[62]

James E. Campbell, a political scientist at the University of Buffalo, has supported Swain's findings. Campbell found that in 1994, over 60 percent of congressional districts in which minorities were the majority ranked in the bottom *quintile* in levels of voter turnout.[63] The most recently published review of the scholarly literature on this subject is a 2007 article by Harvard political scientist Claudine Gay.[64] Summing up what we have learned from previous investigations, Gay observed: "Limited electoral competition and low voter turnout are widely viewed as defining features of districts with black or Latino majorities." The "lack of competition" serves to "discourage participation" and reduces "the incentive for candidates or parties to mobilize voters." Thus, "the unique opportunity that majority-minority districts offer for minority self-determination only partially offsets . . . the decrease in turnout associated with noncompetitive electoral environments."[65]

Gay added further empirical evidence showing that the creation of majority-minority districts tends to depress minority voter turnout, and thus generates political disengagement and apathy. In the districts from which members of the California Assembly were elected in 1996, voter turnout exceeded 60 percent (of registered voters) in only *a quarter* of the majority-minority districts. Turnout levels were above 60 percent, by contrast, in *90 percent* of the white-majority districts.[66] In sum, majority-minority districts probably lower the level of black political participation—a significant cost overlooked by advocates of race-based constituencies.

Thus, the pressure on jurisdictions to create race-based districts ultimately has the perverse effect of suppressing minority turnout and diminishing electoral competition within districts. Race-conscious districting also contributes to the larger problem of political polarization among districts. It tends to reduce the diversity of adjoining districts. As Georgetown University law professor Sheryll Cashin has put the point, "Racial gerrymandering that creates both majority-minority districts and 'safe' Republican . . . districts reduces the number of competitive races and contributes to a balkanized electorate."[67]

Finally, majority-minority districts, with their insularity, may encourage dangerous black pessimism. A 2006 CNN poll found that 40 percent of blacks believed "many" or "almost all" white people disliked blacks.[68] A Gallup poll almost three years earlier had discovered that only 38 percent of blacks believed they were treated "fairly" or "somewhat fairly" in our society. For blacks who had attended college—those best equipped to take advantage of the opportunities opened up since the civil rights revolution—the figure was an even lower 26 percent.[69] The congressionally sanctioned narrative of an America still steeped in white racism and thus in need of another quarter-century of careful federal oversight over covered jurisdictions is not benign.

Pessimism had an impact in the early months of the campaign for the 2008 election. Polling before the first primary ballots were cast showed Barack Obama as having only modest support from black voters. African Americans, it appeared, were lukewarm toward Obama because they believed he had no chance of winning.[70] Robert Ford, a black state senator in South Carolina, for instance, told a *Time* magazine reporter in January 2007 that "Obama would need 43% of the white vote in some states to win, and that's humanly impossible." Southern blacks "don't believe this country is ready to vote for a black president," he added.[71] Referring to Obama's opponent, Hillary Rodham Clinton, Jesse Jackson said, "A white female has an advantage over a black male."[72] And, after the first three contests, political scientist Philip Klinkner was ready to conclude that there was a "ceiling" on potential white support for Obama of about 35 percent.[73]

That pessimism, woven into the fabric of the Voting Rights Act and broadcast as part of civil rights orthodoxy, is belied by polling data on white racial attitudes and by the facts on the ground. In 2007, for instance, only 5 percent of Americans said they were unwilling to vote for a "qualified African American candidate," according to a Gallup Organization survey.[74] Before the Reverend Jeremiah Wright, Obama's longtime pastor, surfaced with his racist, anti-American rhetoric, the Illinois senator had won the majority of white votes in the Democratic primaries in Virginia, New Mexico, Wisconsin, Illinois, and Utah, and had received impressive vote totals among whites in other states' primaries, as well. And in November, as noted above, he received 43 percent of the white vote nationally.

In February 2008, voters in an Alabama county more than 96 percent white sent a black man, James Fields, as their representative to the state House of Representatives. "Really, I never realize he's black," a white woman, smiling, told a *New York Times* reporter.[75] How many Americans today look at the president and think, "black"? I know of no polling in which that question has been asked, but I suspect the answer is, relatively few. They look to him for leadership in the face of extraordinarily urgent economic and foreign policy problems; if previous surveys are any indication, they are unlikely to judge his accomplishments through the lens of race. America has come a very long way in the decades since the Voting Rights Act was passed.

In Conclusion

Harold Ford Jr., quoted in the epigraph, looked at a room full of black CEOs and saw the America that Martin Luther King only dreamed about. Ford exaggerated, but understandably so. We have moved toward that dream much faster than most black Americans thought possible before Obama's election. By now, as Stanford law professor Richard Thompson Ford has written, racial bias has become "unlawful, immoral, and perhaps more important, déclassé."[76] For those of us who remember an earlier era, that is a most remarkable turn of events.

I grew up in a peculiar small corner of American society. My parents and all their friends were Communist Party sympathizers, if not actual members. They sent me to private schools that matched their politics; my high school, for instance, was the one attended by the children of Julius and Ethel Rosenberg after their parents were executed as Soviet spies. Pete Seeger came and sang songs with us. This little American subculture used blacks for its own political and psychological purposes (Richard Wright had something to say about that phenomenon in *Native Son*). Nevertheless, I remain grateful that I grew up with blacks who were friends, not strangers, in our largely segregated nation.

In a small gesture of solidarity with the larger civil rights movement that would begin the quiet revolution that ended white hegemony and black subordination, my husband and I picketed Woolworths in the spring of 1960. And yet, many years later, I found myself at odds with the established civil rights groups over racial preferences. I never abandoned my commitment to racial equality; I felt—and still feel—that those groups rejected the principles that were so central to the civil rights ethos of the early 1960s and to which I was so deeply intellectually and emotionally committed.

Those principles—enduringly articulated by Martin Luther King, Jr.— have been at the core of my own self-definition. Questions involving race and ethnicity have occupied the center of my professional life. More than twenty years ago I wrote another book on the Voting Rights Act—*Whose Votes Count?*—but then moved on to other topics. I have returned to it now as unfinished business. It is both the least understood of all current race-related areas of public policy and in some ways the hardest to sort out. The subtitle of this book—*The Elusive Quest for Racially Fair Elections*—makes the point. It is very difficult to arrive at a definition of representational equity among racial and ethnic groups.

The 1965 Voting Rights Act was a remarkable triumph, but its passage was the beginning of an important conversation, not the end. Richard Pildes described the statute as one of the world's "most ambitious legislative

efforts . . . to define the appropriate balance between the political representation of majorities and minorities in the design of democratic institutions."[77] Courts, Congress, and the Justice Department have struggled over
four decades to find that balance; they have not succeeded. I have wrestled
with the question in this book; I do not claim to offer more than a serious
effort at framing the issue in ways that I hope will provoke further thought.
The act has become an incoherent, and in some ways unprincipled, mess;
the importance of the issue demands an intellectually serious and honest
discussion. By 2009, the starting point of such discussion should be the
recognition of a racially transformed America.

I have argued that race-conscious districting was a necessary jumpstart
for African Americans in the aftermath of Jim Crow—but also that the time
for such protective arrangements has passed. I do not believe racially protective measures have been equally legitimate in other spheres—education,
employment, and contracting—except where intentional racism has been
proved in a court of law. But in 1965 and beyond there was no need to prove
intentional racial exclusion in southern federal courts; the record was clear.
In fact, in the years leading up to the passage of the Voting Rights Act,
proving voting discrimination on a case-by-case basis in states like
Mississippi and Alabama had been tried and found almost totally ineffective;
for one thing, racially hostile white judges frequently presided over the
courts. Closing those southern courts to litigation under the statute, sending
federal registrars to the South, banning literacy and understanding tests,
stopping the institution of new voting procedures until federal approval was
obtained—all these constitutionally drastic measures were needed if
Fifteenth Amendment rights were finally to be realized.

When will we reach true racial equality in American politics? And how will
we know the moment when it comes? I have argued strongly against proportional racial representation as the measure of electoral fairness. Much continues
to be made of "racial polarization" in voting patterns, but if the definition of
nonpolarized voting is whites and blacks voting alike, it is much too crude.
Close to half of blacks would have to become Republicans. There is nothing
morally wrong with group members generally having a strong political identity
of their own. Mormons and Episcopalians tend to vote differently, as do women
and men, gays and straights, Irish and Italians, gun owners and gun control
advocates, married women with children and single women—and so forth.

Group political preferences should be of no concern. But there is something wrong when blacks who break with the Democratic Party are considered, in effect, not black; such ideological coercion robs individuals of freedom and personal dignity. There is also no reason to protest when a president or other elected official engages in old-fashioned ticket-balancing. If a politician caters to farmers, Hispanics, or members of Emily's List, he or she is engaging in the normal process of building an effective political coalition. Voters care about seeing "one of their own" in public life; that, too, is as American as apple pie.

I do not think we should expect a society in which ethnicity or race is irrelevant to political behavior. We want, I believe, a politics in which being an African American is no more salient than being Jewish or Catholic. And we do not want that salience determined by government bureaucrats, but rather by individuals free to choose their own identities. Race-conscious districting served an important but temporary purpose in a particular time and place; it has become positively dangerous in the changed racial landscape of America today, and it will serve us ill in the future. If federal authorities continue to group people together on the basis of racial and ethnic identity, the practice will reinforce pernicious racial stereotyping, as Justice O'Connor warned. It will not move America forward. The Voting Rights Act has become a brake on true racial progress today.

"Minority voters are not immune from the obligation to pull, haul, and trade to find common political ground, the virtue of which is not to be slighted in applying a statute meant to hasten the waning of racism in American politics," Justice David Souter noted in 1994.[78] Wise words. There is something demeaning about the erroneous assumption that blacks are incapable of organizing for political ends, Souter was suggesting. Civil rights policies by now have become laced with such demeaning assumptions—at a time when the majority of voters have just put race aside in voting for a black president. It is time for a voting rights law that expresses confidence in the racial decency of most Americans.

The emergency provisions of the Voting Rights Act were passed when the South was in the grip of a great evil. That time has passed, and today they are the wrong remedies for the very different voting problems we now face. Let us move on—immensely proud of what we have accomplished, but never indifferent to racial inequality in its many remaining forms.

Appendix A

Jurisdictions Covered by Section 5 of the Voting Rights Act

SECTION 5 COVERED JURISDICTIONS

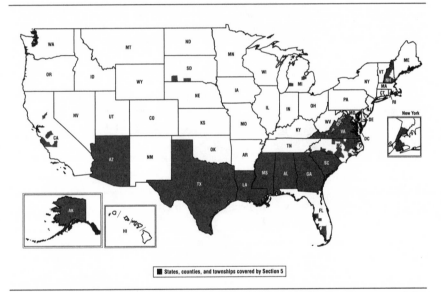

States, counties, and townships covered by Section 5

SOURCE: United States Department of Justice website, http://www.usdoj.gov/crt/voting/sec_5/covered.php.
NOTE: Fifteen political subdivisions in Virginia (Augusta, Botetourt, Essex, Frederick, Greene, Middlesex, Pulaski, Roanoke, Rockingham, Shenandoah, and Warren Counties and the Cities of Fairfax, Harrisonburg, Salem and Winchester) have "bailed out" from coverage pursuant to Section 4 of the Voting Rights Act. The United States consented to the declaratory judgment in each of those cases.

STATES COVERED AS A WHOLE

States	Applicable Date	Federal Register	Date
Alabama	Nov. 1, 1964	30 FR 9897	Aug. 7, 1965
Alaska	Nov. 1, 1972	40 FR 49422	Oct. 22, 1975
Arizona	Nov. 1, 1972	40 FR 43746	Sept. 23, 1975
Georgia	Nov. 1, 1964	30 FR 9897	Aug. 7, 1965
Louisiana	Nov. 1, 1964	30 FR 9897	Aug. 7, 1965
Mississippi	Nov. 1, 1964	30 FR 9897	Aug. 7, 1965
South Carolina	Nov. 1, 1964	30 FR 9897	Aug. 7, 1965
Texas	Nov. 1, 1972	40 FR 43746	Sept. 23, 1975
Virginia[1]	Nov. 1, 1964	30 FR 9897	Aug. 7, 1965

SOURCE: United States Department of Justice website, http://www.usdoj.gov/crt/voting/sec_5/covered.php.
NOTE: 1. Fifteen political subdivisions in Virginia (Augusta, Botetourt, Essex, Frederick, Greene, Middlesex, Pulaski, Roanoke, Rockingham, Shenandoah, and Warren Counties and the Cities of Fairfax, Harrisonburg, Salem and Winchester) have "bailed out" from coverage pursuant to Section 4 of the Voting Rights Act. The United States consented to the declaratory judgment in each of those cases.

COVERED COUNTIES IN STATES NOT COVERED AS A WHOLE

States and Counties	Applicable Date	Federal Register	Date
California			
Kings County	Nov. 1, 1972	40 FR 43746	Sept. 23. 1975
Merced County	Nov. 1, 1972	40 FR 43746	Sept. 23, 1975
Monterey County	Nov. 1, 1968	36 FR 5809	Mar. 27, 1971
Yuba County	Nov. 1, 1968	36 FR 5809	Mar. 27, 1971
Yuba County	Nov. 1, 1972	41 FR 784	Jan. 5, 1976
Florida			
Collier County	Nov. 1, 1972	41 FR 34329	Aug. 13, 1976
Hardee County	Nov. 1, 1972	40 FR 43746	Sept. 23, 1975
Hendry County	Nov. 1, 1972	41 FR 34329	Aug. 13, 1976
Hillsborough County	Nov. 1, 1972	40 FR 43746	Sept. 23, 1975
Monroe County	Nov. 1, 1972	40 FR 43746	Sept. 23, 1975
New York			
Bronx County	Nov. 1, 1968	36 FR 5809	Mar. 27, 1971
Bronx County	Nov. 1, 1972	40 FR 43746	Sept. 23, 1975
Kings County	Nov. 1, 1968	36 FR 5809	Mar. 27, 1971
Kings County	Nov. 1, 1972	40 FR 43746	Sept. 23, 1975
New York County	Nov. 1, 1968	36 FR 5809	Mar. 27, 1971
North Carolina			
Anson County	Nov. 1, 1964	30 FR 9897	Aug. 7, 1965
Beaufort County	Nov. 1, 1964	31 FR 5081	Mar. 29, 1966

States and Counties	Applicable Date	Federal Register	Date
Bertie County	Nov. 1, 1964	30 FR 9897	Aug. 7, 1965
Bladen County	Nov. 1, 1964	31 FR 5081	Mar. 29, 1966
Camden County	Nov. 1, 1964	31 FR 3317	Mar. 2, 1966
Caswell County	Nov. 1, 1964	30 FR 9897	Aug. 7, 1965
Chowan County	Nov. 1, 1964	30 FR 9897	Aug. 7, 1965
Cleveland County	Nov. 1, 1964	31 FR 5081	Mar. 29, 1966
Craven County	Nov. 1, 1964	30 FR 9897	Aug. 7, 1965
Cumberland County	Nov. 1, 1964	30 FR 9897	Aug. 7, 1965
Edgecombe County	Nov. 1, 1964	30 FR 9897	Aug. 7, 1965
Franklin County	Nov. 1, 1964	30 FR 9897	Aug. 7, 1965
Gaston County	Nov. 1, 1964	31 FR 5081	Mar. 29, 1966
Gates County	Nov. 1, 1964	30 FR 9897	Aug. 7, 1965
Granville County	Nov. 1, 1964	30 FR 9897	Aug. 7, 1965
Greene County	Nov. 1, 1964	30 FR 9897	Aug. 7, 1965
Guilford County	Nov. 1, 1964	31 FR 5081	Mar. 29, 1966
Halifax County	Nov. 1, 1964	30 FR 9897	Aug. 7, 1965
Harnett County	Nov. 1, 1964	31 FR 5081	Mar. 29, 1966
Hertford County	Nov. 1, 1964	30 FR 9897	Aug. 7, 1965
Hoke County	Nov. 1, 1964	30 FR 9897	Aug. 7, 1965
Jackson County	Nov. 1, 1972	40 FR 49422	Oct. 22, 1975
Lee County	Nov. 1, 1964	31 FR 5081	Mar. 29, 1966
Lenoir County	Nov. 1, 1964	30 FR 9897	Aug. 7, 1965
Martin County	Nov. 1, 1964	31 FR 19	Jan. 4, 1966
Nash County	Nov. 1, 1964	30 FR 9897	Aug. 7, 1965
Northampton County	Nov. 1, 1964	30 FR 9897	Aug. 7, 1965
Onslow County	Nov. 1, 1964	30 FR 9897	Aug. 7, 1965
Pasquotank County	Nov. 1, 1964	30 FR 9897	Aug. 7, 1965
Perquimans County	Nov. 1, 1964	31 FR 3317	Mar. 2, 1966
Person County	Nov. 1, 1964	30 FR 9897	Aug. 7, 1965
Pitt County	Nov. 1, 1964	30 FR 9897	Aug. 7, 1965
Robeson County	Nov. 1, 1964	30 FR 9897	Aug. 7, 1965
Rockingham County	Nov. 1, 1964	31 FR 5081	Mar. 29, 1966
Scotland County	Nov. 1, 1964	30 FR 9897	Aug. 7, 1965
Union County	Nov. 1, 1964	31 FR 5081	Mar. 29, 1966
Vance County	Nov. 1, 1964	30 FR 9897	Aug. 7, 1965
Washington County	Nov. 1, 1964	31 FR 19	Jan. 4, 1966
Wayne County	Nov. 1, 1964	30 FR 9897	Aug. 7, 1965
Wilson County	Nov. 1, 1964	30 FR 9897	Aug. 7, 1965
South Dakota			
Shannon County	Nov. 1, 1972	41 FR 784	Jan. 5, 1976
Todd County	Nov. 1, 1972	41 FR 784	Jan. 5, 1976

SOURCE: United States Department of Justice website, http://www.usdoj.gov/crt/voting/sec_5/covered.php.

COVERED TOWNSHIPS IN STATES NOT COVERED AS A WHOLE

States, Counties, and Townships	Applicable Date	Federal Register	Date
Michigan			
Allegan County: Clyde Township	Nov. 1, 1972	41 FR 34329	Aug. 13, 1976
Saginaw County: Buena Vista Township	Nov. 1, 1972	41 FR 34329	Aug. 13, 1976
New Hampshire			
Cheshire County: Rindge Town	Nov. 1, 1968	39 FR 16912	May 10, 1974
Coos County: Millsfield Township	Nov. 1, 1968	39 FR 16912	May 10, 1974
Pinkhams Grant	Nov. 1, 1968	39 FR 16912	May 10, 1974
Stewartstown Town	Nov. 1, 1968	39 FR 16912	May 10, 1974
Stratford Town	Nov. 1, 1968	39 FR 16912	May 10, 1974
Grafton County: Benton Town	Nov. 1, 1968	39 FR 16912	May 10, 1974
Hillsborough County: Antrim Town	Nov. 1, 1968	39 FR 16912	May 10, 1974
Merrimack County: Boscawen Town	Nov. 1, 1968	39 FR 16912	May 10, 1974
Rockingham County: Newington Town	Nov. 1, 1968	39 FR 16912	May 10, 1974
Sullivan County: Unity Town	Nov. 1, 1968	39 FR 16912	May 10, 1974

SOURCE: United States Department of Justice website, http://www.usdoj.gov/crt/voting/sec_5/covered.php.

Appendix B

The Voting Rights Act of 1965
Public Law 89-110, August 6, 1965

To enforce the fifteenth amendment to the Constitution of the United States, and for other purposes.

Be it enacted by the Senate and House of Representatives of the United States of America in Congress assembled, That this Act shall be known as the "Voting Rights Act of 1965."

SECTION 2

[1965]
No voting qualification or prerequisite to voting, or standard, practice, or procedure shall be imposed or applied by any State or political subdivision to deny or abridge the right of any citizen of the United States to vote on account of race or color.

[1982]
(a) No voting qualification or prerequisite to voting or standard, practice, or procedure shall be imposed or applied by any State or political subdivision in a manner which results in a denial or abridgement of the right of any citizen of the United States to vote on account of race or color, or in contravention of the guarantees set forth in section 4(f)(2), as provided in subsection (b).

Sections of the Voting Rights Act not relevant to the issues discussed in this book have been omitted from the statutory language.

(b) A violation of subsection (a) is established if, based on the totality of circumstances, it is shown that the political processes leading to nomination or election in the State or political subdivision are not equally open to participation by members of a class of citizens protected by subsection (a) in that its members have less opportunity than other members of the electorate to participate in the political process and to elect representatives of their choice. The extent to which members of a protected class have been elected to office in the State or political subdivision is one circumstance which may be considered: *Provided*, That nothing in this section establishes a right to have members of a protected class elected in numbers equal to their proportion in the population.

SECTION 3

[1965]

(a) Whenever the Attorney General institutes a proceeding under any statute to enforce the guarantees of the fifteenth amendment in any State or political subdivision the court shall authorize the appointment of Federal examiners by the United States Civil Service Commission in accordance with section 6 to serve for such period of time and for such political subdivisions as the court shall determine is appropriate to enforce the guarantees of the fifteenth amendment (1) as part of any interlocutory order if the court determines that the appointment of such examiners is necessary to enforce such guarantees or (2) as part of any final judgment if the court finds that violations of the fifteenth amendment justifying equitable relief have occurred in such State or subdivision: *Provided*, That the court need not authorize the appointment of examiners if any incidents of denial or abridgement of the right to vote on account of race or color (1) have been few in number and have been promptly and effectively corrected by State or local action, (2) the continuing effect of such incidents has been eliminated, and (3) there is no reasonable probability of their recurrence in the future.

(b) If in a proceeding instituted by the Attorney General under any statute to enforce the guarantees of the fifteenth amendment in any State or political subdivision the court finds that a test or device has been used for the purpose or with the effect of denying or abridging the right of any citizen of the United States to vote on account of race or color, it shall suspend the use of tests and devices in such State or political subdivisions as the court shall determine is appropriate and for such period as it deems necessary.

(c) If in any proceeding instituted by the Attorney General under any statute to enforce the guarantees of the fifteenth amendment in any State or political subdivision the court finds that violations of the fifteenth amendment justifying equitable relief have occurred within the territory of such State or political subdivision, the court, in addition to such relief as it may grant, shall retain jurisdiction for such period as it may deem appropriate and during such period no voting qualification or prerequisite to voting, or standard, practice, or procedure with respect to voting different from that in force or effect, at the time the proceeding was commenced shall be enforced unless and until the court finds that such qualification, prerequisite, standard, practice, or procedure does not have the purpose and will not have the effect of denying or abridging the right to vote on account of race or color: *Provided*, That such qualification, prerequisite, standard, practice, or procedure may be enforced if the qualification, prerequisite, standard, practice, or procedure bas been submitted by the chief legal officer or other appropriate official of such State or subdivision to the Attorney General and the Attorney General has not interposed an objection within sixty days after such submission, except that neither the court's finding nor the Attorney General's failure to object shall bar a subsequent action to enjoin enforcement of such qualification, prerequisite, standard, practice, or procedure.

[1970]

Section 4(a) of the Voting Rights Act of 1965 (79 Stat. 438; 42 U.S.C. 1973(b)) is amended by striking out the words "'five years" wherever they appear in the first and third paragraphs thereof, and inserting in lieu thereof the words "ten years."

SECTION 4

[1965]

(a) To assure that the right of citizens of the United States to vote is not denied or abridged on account of race or color, no citizen shall be denied the right to vote in any Federal, State, or local election because of his failure to comply with any test or device in any State with respect to which the determinations have been made under subsection (b) or in any political subdivision with respect to which such determinations have been made as a separate unit, unless the United States District Court for the District of Columbia in an action for a declaratory judgment brought by such State or subdivision against the United States has determined that no such test or device has been used during the five years preceding the filing of the action for the purpose or with the effect of denying or abridging the right to vote on account of race or color: *Provided,* That no such declaratory judgment shall issue with respect to any plaintiff for a period of five years after the entry of a final judgment of any court of the United States, other than the denial of a declaratory judgment under this section, whether entered prior to or after the enactment of this Act, determining that denials or abridgments of the right to vote on account of race or color through the use of such tests or devices have occurred anywhere in the territory of such plaintiff.

An action pursuant to this subsection shall be heard and determined by a court of three judges in accordance with the provisions of section 2284 of title 28 of the United States Code and any appeal shall lie to the Supreme Court. The court shall retain jurisdiction of any action pursuant to this subsection for five years after judgment and shall reopen the action upon motion of the Attorney General alleging that a test or device has been used for the purpose or with the effect of denying or abridging the right to vote on account of race or color.

If the Attorney General determines that he has no reason to believe that any such test or device has been used during the five years preceding the filing of the action for the purpose or with the effect of denying or abridging the right to vote on account of race or color, he shall consent to the entry of such judgment.

(b) The provisions of subsection (a) shall apply in any State or in any political subdivision of a state which (1) the Attorney General determines maintained on November 1, 1964, any test or device, and with respect to which

(2) the Director of the Census determines that less than 50 per centum of the persons of voting age residing therein were registered on November 1, 1964, or that less than 50 per centum of such persons voted in the presidential election of November 1964. A determination or certification of the Attorney General or of the Director of the Census under this section or under section 6 or section 13 shall not be reviewable in any court and shall be effective upon publication in the Federal Register.

(c) The phrase "test or device" shall mean any requirement that a person as a prerequisite for voting or registration for voting (1) demonstrate the ability to read, write, understand, or interpret any matter, (2) demonstrate any educational achievement or his knowledge of any particular subject, (3) possess good moral character, or (4) prove his qualifications by the voucher of registered voters or members of any other class. (d) For purposes of this section no State or political subdivision shall be determined to have engaged in the use of tests or devices for the purpose or with the effect of denying or abridging the right to vote on account of race or color if (1) incidents of such use have been few in number and have been promptly and effectively corrected by State or local action, (2) the continuing effect of such incidents has been eliminated, and (3) there is no reasonable probability of their recurrence in the future. (e) (1) Congress hereby declares that to secure the rights under the fourteenth amendment of persons educated in American-flag schools in which the predominant classroom language was other than English, it is necessary to prohibit the States from conditioning the right to vote of such persons on ability to read, write, understand, or interpret any matter in the English language.

(2). No person who demonstrates that he has successfully completed the sixth primary grade in a public school in, or a private school accredited by, any State or territory, the District of Columbia, or the Commonwealth of Puerto Rico in which the predominant classroom language was other than English, shall be denied the right to vote in any Federal, State, or local election because of his inability to read, write, understand, or interpret any matter in the English language, except that in States in which State law provides that a different level of education is presumptive of literacy, he shall demonstrate that he has successfully completed an equivalent level of education in a public school in, or a private school accredited by, any State or territory, the District of Columbia, or the Commonwealth of Puerto Rico in which the predominant classroom language was other than English.

[1970]

Section 4(b) of the Voting Rights Act of 1965 (79 Stat. 438; §2 U.S.C. 1973) is amended by adding at the end of the first paragraph thereof the following new sentence: "On and after August 6, 1970, in addition to any State or political subdivision of a State determined to be subject to subsection (a) pursuant to the previous sentence, the provisions of subsection (a) shall apply in any State or any political subdivision of a State which (i) the Attorney General determines maintained on November 1, 1968, any test or device, and with respect to which (ii) the Director of the Census determines that less than 50 per centum of the persons of voting age residing therein were registered on November 1, 1968, or that less than 50 per centum of such persons voted in the presidential election of November 1968."

[1975]

Section 4 (a) of the Voting Rights Act of 1965 is amended by striking out "ten" each time it appears and inserting in lieu thereof "seventeen."

Section 4 (a) of the Voting Rights Act of 1965 is amended by—
(1) inserting immediately after the "determinations have been made under" the following: "the first two sentences of";

(2) adding at the end of the first paragraph thereof the following new sentence: "No citizen shall be denied the right to vote in any Federal, State, or local election because of his failure to comply with any test or device in any State with respect to which the determinations have been made under the third sentence of subsection (b) of this section or in any political subdivision with respect to which such determinations have been made as a separate unit, unless the United States District Court for the District of Columbia in an action for a declaratory judgment brought by such State or subdivision against the United States has determined that no such test or device has been used during the ten years preceding the filing of the action

for the purpose or with the effect of denying or abridging the right to vote on account of race or color, or in contravention of the guarantees set forth in section 4(f) (2): *Provided*, That no such declaratory judgment shall issue with respect to any plaintiff for a period of ten years after the entry of a final judgment of any court of the United States, other than the denial of a declaratory judgment under this section, whether they entered prior to or after the enactment of this paragraph, determining that denials or abridgments of the right to vote on account of race or color, or in contravention of the guarantees set forth in section 4 (f) (2) through the use of tests or devices have occurred anywhere in the territory of such plaintiff";

Section 4(b) of the Voting Rights Act of 1965 is amended by adding at the end of the first paragraph thereof the following: "On and after August 6, 1975, in addition to any State or political subdivision of a State determined to be subject to subsection (a) pursuant to the previous two sentences, the provisions of subsection (a) shall apply in any State or any political subdivision of a State which (i) the Attorney General determines maintained on November 1, 1972, any test or device, and with respect to which (ii) the Director of the Census determines that less than 50 per centum of the citizens of voting age were registered on November 1, 1972, or that less than 50 per centum of such persons voted in the Presidential election of November 1972."

Section 4 of the Voting Rights Act of 1965 is amended by adding the following new subsection: "(f) (1) The Congress finds that voting discrimination against citizens of language minorities is pervasive and national in scope. Such minority citizens are from environments in which the dominant language is other than English. In addition they have been denied equal educational opportunities by State and local governments, resulting in severe disabilities and continuing illiteracy in the English language. The Congress further finds that, where State and local officials conduct elections only in English, language minority citizens are excluded from participating in the electoral process. In many areas of the country, this exclusion is aggravated by acts of physical, economic, and political intimidation. The Congress declares that, in order to enforce the guarantees of the fourteenth and fifteenth amendments to the United States Constitution, it is necessary to eliminate such discrimination by prohibiting English-only elections, and by prescribing other remedial devices. "(2) No voting qualification or prerequisite to voting, or standard, practice, or procedure shall be imposed or applied by any State or political subdivision to deny or abridge the right of any citizen of the United States to vote because he is a member of a language minority group.

"(3) In addition to the meaning given the term under section 4 (c) the term 'test or device' shall also mean any practice or requirement by which any State or political subdivision provided any registration or voting notices, forms, instructions, assistance, or other materials or information relating to the electoral process, including ballots, only in the English language, where the Director of the Census determines that more than five per centum of the citizens of voting age residing in such State or political subdivision are members of a single language minority. With respect to section 4(b), the term 'test or device,' as defined in this subsection, shall be employed only in making the determinations under the third sentence of that subsection.

"(4) Whenever any State or political subdivision subject to the prohibitions of the second sentence of section 4(a) provides any registration or voting notices, forms, instructions, assistance, or other materials or information relating to the electoral process, including ballots, it shall provide them in the language of the applicable language minority group as well as in the English language: *Provided*, That where the language of the applicable minority group is oral or unwritten, the State or political subdivision is only required to furnish oral instructions, assistance, or other information relating to registration and voting."

Section 4 (a) of the Voting Rights Act of 1965 is amended by striking out "ten" each time it appears and inserting in lieu thereof "seventeen."

SECTION 5

[1965]

Whenever a State or political subdivision with respect to which the prohibitions set forth in section 4(a) are in effect shall enact or seek to administer any voting qualification or prerequisite to voting, or standard, practice, or procedure with respect to voting different from that in force or effect on November 1, 1964, such State or subdivision may institute an action in the United States District Court for the District of Columbia for a declaratory judgment that such qualification, prerequisite, standard, practice, or procedure does not have the purpose and will not have the effect of denying or abridging the right to vote on account of race or color, and unless and until the court enters such judgment no person shall be denied the right to vote for failure to comply with such qualification, prerequisite, standard, practice, or procedure: *Provided,* That such qualification, prerequisite, standard, practice, or procedure may be enforced without such proceeding if the qualification, prerequisite, standard, practice, or procedure has been submitted by the chief legal officer or other appropriate official of such State or subdivision to the Attorney General and the Attorney General has not interposed an objection within sixty days after such submission, except that neither the Attorney General's failure to object nor a declaratory judgment entered under this section shall bar a subsequent action to enjoin enforcement of such qualification, prerequisite, standard, practice, or procedure. Any action under this section shall be heard and determined by a court of three judges in accordance with the provisions of section 2284 of title 28 of the United States Code and any appeal shall lie to the Supreme Court.

[1970]

Section 5 of the Voting Rights Act of 1965 (79 Stat. 439; 42 U.S.C. 1973) is amended by (1) inserting after "section 4(a)" the following: "based upon determinations made under the first sentence of section 4 (b)," and (2) inserting after "1964," the following: "or whenever a State or political subdivision with respect to which the prohibitions set forth in section 4(a) based upon determinations made under the second sentence of section 4(b) are in effect shall enact or seek to administer any voting qualification or prerequisite to voting, or standard, practice, or procedure with respect to voting different from that in force or effect on November 1, 1968."

[1975]

Section 5 of the Voting Rights Act of 1965 is amended by inserting after "November 1, 1968," the following: "or whenever a State or political subdivision with respect to which the prohibitions after 'November 1, 1968,' or whenever a State or political subdivision with respect to which the prohibitions set forth in section 4(a) based upon determinations made under the third sentence of section 4(b) are in effect shall enact or seek to administer any voting qualification or prerequisite to voting, or standard, practice, or procedure with respect to voting different from that in force or effect on November 1, 1972."

OTHER SECTIONS OF THE ACT
SECTION 14.

[1965]

(b) No court other than the District Court for the District of Columbia or a court of appeals in any proceeding under section 9 shall have jurisdiction to issue any declaratory judgment pursuant to section 4 or section 5 or any restraining order or temporary or permanent injunction against the execution or enforcement of any provision of this Act or any action of any Federal officer or employee pursuant hereto.

(c) (1) The terms "vote" or "voting" shall include all action necessary to make a vote effective in any primary, special, or general election, including, but not limited to, registration, listing pursuant to this Act, or other action required by law prerequisite to voting, casting a ballot, and having such ballot counted properly and included in the appropriate totals of votes cast with respect to candidates for public or party office and propositions for which votes are received in an election.

(2) The term "political subdivision" shall mean any county or parish, except that where registration for voting is not conducted under the supervision of a county or parish, the term shall include any other subdivision of a State which conducts registration for voting.

[1975]

SECTION 205. Sections 3 and 6 of the Voting Rights Act of 1965 are each amended by striking out "fifteenth amendment" each time it appears and inserting in lieu thereof "fourteenth or fifteenth amendment."

SECTION 206. Sections 2, 3, the second paragraph of section 4(a), and sections 4(d), 5, 6, and 13 of the Voting Rights Act of 1965 are each amended by adding immediately after "on account of race or color" each time it appears the following: "or in contravention of the guarantees set forth in section 4(f) (2)."

SECTION 207. Section 14(c) is amended by adding at the end the following new paragraph: "(3) The term 'language minorities' or 'language minority group' means persons who are American Indian, Asian American, Alaskan Natives or of Spanish heritage."

Fannie Lou Hamer, Rosa Parks, and Coretta Scott King Voting Rights Act Reauthorization and Amendments Act of 2006 (VRARA)

SECTION. 1. SHORT TITLE.

This Act may be cited as the "Fannie Lou Hamer, Rosa Parks, and Coretta Scott King Voting Rights Act Reauthorization and Amendments Act of 2006."

SEC. 2. CONGRESSIONAL PURPOSE AND FINDINGS.

(a) Purpose—The purpose of this Act is to ensure that the right of all citizens to vote, including the right to register to vote and cast meaningful votes, is preserved and protected as guaranteed by the Constitution.

(b) Findings—The Congress finds the following:

(1) Significant progress has been made in eliminating first generation barriers experienced by minority voters, including increased numbers of registered minority voters, minority voter turnout, and minority representation in Congress, State legislatures, and local elected offices. This progress is the direct result of the Voting Rights Act of 1965.

Sections of the VRARA not relevant to the issues discussed in this book have been omitted from the statutory language.

(2) However, vestiges of discrimination in voting continue to exist as demonstrated by second generation barriers constructed to prevent minority voters from fully participating in the electoral process.

(3) The continued evidence of racially polarized voting in each of the jurisdictions covered by the expiring provisions of the Voting Rights Act of 1965 demonstrates that racial and language minorities remain politically vulnerable, warranting the continued protection of the Voting Rights Act of 1965.

(4) Evidence of continued discrimination includes—

(A) the hundreds of objections interposed, requests for more information submitted followed by voting changes withdrawn from consideration by jurisdictions covered by the Voting Rights Act of 1965, and section 5 enforcement actions undertaken by the Department of Justice in covered jurisdictions since 1982 that prevented election practices, such as annexation, at-large voting, and the use of multi-member districts, from being enacted to dilute minority voting strength;

(B) the number of requests for declaratory judgments denied by the United States District Court for the District of Columbia;

(C) the continued filing of section 2 cases that originated in covered jurisdictions; and

(D) the litigation pursued by the Department of Justice since 1982 to enforce sections 4(e), 4(f)(4), and 203 of such Act to ensure that all language minority citizens have full access to the political process.

(5) The evidence clearly shows the continued need for Federal oversight in jurisdictions covered by the Voting Rights Act of 1965 since 1982, as demonstrated in the counties certified by the Attorney General for Federal examiner and observer coverage and the tens of thousands of Federal observers that have been dispatched to observe elections in covered jurisdictions.

(6) The effectiveness of the Voting Rights Act of 1965 has been significantly weakened by the United States Supreme Court decisions in *Reno v. Bossier Parish II* and *Georgia v. Ashcroft*, which have misconstrued Congress' original intent in enacting the Voting Rights Act of 1965 and narrowed the protections afforded by section 5 of such Act.

(7) Despite the progress made by minorities under the Voting Rights Act of 1965, the evidence before Congress reveals that 40 years has not been a sufficient amount of time to eliminate the vestiges of discrimination following nearly 100 years of disregard for the dictates of the 15th amendment and to ensure that the right of all citizens to vote is protected as guaranteed by the Constitution.

(8) Present day discrimination experienced by racial and language minority voters is contained in evidence, including the objections interposed by the Department of Justice in covered jurisdictions; the section 2 litigation filed to prevent dilutive techniques from adversely affecting minority voters; the enforcement actions filed to protect language minorities; and the tens of thousands of Federal observers dispatched to monitor polls in jurisdictions covered by the Voting Rights Act of 1965.

(9) The record compiled by Congress demonstrates that, without the continuation of the Voting Rights Act of 1965 protections, racial and language minority citizens will be deprived of the opportunity to exercise their right to vote, or will have their votes diluted, undermining the significant gains made by minorities in the last 40 years.

SEC. 4. RECONSIDERATION OF SECTION 4 BY CONGRESS.

Paragraphs (7) and (8) of section 4(a) of the Voting Rights Act of 1965 (42 U.S.C. 1973b(a)) are each amended by striking "Voting Rights Act Amendments of 1982" and inserting "Fannie Lou Hamer, Rosa Parks, and Coretta Scott King Voting Rights Act Reauthorization and Amendments Act of 2006."

242 VOTING RIGHTS—AND WRONGS

SEC. 5. CRITERIA FOR DECLARATORY JUDGMENT.

Section 5 of the Voting Rights Act of 1965 (42 U.S.C. 1973c) is amended—

(1) by inserting "(a)" before "Whenever";

(2) by striking "does not have the purpose and will not have the effect" and inserting "neither has the purpose nor will have the effect"; and

(3) by adding at the end the following:

> "(b) Any voting qualification or prerequisite to voting, or standard, practice, or procedure with respect to voting that has the purpose of or will have the effect of diminishing the ability of any citizens of the United States on account of race or color, or in contravention of the guarantees set forth in section 4(f)(2), to elect their preferred candidates of choice denies or abridges the right to vote within the meaning of subsection (a) of this section.

> "(c) The term 'purpose' in subsections (a) and (b) of this section shall include any discriminatory purpose.

> "(d) The purpose of subsection (b) of this section is to protect the ability of such citizens to elect their preferred candidates of choice."

PURPOSE AND SUMMARY

The purpose of H.R. 9 is to: (1) extend Section 4(a)(8) and Section 203(b)(1), the temporary provisions of the Voting Rights Act of 1965 currently set to expire on August 6, 2007, for another 25 years; and (2) amend Section 3(a), Section 4, Section 5, Section 6, Section 7, Section 8, Section 9, Section 14, and Section 203. These changes are necessary to update certain provisions of the Voting Rights Act of 1965 (the "VRA") to reflect the current voting environment and to restore the original intent of Congress in enacting the temporary provisions of the VRA.

Notes

Introduction

1. David L. Epstein, Richard H. Pildes, Rodolfo O. de Garza, and Sharyn O'Halloran, eds., introduction to *The Future of the Voting Rights Act* (New York: Russell Sage Foundation, 2006), xiv.

2. Kevin Merida, "America's History Gives Way to Its Future," *Washington Post*, November 5, 2008, A01.

3. Steve Cohen, a Democrat from Tennessee, is currently the only white member of the U.S. House of Representatives elected from a majority-black district. His 60 percent African-American district includes Memphis, and he gained his congressional seat in 2006 after a crowded field of black candidates splintered the vote. With a voting record that the Leadership Conference on Civil Rights called the most liberal in the state, he was reelected in 2008. See Leadership Conference on Civil Rights, LCCR Voting Record, 33, http://www.civilrights.org/resources/voting/2008/lccr_voting_record_110th_congress.pdf (accessed December 22, 2008). One might think that the winner in a majority-black district would be regarded as speaking for black interests, but Representative Cohen's request to join the Congressional Black Caucus was rejected. See Michael Barone, ed., *The Almanac of American Politics 2008*, web edition, NationalJournal.com, entry for Steve Cohen.

4. "In four southern states, Alabama, Arkansas, Louisiana and Mississippi, [Obama] received a smaller share of the white vote than John Kerry received in 2004. Given the political environment of 2008, these results certainly suggest that the race variable was a factor," political scientist David A. Bositis concluded in an analysis of the 2008 election returns. *Blacks and the 2008 Elections: A Preliminary Analysis* (Washington, D.C.: Joint Center for Political and Economic Studies, 2008). But the issues were not the same in the two elections, and while race may have been a factor, it was certainly not decisive, since those four states were safely Republican.

5. *Brown v. Board of Education*, 347 U.S. 483 (1964). For registration figures prior to 1965, see U.S. Commission on Civil Rights, *The Voting Rights Act: Ten Years After* (Washington, D.C.: Government Printing Office, 1975), 43, table 3; and Stephan Thernstrom and Abigail Thernstrom, *America in Black and White: One Nation, Indivisible*

(New York: Simon and Schuster, 1987), 152. It should be noted that estimates of black registration and turnout prior to the passage of the Voting Rights Act vary widely. Figures are drawn from unofficial estimates by county personnel, the Justice Department, the Voter Education Project, and other unofficial sources. Only Louisiana kept official data on registration by race in 1965. Pre-act progress was greatest in the large cities and least in rural areas, particularly those with a high percentage of blacks. In only two states—Florida and Tennessee—was black registration above 50 percent. In the region as a whole in 1964, the voting-age black registration rate had risen to 42 percent, but it remained abysmally low (under 7 percent) in Mississippi, most notably.

6. For an extensive discussion of this history see Thernstrom and Thernstrom, *America in Black and White*, chapters 1–6.

7. The Civil Rights Act of 1957 did authorize the Department of Justice to bring suits on behalf of citizens denied the right to vote on account of race, but such lawsuits were extremely time-consuming, and federal district judges were generally hostile to black voting rights. Relief depended on courts of appeal. Thus, although the Justice Department filed seventy-one suits in the years 1958–64, southern black registration levels remained exceedingly low. Title I of the 1964 Civil Rights Act additionally barred unequal application of voter registration requirements, but still left enforcement up to local federal judges, who were instructed "to assign the case for hearing at the earliest practicable date and to cause the case to be in every way expedited." The instruction amounted, in effect, to an invitation to foot-dragging; in addition, the statute did nothing to eliminate literacy tests and other barriers to registration.

8. Lisa Cozzens, "The Civil Rights Movement 1955–1965: Selma," in *African American History: A Project Documenting Important Events in African American History*, http://www.watson.org/~lisa/blackhistory/civilrights-55-65/selma.html (accessed March 19, 2009).

9. For questions about the legitimacy of the 1964 act, see, for example, Richard A. Epstein, *Forbidden Grounds: The Case against Employment Discrimination Law* (Cambridge, Mass.: Harvard University Press, 1992). Justice Black and other congressional southerners, in objecting to the bill, saw the ghost of Reconstruction. See, for a discussion of the point, Abigail Thernstrom, *Whose Votes Count? Affirmative Action and Minority Voting Rights* (Cambridge, Mass.: Harvard University Press, 1987), 19–20. But Justice Black (from Alabama) made a constitutionally serious argument when the Supreme Court reviewed the constitutionality of the statute in 1966. His concurring and dissenting opinion in *South Carolina v. Katzenbach*, 383 U.S. 301 (1966), will be discussed in chapter 1.

10. *City of Boerne v. Flores*, 521 U.S. 507 (1997).

11. Carl M. Brauer, *John F. Kennedy and the Second Reconstruction* (New York: Columbia University Press, 1977), 118.

12. Frank R. Parker, *Black Votes Count: Political Empowerment in Mississippi after 1965* (Chapel Hill: University of North Carolina Press, 1990), 25. Freedom Summer was also instrumental in the formation of the Mississippi Freedom Democratic Party (MFDP),

which unsuccessfully challenged the all-white official state delegation at the 1964 Democratic National Convention. Ibid., 25–26.

13. Martin Luther King Jr., "I Have a Dream" (speech at the Lincoln Memorial, Washington, D.C., August 28, 1963).

14. U.S. Commission on Civil Rights, *The Voting Rights Act: Ten Years After*, 43. Other states showed more modest gains mainly because the starting point was higher black registration than in Mississippi. Thus, black registration in Alabama, for instance, was an estimated 19.3 percent in March 1965, but rose to 51.6 percent two years later.

15. The Tenth Amendment to the Constitution states that "powers not delegated to the United States . . . are reserved to the States respectively, or to the people."

16. Nathaniel Persily, *The Promise and Pitfalls of the New Voting Rights Act*, 117 Yale L.J. 174, 177 (2007).

17. In fact, when section 5 was renewed for the third time in 1982, many representatives of the civil rights community voiced their frustration with the temporary nature of preclearance. For instance, in 1980, the President's Commission for a National Agenda, chaired by Benjamin Hooks, referred to the temporary status of the special provisions as a "built-in defect" that marred the act. President's Commission for a National Agenda for the Eighties, *Report of the Panel on Government for the Advancement of Social Justice, Health, Welfare, Education, and Civil Rights* (Washington, D.C.: Government Printing Office, 1980), 15. For other examples, see Thernstrom, *Whose Votes Count?* 93.

18. *Katzenbach*, 383 U.S. at 334.

19. These explicitly named "language-minority groups" were entitled to federal protection against changes in election law that were arguably discriminatory in intent or effect, but only where they comprised more than 5 percent of the population in a jurisdiction covered by section 5.

20. *Beer v. United States*, 425 U.S. 130, 141 (1976).

21. My focus here is entirely on the near-unanimity behind the renewal of section 5. There are topics I do not cover in this book, and one of them is section 203, which governs the provision of bilingual ballots and other election materials. A majority of Republicans in the House wanted to see that provision amended. On the question of amending section 203, see Roger Clegg and Linda Chavez, *An Analysis of the Reauthorized Sections 5 and 203 of the Voting Rights Act of 1965: Bad Policy and Unconstitutional*, 5 Geo. J.L. & Pub. Pol'y 561 (2007).

22. *Johnson v. De Grandy*, 512 U.S. 997, 1020 (1994).

23. "The 1963 Inaugural Address of Governor George C. Wallace," Alabama Department of Archives and History, http://www.archives.state.al.us/govs_list/inaugural speech.html (accessed January 2, 2009).

24. Letter from H. Lee Scott Jr. to George W. Bush, June 7, 2005, posted to Votelaw.com by Edward Still, June 16, 2005, http://www.votelaw.com/blog/blogdocs/Wal-Mart%20letter.pdf (accessed January 14, 2008). Of course, Scott's letter would not merit our attention if only he had drawn such a misleading picture of an expiring Voting Rights Act, but he had plenty of company. See, for instance, Kevin C.

Peterson, "Renew Voting Rights Act Now," *Boston Globe*, March 26, 2005, A11 ("Nearly 40 years old, the Voting Rights Act is scheduled to expire in 2007"); and Jesse Jackson, "Republicans Maneuvering to Get Voting Rights Act Killed," *Chicago Sun Times*, March 8, 2005 ("In 2007, the Voting Rights Act must be reauthorized"). The ACLU in March 2005 did acknowledge that the issue involved only "portions" of the statute up for renewal, but its press release included the following quote from the director of the organization's national office: "Voting gives citizens a voice in the national dialogue, and if the Voting Rights Act expires, that important voice will be silenced." Organizations for civil rights, women's rights, and labor, the press release continued, "are calling for a reauthorization of the Voting Rights Act of 1965." American Civil Liberties Union, "ACLU Joins National Call for the Renewal of the Voting Rights Act; Stands with Civil Rights, Women's Rights and Labor Organizations," press release, March 21, 2005, http://www.aclu.org/VotingRights/VotingRights.cfm?ID=17777&c=32 (accessed January 10, 2008). Some of the misleading rhetoric was clearly politically calculated—part of an effort to rally the troops and pressure members of Congress—but some seems to have represented genuine confusion.

25. United States House of Representatives Judiciary Committee, Subcommittee on the Constitution, H. R. Rep. 109-478, at 6 (2006).

26. Voting Rights Act Reauthorization and Amendments Act, Pub. L. No. 109-246, § 2(b)(2), 120 Stat. 577, 577 (2006) (codified at 42 U.S.C. § 1973c) ("2006 Amendments").

27. Charles S. Bullock III and Ronald Keith Gaddie, *Good Intentions and Bad Social Science Meet in the Renewal of the Voting Rights Act*, 5 Geo. J.L. & Pub. Pol'y 1, at 4, 6 (2007).

28. On S. 53, S. 1761, S. 1992, and H.R. 3112. Bills to Amend the Voting Rights Act of 1965: Hearings on the Voting Rights Act Before the Subcomm. on the Constitution of the S. Comm. on the Judiciary, 97th Cong., 1, 444 (1982) (testimony of Barry Gross, Professor, York College, City University of New York) (hereafter 1982 Senate hearings).

29. Ibid., 1247. The "horizons of trust" argument is from Michael Walzer, *Spheres of Justice: A Defense of Pluralism and Equality* (New York: Basic Books, 1983), 149–50.

30. Vanderbilt Law School professor James Blumstein made this point at the 1982 Senate hearings, declaring that the substitution of discriminatory effect for that of intent turned a "fair shake" into a "fair share." 1982 Senate hearings, 1334.

31. *Hirabayashi v. United States*, 320 U.S. 81, 100 (1943).

32. *Thornburg v. Gingles*, 478 U.S. 30, 75 n.35 (1986).

33. Ibid., 40. It is not possible to create a timeline of racial change showing the clear point at which black political exclusion switches to black participation. Different scholars read the data differently. I am impressed by the level of black electoral success in overwhelmingly white multimember districts in North Carolina in 1982. On the other hand, testifying at 2006 Senate hearings on the VRARA, voting rights scholar Richard Pildes stated, "Even in 1982, blacks were still virtually invisible in elective offices; the South remained, for state and local elections, the virtual one-party monopoly it had

been throughout the 20th century." On the Continuing Need for Section 5 Pre-Clearance, Hearing on S. 2703 before the S. Comm. on the Judiciary, 109th Cong. (May 16, 2006) (testimony of Professor Richard H. Pildes, Sudler Family Professor of Constitutional Law, NYU School of Law). The important point is that by now, surely, the line dividing exclusion from inclusion has been clearly crossed.

34. "Is an All White Congress Inevitable?" *Ethnic NewsWatch: New York Beacon* 2, no. 96 (December 13, 1995): 2.

35. The "max-black" description is quoted in *Miller v. Johnson*, 515 U.S. 900, 907 (1995).

36. The two outside the South were in Maryland and Pennsylvania. Alabama, Louisiana, South Carolina, Texas, and Virginia each created one; Georgia and North Carolina, two apiece; Florida, three.

37. This point is made at greater length on the page in *Whose Votes Count?* (239) from which the Tom McCain quotation is taken. The source of the quote was the American Civil Liberties Union, *Civil Liberties*, June 1981.

38. *Regents of the Univ. of Cal. v. Bakke*, 438 U.S. 265, 407 (1978) (Blackmun, J., concurring in part, dissenting in part).

39. *Green v. County School Board*, 391 U.S. 430 (1968); *Swann v. Charlotte-Mecklenburg Board of Education*, 401 U.S. 1 (1971).

40. *City of Richmond v. J. A. Croson Co.*, 488 U.S. 469, 524 (1989) (Scalia, J., concurring). The case involved municipal contracting set-asides; Scalia provided the school desegregation example in distinguishing legitimate from illegitimate race-conscious policies.

41. See *Grutter v. Bollinger*, 539 U.S. 306 (2003), and *Gratz v. Bollinger*, 539 U.S. 244 (2003).

42. See Abigail Thernstrom and Stephan Thernstrom, "Secrecy and Dishonesty: The Supreme Court, Racial Preferences, and Higher Education," *Constitutional Commentary* (Symposium: From *Brown* to *Bakke* to *Grutter*: Constitutionalizing and Defining Racial Equality, Spring 2004), 251–74; Stephan Thernstrom and Abigail Thernstrom, *Reflections on The Shape of the River*, 46 UCLA L. Rev. 1583, 1583–1632 (1999).

43. *Georgia v. Ashcroft*, 195 F. Supp. 2d 25, 92 (D.D.C. 2002). It is important to note, however, that Lewis took the point back later when the proposed 2006 VRARA was before Congress, and voting rights advocates were successfully working to overturn the Supreme Court's 2003 decision that adopted the view of Lewis and black state legislators.

44. Charles S. Bullock and Mark J. Rozell, eds., *The New Politics of the Old South: An Introduction to Southern Politics*, 2d edition (New York: Rowman and Littlefield, 2003), 12. As Bullock and Rozell have noted, "Since the implementation of the 1965 Voting Rights Act, black votes have become the mainstay of the Democratic Party—the vote without which few Democrats can win statewide" (1).

45. In the North, urban majority-black districts are more likely to abut areas dominated by white liberals. In 1987 in *Whose Votes Count?* I argued that Republicans

benefited politically from racially gerrymandered districts in the South. At the time, my point about Republican gains was widely dismissed, but by now it is a well-understood phenomenon, although different scholars estimate Republican gains as a consequence of majority-minority districts differently. For a discussion of the varying estimates with respect to the 1992 and 1994 congressional races, see David Lublin, *The Paradox of Representation: Racial Gerrymandering and Minority Interests in Congress* (Princeton, N.J.: Princeton University Press, 1997), 111–12. Lublin estimates that racial redistricting accounted for at least half of the Republican gains in 1992. On the rise of the Republicans in the South, see Earl Black and Merle Black, *The Rise of Southern Republicans* (Cambridge, Mass.: Harvard University Press, 2002).

46. Richard Thompson Ford, *The Race Card: How Bluffing about Bias Makes Race Relations Worse* (New York: Farrar, Straus and Giroux, 2008), 277. "Taking the 1896 Supreme Court opinion in *Plessy v. Ferguson* one better, the claim here is not separate *but* equal; it is separate *therefore* equal," Ford continues.

47. *National Journal*, "Minority Groups in the House," March 3, 2007, NationalJournal.com/voteratings/pdf/06womenminorities.pdf (accessed June 5, 2008).

48. Lublin, *The Paradox of Representation*, 36.

49. Gwen Ifill, *The Breakthrough: Politics and Race in the Age of Obama* (Amazon Kindle edition, 2009), location 3641–46.

50. *League of United Latin American Citizens v. Clements*, 999 F.2d 831, 837 (5th Cir. 1993) (en banc).

51. *Shaw v. Reno*, 509 U.S 630, 646–47 (1993).

52. Ibid., 643.

53. Ibid., 674 (White, J., dissenting). He was quoting from *Gaffney v. Cummings*, 412 U.S. 735, 754 (1973).

54. Gunnar Myrdal, *An American Dilemma* (New York: Harper and Row, 1944).

55. Richard Pildes, *The Future of Voting Rights Policy: From Anti-Discrimination to the Right to Vote*, 49 How. L.J. 741, 748 (2006). Rather than the 2006 renewal and amendment of section 5, Pildes would have preferred a shift from process to substance with legislation modeled on the 1993 National Voter Registration Act or the 2002 Help America Vote Act. I do not mean to suggest, however, that there were not section 2 suits in the North as well as South, but the Voting Rights Act was irrelevant to the voting problems that have made national news—as in Ohio in 2004.

56. *Gingles*, 478 U.S. 30. I have simplified the holding, which will be discussed at length in chapter 3, but the bottom line is as I describe it.

57. Motion for Leave to File a Brief and Brief of the NAACP, Cindy Moore, Milford Farrior, and Mary Jordan as Amici Curiae, in support of Petitioners, *Bartlett v. Strickland*, 129 S. Ct. 1231 (2009) No. 07-689. *Bartlett* will be discussed in the conclusion.

58. *Vecinos De Barrio Uno v. City of Holyoke*, 72 F.3d 973, 977 (1st Cir. 1995).

Chapter 1: The Fundamentals

1. "President Lyndon B. Johnson's Remarks in the Capitol Rotunda at the Signing of the Voting Rights Act, August 6, 1965," Lyndon Baines Johnson Library and Museum, National Archives and Records Administration, http://www.lbjlib.utexas.edu/johnson/archives.hom/speeches.hom/650806.asp (accessed May 16, 2008).

2. This discussion of the structure and logic of the act borrows heavily from Abigail Thernstrom, *Whose Votes Count? Affirmative Action and Minority Voting Rights* (Cambridge, Mass.: Harvard University Press, 1987).

3. *Allen v. State Board of Elections*, 393 U.S. 544 (1969).

4. That single aim was apparent throughout the 1965 congressional hearings, as the introduction noted. See H.R. 6400 and Other Proposals to Enforce the Fifteenth Amendment to the Constitution of the United States: Hearings before Subcomm. No. 5 of the H. Comm. on the Judiciary, 89th Cong., 17, 21 (1965) (hereafter cited as 1965 House hearings). Witnesses poured forth in detail the continuing obstacles to rudimentary electoral participation.

5. U.S. Commission on Civil Rights, *The Voting Rights Act: Ten Years After* (Washington, D.C.: Government Printing Office, 1975), 43, table 3 (hereafter cited as USCCR, VRA), and U.S. Department of Commerce, *Statistical Abstract of the United States: 1970* (Washington, D.C.: U.S. Government Printing Office, 1970), 369.

6. As was mentioned above, in the introduction. How widespread those fears were is impossible to tell. In February 2006, the Frederick Douglass Republican Club of Central Florida said it was trying to counteract the rumor that if the temporary provisions were not renewed, blacks would lose the right to vote. Bill Rufty, "Voting Rights Act Deadline Creates a Stir: Black Republicans Club Works to Spread the Word Minorities Won't Lose the Right to Vote," *The Ledger* (Lakeland, Fla.), February 20, 2006, http://www.theledger.com/article/20060220/NEWS/602200373&SearchID= 73313460763226 (accessed May 16, 2008). The NAACP Legal Defense and Educational Fund also acknowledged "myths . . . circulating that African Americans will lose their right to vote in 2007, or that the Voting Rights Act expires in 2007," and went on to say that "these rumors are false." NAACP Legal Defense and Educational Fund, "Dispelling Myths about the Voting Rights Act," June 1, 2004, http://www.naacpldf.org/content.aspx?article=313 (accessed May 16, 2008). Nonetheless, some in the civil rights community certainly did their best to obscure the fact that the core provisions of the Voting Rights Act were permanent. Thus, shortly before the 2004 elections, the local NAACP branch in Tacoma, Washington, sent out a newsletter that contained an excerpt from a speech by Camille Cosby in which she declared, "In the year 2007 we could lose the Right to vote!" and urged black voters to contact members of Congress. Tacoma Branch NAACP, "Voting Rights: Will We Still Have Them in 2007?" *Tacoma Branch NAACP Newsletter,* September 3, 2004, http://www.tacoma-naacp.org/docs/naacpSept04.pdf (accessed February 5, 2008). The rumor was of sufficient concern to the U.S. Justice Department that it

posted a "clarification" on its website saying, "The voting rights of African Americans are guaranteed by the United States Constitution and the Voting Rights Act, and those guarantees are permanent and do not expire." U.S. Department of Justice, Civil Rights Division Voting Section, "Voting Rights Act Clarification" (undated, accessed June 1, 2006), http://www.usdoj.gov/crt/voting/misc/ clarify3.htm.

7. Rather confusingly, the statute did not contain a section 1, although it can be said that its opening title ("An act to enforce the fifteenth amendment to the Constitution of the United States, and for other purposes") was, in effect, section 1, although not labeled as such. In addition to sections 2 and 3, the permanent provisions included section 208, which enabled illiterate voters to have someone of their choice assist them at the polls. Other permanent sections provided for criminal and civil penalties for stopping otherwise eligible citizens from voting. Section 3, in addition to enabling a court to certify a jurisdiction for examiners (registrars) and observers, allowed the judicial imposition of the preclearance provision on jurisdictions not otherwise covered. Preclearance will be explained in subsequent pages. The core of the statute was the enforcement of Fifteenth Amendment rights, but the equal protection clause of the Fourteenth Amendment was relevant to certain provisions. Thus, the act stated, "Congress hereby declares that to secure the rights under the fourteenth amendment of persons educated in American-flag schools [in Puerto Rico, mainly] in which the predominant classroom language was other than English, it is necessary to prohibit the States from conditioning the right to vote of such persons on ability to read, write, understand, or interpret any matter in the English language" (sections 4 and 203).

8. The statutory language refers to total voting-age population registration or turnout (black and white together), but the registration figure was, in fact, irrelevant. If any southern state had had registration of, say, 51 percent, but turnout of only 30 percent, that turnout of under 50 percent would trigger coverage.

9. The constitutionality of literacy tests was upheld in *Lassiter v. Northampton County Board of Elections*, 306 U.S. 45 (1959). Every historian of voting in the South prior to the passage of the 1965 act has noted the fraudulent nature of the southern literacy test. See, for example, V. O. Key, who in his seminal 1949 work on southern politics said that "no matter from what direction one looks at it, the Southern literacy test is a fraud and nothing more." Key, *Southern Politics in State and Nation* (New York: Vintage Books, 1949), 576.

10. H. Comm. on the Judiciary, The Voting Rights Act of 1965, H.R. Rep. 89-439, at 45 (1965) (Republican views).

11. Examiners were last used in 1982 and 1983 to register voters in only eight counties nationwide. U.S. Commission on Civil Rights, *Voting Rights Enforcement and Reauthorization* (Washington, D.C.: Government Printing Office, 2006), 53. The National Voter Registration Act of 1993 now governs registration procedures. On the other hand, as the report points out, the Department of Justice continues to send observers, who are hired by the U.S. Office of Personnel Management (OPM), to monitor elections. Indeed, despite the fact that the attorney general's power (in contrast to

that of a federal court) extends only to the jurisdictions covered by the special, temporary provisions, the DOJ sends its own staff lawyers to locations not identified by the section 4 trigger, by agreement with the jurisdictions themselves.

12. See introduction. Originally, section 5 applied only to Alabama, Georgia, Louisiana, Mississippi, South Carolina, Virginia, and most counties in North Carolina. These were the jurisdictions identified in 1965 by the section 4 statistical trigger.

13. 1965 House hearings, 60.

14. Ibid.

15. Ibid., 379.

16. Ibid., 456.

17. *South Carolina v. Katzenbach*, 383 U.S. 301, 309 (1966).

18. Ibid., 358.

19. It is because a judge from the D.C. Court of Appeals already sits on the three-judge panel that appeals from the decisions of the lower court go directly to the Supreme Court, 42 U.S.C. § 1973c(a), but the appeal must be filed within sixty days of a final district court decision, 28 U.S.C. § 2101(b). The sixty-day requirement has been an issue in several suits. See, for instance, *Riley v. Kennedy*, 128 S.Ct. 1970 (2008).

20. Daniel Hays Lowenstein, *You Don't Have to Be Liberal to Hate the Racial Gerrymandering Cases*, 50 Stan. L. Rev. 779, 814 (1998).

21. This is an old story. See Howard Ball, Dale Krane, and Thomas P. Lauth, *Compromised Compliance: Implementation of the 1965 Voting Rights Act* (Westport, Conn.: Greenwood Press, 1982), 79. That the process has remained as it was more than two decades ago has been confirmed for me through confidential conversations with current members of the voting section of the DOJ.

22. USCCR, VRA, 43.

23. *Allen*, 393 U.S. 544.

24. In an at-large system, the institution of which was a central issue in *Allen*, all voters in the jurisdiction choose all representatives on the county council or other governing body. In some at-large systems, a candidate must run for a specific seat and reside in a district to which the seat is assigned, although voters in every district elect such candidates. That modification prevents all candidates from living in the same neighborhood. In a system of single-member districts, the political unit—a city, for instance—is divided into districts, each of which elects one representative to the governing body. The institution of countywide voting as a replacement for single-member districts was the central issue in *Allen*. But, over time, the list of changes covered by section 5 became extensive. The provision now covers changes

- in redistricting plans;
- in the method of electing officials;
- in the designation of public officials as appointed or elected;
- in the number of elected officials;
- in municipal boundaries, through a process of annexation or deannexation that alters the voting constituency for electing officials;

- in voting precinct lines, polling place locations, and absentee or early-voting rules;
- in the format of ballots and the rules governing them;
- in the rules governing the discretionary setting of special-election dates;
- in voter registration procedures;
- in the procedures and standards for becoming a candidate for elective office;
- in campaign finance requirements;
- in rules governing ballot initiatives, referenda, and recall procedures adopted by political parties that relate to their public electoral functions;
- and in the languages in which jurisdictions provide voting materials and information to the public.

However, changes ordered by a federal court that do not reflect the policy choices of the covered jurisdiction do not require preclearance—see *Connor v. Johnson*, 402 U.S. 690 (1971)—nor do changes in the powers and duties of elected officials—see *Presley v. Etowah County*, 502 U.S. 491 (1992).

25. Since, as noted above, jurisdictions so seldom use the D.C. court to obtain preclearance, I simply assume throughout much of this book that the Justice Department is the relevant actor.

26. *Reynolds v. Sims*, 377 U.S. 533 (1964). As Daniel Hays Lowenstein has pointed out in an analysis of *Davis v. Bandemer*, 478 U.S. 109 (1986), a 1986 partisan gerrymandering case, in *Reynolds v. Sims* "the Court was invalidating discrimination against individuals rather than groups; it was vindicating voting rights that were 'individual and personal in nature.'" *Reynolds* and other malapportionment cases thus need to be distinguished from those involving group electoral inequality. Lowenstein, "Bandemer's Gap: Gerrymandering and Equal Protection," in *Political Gerrymandering and the Courts*, ed. Bernard Grofman (New York: Agathon Press, 1990), 70.

27. "The effect of state legislative districting schemes which give the same number of representatives to unequal numbers of constituents" is that the right to vote of those living in a densely populated district "is simply not the same right to vote as that of those living in a [sparsely populated] part of the State. Two, five, or 10 of them must vote before the effect of their voting is equivalent to that of their favored neighbor." *Reynolds*, 377 U.S. at 563. "Full and effective participation by all citizens in state government requires . . . that each citizen have an equally effective voice in the election of members of his state legislature." Ibid., 565.

28. Ibid.

29. Justice Harlan's precise words were, "People are not ciphers and . . . legislators can represent their electors only by speaking for their interests—economic, social, political— many of which do reflect the place where the electors live. The Court does not establish, or indeed even attempt to make a case for the proposition that conflicting interests within a State can only be adjusted by disregarding them when voters are grouped for purposes of representation." Ibid., 623–24.

30. *Allen*, 393 U.S. at 569.

31. The jurisdictions newly covered as a consequence of the 1970 amendments comprised four districts in Alaska, eight counties in Arizona, two counties in California,

three counties in Connecticut, one county in Idaho, ten towns in New Hampshire, three counties in New York, eighteen towns in Maine, nine towns in Massachusetts, and one county in Wyoming. There were two other amendments, though not relevant here. The first lowered the voting age to eighteen; it was later struck down as partially unconstitutional but was revived as a constitutional amendment. See *Oregon v. Mitchell*, 400 U.S. 112 (1970), in which the Supreme Court held that states could set their own age limits for state elections. The second abolished durational residency requirements in voting for president and vice president.

32. *United Jewish Organizations v. Carey*, 430 U.S. 144, 151–52 (1977).

33. As will be noted below, bilingual ballots were regarded by voting rights advocates as an inadequate remedy because they did not address the problem of alleged language-minority group "disfranchisement" by districting plans and other methods of voting said to dilute the impact of the Hispanic vote. "A provision for bilingual ballots was thus only one component in the package of changes in 1975." Bilingual election materials were required in every state or county that met the criteria of the new trigger: English-only ballots and a language-minority concentration, combined with low voter turnout. Bilingual ballots and other materials were also required in every county (whatever the level of electoral participation) where the language-minority citizens had an illiteracy rate higher than the national average. Section 203 of the Voting Rights Act defined illiteracy as "failure to complete the fifth primary grade." This book does not address the question of the need for such ballots.

34. Confidential interview conducted by the author, May 1981. This and other interviews cited in this book took place in the course of researching *Whose Votes Count?*

35. Other leading civil rights spokesmen concurred with the MALDEF representative. Joseph Rauh, counsel for the Leadership Council on Civil Rights, admitted, "You do not have the same situation . . . the murders, the awful things that happened to blacks." Extension of the Voting Rights Act: Hearings on S. 407, S. 903, S. 1297, and S. 1443, Before the Subcomm. on Constitutional Rights of the S. Comm. on the Judiciary, 94th Cong. 60 (1975) (hereafter cited as 1975 Senate hearings). A U.S. Commission on Civil Rights memorandum made the same point: "Statistics on [language] minority registration and voting and the election of minorities to office do not paint the shocking picture that, for example, the 1965 statistics on [blacks in] Mississippi did." U.S. Commission on Civil Rights, "Expansion of the Coverage of the Voting Rights Act," staff memorandum, 47 (June 5, 1975).

36. 1975 Senate hearings, 543–44.

37. H. Comm. on the Judiciary, "Voting Rights Act Extension," H.R. Rep. No. 94-196 at 30 (1975) (hereafter cited as House Judiciary Committee report).

38. S. Comm. on the Judiciary, "Voting Rights Extension," S. Rep. No. 94-295 at 24 (1975).

39. House Judiciary Committee report, 18.

40. 1975 Senate hearings, 8.

41. Ibid., 162.

42. Extension of the Voting Rights Act: Hearings on H.R. 939, H.R. 2148, H.R. 3247, and H.R. 3501 Before the Subcomm. on Civil and Constitutional Rights of the H. Comm. on the Judiciary, 94th Cong. 26 (1975) (hereafter cited as 1975 House hearings).

43. The fact that some Hispanics thought of themselves as white affected their sense of group solidarity, and their relative economic mobility lessened their dependence on ethnic politics as an avenue of advancement. In addition, considerable residential integration made majority-Hispanic districts harder to draw. The scholarly literature on the Mexican-American experience prior to the amendments of 1975 includes Clifton McClesky and Bruce Merrill, "Mexican American Political Behavior in Texas," *Social Science Quarterly* 53 (March 1973): 785–98; O. Douglas Weeks, "The Texas-Mexican and the Politics of South Texas," *American Political Science Review* 24 (August 1930): 606–27; Harry P. Pachon, "Political Mobilization in the Mexican-American Community," and Donald Horowitz, "Conflict and Accommodation: Mexican-Americans in the Cosmopolis," in *Mexican-Americans in Comparative Perspective*, ed. Walker Connor (Washington, D.C.: Urban Institute Press, 1985); Harry P. Pachon and Joan W. Moore, "Mexican-Americans," *Annals of the American Academy of Political and Social Science* 454, no. 1 (March 1981): 111–24; Leo Grebler, Joan W. Moore, and Ralph Guzman, *The Mexican-American People* (Glencoe, Ill.: Free Press, 1970); George Antunes and Charles M. Gaitz, "Ethnicity and Participation: A Study of Mexican-Americans, Blacks, and Whites," *American Journal of Sociology* 80, no. 5 (March 1975): 1192–1211; Delbert Taebel, "Minority Representation on City Councils: The Impact of Structure on Blacks and Hispanics," *Social Science Quarterly* 59 (June 1978): 142–52; and Peter Skerry, *Mexican-Americans: The Ambivalent Minority* (New York: Free Press, 1993).

44. House Judiciary Committee report, 19. "These structures effectively *deny* Mexican-American and black voters in Texas political access," the report said (emphasis added). The reference to the numbered-place system was to at-large systems in which a candidate runs for a specific seat and must reside in the district to which the seat is assigned, although voters in every district elect that candidate. That modification prevents all candidates from living in the same neighborhood, as noted in note 24, above. The majority runoff rule prevents candidates who receive a plurality of votes from taking seats. So take, for instance, a citywide (at-large) election, with five open seats but only one Hispanic candidate. If Hispanics choose to concentrate all their ballots on that one candidate (a strategy called bullet voting), ignoring their option to participate in the white-on-white contests for other seats, their candidate will not have won if he or she received only a plurality of the votes. The system requires a runoff, and, in a majority-white city, the Hispanic candidate might fail to get a majority in that second round of voting.

45. *Reynolds*, 377 U.S. at 565. That one-person, one-vote decision provided the theoretical foundation for the constitutional cases involving minority-vote dilution, as well as for *Allen* and others resting on section 5.

46. *White v. Regester*, 412 U.S. 755, 766 (1973).

47. Ibid., 768.

48. *City of Mobile v. Bolden*, 446 U.S. 55 (1980).

49. 42 U.S.C. § 1973 (1982).

50. Impact can, of course, indicate illicit purpose, the Supreme Court has recognized. And thus the Court in *Mobile v. Bolden* acknowledged that racially disparate effect is an important starting point in an equal protection inquiry, citing both *Washington v. Davis*, 426 U.S. 229, 242 (1976), and *Arlington Heights v. Metropolitan Housing Development Corp.*, 429 U.S. 252, 264–65 (1977). It noted, however, that "where the character of a law is readily explainable on grounds apart from race, as would nearly always be true where, as here, an entire system of local governance is brought into question, disproportionate impact alone cannot be decisive, and courts must look to other evidence to support a finding of discriminatory purpose." *Bolden*, 446 U.S. at 70.

51. Substituting at-large elections for voting by ward was a favorite cause of municipal reformers in the Progressive Era. Citywide voting was implemented in a great many cities, large and small, as part of the "good government" attack on corrupt urban political machines. Elected officials who were not dependent upon the electorate in a single ward, reformers thought, would be less parochial and have a larger vision of the interests of the city as a whole. A thinly researched 1964 article by Samuel P. Hays, "The Politics of Reform in Municipal Government in the Progressive Era," in the *Pacific Northwest Quarterly* 55, no. 4 (October 1964): 157–69, argued instead that the reformers sought to reduce the power of working class and immigrant voters. For a time, this became the common view of historians of the subject. But recent work suggests that the motivations of reformers were more complex than Hays allowed, and that the adoption of at-large elections in fact brought cleaner and more efficient government that benefited city-dwellers in general. The assumption that the ward-based political machines worked to benefit ordinary people has been undermined by studies such as James J. Connolly's *The Triumph of Ethnic Progressivism: Urban Political Culture in Boston, 1900–1925* (Cambridge, Mass.: Harvard University Press, 1998).

52. *Gingles*, 478 U.S. at 91 (O'Connor, J., concurring). Her concurrence will be discussed at length in chapter 3.

53. *New York Times*, March 11, 1970, 21.

54. *New York Times*, June 20, 1969, 23.

Chapter 2: Interpreting Section 5:
The Mess the Courts Have Made

1. Richard L. Hasen, *Congressional Power to Renew the Preclearance Provisions of the Voting Rights Act after Tennessee v. Lane*, 66 Ohio St. L.J. 178 (2005).

2. Extension of the Voting Rights Act: Hearings on H.R. 939, H.R. 2148, H.R. 3247, and H.R. 3501 Before the Subcomm. on Civil and Constitutional Rights of the H.

Comm. on the Judiciary, 94th Cong. 26, 26 (1975) (statement of Arthur S. Flemming) (hereafter cited as 1975 House hearings).

3. Extension of the Voting Rights Act: Hearings on S. 407, S. 903, S. 1297, and S. 1443, Before the Subcomm. on Constitutional Rights of the S. Comm. on the Judiciary, 94th Cong. 60, 131 (1975) (hereafter cited as 1975 Senate hearings).

4. 1975 House hearings, 169.

5. *Georgia v. Ashcroft*, 539 U.S. 461, 480 (2003).

6. H.R. 6400 and Other Proposals to Enforce the Fifteenth Amendment to the Constitution of the United States: Hearings before Subcomm. No. 5 of the H. Comm. on the Judiciary, 89th Cong., 456 (1965) (hereafter cited as 1965 House hearings).

7. *Allen v. State Board of Elections*, 393 U.S. 544, 565 (1969) (Warren, C.J.).

8. Ibid., 564, quoting Attorney General Katzenbach.

9. Ibid., 568, quoting Attorney General Katzenbach at 1965 House hearings, 65.

10. Ibid., 569.

11. *Holder v. Hall*, 512 U.S. 874, 893 (1994) (Thomas, J., concurring).

12. *Allen*, 393 U.S. at 584 (Harlan, J., concurring in part and dissenting in part).

13. *Perkins v. Matthews*, 400 U.S. 379 (1971). The Supreme Court held that annexations had the potential to dilute the weight of black votes, and thus constituted changes in "practice or procedure with respect to voting."

14. For a good discussion of the problem of proportionality as the measure of racial fairness once disparate impact becomes the test for discrimination, see *Wards Cove Packing Co. v. Atonio*, 490 U.S. 642 (1989). The erroneous opinion of the lower court, Justice Bryon White wrote for the majority, "would mean that any employer who had a segment of his work force that was—for some reason—racially imbalanced, could be hauled into court and forced to engage in the expensive and time-consuming task of defending the 'business necessity' of the methods used to select the other members of his work force. The only practicable option for many employers would be to adopt racial quotas, insuring that no portion of their work forces deviated in racial composition from the other portions thereof." Ibid., 652.

15. The subsequent "coverage" cases have included, for example, *Presley v. Etowah County Commission*, 502 U.S. 491 (1992), which involved changes made to the authority of county commissioners in two Alabama counties. Supervising and maintenance of the roads is the main job of county commissioners in the state, and after a black man was elected to one of the seats, the majority voted to end the practice of allowing each commissioner to determine how to spend funds allocated to his own road district. Elected blacks in Etowah and other counties sued, arguing the change had not been precleared. The Court held that preclearance was not required for alterations in the powers and duties of elected officials.

16. *South Carolina v. Katzenbach*, 383 U.S. 301, 584 (1966).

17. Report, Subcomm. on the Constitution of the H. Comm. on the Judiciary, H. R. Rep. 109-478, at 93 (2006) (page number from http://frwebgate.access.gpo.gov/cgi-bin/getdoc.cgi?dbname=109_cong_reports&docid=f:hr478.109.pdf).

18. Courts have agreed that annexations are a "voting change," but the section 5 regulations are so vaguely worded as to allow the Justice Department to add other election-related decisions made by states and local authorities which, in my view, do not belong on the list of "voting changes" requiring preclearance. For instance, 28 C.F.R. § 51.13 (k) includes "any change affecting the right or ability of persons to participate in political campaigns which is effected by a jurisdiction subject to the requirement of section 5." That section has been read to mandate the preclearance of state campaign finance laws, for instance, which opens the door to the use of the Voting Rights Act to control what it sees as the influence of money in covered jurisdictions, whether or not that influence bears any relation to minority representation.

19. *City of Petersburg v. United States*, 354 F. Supp. 1021, 1023 (D.D.C. 1972), *aff'd*, 410 U.S. 962 (1973).

20. As indicated in chapter 1, jurisdictions that seek a declaratory judgment from the D.C. District Court after the attorney general has objected to the plan begin *de novo*; their doing so is not an appeal from the DOJ decision, in other words. But the district court, as it said in *Petersburg*, generally regards the attorney general's "interpretation of this section of the statute . . . [as] entitled to deference." 354 F. Supp. at 1031. It is thus difficult to prevail once the DOJ has filed an objection, and, indeed, the full weight of the Justice Department is thrown into arguing the views of the United States before the three-judge panel.

21. Ibid., 1025, 1028–29.

22. Ibid., 1031.

23. Ibid., 1029.

24. *City of Richmond v. United States*, 376 F. Supp. 1344, 1352 (D.D.C.), *vacated and remanded*, 422 U.S. 358 (1975). "The primary thrust of Richmond's present arguments before this court . . . is that any discriminatory purpose and effect of the annexation was purged by the City's adoption, on April 25, 1973, of a single-member district, nine-ward plan for future councilmanic elections . . . Richmond undertook to develop a ward plan after the decision in *City of Petersburg, Va. v. United States*."

25. *City of Richmond*, 376 F. Supp. at 1349. "The period of the suit's dormancy witnessed a significant growth in black voting strength in Richmond. Blacks were rapidly becoming a majority of the population." Ibid.

26. Ibid., 1356.

27. Ibid., 1354 n.50.

28. Ibid., 1353 (emphasis added).

29. Ibid., 1355.

30. Ibid., 1357.

31. *City of Richmond v. United States*, 422 U.S. 358 (1975).

32. Ibid., 371.

33. Ibid., 373 (emphasis added).

34. *Beer v. United States*, 425 U.S. 130 (1976).

35. *Beer v. United States*, 374 F. Supp. 363, 371 (D.D.C. 1974). The city had submitted an earlier plan, as well, which contained no majority-black districts. The one referred to here was a second attempt to meet Justice Department standards.

36. Ibid., 388.

37. Ibid.

38. The "no Negro will win" quotation is from Justice Byron White, summarizing the district court findings. *Beer*, 425 U.S. at 143 (White, J., dissenting). The reality in New Orleans was quite different from that depicted by the district court and by the four dissenters in the high Court's decision. Four blacks had been elected at large to offices other than the city council. The black population, and thus black political strength, was growing so rapidly that before long whites would lose the city's two at-large councilmanic seats, and four years after *Beer* the city would have its first black mayor.

39. Ibid., 141.

40. Ibid.

41. Ibid., 146 (Marshall, J., dissenting). I will return to the question of ongoing discontent with the *Beer* standard below. But it is worth noting, as Daniel Hays Lowenstein and Richard L. Hasen have pointed out, that in the 1970s there were so few majority-minority districts that the question of retrogression seldom arose, and in the 1980s and 1990s, legal and sometimes political pressure compelled legislators to create additional safe minority districts. As a result, *reducing* the number of majority-minority districts often was not even possible and almost never was likely as a practical matter. Whatever could be said for or against *Beer* as a matter of statutory construction, for practical purposes the decision seemed to make section 5 marginal at best in the districting process. Daniel Hays Lowenstein and Richard L. Hasen, *Election Law: Cases and Materials*, 3d ed. (Durham, N.C.: Carolina Academic Press, 2004), 167–68.

42. Maurice T. Cunningham, *Maximization, Whatever the Cost: Race, Redistricting, and the Department of Justice* (Westport, Conn.: Praeger, 2001), 70.

43. See *County Council v. United States*, 596 F. Supp. 35, 37 (D.D.C. 1984) (per curiam). The court found that a "fairly drawn" single-member district plan would be "likely to allow black citizens to elect candidates of their choice in three of seven districts (or 42.8 percent of the representation on the Council)"—providing roughly proportional officeholding. The county's appointed council had been replaced with one elected at large. Since the county was 44.1 percent black, any method of election—even one that was countywide—would seem to have offered blacks a greater chance to elect candidates of their choice. But the district court found the plan retrogressive, given the availability of "a fairly drawn single-member election plan." Needless to say, such a holding directly contradicted *Beer*, in which the Supreme Court had explicitly rejected arguments based on the superiority of alternative plans. Other examples illustrating the degree to which the D.C. court ignored the decision in *Beer* will be apparent in the cases discussed below.

44. For the views of that minority of justices still opposed to the retrogression test, see, for instance, the dissents of Justices Stevens, Breyer, Souter, and Ginsburg in

Reno v. Bossier Parish School Board, 528 U.S. 320, 342 (2000) (*Bossier II*) in which all four concurred that "the Court was mistaken in *Beer* when it restricted the effect prong of § 5 to retrogression." The retrogression test, however, was reaffirmed in *City of Lockhart v. United States*, 460 U.S. 125 (1983), *rev'd*, 559 F.Supp. 581 (D.D.C. 1981). *Lockhart* overturned a district court ruling that made clear the lower court's persistent commitment to subverting the high Court's test.

45. Revision of Procedures for Administration of Section 5 of the Voting Rights Act of 1965, 52 Fed. Reg. 486 (Jan. 6, 1987). See 28 C.F.R. § 51 for the current guidelines, which have been revised numerous times. The decision to merge section 2 standards into section 5 was the result of a well-organized campaign by the civil rights community. See Cunningham, *Maximization*, 26–27. The DOJ decision will be discussed at greater length in chapter 5.

46. *Reno v. Bossier Parish Sch. Bd.*, 520 U.S. 471 (1997) (*Bossier I*). There was, it is true, a footnote in the 1982 Senate report that read, "In light of the amendment to Section Two, it is intended that a Section Five objection also follows if a new voting procedure so discriminates as to violate Section Two." Report of the Subcomm. on the Constitution to the S. Comm. on the Judiciary, reprinted in the Report of the Comm. on the Judiciary, S. Rep. No. 97-417, at 12 n.31 (1982). That footnote was engineered by civil rights advocacy groups who knew that the vote on the act was imminent and that only proponents would notice it. But in *Bossier I*, the Court did not buy the footnote story. "We doubt," it said, "that Congress would depart from the settled interpretation of § 5 and impose a demonstrably greater burden on the jurisdictions covered by § 5 . . . by dropping a footnote in a Senate Report instead of amending the statute itself." *Bossier I*, 520 U.S. at 484.

47. *Bossier I*, 520 U.S. 471.

48. Ibid., 475.

49. Ibid., 477. The decision was followed by an amendment (in 1998) of the Justice Department regulations governing the enforcement of section 5. The change eliminated the reference to a "clear violation" of section 2 as a basis to deny preclearance. 28 C.F.R. § 51.54 (2001).

50. *Bossier I*, 520 U.S. at 479–80.

51. Ibid., 494 (Breyer, J., dissenting).

52. *Bossier II*, 528 U.S. 320.

53. Numerous commentators have asserted that before *Bossier II*, the definition of discriminatory purpose was, in fact, perfectly clear. It was the same as that used in Fourteenth and Fifteenth Amendment cases. They point, for instance, to Justice White's majority opinion in *City of Richmond*, 422 U.S. at 378, in which he stated that "an official action, whether an annexation or otherwise, taken for the purpose of discriminating against Negroes on account of their race has no legitimacy at all under our Constitution or under the statute." But that does not answer the question, never directly addressed by the Supreme Court, of whether the definition of purpose was the same in the statute and the Constitution.

54. *Bossier II*, 528 U.S. at 329.

55. Ibid., 335.

56. Peyton McCrary, Christopher Seaman, and Richard Valelly, "The Law of Preclearance: Enforcing Section 5," in *The Future of the Voting Rights Act*, ed. David L. Epstein, Richard H. Pildes, Rodolfo O. de la Garza, and Sharyn O'Halloran (New York: Russell Sage Foundation, 2006), 21.

57. Laughlin McDonald, "Why the Renewed Voting Rights Act Will Pass Constitutional Muster—Despite Predictions that the Roberts Court May Strike It Down," *FindLaw Legal News and Commentary*, June 9, 2006, http://writ.news.findlaw.com/commentary/20060609_mcdonald.html (accessed May 21, 2008).

58. The annexation submission is mentioned in McCrary et al., "The Law of Preclearance," 27–28. It involved the town of North, South Carolina.

59. Ibid., 21.

60. *Georgia v. Ashcroft*, 539 U.S. 461, 481 (2003).

61. Ibid., 482.

62. *Ashcroft*.

63. The ACLU's Laughlin McDonald viewed *Ashcroft* as dangerous, in that it might "allow states to turn black and other minority voters into second-class voters, who can 'influence' the election of white candidates, but cannot elect candidates of their choice, or, if they so choose, of their own race. That is a result Section 5 was enacted expressly to avoid." McDonald, "Why the Renewed Voting Rights Act Will Pass Constitutional Muster."

64. Direct testimony of John Lewis, *Georgia v. Ashcroft*, 195 F. Supp. 2d 25 (D.D.C. 2002), quoted in Richard H. Pildes, *Is Voting-Rights Law Now at War with Itself: Social Science and Voting Rights in the 2000s*, 80 N. C. L. Rev. 1517, 1538 (2002). Samuel Issacharoff was also among a number of legal scholars strongly identified with the plaintiffs' bar who saw *Ashcroft* as a welcome recognition of a changed South—a recognition that would actually aid the fulfillment of black political aspirations. See *Is Section 5 a Victim of Its Own Success?* 104 Colum. L. Rev. 1710 (2004).

65. *Georgia v. Ashcroft*, 195 F. Supp. 2d 25 (D.D.C. 2002), *vacated and remanded*, 539 U.S. 461 (2003).

66. *Ashcroft*, 539 U.S. at 491.

67. Ibid., 469.

68. Ibid.

69. *Ashcroft*, 195 F. Supp. 2d at 92. Also see *Ashcroft*, 539 U.S. at 469 (Georgia state senator Brown's statement regarding the design of the senate plan) and 470 (African Americans "have a better chance to participate in the political process under the Democratic majority than we would have under a Republican majority," Charles Walker, the senate majority leader, had testified).

70. *Ashcroft*, 539 U.S. at 480. Justice O'Connor had earlier raised the point in the section 2 context. For instance, in *Thornburg v. Gingles*, she had noted that "the phrase 'vote dilution,' in the legal sense, simply refers to the impermissible discriminatory effect

that a multimember or other districting plan has when it operates 'to cancel out or minimize the voting strength of racial groups.' This definition, however, conceals some very formidable difficulties. Is the 'voting strength' of a racial group to be assessed solely with reference to its prospects for electoral success, or should courts look at other avenues of political influence open to the racial group?" 478 U.S. 30, 87–88 (1986) (O'Connor, J., concurring) (internal citations omitted).

71. See *Ashcroft*, 539 U.S. at 483. "The State may choose, consistent with § 5, that it is better to risk having fewer minority representatives in order to achieve greater overall representation of a minority group by increasing the number of representatives sympathetic to the interests of minority voters."

72. Ibid., 479, 480 (citing *Beer*, 425 U.S. at 141).

73. Ibid., 482 (quoting *Gingles*, 478 U.S. at 99 [O'Connor, J., concurring]).

74. Ibid., 482.

75. In actuality, in turned out to be no risk at all. In two of the districts in which the black population had been reduced, those incumbents won overwhelmingly under the revised plan. The incumbent in a third district in which the black proportion had been lowered was white. This history of electoral success in the districts at issue in the litigation is summarized in Richard Pildes, "Response to Written Questions from Senator John Cornyn," Supplement to Original Testimony Before Senate Judiciary Committee on May 16, 2006, hearing on "The Continuing Need for Section 5 Preclearance."

76. The black caucus in the Georgia State Senate "wanted to maintain" the existing majority-minority districts and at the same time "not waste" black votes, the director of Georgia's Legislative Redistricting Office testified. *Ashcroft*, 539 U.S. at 469. Black votes were "wasted" when a majority-black district contained more black voters than black candidates needed to prevail.

77. Robert F. Bauer, "Thinking about the Politics of *Georgia v. Ashcroft* and Its Critics," posting on *More Soft Money Hard Law* blog, June 6, 2006, http://moresoftmoney hardlaw.com/updates/voting_rights_act_redistricting_issues.html?AID=742 (accessed March 17, 2009).

78. *Ashcroft*, 539 U.S. at 485–87.

79. Daniel Hays Lowenstein, *You Don't Have to Be Liberal to Hate the Racial Gerrymandering Cases*, 50 Stan. L. Rev. 779, 810–11 (1998).

80. In dissent, Justice Souter wrote: "Whatever one looks to . . . how does one put a value on influence that falls short of decisive influence through coalition? Nondecisive influence is worth less than majority-minority control, but how much less? Would two influence districts offset the loss of one majority-minority district? Would it take three? Or four? The Court gives no guidance for measuring influence that falls short of the voting strength of a coalition member, let alone a majority of minority voters. Nor do I see how the Court could possibly give any such guidance. The Court's 'influence' is simply not functional in the political and judicial world." *Ashcroft*, 539 U.S. at 495 (Souter, J., dissenting). Numerous scholars have expressed frustration with the *Ashcroft* Court's

notion of influence. See, most notably, Pamela S. Karlan, Georgia v. Ashcroft *and the Retrogression of Retrogression*, 3 Election L.J. 21 (2004).

81. In a famous concurrence, Justice Stewart quipped that while hardcore pornography is hard to define, "I know it when I see it." *Jacobellis v. Ohio*, 378 U.S. 184, 197 (1964) (Stewart, J., concurring). Political scientist Bernard Grofman has made an interesting attempt to "to elucidate the concept of minority influence from a social science perspective," while confessing "to more than a little doubt that anything we or anyone else suggests can fully rescue the Court's approach from its inherent internal contradictions." Bernard Grofman, *Operationalizing the Section 5 Retrogression Stand of the Voting Rights Act in the Light of* Georgia v. Ashcroft: *Social Science Perspectives on Minority Influence, Opportunity, and Control*, 5 Election L.J. 250, 252 (2006). His analysis of the complexity of assessing influence is careful and impressive, but its starting point is one with which I disagree—namely that, ultimately, even today the important question should be whether minority voters are able to elect the candidates of their choice. Surely, at some point, we should hope that the law would be able to treat black voters as American voters, entitled to no unique privileges in the way of protective measures. Grofman undoubtedly would agree, while arguing that we are still far from that day. He writes, "Even today, in the deep South, congressional districts with less than 40% black voting age population never elect black candidates who are the first choices of the African American community" Ibid., 258. But how many under–40 percent black congressional districts in the Deep South elect Democrats, whether white or black? The whole question of black legislative representation in contemporary America is one to which I will return.

82. Issacharoff, *Is Section 5 of the Voting Rights Act a Victim of Its Own Success?* 1720.

83. *Katzenbach*, 383 U.S. 301 at 358.

84. Grofman, *Operationalizing the Section 5 Retrogression Stand*, 251.

Chapter 3: Interpreting Section 2:
Judges Lost in a Political Thicket

1. Lani Guinier, *The Supreme Court, 1993 Term: [E]racing Democracy: The Voting Rights Cases*, 108 Harv. L. Rev. 109, 113 (1994).

2. The first desegregation decision to require busing was *Swann v. Charlotte-Mecklenburg Board of Education*, 402 U.S. 1 (1971). I am not suggesting that the Court's frustration with resistance to desegregation was inappropriate seventeen years after the decision in *Brown v. Board of Education*, but simply that the zeitgeist had so changed as to make the actual language of the 1964 act basically irrelevant. *Swann* was a Fourteenth Amendment case, but the decision did refer explicitly to the problem of the 1964 statute. "The legislative history of Title IV," the Court unanimously held, "indicates that Congress was concerned that the Act might be read as creating a right of action under the Fourteenth Amendment in the situation of so-called 'de facto segregation,' where

racial imbalance exists in the schools but with no showing that this was brought about by discriminatory action of state authorities. In short, there is nothing in the Act that provides us material assistance in answering the question of remedy for state-imposed segregation in violation of *Brown I*." 402 U.S. at 17–18. It was an imaginative reading of the legislation—but one the Court would never have given it in 1964.

3. See Stephan Thernstrom and Abigail Thernstrom, *America in Black and White: One Nation, Indivisible* (New York: Simon and Schuster, 1987), chapter 15.

4. *Whitcomb v. Chavis*, 403 U.S. 124 (1971). Two earlier cases in effect invited minority plaintiffs to initiate litigation challenging electoral arrangements with a discriminatory impact on the voting strength of racial and ethnic groups. See *Fortson v. Dorsey*, 379 U.S. 433 (1965), and *Burns v. Richardson*, 384 U.S. 73 (1966).

5. *Swann*, 402 U.S. at 26. The employment case was *Griggs v. Duke Power Company*, 401 U.S. 424 (1971).

6. "Legislators," Harlan wrote, "can represent their electors only by speaking for their interests—economic, social, political—many of which do reflect the place where the electors live. The Court does not establish, or indeed even attempt to make a case for the proposition that conflicting interests within a State can only be adjusted by disregarding them when voters are grouped for purposes of representation." *Reynolds v. Sims*, 377 U.S. 533, 624 (1964) (Harlan, J., dissenting).

7. Arguably, members of a racial group do not enjoy complete equality as long as there are, for instance, socioeconomic disparities that affect turnout. But the Fourteenth Amendment guarantee does not extend to all group inequalities.

8. *Whitcomb*, 403 U.S. 124.

9. *Chavis v. Whitcomb*, 305 F. Supp. 1364 (S.D. Ind. 1969), *rev'd*, 403 U.S. 124 (1971).

10. It has come to be known by that name, but in fact it was the *Report of the National Advisory Commission on Civil Disorders* (Washington, D.C.: Government Printing Office, 1968), chaired by Illinois governor Otto Kerner Jr. The commission had been created in July 1967 by President Lyndon B. Johnson to investigate the causes of the 1967 race riots, and its report was released the following February. "Our nation is moving toward two societies, one black, one white—separate and unequal," it famously concluded. Ibid., 1.

11. *Whitcomb*, 403 U.S. at 153.

12. Ibid., 149.

13. *White v. Regester*, 412 U.S. 755 (1973).

14. James Blacksher and Larry Menefee, "At-Large Elections and One Person, One Vote: The Search for the Meaning of Vote Dilution," in *Minority Vote Dilution*, ed. Chandler Davidson (Washington, D.C.: Howard University Press, 1984), 215.

15. *Zimmer v. McKeithen*, 485 F.2d 1297 (5th Cir. 1973).

16. Ibid., 1305.

17. In *Zimmer* the court had found disparities in the electoral opportunities open to whites and blacks. Yet the facts of the case could have supported a contrary finding. For

example, there was no indication that single-member districts were especially advantageous to black candidates or constituents; three blacks had been elected when voting was by wards and three under the new at-large system. In the latter case, blacks had won with the help of the white vote, but the court dismissed this support, suggesting that the right votes had been cast for the wrong reasons. In addition, the parish was a majority-black one; if voting remained at-large and blacks registered in proportion to their numbers, black candidates in the future could win every legislative seat.

18. James F. Blumstein, *Defining and Proving Race Discrimination: Perspectives on the Purpose vs. Results Approach from the Voting Rights Act*, 69 Va. L. Rev. 645 (1983). Blumstein's reference was actually to the section 2 "results" test, but since that test incorporated the legal standards contained in the constitutional cases, his point was also about that line of decisions, including *Zimmer*.

19. On S. 53, S. 1761, S. 1992, and H.R. 3112. Bills to Amend the Voting Rights Act of 1965: Hearings on the Voting Rights Act Before the Subcomm. on the Constitution of the S. Comm. on the Judiciary, 97th Cong. vol. 2, Appendix, at 478 (1982) (Timothy G. O'Rourke, "The Legal Status of Local At-Large Elections: Racial Discrimination and the Remedy of 'Affirmative Representation'") (hereafter cited as 1982 Senate hearings). These hearings (and indeed the entire history of the passage of the 1982 amendments) are discussed at great length in chapters 5 and 6 of Abigail Thernstrom, *Whose Votes Count? Affirmative Action and Minority Voting Rights* (Cambridge, Mass.: Harvard University Press, 1987).

20. *City of Mobile v. Bolden*, 446 U.S. 55 (1980).

21. *Washington v. Davis*, 426 U.S. 229, 239–40 (1976). See also *Keyes v. School District No. 1*, 413 U.S. 189, 205 (1973), holding that racially identifiable schools are not necessarily unconstitutional; the alleged segregation must result from intentional state action. Other Fourteenth Amendment decisions in which the Court demanded direct or indirect evidence of purposeful discrimination include *Village of Arlington Heights v. Metropolitan Housing Development Corp.*, 429 U.S. 252 (1977), and *Personnel Administrator v. Feeney*, 442 U.S. 256 (1979).

22. During the subsequent Senate hearings on the amendment of section 2, the Supreme Court's demand was described as "a requirement of a smoking gun" (Senator Charles Mathias); "impossible" (Benjamin Hooks, executive director of the NAACP); and "impossible, short of having the smoking pistol, the body buried in the shallow grave" (Laughlin McDonald, director of the ACLU Southern Regional Office). 1982 Senate hearings, 199, 268, and 371. In fact, courts had long accepted circumstantial evidence of discriminatory intent in Fourteenth Amendment decisions. See, for example, *Village of Arlington Heights*, according to which "determining whether invidious discriminatory purpose was a motivating factor demands a sensitive inquiry into such circumstantial and direct evidence of intent as may be available." 429 U.S. at 252. See also *Personnel Administrator*, 442 U.S. at 276. Overturning at-large voting in Burke County, Georgia, two years after the decision in *Bolden*, the Court found evidence of discriminatory intent that was no greater than that on which lower courts

had erroneously relied in *Bolden. Rogers v. Lodge*, 458 U.S. 613 (1982). The "smoking pistol" standard was never contemplated by the Court, in other words. Moreover, in the 1990s especially, the Department of Justice used findings of suspected discriminatory purpose to find districting plans and other electoral practices retrogressive and, thus, in violation of section 5, although objections to changes on section 5 grounds demanded no more than a speculative finding that the voting change submitted for preclearance might have been animated by invidious purpose—a very easy standard to meet.

23. "We are asking merely a return to the *White v. Regester* standards," Joaquin Avila, associate counsel to the Mexican American Legal Defense and Education Fund (MALDEF) said at the Senate hearings. 1982 Senate hearings, 564. Numerous other witnesses made the same point, which was one on which all advocates of the amendment agreed.

24. The history of the passage of the 1982 amendments is discussed in great detail in chapters 5 and 6 of Thernstrom, *Whose Votes Count?* Senator Dole believed his compromise guaranteed equal opportunity to participate, rather than proportionate results.

25. *Bolden*, 446 U.S. at 61.

26. The argument that the amendment was aimed only at a clarification of section 2 was made repeatedly throughout the 1982 hearings on the bill. See, for instance, statement of Jesse Jackson in Extension of the Voting Rights Act: Hearings before the Subcomm. on Civil and Constitutional Rights of the H. Comm. on the Judiciary, 97th Cong., 171 (1971), and that of the president of the League of Women Voters, ibid., 197.

27. Quoted by Senator Orrin Hatch, 1982 Senate hearings, 252.

28. It was clear that at-large voting was "the principal immediate target" of the amendment to section 2, the report of the Senate Subcommittee on the Constitution asserted. In 1975, seven years earlier, when the question of extending section 5 was before Congress, voting rights attorney Armand Derfner had flatly announced his hope "that maybe ten years from now we would have learned and progressed enough to say that . . . we might want to put in [the act] permanent bans that bar at-large elections not only in the covered states but perhaps in the rest of the country as well." Derfner and the civil rights community had not forgotten that hope. Report of the Subcomm. on the Constitution to the S. Comm. on the Judiciary on the Voting Rights Act, reprinted in the Report of the Comm, on the Judiciary, S. Rep. No. 97-417, 109 and n.4 (1982) (hereafter cited as 1982 Senate report).

29. The "fair share," "fair shake" distinction is that of James F. Blumstein. 1982 Senate hearings, 1334. In contrast to the 1982 debate in the House (which was concerned with whether to make section 5 permanent, while allowing jurisdictions to bail out from coverage more easily), in the Senate the focus was on section 2.

30. 1982 Senate report, 9. The list of factors was as follows: "The extent of any history of official discrimination in the state or political subdivision that touched the right of members of the minority group to register, to vote, or otherwise to participate in the democratic process; the extent to which voting . . . is racially polarized; the extent to which the state or political subdivision has used unusually large election districts,

majority-vote requirements, anti-single shot provisions, or other voting practices or procedures that may enhance the opportunity for discrimination . . . ; whether minorities have been denied access to [a candidate slating process] . . . ; the extent to which members of the minority group . . . bear the effects of discrimination in such areas as education, employment, and health, which hinder their ability to participate effectively in the political process; whether political campaigns have been characterized by overt or subtle racial appeals; the extent to which members of the minority group have been elected to public office in the jurisdiction." Two other factors of more limited relevance were listed: a lack of responsiveness on the part of elected officials to the particularized needs of minority group members, and whether the policy underlying voting procedures was "tenuous."

31. *McCain v. Lybrand*, No. 74-281 (D.S.C. April 17, 1980).

32. 1982 Senate report, 148–49.

33. Ibid., 32 (emphasis added).

34. 1982 Senate hearings, 2.

35. Testimony of Armand Derfner, 1982 Senate hearings, 803 and 810. Some of Derfner's commentary was directed to the question of vote dilution in an at-large scheme, but the test for unequal access was surely the same whether voting was, say, citywide or within single-member districts.

36. Ibid., 803.

37. *McNeil v. Springfield Park District*, 851 F.2d 937, 942 (7th Cir. 1988), *cert denied*, 490 U.S. 1031 (1989).

38. See, for instance, the 1982 Senate report, 28, 103. "In adopting the 'results standard' as articulated in *White v. Regester*," the report stated, "the Committee has codified the basic principle in the case as it was applied prior to the *Mobile* litigation." Ibid., 103.

39. Katharine Inglis Butler, *Constitutional and Statutory Challenges to Election Structures: Dilution and the Value of the Right to Vote*, 42 La. L. Rev. 888 (1982).

40. Katharine Inglis Butler, *Reapportionment, the Courts, and the Voting Rights Act: A Resegregation of the Political Process*, 56 U. Colo. L. Rev. 1, 21 (1984).

41. *Thornburg v. Gingles*, 478 U.S. 30 (1986).

42. *Gingles v. Edmisten*, 590 F. Supp. 345, 365–72 (E.D.N.C. 1984), *aff'd in part, rev'd in part*, 478 U.S. 30 (1986). The cited pages analyze the election results district by district. The bottom line is that in four out of the five districts, blacks had been elected at some point to the state legislature, and in all five, they had captured local offices. White support for these candidates was often substantial.

43. *Gingles*, 478 U.S. at 44.

44. Ibid., 45.

45. 1982 Senate hearings, 201.

46. Ibid., 599 and 601.

47. *Gingles*, 478 U.S. at 50. These three preconditions did not follow either from the legislative history of section 2 or the key constitutional decisions—*Whitcomb, White,* and *Zimmer.* It was mainly inspired by a law review article written by two lawyers for

the plaintiffs in *Bolden*. James U. Blacksher and Terry T. Menefee, *From* Reynolds v. Sims *to* City of Mobile v. Bolden: *Have the White Suburbs Commandeered the Fifteenth Amendment?*, 34 Hastings L.J. 1 (1982). It is important to stress that these were specifically labeled by the *Gingles* Court as threshold questions, allowing a section 2 claim to proceed. Too often federal courts trying voting rights cases treat those three threshold questions as the beginning and end of a section 2 inquiry.

48. *Gingles*, 478 U.S. at 55.

49. Ibid., 47.

50. Ibid., 64–65, 67, 69.

51. Ibid., 83 and 98.

52. Ibid., 88.

53. Ibid., 92. "If the minority can prove that it could constitute a majority in a single-member district, that it supported certain candidates, and that those candidates have not usually been elected, then a finding that there is 'legally significant white bloc voting' will necessarily follow. Otherwise, by definition, those candidates would usually have won rather than lost."

54. 1982 Senate report, 28–29.

55. "The overall vote dilution inquiry neither requires nor permits an arbitrary rule against consideration of all evidence concerning voting preferences other than statistical evidence of racial voting patterns. Such a rule would give no effect whatever to the Senate Report's repeated emphasis on 'intensive racial politics,' on 'racial political considerations,' and on whether 'racial politics . . . dominate the electoral process' as one aspect of the 'racial bloc voting' that Congress deemed relevant to showing a [section] 2 violation." *Gingles*, 478 U.S. at 101.

56. Ibid., 88.

57. *Baker v. Carr*, 369 U.S. at 186, 300 (1962) (Frankfurter, J., dissenting).

58. *Allen v. State Board of Elections*, 393 U.S. 544, 586 (1969) (Harlan, J., dissenting).

59. *Gingles*, 478 U.S. at 90–91.

60. Ibid., 91.

61. James Blumstein, 1982 Senate hearings, 1335.

62. Donald Horowitz, 1982 Senate hearings, 1309.

63. See, for instance, Davidson, *Minority Vote Dilution*, introduction. There was nothing unusual about the belief in statistical parity in the voting rights context; it pervaded the thinking of civil rights groups as early as the mid-1960s. For a discussion of the evolution of civil rights norms in the employment and contracting context, see Thernstrom and Thernstrom, *America in Black and White*, 423–36.

64. In *Bartlett v. Strickland*, decided in 2009 and discussed in chapter 6, North Carolina and the civil rights community teamed up to argue that the majority-minority requirement was out of date, and reliable white crossover voting should be a criterion in deciding whether the first *Gingles* requirement had been met. But the *Gingles* Court read section 2 as it was written.

65. As Judge Schroeder explained in *Garza v. County of Los Angeles*, 918 F.2d 763, 774 (9th Cir. 1990): "In *Reynolds*, the Supreme Court applied to the apportionment of state legislative seats the standard enunciated in *Wesberry v. Sanders*, that 'the fundamental principle of representative government is one of equal representation for equal numbers of people, without regard to race, sex, economic status, or place of residence within a state.' This standard derives from the constitutional requirement that members of the House of Representatives are elected 'by the people' . . . 'from districts founded on the aggregate number of inhabitants of each state' (James Madison, *The Federalist*, No. 54). . . . The framers were aware that this apportionment and representation base would include categories of persons who were ineligible to vote—women, children, bound servants, convicts, the insane, and, at a later time, aliens . . . Nevertheless, they declared that government should represent all the people. In applying this principle, the *Reynolds* Court recognized that the people, including those who are ineligible to vote, form the basis for representative government. Thus population is an appropriate basis for state legislative apportionment" (case citations omitted).

66. The 65 percent rule, which has been modified by now, was clearly operative in the 1970s and 1980s. See, for instance, *United Jewish Organizations v. Carey*, 430 U.S. 144, 151 (1977): "A staff member of the legislative reapportionment committee testified that in the course of meetings and telephone conversations with Justice Department officials, he 'got the feeling . . . that 65 percent would be probably an approved figure' for the nonwhite population in the assembly district in which the Hasidic community was located, a district approximately 61% nonwhite under the 1972 plan. To attain the 65% figure, a portion of the white population, including part of the Hasidic community, was reassigned to an adjoining district." See also *Barnett v. City of Chicago*, 141 F.3d 699, 702 (7th Cir. 1998), describing as "a rule of thumb that blacks must be at least 65 percent of the total population of a district in order to be able to elect a black."

When William Bradford Reynolds was President Ronald Reagan's assistant attorney general for civil rights, that rule of thumb was frequently acknowledged in both Justice Department internal memos and the DOJ's communications with localities. Thus, a staff attorney, writing up notes on a meeting with a representative of the Independent School District of Nacagdoches, Texas, recalled informing the representative that "65%+ minority districts were rule of thumb." "Minority contacts," he went on, had "confirmed" the department's view that districts less heavily black were not likely to elect a black. See Thernstrom, *Whose Votes Count?* 172. I had access to internal Justice Department memos in the mid-1980s.

67. For instance, in the Texas redistricting case that became *League of United Latin American Citizens [LULAC] v. Perry*, 548 U.S. 399 (2006), Representative Rubén Hinojosa, elected from Congressional District 15, testified at the trial that because of low turnout rates, Hispanic concentrations of approximately 57–58 percent were necessary to give Latinos the opportunity to elect. State Appellees' Brief at 95 n.107, *League of United Latin American Citizens v. Perry*, 548 U.S. 399 (2006) (No. 05-204).

68. *Vera v. Richards*, 861 F. Supp. 1304, 1320–21 (S.D. Tex. 1994). The reference to homeowners was actually made by Representative Fred Blair but was described by the district court as "consistent with Congresswoman Johnson's view." This was a Fourteenth Amendment challenge to Texas congressional districts that eventually morphed into a section 2 suit, decided by the Supreme Court in *LULAC v. Perry*, 548 U.S. at 399, cited above and discussed below.

69. *Dillard v. Baldwin County Board of Education*, 686 F. Supp. 1459, 1466 (M.D. Ala. 1988).

70. For a fuller discussion of the record of the lower courts in the years immediately following *Gingles*, see Bernard Grofman, Lisa Handley, and Richard G. Niemi, *Minority Representation and the Quest for Voting Equality* (New York: Cambridge University Press, 1992), 64–66. "Despite the Supreme Court's use of the term compact, lower courts have, almost without exception, interpreted this part of the first prong [of the *Gingles* test] to mean only contiguity—that is, that all parts of the district are joined together," the authors concluded. Ibid., 64. On the other hand, they noted, "approximately half the states have some sort of compactness requirement in their state constitutions or statutes." Ibid., 66.

71. This was particularly true after *Growe v. Emison*, 507 U.S. 25 (1993), in which the Supreme Court extended the reasoning of *Gingles* to single-member districts. As Richard H. Pildes and Richard G. Niemi have written, "In the multimember context, the conflict [between territory and group interest] is more diminished because the existing district boundary lines define the limited geographic territory within which to locate replacement single-member districts. One must still define compactness, but within a relatively small, predefined physical territory. In contrast, in challenges to existing single-member districting plans for congressional or state legislative seats, the only fixed boundary lines are those of the state itself. Within those boundaries, an unlimited number of districting plans and individual district shapes are possible. Defining 'geographically compact' in this context is more necessary and more difficult." Richard H. Pildes and Richard G. Niemi, *Expressive Harms, 'Bizarre Districts,' and Voting Rights: Evaluating Election-District Appearances After* Shaw v. Reno, 92 Mich. L. Rev. 489 (1993).

72. *Vera*, 861 F. Supp. at 1320.

73. Beginning in 1994, the Supreme Court did set some limits on how distorted districts could become. *Miller v. Johnson*, 515 U.S. 900 (1995). The cases in which the Court found race-driven, contorted districts a violation of the Fourteenth Amendment were all responding to lines drawn to comply with section 5, however—not section 2. Chapter 5 will discuss these cases at length.

74. On this point, see Judge Edith Jones writing for the court in *Vera*, 861 F. Supp. at 1335, n.43: "Organized political activity takes place most effectively within neighborhoods and communities; on a larger scale, these organizing units may evolve into media markets and geographic regions. When natural geographic and political boundaries are arbitrarily cut, the influence of local organizations is seriously diminished. After the civic and veterans groups, labor unions, chambers of commerce, religious congregations, and

school boards are subdivided among districts, they can no longer importune their Congressman and expect to wield the same degree of influence that they would if all their members were voters in his district. Similarly, local groups are disadvantaged from effectively organizing in an election campaign because their numbers, money, and neighborhoods are split. Another casualty of abandoning traditional districting principles is likely to be voter participation in the electoral process. A citizen will be discouraged from undertaking grass-roots activity if, for instance, she has attempted to distribute leaflets in her congressman's district only to find that she could not locate its boundaries. . . . [As] the influence of truly local organizations wanes, that of special interests waxes. . . . The bedrock principle of self-government, the interdependency of representatives and their constituents, is thus undermined by ignoring traditional districting principles."

75. *Gingles*, 478 U.S. at 31 (emphasis added).

76. *LULAC v. Perry*, 548 U.S. at 399. The question of Martin Frost–like districts came before the Supreme Court once again in its 2008-9 term. In March 2008, the Court granted a petition for certiorari in *Bartlett v. Strickland*, in which the issue is whether a minority group that constitutes less than 50 percent of the population in a district can nonetheless state a section 2 vote dilution claim. The court decided the case on March 9, 2009. *Bartlett v. Strickland*, 129 S. Ct. 1231 (2009).

77. *Vera*, 861 F. Supp. at 1316. The first quotation in the court's opinion is from a plaintiff's exhibit and the second from expert witness Richard Murray.

78. *League of United Latin American Citizens v. Midland Independent School District*, 812 F.2d 1494, 1504 (5th Cir. 1987). *Gingles* had involved the familiar question of the submergence of the black vote in majority-white multimember districts, but cases in Texas and other settings with significant Hispanic populations added further complexity to the Brennan preconditions, which were, to begin with, only simple on their face.

79. Katharine I. Butler and Richard Murray, *Minority Vote Dilution Suits and the Problem of Two Minority Groups: Can a 'Rainbow Coalition' Claim the Protection of the Voting Rights Act?*, 21 Pac. L.J. 619, 648–649 (1990).

80. *Nixon v. Kent County*, 76 F.3d 1381, 1386 (6th Cir. 1996) (en banc) (emphasis added).

81. It can be argued, of course, that the obstacles to black candidates are all related, at the very least, as a legacy of the history of racial discrimination, and, thus, different black and white voting patterns always reflect American racism. By this reasoning, the distinction between racial and partisan motivation is a distinction without a difference. But since some sort of history of racial discrimination can always be found, this assumption permits the finding of a section 2 violation everywhere a remedy can be fashioned.

82. Samuel Issacharoff, *Polarized Voting and the Political Process: The Transformation of Voting Rights Jurisprudence*, 90 Mich. L. Rev. 1851 (1992).

83. An early section 5 annexation case did state that "although state-imposed segregation has been abated, its long continuance in the past caused a dramatic polarization of the races in Petersburg with respect to voting and this result has not been

obliterated." *City of Petersburg v. United States*, 354 F. Supp. 1021, 1025 (D.D.C. 1972). But there was no similar reference in *City of Richmond v. United States*, 422 U.S. 358 (1975); nor was there any in the most important of the section 5 decisions, *Beer v. United States*, 425 U.S. 130 (1976), which set the retrogression standard (discussed in chapter 2).

84. *Gingles*, 478 U.S. at 83 (White, J., concurring). Justice White, it may be recalled, wrote the Court's opinion in both *Whitcomb v. Chavis*, 403 U.S. 124 (1971), and *White v. Regester*, 412 U.S. 755 (1973), the Fourteenth Amendment cases that laid the foundation for the revision of section 2.

85. *Gingles*, 478 U.S. at 57.

86. Ibid., 75.

87. *Vecinos De Barrio Uno v. City of Holyoke*, 72 F.3d 973, 981 (1st Cir. 1995).

88. *League of United Latin American Citizens v. Clements*, 999 F.2d 831 (5th Cir. 1993) (en banc).

89. Ibid., 857.

90. Ibid., 850.

91. Statement of Drew Days, Associate Professor of Law, Yale University, 1982 Senate hearings, vol. 1, 1367–68 (emphasis added). Days had served as assistant attorney general in the Carter administration.

92. *Clements*, 999 F.2d at 855.

93. Ibid., 858.

94. *Nipper v. Smith*, 39 F.3d 1494, 1497 (11th Cir. 1994) (en banc).

95. Ibid., 1515.

96. "The VRA is designed to ensure that the electoral process is fair and the opportunities for access to it are equal. Forcing courts to turn a blind eye to other causes of majoritarian bloc voting serves neither of these ends, but, rather, facilitates a back-door approach to proportional representation." *Vecinos De Barrio Uno*, 72 F.3d at 982.

97. Daniel Polsby and Robert Popper, *Ugly: An Inquiry Into the Problem of Racial Gerrymandering Under the Voting Rights Act*, 92 Mich. L. Rev. 659 (1993).

98. Daniel H. Lowenstein, "Race and Representation in the Supreme Court," in *Voting Rights and Redistricting in the United States*, ed. Mark E. Rush (Westport, Conn.: Greenwood Press, 1998), 62.

99. See *Jenkins v. Red Clay School District*, 4 F.3d. 1103, 1135 (3rd Cir.1993): "It will be only the very unusual case in which the plaintiffs can establish the existence of the three *Gingles* factors but still have failed to establish a violation of § 2 under the totality of circumstances. In such cases, the district court must explain with particularity why it has concluded, under the particular facts of that case, that an electoral system that routinely results in white voters voting as a bloc to defeat the candidate of choice of a politically cohesive minority group is not violative of § 2 of the Voting Rights Act." On the other hand, in *Johnson v. De Grandy*, 512 U.S. 997 (1994) the Supreme Court did hold that the three preconditions to establishing a section 2 violation were only the beginning of the inquiry—that the lower courts must look at the totality of the circumstances

in the case. But the facts in *De Grandy*, involving as it did a districting plan that already provided roughly proportional representation for minority voters, fell precisely into that "very unusual case" category to which *Red Clay* referred.

100. See, for instance, *Gossby v. Town Board*, 180 F.3d 476 (2nd Cir. 1999).

101. Issacharoff, "Polarized Voting and the Political Process," 1834–35. In a footnote, Issacharoff does call the three parts of the threshold test "prerequisites," but in the text itself he suggests that *Gingles* had eliminated the totality of circumstances inquiry. Issacharoff argues that *Gingles* itself discarded the "multidimensional statutory 'totality of circumstances' inquiry," substituting a "simplified test." Ibid., 1834. That is undoubtedly how many lower courts saw the Supreme Court's decision, but Brennan did refer to the need for "a searching practical evaluation of the 'past and present reality.'" *Gingles*, 478 U.S. at 45 (quoting the 1982 Senate report at 30).

102. The "simplified test" made all Republican victories in jurisdictions with significant black or Hispanic populations racially suspect, as noted above.

103. New York University law professor Richard H. Pildes and others who normally identify with the civil rights community have raised questions about the analogy between blacks in the 1980s and the Hispanic experience today. Pildes has asked, do Hispanic voters today require majority-minority, single-member districts to elect the candidates of their choice? Richard H. Pildes, *Election Law Blog*, posted December 9, 2006 (http://electionlawblog.org/).

104. *Vecinos De Barrio Uno*, 72 F.3d at 988.

105. *White*, 412 U.S. at 769.

106. *Nipper*, 39 F.3d at 1527.

107. *Gingles*, 478 U.S. at 99 (quoting *Davis v. Bandemer*, 478 U.S. 109 [1986]).

108. *De Grandy*, 512 U.S. at 1017.

109. Ibid., 1020.

110. *Regents of the University of California v. Bakke*, 438 U.S. 265, 407 (1978).

111. For an extended discussion of *Ashcroft*, see chapter 2.

112. *LULAC v. Perry*, 548 U.S. 399 (2006).

113. Reply Brief of Jackson Appellants at 2, *Jackson v. Perry*, 548 U.S. 399, No. 05-276 (2006) (companion case to *LULAC v. Perry*). Indeed, "the only reason that this law was even considered, let alone passed, was to help one political party gain more seats in the Congress at the expense of the other," Paul Smith complained when the case was heard on March 1. Transcript of Oral Argument at 5, *Jackson v. Perry*, 548 U.S. at 399. "Wow. That's a surprise," Justice Scalia replied. "Imagine that: politics driving the redistricting process." Ibid.

114. The 2001 court-drawn map essentially retained the lines of a 1991 map that was mainly the work of Representative Martin Frost, at a time when Democrats still controlled both houses of the state legislature. It was described by Michael Barone as the "shrewdest gerrymander of the 1990s." Barone, *The Almanac of American Politics 2002* (Washington, D.C.: National Journal Group, 2001), 1448. When the lines were redrawn in 2003, substantial political credit went to House Majority Leader Tom DeLay,

and, for a scandal-loving media, the weighty hand of DeLay gave particular credence to a charge of illegal political gerrymandering. But in 2004, the Supreme Court had refused to strike down a Pennsylvania partisan gerrymander, *Veith v. Jubelirer*, 541 U.S. 267 (2004), and in the oral argument in the Texas case, the court basically yawned, suggesting it was an issue going nowhere—as, in fact, turned out to be the case. Section 2 was the core issue in *LULAC v. Perry*.

115. The legal analyst Stuart Taylor opened his analysis of the decision with a useful and dismaying picture of that cacophony of voices: "KENNEDY, J., announced the judgment of the Court and delivered the opinion of the Court with respect to Parts II -- A and III, in which STEVENS, SOUTER, GINSBURG, AND BREYER, JJ., joined, an opinion with respect to Parts I and IV, in which ROBERTS, C.J., and ALITO, J., joined, an opinion with respect to Parts II -- B and II -- C, and an opinion with respect to Part II -- D, in which SOUTER and GINSBURG, JJ., joined. STEVENS, J., filed an opinion concurring in part and dissenting in part, in which BREYER, J. joined as to Parts I and II. SOUTER, J., filed an opinion concurring in part and dissenting in part, in which GINSBURG, J., joined. BREYER, J., filed an opinion concurring in part and dissenting in part. ROBERTS, C.J., filed an opinion concurring in part, concurring in the judgment in part, and dissenting in part, in which ALITO, J., joined. SCALIA, J., filed an opinion concurring in the judgment in part and dissenting in part, in which THOMAS, J., joined, and in which ROBERTS, C.J., and ALITO, J., joined as to Part III." *National Journal*, "Opening Argument—Supreme Confusion," July 1, 2006, 17.

116. *LULAC v. Perry*, 548 U.S. at 438–39, 440.

117. Transcript of Oral Argument at 15, *LULAC v. Perry*, 548 U.S. at 399 (No. 05-204). Perales refers to "race," although Hispanics are not, technically, a racial group; the terms "race" and "ethnicity" are often used interchangeably, however.

118. Ibid., 19–21.

119. *LULAC v. Perry*, 548 U.S. at 432. In describing "different communities of interest," Kennedy was quoting from the district court finding in the case.

120. Ibid., 424. The phrase "needs and interests" is taken from the district court opinion in *Session v. Perry*, 298 F. Supp. 2d 451, 512 (E.D. Tex. 2004) (per curiam).

121. *LULAC v. Perry*, 548 U.S. at 434.

122. Ibid., 438.

123. Ibid., 501 (emphasis added). The quoted description of the district is from the trial testimony of T. Giberson.

124. And yet the district court (whose factual findings were owed deference) had found CD 25 to be "a more effective Latino majority district than old District 23 ever was." Indeed, the lower court had concluded that "the Hispanic-preferred candidate [would win] every primary and general election examined in District 25," compared to the partial success such candidates enjoyed in former District 23. *LULAC v. Perry*, 548 U.S. at 442, citing *Session v. Perry*, 298 F. Supp. 2d at 503 (per curiam) (emphasis in original).

125. *LULAC v. Perry*, 548 U.S. at 503 (emphasis in original).

126. *De Grandy*, 512 U.S. at 1021–22. The argument for looking at proportionality statewide, the Court said, "would recast these cases as they come to us, in order to bar consideration of proportionality except on statewide scope, whereas up until now the dilution claims have been litigated on a smaller geographical scale."

127. *LULAC v. Perry*, 548 U.S. at 509. Even looking at the statewide picture, it was hard to argue gross underrepresentation. There were six "Latino opportunity districts" out of thirty-two, or 19 percent of the seats, which was "roughly proportional" to the Latino 22 percent of the population.

128. Ibid., 497.

129. Ibid., 506 (quoting *Shaw v. Hunt*, 517 U.S. 899, 917 n.9 [1996]).

130. Ibid., 506.

131. Ibid., 443.

132. Ibid., 444.

133. Ibid., 445, trial testimony of Eddie Bernice Johnson. Johnson had been deeply involved in the redistricting, as noted above.

134. Ibid., 445–446. Justice Stevens, in response, argued that dismantling CD 24 violated the protection against retrogression embedded in the preclearance provision. "Judges," he wrote, "are frequently called upon to consider whether a redistricting plan violates § 5, because a covered jurisdiction has the option of seeking to achieve preclearance by either submitting its plan to the Attorney General or filing a declaratory judgment action in the District Court for the District of Columbia, whose judgment is subject to review by this Court." Ibid., 480–81. The state's map left minority voters with less power than they previously had. But Stevens's view was completely bizarre; this was not a section 5 case, and it did not come on appeal from the D.C. District Court. Ibid., 480. Justices Souter and Ginsburg also weighed in. On the question of District 24, specifically, they argued that the state's failure to preserve Frost's district was a violation of section 2, and they urged sending the matter back to the lower court. Blacks constituted a majority in the Democratic primary, which meant they determined the outcome of the election. In the general election a coalition of black and white Democrats kept Frost in office. "The integrity of the minority voting population in a coalition district should be protected much as a majority-minority bloc would be," they wrote. Ibid., 485. Justices Souter and Ginsburg were writing before section 5 was amended to supersede *Georgia v. Ashcroft*, and used that case as a basis on which to build the argument for protecting coalitions.

135. Ibid., 515 (Scalia, J.).

136. *Holder v. Hall*, 512 U.S. 874 (1994). The case involved Bleckley County, Georgia, which, like many other counties in the state, had a single-commissioner form of government. The Court held that the size of a governing authority was not subject to a vote dilution challenge under section 2; there was no objective and workable benchmark against which to measure proper government size.

137. *LULAC v. Perry*, 548 U.S. at 512 (Scalia, J., concurring in part, dissenting in part).

138. *Holder*, 512 U.S. at 914.

139. Ibid., 901–2.

140. See the epigraph at the beginning of this chapter.

141. The number of counties, cities, school districts, and other jurisdictions that either did not wait to redistrict until a section 2 suit challenged their method of voting or quickly settled out of court once litigation began is impossible to count. But there is no doubt that the amended provision forced the drawing of majority-minority districts wherever they could be fashioned. For a useful review of the impact of section 2, written from the perspective of advocates of race-based districting, see Chandler Davidson and Bernard Grofman, eds., *Quiet Revolution in the South: The Impact of the Voting Rights Act, 1965–1990* (Princeton, N.J.: Princeton University Press, 1994).

142. Representative Harold Ford, a Democrat from Tennessee, lost his bid in November 2006 to become the first southern black elected to the Senate since Reconstruction, but by less than three percentage points. Ford himself, along with a number of election analysts, attributed his defeat to the weakness of the Democratic Party in the state, rejecting the idea that white racism explained his defeat. See Beth Ruker, "After Senate Defeat, What's Harold Ford Jr.'s Next Move?" posted on the website of WKRN.com, November 12, 2006. In 2000, Bill Frist, whose vacant seat Ford hoped to fill, had won the state with 65 percent of the vote, and in the presidential contest in 2004, George W. Bush had won with 57 percent of the vote. Michael Barone and Richard E. Cohen, *Almanac of American Politics* 2006 (Washington, D.C.: National Journal Group, 2005), 1536, 1540.

143. Gerard Alexander, "The Myth of the Racist Republicans," *Claremont Review of Books*, Spring 2004.

144. *De Grandy*, 512 U.S. at 1020.

145. *LULAC v. Perry*, 548 U.S. at 399.

146. Ibid., 511.

147. *Holder*, 512 U.S. at 892.

148. Ibid., 914.

Chapter 4: Section 5 Enforcement:
The Mischief That Government Bureaucrats Can Make

1. Quoted in *Johnson v. Miller*, 864 F. Supp. 1354, 1361 (S.D. Ga. 1994).

2. The tension between the interests of blacks as Democrats and their desire to maximize minority officeholding was refreshingly acknowledged, it might be recalled, by Representative John Lewis in his deposition in *Georgia v. Ashcroft* (see chapter 2). The connection between Republican gains and race-based districting is a point that has been made frequently by scholars and journalists. See, for example, Abigail Thernstrom, *Whose Votes Count? Affirmative Action and Minority Voting Rights* (Cambridge, Mass.: Harvard University Press, 1987), 6. See also Abigail Thernstrom, "A Republican–Civil Rights Conspiracy," *Washington Post*, September 23, 1991, A11; David Lublin, *The Paradox of Representation: Racial Gerrymandering and Minority Interests in Congress*

(Princeton, N.J.: Princeton University Press, 1997); David Lublin, *The Republican South: Democratization and Partisan Change* (Princeton, N.J.: Princeton University Press, 2004); Earl Black and Merle Black, *The Rise of Southern Republicans* (Cambridge, Mass.: Harvard University Press, 2002).

3. In 1975, preclearance protection was also extended to American Indians, Asian Americans, and Alaskan Natives, but voting changes involving the electoral power of members of these groups play such a minor role in the enforcement of the Voting Rights Act that they are not discussed in this book.

4. "While many of their members were veterans of past redistricting wars, the legislators could not have known what the DOJ would require by way of compliance with sections 2 and 5 of the VRA." *Johnson v. Miller*, 864 F. Supp. at 1360.

5. *Beer v. United States*, 425 U.S. 130, 141 (1976). See chapter 2 for an extensive discussion of the case.

6. *Miller v. Johnson*, 515 U.S. 900, 907 (1995).

7. Ibid. An earlier letter had referred to both discriminatory effect and purpose, but since there was no retrogression from the previous congressional districting plan, the reference to discriminatory effect was just idly thrown in.

8. Ibid., 912.

9. *Johnson v. Miller*, 864 F. Supp. at 1365.

10. Ibid., 1363–64. "Ms. Wilde was not simply one of various advocates. Her work was of particular importance to DOJ lawyers, whose criteria for and opinions of Georgia's submissions were greatly influenced by Ms. Wilde and her agenda." Ibid., 1362.

11. Ibid., 1364 n.8.

12. *Miller v. Johnson*, 515 U.S. at 915–16.

13. *Johnson v. Miller*, 864 F. Supp. at 1367.

14. Ibid.,

15. Ibid., 1362.

16. Ibid., 1368.

17. Ibid., 1362, 1368.

18. Since 1969, when the number of submissions for preclearance skyrocketed in the wake of *Allen v. State Board of Elections*, 393 U.S. 544 (1969), there has been a separate voting section within the Civil Rights Division. See below for more on the increase in submissions.

19. Court-drawn plans could be a risk to either side of a redistricting dispute. In *Smith v. Beasley*, the district court noted that the three-judge panel had already drawn an alternative map for the South Carolina Senate, but that the ACLU and a black caucus member "had advised the DOJ attorneys that everything should be done to avoid delaying preclearance because the court plan was not as advantageous to minorities as the plan adopted by the House." 946 F. Supp. 1174, 1191 (D.S.C. 1996).

20. *City of Lockhart v. United States*, 460 U.S. 125 (1983).

21. Thus, the 2006 House Judiciary Committee report referred (in mangled prose) to *Beer* as the controlling decision in the interpretation of the section 5 effects test

for discrimination: "Since the Supreme Court's decision in *Beer v. United States*, it [has been] accepted that if 'the ability of minority group's ability to elect candidates of choice to office is diminished, Section 5 requires the denial of preclearance.'" Report, Subcomm. on the Constitution of the H. Comm. on the Judiciary, H.R. Rep. No. 109-478, 12 (2006).

22. Procedures for Administration of Section 5 of the Voting Rights Act of 1965, 28 C.F.R. § 51, *et seq*. First released in 1971, these procedures have been revised numerous times, as chapter 3 noted. The sixty-day timetable can be extended if new information is required from the jurisdiction.

23. Maurice T. Cunningham, *Maximization, Whatever the Cost: Race, Redistricting, and the Department of Justice* (Westport, Conn.: Praeger, 2001), 9.

24. Cunningham, *Maximization*, 50–51, has a good discussion of the belief on the part of Civil Rights Division attorneys that "their work promotes justice."

25. U.S. Commission on Civil Rights, *Voting Rights Enforcement and Reauthorization* (Washington, D.C.: Government Printing Office, 2006), 68–69, tables A-3 and A-4. The number of submissions in 1992 reflected the need to submit the new maps after the 1990 census returns forced redistricting. *Allen* is discussed at length in chapter 2.

26. See, for instance, Dan Eggen, "Politics Alleged in Voting Cases: Justice Officials Are Accused of Influence," *Washington Post*, January 23, 2006, A01.

27. Quoted in Cunningham, *Maximization*, 56.

28. Hiroshi Motomura, *Preclearance under Section 5 of the Voting Rights Act*, 61 N.C. L. Rev. 192 (1983).

29. Howard Ball, Dale Krane, and Thomas P. Lauth, *Compromised Compliance: Implementation of the 1965 Voting Rights Act* (Westport, Conn.: Greenwood Press, 1982), 89.

30. Procedures for the Administration of Section 5 of the Voting Rights Act of 1965, as Amended, 28 C.F.R. § 51 (1971).

31. That point was reiterated time and again by the department. "In the conduct of our preclearance function under section 5 of the Voting Rights Act, we traditionally have considered ourselves to be a surrogate of the district court, seeking to make the kind of decision we believe the court would make if the matter were before it," an objection letter to Port Arthur, Texas, stated. Letter of objection, March 12, 1982, as quoted in Motomura, *Preclearance under Section 5*, 191 n.15.

32. Katharine Inglis Butler, *Reapportionment, the Courts, and the Voting Rights Act: A Resegregation of the Political Process?*, 56 U. Colo. L. Rev. 1, 28 n.123 (1984).

33. These two examples are taken from Luis Fuentes-Rohwer and Guy-Uriel E. Charles, *Preclearance, Discrimination, and the Department of Justice: The Case of South Carolina*, 57 S. C. L. Rev. 827, 845, 847 (2006). The authors examined objection letters from the DOJ to the state of South Carolina. Cunningham, *Maximization*, 77, also has a very good discussion of the opaque language of objection letters in the 1990s.

34. 28 C.F.R. § 51. The revision of procedures was sent out for comment on May 6, 1985, and adopted on January 6, 1987.

35. *Vecinos De Barrio Uno v. City of Holyoke*, 72 F.3d 973, 988 (1st Cir. 1995). This description by Judge Selya might be recalled from the previous chapter.

36. Timothy O'Rourke, telephone conversation, July 1, 1985, quoted in Thernstrom, *Whose Votes Count?* 162.

37. That bright-line assumption runs through Cunningham, *Maximization*, for instance.

38. Thernstrom, *Whose Votes Count?* has an extensive discussion of the detours around the law that the Justice Department created in the 1980s; many of the submissions for preclearance discussed in that work were gathered from the internal department files.

39. This early embrace of "influence" districts was striking. As chapter 2 indicated, in 2003 the Supreme Court would include them in calculating minority electoral strength, but in 2006 the civil rights groups persuaded Congress to overturn that decision.

40. Such calculations were almost always based on voting-age numbers, but after 1975, when Hispanics were added to the list of protected groups, it became important to look at the citizen voting-age population as well. A 65 percent Hispanic voting-age population would not be a majority-minority constituency if half the residents were ineligible to vote.

41. The quotations in this paragraph and two following are from internal Justice Department memos, obtained from the voting section in the Civil Rights Division in the course of researching Thernstrom, *Whose Votes Count?* The findings were written up in a memo for the U.S. Commission on Civil Rights entitled *Memo on Submissions to the Department of Justice Involving Redistricting*, 1985 (hereafter cited as USCCR memo), which was more extensively cited in *Whose Votes Count?*

42. Letter of U.S. Assistant Attorney General William Bradford Reynolds to Virginia Attorney General Gerald L. Bailes, Objection to Virginia on House of Delegates Districts (March 12, 1982); Letter of U.S. Assistant Attorney General William Bradford Reynolds to Jeffrey A. Davis, Esq., Objection to Uvalde County, Texas (February 18, 1982); Letter of U.S. Assistant Attorney General William Bradford Reynolds to Texas Secretary of State David Dean, Objection to Texas (January 29, 1982). USCCR memo.

43. USCCR memo, 14. No names were attached to such comments by voting section staff.

44. With respect to Sumter County, Gerald Jones, the chief of the voting section, said explicitly: "We took the unusual step of going down and helping them work out an acceptable solution which, apparently, they have rejected, along with other fairly drawn alternatives, for no racially neutral reason." USCCR memo, 8.

45. Letters of objection from the time contained a standard sentence: "Under these circumstances we are unable to conclude, as we must under the Voting Rights Act, that the submitted plan does not have the purpose and will not have the effect of abridging the right to vote." USCCR memo, passim.

46. NAACP-Defendant's Supplemental Response to Interrogatories at 3–4, *South Carolina v. United States*, No. 83-3626 (D.D.C. April 2, 1984): "The redistricting

plan as drawn avoidably and deliberately denies Blacks the equal opportunity to elect a candidate of their choice. . . . Moreover, the State . . . failed and or refused to implement suggestions for redistricting made by the NAACP Defendants, as well as other minority organizations."

47. Thus, an October 1981 "Legal Analysis and Recommendation" reviewing the submission by Barbour County, Alabama, referred to a new plan as an improvement over that to which the department had objected in July. But the plan still failed to meet the Justice Department standard. "It appears that the county, which, due to our July 21, 1981 letter, is on notice of its obligation to adopt a fairly-drawn plan, has done otherwise," a staff attorney wrote. "Thus . . . considering the notice which the county has and the configuration of District 3, it . . . appears that the county has deliberately drawn the plan to dilute black voting strength." Once the county had been told to draw a "fair" plan, its failure to adhere to the department's particular definition of fairness left it open to the charge of purposeful discrimination. USCCR memo, 3.

48. Memorandum for the United States in Opposition to South Carolina's Motion for Partial Summary Judgment at 9, *South Carolina v. United States and the NAACP*, Civil Action No. 83-3626 (D.D.C. 1984).

49. *Smith v. Beasley*, 946 F. Supp. 1174.

50. Ibid., 1185.

51. Ibid., 1208.

52. Ibid., 1209.

53. Ibid., 1185.

54. In 1996, the Department of Justice agreed to settle the plaintiffs' claims for attorneys' fees and costs for $282,500. Letter from William E. Moschella, Assistant Attorney General, Office of Legislative Affairs, U.S. Department of Justice, to F. James Sensenbrenner, Chairman, Committee on the Judiciary, U.S. House of Representatives (April 12, 2006).

55. USCCR memo, 10. The staff attorney's visit was made on January 1, 1983.

56. *Hays v. Louisiana*, 839 F. Supp. 1188, 1196 (W.D. La. 1993).

57. Ibid. The assistant attorney general at the time was still John Dunne, who had been appointed by the first President Bush but who did step down in 1993. Deval Patrick, Clinton's appointee, did not assume office until 1994, as a consequence of the firestorm the president ran into when he tried to nominate Lani Guinier, his first choice.

58. *Hays v. Louisiana*, 936 F. Supp. 360, 369 (W.D. La. 1996) (per curiam).

59. *Hays v. Louisiana*, 839 F. Supp. at 1196 n.21.

60. Ibid. The first racially gerrymandered plan had been declared unconstitutional. In insisting, once again, that the state draw two black districts, the DOJ was saying, in effect, that although the Court had declared the state's first gerrymandered map unconstitutional, that did not mean that a revised map with two differently configured majority-black districts would also be unconstitutional. The Court had not ruled on the statutory mandate, but only on the constitutionality of the gerrymandered districts, and

in so confining itself, it had left the Justice Department free to read the statute as demanding two black districts.

61. The description of the Texas district is in *Terrazas v. Slage*, 789 F. Supp. 828, 834 (W.D. Tex. 1991). The metaphors describing North Carolina's District 1 are from *Shaw v. Reno*, 509 U.S. 630, 635 (1993) (*Shaw*). Katharine Inglis Butler, *Racial Fairness and Traditional Districting Standards: Observations on the Impact of the Voting Rights Act on Geographic Representation*, 57 S.C. L. Rev. 749 (2006) has some very useful maps of egregiously gerrymandered districts drawn in the early 1990s.

62. Cunningham, *Maximization*, 4.

63. That important phrase—an invitation to a wide variety of creative interpretations—is contained in the *Beer* decision itself. 425 U.S. at 141.

64. John R. Dunne, remarks at National Conference of State Legislators (August 13, 1991), quoted in Cunningham, *Maximization*, 74.

65. Remarks of John R. Dunne, 14 Cardozo L. Rev. 1127, 1128–29 (1993).

66. *Shaw*, 509 U.S. 630.

67. Cunningham, *Maximization*, 106.

68. Remarks of John R. Dunne, 14 Cardozo L. Rev. 1133.

69. Quoted in Cunningham, *Maximization*, 99.

70. Ibid., 77.

71. Letter from Moschella to Sensenbrenner.

72. *United States v. Jones*, 125 F.3d 1418, 1431 (11th Cir. 1997).

73. *Miller v. Johnson*, 515 U.S. at 926 (quoting H. R. Rep. No. 91-397, at 8 [1969]).

74. See the discussion of *Reno v. Bossier Parish School Board*, 528 U.S. 320 (2000) (*Bossier II*), in chapter 2. The 2006 amendments of section 5—the Voting Rights Act Reauthorization and Amendments Act (VRARA)—superseded that decision.

75. The announcement at the APSA convention was reported by Howard Kurtz in "Justice Dept. Won't Assess Possible Bias in Election Plans," *Washington Post*, August 30, 1986, A1. Subsequently, the House Judiciary Subcommittee on Constitutional and Civil Rights held oversight hearings and in 1986 issued a report in which it concluded "that it is a proper interpretation of the legislative history of the 1982 amendments to use Section 2 standards in the course of making Section 5 determinations." House Subcomm. on Civil and Constitutional Rights of the Comm. on the Judiciary, Proposed Changes to Regulations Governing Section 5 of the Voting Rights Act, 99th Cong. (1986). For a discussion of this history, see Cunningham, *Maximization*, 26–27, and *Reno v. Bossier Parish School Board*, 520 U.S. 471, 507 n.9 (1997) (*Bossier I*) (Stevens, J., dissenting).

76. The official switch in Reynolds' position was announced when the Justice Department issued new regulations governing section 5 on January 6, 1987. Mary Thornton, "New Rules Strengthen Voting Act: Justice Dept. Shifts On Election Change," *Washington Post*, January 7, 1987, A1. U.S. Department of Justice, "Revision of Procedures for the Administration of Section 5 of the Voting Rights Act of 1965 as Amended, Final Rule," 28 C.F.R. § 51 (January 6, 1987).

77. The footnote, as previously mentioned in chapter 2, note 46, read: "In light of the amendment to Section Two, it is intended that a Section Five objection also follows if a new voting procedure so discriminates as to violate Section Two." S. Rep. No. 97-417, at 12 n.31 (1982).

78. Only 1 percent of objections were based on violations of section 2 in the 1980s, with the figure rising to 2 percent in the 1990s, Peyton McCrary, Christopher Seaman, and Richard Valelly found. "The Law of Preclearance: Enforcing Section 5," in *The Future of the Voting Rights Act*, ed. David Epstein, Richard H. Pildes, Rodolfo O. de la Garza, and Sharyn O'Halloran (New York: Russell Sage Foundation, 2006), 26, table 2.2.

79. Ibid., 26; *Bossier I*, 520 U.S. 471; *Bossier II*, 528 U.S. 320.

80. A good summary of this transformation is contained in Butler, *Racial Fairness*, 57 S.C. L. Rev. 769. Butler also has a good description of the change in the information available from the Census Bureau in *Affirmative Racial Gerrymandering: Rhetoric and Reality*, 26 Cumberland L. Rev. 313 (1996).

81. *Shaw v. Hunt*, 861 F. Supp. 408, 457 (E.D.N.C. 1994). On the use of computer technology, see also *Vera v. Richards*, 861 F. Supp. 1304, 1308 (S.D. Tex. 1994).

82. *Shaw*, 509 U.S. at 641.

83. Ibid., 640, quoting Eric Foner, *Reconstruction: America's Unfinished Revolution, 1863–1877* (New York: Harper and Row, 1988), 590.

84. Ibid., 635–36 (citations omitted).

85. Cunningham, *Maximization*, 105. "The Republicans moved early and aggressively in the 1990 redistricting cycle." Ibid. An organization that the Republican National Committee set up "offered free software . . . [that] attracted the NAACP, MALDEF, the Lawyers' Committee, Southwest Voter Education Project, Civil Rights Division officials—and even suspicious representatives of the Democratic Party, who could hardly be denied a display by a tax-exempt organization." Ibid.

86. *Georgia v. Ashcroft*, 539 U.S. 461 (2003). The decision is discussed at length in chapter 2.

87. Ibid., 480.

88. Ibid., 496.

89. *League of United Latin American Citizens [LULAC] v. Perry*, 548 U.S. 399 (2006).

90. U.S. Department of Justice, Voting Section, Section 5 Recommendation Memorandum (December 12, 2003) (hereafter cited as DOJ memorandum). It was posted by the *Washington Post* as a supplement to Dan Eggen, "Justice Staff Saw Texas Districting as Illegal: Voting Rights Finding on Map Pushed by DeLay Was Overruled," December 2, 2005, A01, www.washingtonpost.com/wp-dyn/content/article/2005/12/01/AR2005120101927.html (accessed March 18, 2009).

91. Ibid.

92. A confidential source within the Justice Department provided me with a copy of this second memorandum. It was prepared by a career lawyer and two political appointees.

93. As a Justice Department white paper explained, "It is not improper to consider political affiliations when hiring for political positions. However . . . both Department policy and federal civil service law prohibit discrimination in hiring for career positions on the basis of political affiliations." U.S. Department of Justice, Office of Professional Responsibility and Office of the Inspector General, An Investigation of Allegations of Politicized Hiring by Monica Goodling and Other Staff in the Office of the Attorney General, July 28, 2008, 4, http://www.usdoj.gov/oig/special/s0807/final.pdf (accessed March 18, 2009).

94. Numerous critics have charged the George W. Bush administration with allowing a corruption of the Civil Rights Division. See, for instance, William L. Taylor, Dianne M. Piché, Crystal Rosario, and Joseph D. Rich, eds., *The Erosion of Rights: Declining Civil Rights Enforcement Under the Bush Administration*, Center for American Progress, March 21, 2007, http://www.americanprogress.org/issues/2007/03/erosion_of_rights.html (accessed March 18, 2009). Joseph Rich had been the chief of the voting section of the Civil Rights Division from 1999 to 2005 and then took a well-worn path to the Lawyers' Committee for Civil Rights Under Law. See also Mark Posner, "The Politicization of Justice Department Decisionmaking Under Section 5 of the Voting Rights Act: Is It a Problem and What Should Congress Do?" American Constitution Society for Law and Policy, January 2006, http://www.acslaw.org/files/Section%205%20decisionmaking%201-30-06.pdf (accessed March 18, 2009). For a rejoinder to these critics, see Hans A. von Spakovsky, "Revenge of the Liberal Bureaucrats: A New Report on Bush Administration Hiring Practices at Justice," *Weekly Standard*, January 23, 2009.

95. *Balderas v. Texas*, No. 6:01-158, 2001 WL 35673968 (E.D. Tex. Nov. 14, 2001) (per curiam) *summarily aff'd*, 536 U.S. 9191 (2002).

96. Quoted in Justice William Rehnquist's dissent, *United Steel Workers of America v. Weber*, 443 U.S. 193, 242 n.20 (1979).

97. Alfred W. Blumrosen, *Black Employment and the Law* (New Brunswick, N.J.: Rutgers University Press, 1971), 53.

98. Ibid., 58.

99. Ibid., 71–73.

100. Hugh Davis Graham, *The Civil Rights Era: Origins and Development of National Policy* (New York: Oxford University Press, 1990), 343.

Chapter 5: The Fourteenth Amendment Cases: Trafficking in Racial Stereotyping

1. *Shaw v. Reno*, 509 U.S 630, 647 (1993) (*Shaw*).

2. *City of Mobile v. Bolden*, 446 U.S. 55 (1980).

3. *Shaw*, 509 U.S at 630. The other two were *Growe v. Emison*, 507 U.S. 25 (1993), and *Voinovich v. Quilter*, 507 U.S. 146 (1993). *Shaw* was unquestionably the most important of the three.

4. *Beer v. United States*, 425 U.S. 130 (1976).

5. District 1, it might be recalled, had been described by the *Wall Street Journal* as resembling a "bug splattered on a windshield." *Shaw*, 509 U.S at 635.

6. *Regents of the University of California v. Bakke*, 438 U.S. 265 (1978); *City of Richmond v. J. A. Croson Co.*, 488 U.S. 469 (1989).

7. *J. A. Croson Co.*, 488 U.S. at 494.

8. *Whitcomb v. Chavis*, 403 U.S. 124 (1971); *White v. Regester*, 412 U.S. 755 (1973). Both decisions are discussed in chapter 3.

9. In three previous, but quite different, cases, the Supreme Court had addressed the question of race-conscious districting: *Gomillion v. Lightfoot*, 364 U.S. 340 (1960); *Wright v. Rockefeller*, 376 U.S. 52 (1964); and *United Jewish Organizations v. Carey*, 430 U.S. 144 (1977) (*UJO*). *Gomillion*, however, was not a Fourteenth Amendment legislative redistricting case; it involved the almost total exclusion of black voters from the city of Tuskegee, Alabama, which left all whites within redrawn boundaries. The municipal boundary change was ruled a violation of the Fifteenth Amendment; it denied black voters the right to vote in municipal elections. In any case, municipal boundary changes are not usually regarded as districting alterations. Indeed, in the annexation cases discussed in chapter 2, the Court developed legal standards by which to judge a section 5 violation that were very different from those it arrived at in 1976 in *Beer*, in which new district lines were the issue. The *Wright* Court found the plaintiffs had not carried their burden of proving the districts in question were race-driven, and thus it did not get to the question of the constitutionality of such race-conscious maps. The majority opinion in *UJO* had dismissed the equal protection claim of Hasidic Jews on the ground that, since white voters as a whole (whites being fungible members of one group) were not underrepresented, their voting strength had not been diluted. Moreover, the plaintiffs did not allege, the *Shaw* court argued, that contorted district lines suggested an effort to segregate voters. None of these decisions, therefore, settled the issue raised in the new line of the Fourteenth Amendment cases: Were districting lines analogous to suspect racial classifications in employment, contracting, and other contexts? If they were, as *Washington v. Davis*, 426 U.S. 229 (1976), had made clear, their constitutionality would not be settled by their disparate impact on either white or minority voters.

10. *Shaw*, 509 U.S at 646–47.

11. Ibid., 642.

12. Strict scrutiny dates back to *Korematsu v. United States*, which was the first decision to make explicit the point that racial classifications were inherently suspect. Justice Hugo Black, writing for the majority, stated, "It should be noted, to begin with, that all legal restrictions which curtail the civil rights of a single racial group are immediately suspect. That is not to say that all such restrictions are unconstitutional. It is to say that courts must subject them to the most rigid scrutiny. Pressing public necessity may sometimes justify the existence of such restrictions; racial antagonism never can." 323 U.S. 214, 216 (1944).

13. For the point that O'Connor had pared down the original argument of the plaintiffs, see Daniel D. Polsby and Robert D. Popper, *Ugly: An Inquiry into the Problem of Racial Gerrymandering under the Voting Rights Act*, 92 Mich. L. Rev. 652, 661 (1993). The "narrowly tailored to meet a compelling state interest" test for racial classifications had been established in *Adarand Constructors, Inc. v. Pena*, 515 U.S. 200, 227 (1995). Earlier, in *Wygant v. Jackson*, 476 U.S. 267, 273–74 (1986), Justice Powell had referred (although in an opinion signed only by a plurality) to a compelling state interest and narrow tailoring as requirements of that "most searching examination" of all racial preferences required by the Constitution. The district court in *Shaw v. Hunt*, 861 F. Supp. 408 (E.D.N.C. 1994), had found the North Carolina plan to be narrowly tailored to further the state's compelling interest in complying with the Voting Rights Act. The Supreme Court subsequently reversed that ruling in *Shaw v. Hunt*, 517 U.S. 899 (1996) (*Shaw II*).

14. *Shaw*, 509 U.S at 642 (quoting *Hirabayashi v. United States*, 320 U.S. 81 [1943]).

15. Ibid., 644.

16. Ibid., 647.

17. Ibid., 643, 657.

18. Ibid., 648.

19. Ibid., 647.

20. Ibid., 659 (White, J., dissenting).

21. Ibid., 660.

22. Ibid., 658.

23. Ibid., 673–74. White viewed the racial gerrymandering cases as indistinguishable from those, like *Gaffney v. Cummings*, 412 U.S. 735 (1973), that dealt with the impact of districting on the partisan distribution of political power. As the Court said in *Gaffney*, he wrote, we have no "constitutional warrant to invalidate a state plan, otherwise within tolerable population limits, because it undertakes, not to minimize or eliminate the political strength of any group or party, but to recognize it and, through districting, provide a rough sort of proportional representation in the legislative halls of the State." *Shaw*, 509 U.S. at 673–74 (citation omitted).

24. *Shaw*, 509 U.S. at 672.

25. Ibid., 666.

26. Ibid., 675.

27. *Brown v. Board of Education*, 347 U.S. 483, 494 (1954): "To separate [children in grade and high schools] from others of similar age and qualifications solely because of their race generates a feeling of inferiority as to their status in the community that may affect their hearts and minds in a way unlikely ever to be undone. The effect of this separation on their educational opportunities was well stated by a finding in the Kansas case by a court which nevertheless felt compelled to rule against the Negro plaintiffs: 'Segregation of white and colored children in public schools has a detrimental effect upon the colored children. The impact is greater when it has the sanction of the law; for the policy of separating the races is usually interpreted as denoting the inferiority of the negro group. A sense of inferiority affects the motivation of a child to learn.'"

28. *Shaw v. Hunt*, 861 F. Supp. 408; two years later, in *Shaw II*, the Supreme Court reversed the district court's holding.

29. *Johnson v. Miller*, 864 F. Supp. 1354, 1366 (S.D. Ga. 1994).

30. Ibid., 1368.

31. *Miller v. Johnson*, 515 U.S. 900, 921, 925 (1995).

32. Ibid., 909. The Court quotes from M. Barone and G. Ujifusa, *Almanac of American Politics* (Washington, D.C.: National Journal Group, 1994), 356, in describing the Eleventh Congressional District: "Geographically, it is a monstrosity, stretching from Atlanta to Savannah. Its core is the plantation country in the center of the state, lightly populated, but heavily black. It links by narrow corridors the black neighborhoods in Augusta, Savannah and southern DeKalb County."

33. *Shaw*, 509 U.S. at 672 (White, J., dissenting). "'Compactness or attractiveness has never been held to constitute an independent federal constitutional requirement for state legislative districts' [citing *Gaffney v. Cummings*, 412 U.S. 735 (1973)]. . . . A regularly shaped district can just as effectively effectuate racially discriminatory gerrymandering as an odd-shaped one."

34. *Miller*, 515 U.S. at 912–13.

35. Ibid., 916.

36. Letter from William E. Moschella, Assistant Attorney General, Office of Legislative Affairs, U.S. Department of Justice, to F. James Sensenbrenner, Chairman, Committee on the Judiciary, U.S. House of Representatives (April 12, 2006).

37. *Miller*, 515 U.S. at 916.

38. The quoted phrase is from the district court opinion in *Johnson v. Miller*, 922 F. Supp. 1556, 1563 (S. D. Gra. 1995).

39. *Shaw II*, 517 U.S. 899; and *Bush v. Vera*, 517 U.S. 952 (1996).

40. *Hays v. Louisiana*, 936 F. Supp. 360 (W.D. La. 1996) (per curiam).

41. Ibid., 369, 372. In 1999, the Department of Justice agreed to pay $1,147,228 to settle claims against it for attorneys' fees, expenses, and costs in this case. Letter from Moschella to Sensenbrenner.

42. *Abrams v. Johnson*, 521 U.S. 74 (1997).

43. *Hunt v. Cromartie*, 526 U.S. 541 (1999) (*Cromartie I*); *Easley v. Cromartie*, 532 U.S. 234 (2001) (*Cromartie II*).

44. The description is that of M. Barone and Richard E. Cohen, eds., *The Almanac of American Politics, 2006* (Washington, D.C.: National Journal Group, 2005), 1279.

45. *Cromartie I*, 526 U.S. at 544. It had become "wider and shorter" than it was before, which did not change the basic snakelike (tracking I-85) picture, however.

46. *Cromartie II*, 532 U.S. at 257.

47. Daniel P. Tokaji, "The Story of *Shaw v. Reno*: Representation and Raceblindness," *Public Law and Legal Theory Working Paper Series No. 53*; and Center for Interdisciplinary Law and Policy Studies, Moritz College of Law, Ohio State University, Working Paper Series No. 34 (February 2006), 45. Downloaded from Social Science Research Network Electronic Paper Collection: http://ssrn.com/.

48. *Jet Magazine*, "Deval Patrick is Sworn in as Assistant Attorney General for Civil Rights," May 2, 1994, http://www.encyclopedia.com/doc/1G1-15407619.html (accessed April 14, 2009).

49. Deval Patrick, remarks (NAACP National Convention, Chicago, July 12, 1994), quoted in Maurice T. Cunningham, *Maximization, Whatever the Cost: Race, Redistricting, and the Department of Justice* (Westport, Conn.: Praeger, 2001), 60.

50. Deval Patrick, remarks for Fall 1994 Rubin Lecture (Columbia School of Law, New York, November 2, 1994), quoted in Cunningham, *Maximization*, 60.

51. *Columbus Times*, "Supreme Court Decision May Lead to Second Reconstruction," September 7, 1993, 3.

52. Brenda Wright, "Toward a Politics of Inclusion," *ABA Journal*, July 1993, 44.

53. "Is an All White Congress Inevitable?" *Ethnic NewsWatch: New York Beacon* 2, no. 96 (December 13, 1995): 2.

54. Ibid.

55. Ronald K. Gaddie, "The Problem, the Opportunity, and Some Thoughts for Discussion of the Renewal of Section 5 of the Voting Rights Act," in U.S. Commission on Civil Rights Briefing Report, *Reauthorization of the Temporary Provisions of the Voting Rights Act: An Examination of the Act's Section 5 Preclearance Provision*, February 2006, 31.

56. Charles S. Bullock III and Mark J. Rozell, eds., "Southern Politics in the Twenty-first Century," in *The New Politics of the Old South* (Lanham, Md.: Rowman and Littlefield, 2003), 12.

57. Katharine Butler, *Affirmative Racial Gerrymandering: Rhetoric and Reality*, 26 Cumberland L. Rev. 313, 317 (1996). See also James F. Blumstein, *Racial Gerrymandering and Vote Dilution: Shaw v. Reno in Doctrinal Context*, 26 Rutgers L.J. 517 (1995). As noted above, *Korematsu*, 323 U.S. 214, decided in 1944, was the first case to hold that racial classifications were inherently suspect.

58. Butler, *Affirmative Racial Gerrymandering*, 356. "Many black students assigned to segregated schools would have been assigned to the same school under standard neighborhood or geographic based school assignments. The evil in both cases is that the district and the school were created by racial sorting and were designed to serve a racial purpose."

59. Ibid., 337 ("Creating districts with race as the primary criterion is like segregating schools.").

60. Ibid., 357.

61. *Gratz v. Bollinger*, 539 U.S. 244, 305 (2003) (Ginsburg, J., concurring) (emphasis added). For a lengthy discussion of both *Gratz* and the law school case, *Grutter v. Bollinger*, 539 U.S. 306 (2003), decided the same day, see Abigail Thernstrom and Stephan Thernstrom, "Secrecy and Dishonesty: The Supreme Court, Racial Preferences, and Higher Education," *Constitutional Commentary* (Symposium: From *Brown* to *Bakke* to *Grutter*: Constitutionalizing and Defining Racial Equality), Spring 2004, 251–74.

62. T. Alexander Aleinikoff and Samuel Issacharoff, *Race and Redistricting*, 92 Mich. L. Rev. 592 (1993).

63. Pamela Karlan, *Still Hazy After All These Years: Voting Rights in the Post-*Shaw *Era*, 26 Cumberland L. Rev. 311 (1996).

64. Ibid., 300.

65. Aleinikoff and Issacharoff, *Race and Redistricting*, 623.

66. Ibid., 602–3.

67. Daniel Hays Lowenstein, *You Don't Have to Be Liberal to Hate the Racial Gerrymandering Cases*, 50 Stan. L. Rev. 779, 805 (1998).

68. Ibid., 802.

69. Aleinikoff and Issacharoff, *Race and Redistricting*, 636.

70. Ibid., 637. "The concept of 'geographical coherence' may be far less relevant in defining primary communities of interest in today's society. The census demographic data reveal a highly fluid society in which changes of residence are far from unexpected, and in which the growth of 'exurbs'—defined by proximity to the highway networks—have replaced any preexisting sense of geographic coherence. To the extent that political communities of interest do not fall within neat geographic contours—as with, for example, feminist concerns, environmentalism, foreign policy preferences—the persistent use of geographically based districts reflects arbitrariness and heavy-handedness on the part of government line drawers."

71. Ibid., 627.

72. Ibid., 627–28. The best-known advocate for a system of proportional representation among voting rights scholars is Lani Guinier, who wrote that "in a system shaped by irrational, majority prejudice, remedial mechanisms that eliminate pure majority rule and enforce principles of interest proportionality may provide better proxies for political fairness." Single-member districts, in her view, did not solve the problem that "black legislators, especially those representing geographically segregated districts, may be victims of prejudice" in a white-dominated legislative body. She advocated what she called "proportionate interest representation." Lani Guinier, *The Triumph of Tokenism: The Voting Rights Act and the Theory of Black Electoral Success*, 89 Mich. L. Rev. 1077, 1102, 1137 (1991).

73. Richard H. Pildes and Richard G. Niemi, *Expressive Harms, "Bizarre Districts," and Voting Rights: Evaluating Election-District Appearances after* Shaw v. Reno, 92 Mich. L. Rev. 483, 483 (1993).

74. Polsby and Popper, *Ugly: An Inquiry into the Problem of Racial Gerrymandering*, 670.

75. Ibid., 671.

76. See also the introduction. In 2006, other members of the CBC with relatively low liberal scores were David Scott, of Georgia, who had a score of 63.2, and Artur Davis of Alabama, 60.0. *National Journal*, "Minority Groups in the House," March 3, 2007, NationalJournal.com/voteratings/pdf/06womenminorities.pdf (accessed June 5, 2008).

77. *Shaw*, 509 U.S. at 647.

78. See, for instance, Abigail Thernstrom, "*Shaw v. Reno*: Notes from a Political Thicket," in *The Public Interest Law Review*, ed. Roger Clegg and Leonard Leo, 35–56

(Washington, D.C.: National Legal Center for the Public Interest, 1994), 56: "We need electoral arrangements that deliver the right messages. . . . The messages that we deliver in our public policies are important. They help to shape the society."

79. Pildes and Niemi, *Expressive Harms*, 485.

80. Ibid., 500–501.

81. Ibid., 501, 507.

82. Ibid., 507.

83. Ibid., 484.

84. The case was *United Jewish Organizations v. Carey*, 430 U.S. 144, referred to in chapter 1, note 32, chapter 3, note 66, and chapter 5, note 9. Aleinikoff and Issacharoff wrote: "The Court's focus on the noninvidiousness (indeed, positive good) behind the districting plan led it to indulge in a form of race 'essentialism'—that is, the assumption that 'white' voters share outlooks and interests simply on the basis of their race—that it would later attack in *Shaw v. Reno*. The political theory of 'virtual representation' and an unstated sociological assumption about the nature of 'whiteness' made the harm visited on the Brooklyn Hasidim unproblematic in the eyes of the Court." Aleinikoff and Issacharoff, *Race and Redistricting*, 596.

85. Aleinikoff and Issacharoff, *Race and Redistricting*, 610.

86. Lowenstein, *You Don't Have to Be Liberal*, 828.

87. "As a result, the claim of a right of effective participation in an electoral system not only entails the recognition of an affirmative group right, but—given the zero-sum quality of representation—the claim also assumes the right to subordinate electorally some other group or groups." Aleinikoff and Issacharoff, *Race and Redistricting*, 601.

88. Ibid.

89. Ibid., 631.

90. *Shaw*, 509 U.S. at 635.

91. Lowenstein, *You Don't Have to Be Liberal*, 779.

92. Ibid., 786.

93. Ibid.

94. Ibid.

Chapter 6: The Serbonian Bog

1. *Vecinos De Barrio Uno v. City of Holyoke*, 72 F.3d 973, 977 (1st Cir. 1995).

2. *Georgia v. Ashcroft*, 539 U.S. 461, 479 (2003) (O'Connor, J., concurring).

3. *Allen v. State Board of Elections*, 393 U.S. 544, 569 (1969).

4. *Shaw v. Reno*, 509 U.S. 630, 635 (1993).

5. The current case is *Northwest Austin Municipal Utility District No. One v. Holder*, No. 08-322 (U.S. oral argument April 29, 2009) (*NAMUDNO*). The "divvying up" point was made by the chief justice in *League of United Latin American Citizens [LULAC] v. Perry*, 548 U.S. 399, 511 (2006) (Roberts, C. J.).

6. *Wards Cove Packing Co. v. Atonio*, 490 U.S. 642, 652 (1989).

7. *City of Richmond v. J. A. Croson Co.*, 488 U.S. 469, 493 (1989).

8. Ibid., 499. In a number of other decisions, the Court made essentially the same point. See, for instance, *Washington v. Davis*, decided more than a decade earlier: "The Court has also recently rejected allegations of racial discrimination based solely on the statistically disproportionate racial impact of various provisions of the Social Security Act because '[t]he acceptance of appellants' constitutional theory would render suspect each difference in treatment among the grant classes, however lacking in racial motivation and however otherwise rational the treatment might be.'" 426 U.S. 229, 240–41 (1976).

9. *J. A. Croson Co.*, 488 U.S. at 480.

10. *Regents of the University of California v. Bakke*, 438 U.S. 265, 307 (1978).

11. See, for example, David W. Moore, "Public: Only Merit Should Count in College Admissions," Gallup News Service, June 24, 2003. Moore reported on a Gallup Poll finding that 69 percent of Americans and 75 percent of whites believed college applicants "should be admitted solely on the basis of merit, even if that results in few minority students being admitted." Blacks were almost evenly divided, with 44 percent favoring merit-only admissions and 49 percent supporting color-conscious admissions. See also Gallup Organization, "Race Relations Poll," June 4–24, 2007 (unpaginated), as well as Pew Research Center, "Blacks See Growing Values Gap Between Poor and Middle Class," November 2007, 35.

12. William G. Bowen and Derek Bok, *The Shape of the River: Long-Term Consequences of Considering Race in College and University Admissions* (Princeton, N.J.: Princeton University Press, 1998), 41.

13. For clear evidence that minority groups have fared well without racial preferences in admissions since the passage of Proposition 209, see University of California, Office of the President, Office of Admissions, "New Freshman ADMITS by Race/Ethnicity, Fall 1997 through 2008," April 2008, http://www.ucop.com/news/factsheets/2008/fall_2008_admissions_table_1.pdf (accessed April 3, 2009). Although opponents of Prop. 209 warned that it would make the University of California "lily-white," the only group to lose a significant share in its proportion of new admits to the University of California after the abolition of preferences was, in fact, whites.

14. Much other data tell basically the same story. For summaries, see Abigail Thernstrom and Stephan Thernstrom, *Secrecy and Dishonesty: The Supreme Court, Racial Preferences, and Higher Education*, 21 Const. Comment. 251 (2004); Stephan Thernstrom and Abigail Thernstrom, *Reflections on The Shape of the River*, 46 UCLA L. Rev. 1583 (1999); Stephan Thernstrom and Abigail Thernstrom, *America in Black and White: One Nation, Indivisible* (New York: Simon & Schuster, 1997), chapter 14. See also Richard H. Sander, *A Systematic Analysis of Affirmative Action in American Law Schools*, 57 Stan. L. Rev. 367 (2004); and Richard H. Sander, *A Reply to Critics*, 57 Stan. L. Rev. 1963 (2005).

15. *Riley v. Kennedy*, 128 S.Ct. 1970, 1987 (2008) (Stevens, J., dissenting).

16. *South Carolina v. Katzenbach*, 383 U.S. 301, 309 (1966).

17. Senate Judiciary Committee, Fannie Lou Hamer, Rosa Parks, Coretta Scott King, and Cesar E. Chavez Voting Rights Act Reauthorization and Amendments Act of 2006, S. Rep. No. 109-295, at 19, 31, 47, and 52 (2006) (hereafter cited as 2006 Senate report). Cesar E. Chavez's name, which was not included in the House bill's name, was dropped from the Senate bill before the final congressional vote so that the two bills would be identical, eliminating the need for further debate.

18. These examples of testimony that should have raised questions about the continuing use of voter turnout in the 1972 presidential election to trigger section 5 coverage are from Clegg and Chavez, *An Analysis of the Reauthorized Sections 5 and 203*, 5 Geo. J.L.& Pub. Pol'y 561, 567 (2007).

19. *Thornburg v. Gingles*, 478 U.S. 30 (1986). See chapter 3.

20. House Committee on the Judiciary, Fannie Lou Hamer, Rosa Parks, and Coretta Scott King Voting Rights Act Reauthorization and Amendments Act of 2006, H. Rep. No. 109-478 at 6 (2006) (hereafter cited as 2006 House report).

21. A former Justice Department lawyer who was present at a meeting at the White House early in 2005 to discuss the Bush administration's position on renewal has told me that no one there had any interest in getting information from him regarding any actual evidence of continued racial discrimination that would justify renewing section 5: "Their only concern was that the president be seen as supporting the renewal because it would be political suicide to oppose it," he said in a confidential interview. Similarly, he was present at a meeting with staff for House Judiciary Committee chairman James Sensenbrenner, where it was made very clear to him that Sensenbrenner did not want to hear or see any evidence that would impede the renewal of section 5. The Republican congressman saw the renewal as a legacy he wanted to be able to claim for his legislative record. My confidential source also described a debate staged at a private meeting for House Republican congressional leaders between two prominent GOP lawyers who were experts on redistricting, with one arguing that there was no reason to renew section 5, and the other arguing that its renewal would continue to benefit Republican redistricting efforts.

22. Fannie Lou Hamer, Rosa Parks, and Coretta Scott King Voting Rights Act Reauthorization and Amendments Act, Pub. L. No. 109-246, §§ 2(b)(2), 2(b)(9), 120 Stat. 577, 577–78 (2006).

23. In 1990, for instance, 39 percent of blacks reportedly thought AIDS was a racist plot, with college-educated African Americans more likely to believe that rumor than high school graduates. Jennifer L. Hochschild, *Facing Up to The American Dream: Race, Class, and the Soul of the Nation* (Princeton, N.J.: Princeton University Press, 1995), 106, table 5.1.

24. The two decisions are discussed in depth in chapter 2.

25. *Reno v. Bossier Parish Sch. Bd.*, 528 U.S. 320, 335 (2000) (*Bossier II*).

26. See chapter 2.

27. The seminal case of *Arlington Heights v. Metropolitan Housing Development Corp.*, 429 U.S. 252 (1977), involving housing discrimination, established criteria that were

expected to ease the burden on plaintiffs who were required to show discriminatory intent in Fourteenth Amendment cases. "Rarely," the Court held, "can it be said that a legislature or administrative body . . . made a decision motivated by a single concern, or even that a particular purpose was the 'dominant' or 'primary' one." Circumstantial evidence was thus pertinent to evaluating allegations of discrimination in public housing. 429 U.S. at 265. An informed anonymous source has suggested that, in the wake of the 2006 amendments to section 5, the DOJ is demanding that jurisdictions show an absence of all possible circumstantial evidence (using the *Arlington Heights* criteria) that might indicate invidious intent—an extraordinarily difficult standard to meet, obviously. While *Arlington Heights* made it easier for plaintiffs to prove discriminatory intent, the Justice Department is allegedly making it harder for jurisdictions to show an absence of invidious purpose, as they must in the unique voting rights setting.

28. See chapter 5.

29. 2006 House report, 70. The report was quoting from Oversight Hearing on the Voting Rights Act: The Judicial Evolution of the Retrogression Standard, Subcomm. on the Constitution, H. Comm. on the Judiciary, 109th Cong. 1 (November 9, 2005).

30. For the political history of the passage of the VRARA, see Nathaniel Persily, *The Promise and Pitfalls of the New Voting Rights Act*, 117 Yale L.J. 174 (2007).

31. 2006 House report, 93.

32. See chapter 3.

33. 2006 Senate report, 16. The report was quoting from the testimony of Nina Perales, Southwest Regional Counsel for the Mexican American Legal Defense and Education Fund (MALDEF).

34. Ibid., 17.

35. Ibid.

36. Ibid., 21.

37. Ibid.

38. This is assuming section 5 survives the *NAMUDNO* challenge being heard by the Court this term, to which I referred above.

39. *Gingles*, 478 U.S. at 30. "In recognizing that some [1982] Senate Report factors are more important to multimember district vote dilution claims than others, the Court effectuates the intent of Congress." Ibid., 51 n.15. Those Senate report factors were a checklist, in effect, that was to be used by courts in judging the merits of a vote dilution suit. See chapter 3.

40. See chapter 2.

41. *Bartlett v. Strickland*, 129 S. Ct. 1231 (2009).

42. Motion for Leave to File a Brief and Brief of the NAACP, Cindy Moore, Milford Farrior, and Mary Jordan as Amici Curiae in support of Petitioners, *Bartlett v. Strickland*, 129 S. Ct. 1231 (2009) (No. 07–689).

43. This was an unusual section 2 case; the defendant—the state—was using the 1982 provision to defend its own districting. The plaintiffs had the burden of proving that the state had violated its own constitution, and that no Voting Rights Act violation

would have occurred had the district lines followed the Pender County boundaries. The Voting Rights Act shifts the burden of proof to the defendants in section 5 cases, but not in suits involving section 2. It is an important difference. Where the burden of proof lies always has a significant impact on the outcome of litigation.

44. *Pender County v. Bartlett*, 361 N.C. 491, 649 S.E.2d 364 (2007).

45. *Gingles*, 478 U.S. at 50.

46. J. Gerald Hebert, "50% Rule Gets Its Day in the High Court," *Campaign Legal Center Blog*, http://www.clcblog.org/blog_item-218.html, posted March 17, 2008 (accessed April 1, 2009).

47. See chapter 3 for a discussion of the case.

48. *LULAC v. Perry*, 548 U.S. at 444.

49. Brief for the Respondents at 10, *Bartlett v. Strickland*, 129 S. Ct. 1231 (2009).

50. Ibid., 36.

51. Transcript of Oral Argument at 1, *Bartlett v. Strickland*, 129 S. Ct. at 1231.

52. Ibid., 3–4.

53. *Bartlett*, 129 S. Ct. at 1247.

54. Ibid., 1243.

55. Ibid., 1244.

56. Ibid., 1244–45.

57. Ibid., 1246.

58. Ibid., 1248. A brief reference, in parentheses, is made to an article by Richard Pildes: "(Crossover-district requirement would essentially result in political party 'entitlement to . . . a certain number of seats.')" The article to which the Court refers is: Richard Pildes, *Is Voting-Rights Law Now at War with Itself? Social Science and Voting Rights in the 2000s*, 80 N.C. L. Rev. 1517 (2002).

59. Hearing, Renewing the Temporary Provisions of the Voting Rights Act: Legislative Options after *LULAC v. Perry*, Before the S. Comm. on the Judiciary (testimony of Michael A. Carvin, July 13, 2006), http://judiciary.senate.gov/hearings/testimony.cfm?id=1992&wit_id=5574 (accessed April 14, 2009).

60. No. 08-322 (U.S. oral argument April 29, 2009). It should be noted that the name of the case has changed with successive attorneys general. It started out naming Gonzales as the defendant; his name was replaced by Mukasey; and finally by Holder, the current attorney general.

61. Complaint at 2, *Northwest Austin Mun. Util. Dist. No. One v. Mukasey*, 557 F.Supp. 2d 9 (D.D.C. 2008).

62. Ibid., 6.

63. *Northwest Austin Mun. Util. Dist. No. One v. Mukasey*, 557 F.Supp. 2d 9.

64. Ibid., 11 (citation omitted).

65. *South Carolina v. Katzenbach*, 383 U.S. 301, 309 (1966).

66. Ibid., 308.

67. Ibid., 309.

68. Ibid., 327.

69. Ibid., 324.

70. Ibid., 335. The Court, in deciding *NAMUDNO*, could ask whether the case fits another framework—that spelled out in *City of Boerne v. Flores*, 521 U.S. 507 (1997). *Boerne* was a decision involving the constitutionality of the Religious Freedom Restoration Act of 1993, and the Court held that "there must be a congruence and proportionality between the injury to be prevented or remedied and the means adopted to that end." 521 U.S. at 520. Judge Tatel, in ruling against the utility district, argued that even if section 5 were held to that stricter standard, the twenty-five–year extension qualified as a congruent and proportional response to "the continuing problem of racial discrimination in voting." 557 F.Supp. 2d at 80. The standard of congruence and proportionality is more difficult to meet than *Katzenbach's* rational-basis test, but, since *Boerne* did not involve racial classifications, the Court did not apply strict scrutiny in assessing the constitutionality of the legislation. Whether *Boerne* is relevant to the very different context of a voting rights case is an open question, and one that I do not explore.

71. For instance, New York University law professor Samuel Issacharoff, among others, raised this question in a thoughtful discussion in June 2006. "Any serious discussion of the constitutionality of the bill has to proceed along at least three tracks, each of which introduces huge amounts of uncertainty," he wrote. "The first is what level of scrutiny applies to legislation clearly within the core enforcement concerns of the Reconstruction amendments. Is the Court likely to see this as an extension of *City of Boerne*, or will it apply the laxer standard of review of *Hibbs*? Will the Court be inclined, if faced with a 25-year extension, to continue the deferential treatment of the Voting Rights Act offered up most recently in *Lopez v. Monterey County*? My hunch is that the standard of review will be more exacting than *Hibbs*, but less than *Boerne*. That is, I think the Court is likely to have far greater reluctance to strike down core enforcement statutes dealing with race than it would be with the further reaches of congressional power. But I acknowledge this is a hunch based on wildly incomplete data and a small and internally inconsistent body of decided cases. I find it bizarre that anyone would speak with certainty about the constitutionality or unconstitutionality of the Act without even a clear sense of what the standard of review might be. In fact, I am more inclined to view these arguments as unenlightening advocacy dressed up as constitutional analysis." Samuel Issacharoff, "On the Constitutionality of the VRA Renewal," *Election Law Blog*, June 24, 2006, http://electionlawblog.org/archives/cat_vra_renewal_guest_blogging.html (accessed April 1, 2009).

72. *Adarand v. Pena*, 515 U.S. 200 (1995), held that all racial classifications must be subject to "strict scrutiny."

73. Mark Posner, "Update: More on the VRA Compromise," *Election Law Blog*, June 23, 2006, http://electionlawblog.org/archives/cat_vra_renewal_guest_blogging.html (accessed April 1, 2009).

74. Issacharoff, "On the Constitutionality of the VRA Renewal" (emphasis added).

75. Katz went on to argue, however, that "Section 5 . . . is not new" and consequently doesn't need the same kind of supporting evidence the passage of a new law would

require. The provision, however, was designed to expire in 1970, and all extensions have had termination dates; it would thus seem that there was a built-in expectation that each new extension would have to be justified by relevant and fresh evidence. Ellen D. Katz, "Mission Accomplished?" *Pocket Part: An Online Companion to the Yale Law Journal*, December 10, 2007, http://yalelawjournal.org/2007/12/10/katz.html (accessed April 14, 2009).

76. *Miller v. Johnson*, 515 U.S. 900, 927 (1975); for more on the case, see chapter 5.

77. *Fullilove v. Klutznick*, 448 U.S. 448, 538 (1980) (Stevens, J. dissenting). The case involved a minority set-aside program in federal contracting. The narrow tailoring for a compelling state interest formula is set out in *Adarand v. Pena*, 515 U.S. at 200.

78. Those originally covered states were Alabama, Georgia, Louisiana, Mississippi, South Carolina, and Virginia, with North Carolina not entirely but so substantially covered as to be often included in such calculations.

79. U.S. Commission on Civil Rights, *The Voting Rights Act: Ten Years After* (Washington, D.C.: Government Printing Office, 1975), 43, table 3.

80. 2006 Senate report, 26.

81. Ibid. As University of Oklahoma political scientist Ronald Keith Gaddie testified at the House hearings, "For the last four elections for which there are comparative data, black registration in six of the seven [covered] states (all but Virginia) exceeds black registration rates in the nonsouthern states." To Examine the Impact and Effectiveness of the Voting Rights Act, Hearing Before the Subcomm. on the Constitution, H. Comm. on the Judiciary, 109th Cong. (2005) (Gaddie, "*The Renewal of Section 5 of the Voting Rights Act: Some Facts and Some Thoughts*," at 3, submitted October 21, 2005). The 2006 House report acknowledged that "many of the first generation barriers to minority voter registration and voter turnout that were in place prior to the VRA have been eliminated," but the reference to "many" suggests a continuing problem of some unspecified magnitude. 2006 House report, 12.

82. David A. Bositis, *Blacks and the 2008 Elections: A Preliminary Analysis* (Washington, D.C.: Joint Center for Political and Economic Studies, 2008), 15, table 2.

83. U.S. Bureau of the Census, Current Population Reports, Special Studies, P-23-80, *The Social and Economic Status of the Black Population in the United States: An Historical View, 1790–1978* (Washington, D.C.: U.S. Government Printing Office, 1979), 156–57.

84. That number does not include the two African Americans elected from the District of Columbia and the U.S. Virgin Islands who are nonvoting members of the House.

85. U.S. Census Bureau, *Statistical Abstract of the United States: 2009*, 251, table 398, http://www.census.gov/prod/2008pubs/09statab/election.pdf (accessed April 3, 2009).

86. Joint Center for Political and Economic Studies, *Black Elected Officials: A Statistical Summary, 2000*, Appendix, Black Elected Officials in the U.S., 28.

87. David Lublin, Tom Brunnell, Bernard Grofman, and Lisa Handley, *Has the Voting Rights Act Outlived Its Usefulness? In a Word, No,* January 2009, unpublished paper available at http://papers.ssrn.com.Table 1. Data on voting-age population is drawn from the Census Bureau's American FactFinder 2005–2007 American Community Survey 3-Year Estimates.

88. 2006 Senate report, 14. For a compilation of data on Justice Department objections, see U.S. Commission on Civil Rights, *Voting Rights Enforcement and Reauthorization: The Department of Justice's Record of Enforcing the Temporary Voting Rights Act Provisions* (Washington, D.C.: Government Printing Office, 2006).

89. Bositis, *Blacks and the 2008 Elections,* 13.

90. See, for instance, the testimony of Theodore M. Shaw, President and Director-Counsel of the NAACP Legal Defense and Educational Fund, Inc., in Voting Rights Act: The Judicial Evolution of the Retrogression Standard, Hearing Before the H. Subcomm. on the Constitution of the H. Comm. on the Judiciary, 109th Cong. (November 9, 2005); testimony of Laughlin McDonald, Director of the Voting Rights Project, American Civil Liberties Union, Fnd., in The Voting Rights Act: The Continuing Need for Section 5, Hearing Before the H. Subcomm. on the Constitution of the H. Comm. on the Judiciary, 109th Cong. (October 25, 2005).

91. "For black Americans born in the 20th century, the chasms of experience that separate one generation from the next—those who came of age before the movement, those who lived it, those who came along after—have always been hard to traverse." Matt Bai, "Is Obama the End of Black Politics?" *Sunday New York Times Magazine,* August 10, 2008.

92. *Clarksdale Press Register,* "Voting Rights Act Is Antiquated," June 13, 2008.

93. Eric Holder, U.S. Attorney General, Remarks as Prepared for Delivery by Attorney General Eric Holder at the Department of Justice African American History Month Program, Wednesday, February 18, 2009.

94. Richard L. Hasen, "What Congress Should Consider Before Renewing the Voting Rights Act: A Chance to Preempt Supreme Court Invalidation, and Better Protect Minority Voting Rights," http://writ.news.findlaw.com/commentary/20060530_hasen.html, republished on *Election Law Blog,* May 30, 2006, http://electionlawblog.org.

95. Richard L. Hasen, "The Civil Rights Community's Double Gamble on VRA Renewal," *Election Law Blog,* June 21, 2006, http://electionlawblog.org/archives/2006_06.html (accessed April 7, 2009).

96. Hasen, "What Congress Should Consider."

97. Richard H. Pildes, *The Future of Voting Rights Policy: From Anti-Discrimination to the Right to Vote,* 49 How. L.J. 741, 764 (2006).

98. Issacharoff, "On the Constitutionality of the VRA Renewal."

99. The Continuing Need for Section 5 Preclearance, Hearing Before the S. Comm. on the Judiciary, 109th Cong. (2006) (Testimony of Richard H. Pildes, May 16, 2006).

100. Richard Hasen, "What Congress Should Consider."

101. Richard H. Pildes, *The Future of Voting Rights Policy,* 757.

102. Help America Vote Act, Pub. L. No. 107-252, 116 Stat. 1666 (codified at 42 USC § 15301 [2002]).

Conclusion: Moving On

1. Matt Bai, "Is Obama the End of Black Politics?" *Sunday New York Times Magazine*, August 10, 2008.

2. Gwen Ifill, *The Breakthrough: Politics and Race in the Age of Obama* (Amazon Kindle edition, 2009), locations 432–38.

3. CNNPolitics.com, "Most Blacks Say MLK's Vision Fulfilled, Poll Finds," January 21, 2009, poll conducted January 12–15, 2009, http://www.cnn.com/2009/POLI-TICS/01/19/king.poll (accessed April 8, 2009).

4. Ifill, *The Breakthrough*, locations 316–21.

5. 1964 data from Philip E. Converse et al., *American Social Attitudes Data Sourcebook, 1947–1978* (Cambridge, Mass.: Harvard University Press, 1980), 71. The most recent figure, for 2007, is from the Pew Research Center, "Optimism about Black Progress Declines: Blacks See Growing Values Gap Between Rich and Poor," November 2007, 52. "Fairly close personal friend" is from ABC News Poll, "Contact Between Races Is Up Although Discrimination Remains," June 2005.

6. William Brink and Louis Harris, *Black and White: A Study of U.S. Racial Attitudes Today* (New York: Simon and Schuster, 1967), 132; *Washington Post*/Kaiser Family Foundation/Harvard University, "African American Men Survey," June 2006, 25–26; U.S. Census Bureau, *Statistical Abstract of the United States: 2009*, 52, table 59, http://www.census.gov/prod/2008pubs/09statab/pop.pdf (accessed April 8, 2009).

7. See Converse, et al., *American Social Attitudes Data Sourcebook*, 71.

8. David A. Bositis, *Blacks and the 2008 Elections: A Preliminary Analysis* (Washington, D.C.: Joint Center for Political and Economic Studies, 2008), 1, 13. The final figures will be published in the Census Bureau's "Voting and Registration in the Election of 2008."

9. Ibid., 15. "Although Obama ran behind Kerry in Kerry's home state of Massachusetts, and its neighboring states of Connecticut and Rhode Island, Obama still won all three with 60+ percent of the vote," Bositis reported. He "ran ahead of Sen. Kerry among white voters in such reliably Republican states as Utah (nine points better among whites) and Idaho (seven points better than Kerry)." In four southern states, Alabama, Arkansas, Louisiana, and Mississippi, Obama received a smaller share of the white vote than John Kerry did in 2004.

10. Brief for Nathaniel Persily et al., at 3, *Northwest Austin Mun. Util. Dist. No. One v. Holder*, No. 08-322 (U.S. February 25, 2009).

11. Exit polls are highly imperfect for two reasons. Strong evidence indicates that Republicans are less likely to submit to exit interviews. Second, these polls do not comprehensively cover early voters or those who cast absentee ballots. In 2004,

exit pollsters did telephone surveys of early voters in only twelve states; in 2008, it was eighteen. Mark Blumenthal, "The Overlooked Exit Poll Question," October 28, 2008, and Blumenthal, "How Do Polls and Exit Polls Handle Early Voting?" October 31, 2008. Both analyses can be found on http://pollster.com/blogs/how_do_polls_and_exit_polls_ha.php

12. In theory, jurisdictions that meet certain criteria can bail out from section 5 coverage, but the stringent criteria and the high cost of litigating the cases in the D.C. court have made it exceedingly difficult to do so, with the result that only fifteen political subdivisions, all in Virginia, have done so since 1982 when the criteria for doing so were eased. This list of political subdivisions that have bailed out is available on the U.S. Department of Justice, Civil Rights Division, Voting Section Home Page, Section 5 Covered Jurisdictions. If the trigger date were updated to 2004, the last presidential elections for which figures are available, perhaps Hawaii would be covered, but no other states would qualify. (Some turnout estimates put Hawaii turnout at just above the 50 percent mark.)

13. The full list was provided in chapter 1, note 24.

14. No. 08-322 (U.S. oral argument April 29, 2009) (*NAMUDNO*).

15. For the immigrant figure, see U.S. Census Bureau, *Statistical Abstract of the United States: 2009*, 45, table 44, http://www.census.gov/prod/2008pubs/09statab/pop.pdf (accessed April 8, 2009).

16. Ibid., 12, table 9.

17. U.S. Census Bureau, *2008 National Population Projections*, http://www.census.gov/population/www/projections/2008projections.html (accessed April 3, 2009).

18. William H. Frey, *Diversity Spreads Out: Metropolitan Shifts in Hispanic, Asian, and Black Populations Since 2000*, Metropolitan Policy Program, Brookings Institution, March 2006, http://www.brookings.edu/reports/2006/03demographics_frey.aspx (accessed April 3, 2009).

19. House Committee on the Judiciary, Fannie Lou Hamer, Rosa Parks, and Coretta Scott King Voting Rights Act Reauthorization and Amendments Act of 2006, H. R. Rep. No. 109-478 at 70 (2006) (hereafter cited as 2006 House report).

20. *Bartlett v. Strickland*, 129 S. Ct. at 1231, 1251 (2009) (Souter, J. dissenting).

21. *Shaw v. Reno*, 509 U.S 630, 657 (1993).

22. *Bartlett*, 129 S. Ct. at 1248.

23. *Thornburg v. Gingles*, 478 U.S. 30, 91 (1986) (O'Connor, J., concurring).

24. In section 2 the burden of proof is on the plaintiffs; only in section 5 cases does the customary burden shift.

25. Report of the Subcomm. on the Constitution to the S. Comm. on the Judiciary, reprinted in the Report of the S. Comm. on the Judiciary, S. Rep. 97-417 at 148–49 (1982) (hereafter cited as 1982 Senate report).

26. Ibid., 32 (emphasis added).

27. On S. 53, S. 1761, S. 1992, and H.R. 3112. Bills to Amend the Voting Rights Act of 1965: Hearings on the Voting Rights Act Before the Subcomm. on the

Constitution of the S. Comm. on the Judiciary, 97th Cong. at 803 and 810 (1982) (testimony of Armand Derfner).

28. *Gingles*, 478 U.S. at 100.

29. *League of United Latin American Citizens [LULAC] v. Perry*, 548 U.S. 399, 428 (2006), quoting *Johnson v. De Grandy*, 512 U.S. 997, 1014 n.11 (1994).

30. U.S. Census Bureau, *Statistical Abstract of the United States: 2009*, 251, table 398, http://www.census.gov/ prod/2008pubs/09statab/election.pdf (accessed April 3, 2009).

31. *Gingles*, 478 U.S. at 54 n.21. "The reasons black and white voters vote differently have no relevance to the central inquiry of § 2," Justice William Brennan concluded, writing for a plurality. "It is the difference between the choices made by blacks and whites—not the reasons for that difference—that results in blacks having less opportunity than whites to elect their preferred representatives." Ibid., 63.

32. Richard Pildes, *Is Voting-Rights Law Now at War with Itself? Social Science and Voting Rights in the 2000s*, 80 N.C. L. Rev. 1517, 1564 (2002).

33. Ibid., 1565.

34. No. 08-322 (U.S. oral argument April 29, 2009).

35. The arguments made included, first, that the evidence of ongoing racial discrimination had been shown to be still abundant at the 2006 hearings, and, second, that section 5 actually deterred unconstitutional discrimination by stopping changes in voting procedure before they went into effect, while at the same time safeguarding minority progress by preventing retrogressive changes. Brief for the Federal Appellee, *NAMUDNO*, No. 08-322 (filed March 18, 2009). As noted in chapter 6, the evidence for such assertions was exceedingly thin. It could not be demonstrated that, without preclearance more than four decades after the passage of the act, southern jurisdictions would be ready to engage in some form of disfranchisement once again. Of what would the evidence consist—either for or against the proposition? Indeed, as argued above, a return to an earlier era is a most unlikely scenario—if not out of the question—politically and legally. In addition to the Fifteenth Amendment there are other statutory protections that respond to voting wrongs.

36. These data were collected by the U.S. Commission on Civil Rights, which, on June 6, 2008, held a briefing on "The U.S. Department of Justice Plans for Monitoring the 2008 Presidential Election." The commission has not yet issued a final report. USCCR transcript, posted on http://www.usccr.gov/.

37. *Georgia v. Ashcroft*, 195 F. Supp. 2d 25, 92 (D.D.C. 2002).

38. See *Georgia v. Ashcroft*, 539 U.S. 461 (2003), for Georgia state Senator Brown's statement regarding the design of the senate plan (469), and the testimony of Charles Walker, the senate majority leader, that African Americans "have a better chance to participate in the political process under the Democratic majority than we would have under a Republican majority," 470.

39. Associated Press, "Differing Views in GOP on Voting Rights Case, *New York Times* (online), April 12, 2009. http://www.nytimes.com/aponline/2009/04/12/washington/AP-Voting-Rights-Republicans.html?_r=2 (accessed April 14, 2009).

40. Brief of the Leadership Conference on Civil Rights and the LCCR Education Fund et al., as Amici Curiae in Support of Respondents at 3, *NAMUDNO* (U.S. filed March 25, 2009).

41. Brief for Intervenors-Appellees Rodney and Nicole Louis et al., at 57, *NAMUDNO* (filed March 18, 2009).

42. Ibid., 5.

43. See, for instance, Brief for the States of North Carolina, Arizona, California, Louisiana, Mississippi and New York, as Amici Curiae in Support of Eric H. Holder, Jr., et al. (filed March 25, 2009); and Brief for the Appellee, Travis County (filed March 18, 2009), *NAMUDNO*.

44. Brief for the Federal Appellee, at 53, *NAMUDNO*.

45. Ibid.

46. United States Commission on Civil Rights, "Voting Irregularities in Florida During the 2000 Presidential Election," issued June 2001.

47. Numerous allegations were made of voting wrongs in Ohio in 2004. For a summary of the issues see, for instance, Adam Liptak, "Voting Problems in Ohio Set Off an Alarm," *New York Times*, November 7, 2004.

48. Ellen Katz, "The Misguided Effort to Explain Obama to the Court—or—Why Obama Really Matters and What the Court Should Do About It," *Election Law Blog*, March 26, 2009, http://electionlawblog.org/archives/2009_03.html (accessed April 7, 2009).

49. Some of the young African Americans holding important positions in the Obama administration were profiled in the *Washington Post*, "The New Black Pack," March 22, 2009, E8. Among the ten profiled, the oldest was thirty-three years old.

50. Steven F. Lawson, *Black Ballots: Voting Rights in the South, 1944–1969* (New York: Columbia University Press, 1976), 321. Lewis saw the Supreme Court's decision in *Brown v. Board of Education* as equally important.

51. Daniel Lowenstein, remarks, book event for Anthony A. Peacock, American Enterprise Institute, Washington, D.C., May 5, 2008, edited transcript from audio tapes, http://www.aei.org/events/eventID.1710/event_detail.asp (accessed April 1, 2009).

52. *Shaw*, 509 U.S at 647, 643, 657, and 648.

53. Alex Aleinikoff and Samuel Issacharoff, *Race and Redistricting: Drawing Constitutional Lines After Shaw v. Reno*, 92 Mich. L. Rev. 588, 610 (1993).

54. Pew Research Center, "Optimism About Black Progress Declines: Blacks See Growing Values Gap Between Poor and Middle Class," November 13, 2007, 1, pewresearch.org/pubs/634/black-public-opinion (accessed April 8, 2009).

55. Randall Kennedy, *Sellout: The Politics of Racial Betrayal* (New York: Pantheon Books, 2008), 80.

56. David Lublin, et al, *Has the Voting Rights Act Outlived its Usefulness?* Unpublished paper on file with author.

57. *Bartlett v. Strickland*, 129 S. Ct. 1231.

58. Cass R. Sunstein, *Why Groups Go to Extremes* (Washington, D.C.: AEI Press, 2008).

59. Jesse Jackson, never elected to any office, ran in 1984 and 1988. He raised his national profile, and perhaps his speaking fees, but he had no chance of winning the Democratic nomination. Likewise, in 1972, Representative Shirley Chisholm, a Democrat from New York, declared her candidacy, but she was not a politically serious contender.

60. Michael Carvin, remarks, book event, American Enterprise Institute, May 5, 2008.

61. It should be noted, however, that some scholarly work has found a mixed picture. Kimball Brace, Lisa Handley, Richard Niemi, and Harold Stanley, "Minority Turnout and the Creation of Majority-Minority Districts," *American Politics Quarterly* 23, no. 2 (April 1995): 190–203, for example, found no consistent pattern in elections for the Florida State House and Senate and the U.S. House of Representatives. In some newly created black-majority districts, black turnout rose modestly; in many others it declined. "Overall, we cannot yet conclude that the creation of minority-dominated districts has a consistent effect on minority turnout," the authors wrote.

62. Carol Swain, *Black Faces, Black Interests: The Representation of African Americans in Congress* (Cambridge, Mass.: Harvard University Press, 1993), 203.

63. James E. Campbell, *Cheap Seats: The Democratic Party's Advantage in U.S. House Elections* (Columbus, Ohio: Ohio State University Press, 1996).

64. Claudine Gay, "Legislating Without Constraints: The Effect of Minority Districting on Legislators' Responsiveness to Constituency Preferences," *Journal of Politics* 69, no. 2 (May 2007): 442–56.

65. Ibid., 443.

66. Ibid., 446 n.6.

67. Sheryll D. Cashin, *Democracy, Race, and Multiculturalism in the Twenty-First Century: Will the Voting Rights Act Ever Be Obsolete?* 22 Wash. U. J.L. & Pol'y 71, 90 (2006).

68. CNN.com., "Poll: Most Americans See Lingering Racism—in Others," December 12, 2006, 1, http://www.cnn.com/2006/US/12/12/racism.poll/index.html (accessed April 8, 2009).

69. Gallup Organization (for AARP), "Civil Rights and Race Relations," poll conducted January 2004, 17–18.

70. "Among blacks . . . the surge to Obama since December has been remarkable. In the last pre-primary ABC News/*Washington Post* poll last year, Clinton led Obama among blacks by 52–39 percent. That changed after Obama established his credentials by winning Iowa; across all primaries to date he's won African-Americans by 79–17 percent." Gary Langer, "The Role of Race," *The Numbers: A Run at the Latest Data from ABC's Poobah of Polling*, http://blogs.abcnews.com/thenumbers/2008/02/the-role-of-rac.html, February 15, 2008 (accessed April 7, 2009).

71. Perry Bacon Jr., "Can Obama Count On the Black Vote?" *Time*, January 23, 2007.

72. Adam Nagourney, "The Pattern May Change, If," *New York Times*, December 10, 2006, Week in Review, section 4, 1.

73. Philip Klinkner, "The Obama Ceiling, Again," *PolySigh: The Political Science Take on Things*, March 10, 2008, http://polysigh.blogspot.com/search?q=klinkner (accessed April 8, 2009).

74. Frank Newport and Joseph Carroll, "Analysis: Impact of Personal Characteristics on Candidate Support: Americans Most Comfortable Voting for a Black or Female Candidate," Gallup News Service, March 13, 2007.

75. Adam Nossiter, "Race Matters Less in Politics of South," *New York Times*, February 21, 2008, A1.

76. Richard Thompson Ford, *The Race Card: How Bluffing About Bias Makes Race Relations Worse* (New York: Farrar, Straus and Giroux, 2008), 26.

77. David L. Epstein, Richard H. Pildes, Rodolfo O. de Garza, and Sharyn O'Halloran, eds., introduction to *The Future of the Voting Rights Act* (New York: Russell Sage Foundation, 2006), xiv.

78. *Johnson v. De Grandy*, 512 U.S. 997, 1020 (1994).

Index of Voting Rights Cases

General Index

Abraham, Henry, 12
Affirmative action, *see* Racial preferences
American Indians, 8, 37, 204, 276n3
Alabama, 6, 32, 91, 121, 130, 172, 193, 194, 220, 279n47, 283n9
Alaska, 37, 41, 170, 252n31
Alaskan Natives, 8, 37, 204, 276n3
Aleinikoff, T. Alexander, 158–60, 163–64, 216
Alexander, Gerald, 108
Alito, Samuel, J., 102–4, 106, 109
American Civil Liberties Union (ACLU), 13–14, 65, 111, 113–14, 125, 129, 149, 246n24
American Indians, 8, 37–38, 204, 276n3
Annexation, municipal, 53–58, 124, 257n18
Arizona, 7, 35, 37, 41, 54, 252n31
Asian Americans, 8, 37–38, 204, 207. 276n3
At-large elections, 32–33, 40–45, 55–57, 76, 79, 91, 106–7, 143, 251n24, 255n51, 264n22, 265n28, 266n35
Austin, Tex., 187–91, 211

Barone, Michael, 272n114
Bauer, Robert, 69
Bell, Chris, 137, 139
Bilingual ballots, 38–39, 245n21, 253n33
Bingham, Jonathan, 29, 49
Birmingham, Ala., 202–3

Bishop, Sanford, 162
Black Caucus, *see* Congressional Black Caucus
Black, Hugo, J., 5, 29–30, 72, 283n12
Blackmun, Harry, J., 15–16, 99–100, 147
Blumrosen, Alfred W., 141
Blumstein, James, 80, 85, 89, 246n30, 265n29, 266n47
Bok, Derek, 171
Bond, Julian, 94
Bonilla, Henry, 100–2, 138
Bositis, David A., 200, 243n4
Bowen, William G., 171
Brennan, William, J., 85–88, 92–94, 97, 175
Breyer, Stephen, J., 63, 152–53
Brooks, Tyrone, 111, 155
Browning, Christopher G. Jr., 185
Brown, Joe, 125
Bush, George W., 10, 116, 175
Butler, Katharine I., 85, 92, 156–57

California, 8, 35, 37, 41, 54, 171, 219
Campbell, James E., 218
Carvin, Michael, 187, 218
Cashin, Sheryll, 219
Celler, Emanuel, 46
Center for Equal Opportunity, 174
Chaney, James, 4, 6
Civil Rights Act of 1964, xv, 5–6, 141, 214, 244n7

307

About the Authors

Abigail Thernstrom is an adjunct scholar at the American Enterprise Institute, vice-chair of the U.S. Commission on Civil Rights, and a member of the board of advisers of the U.S. Election Assistance Commission. She was a senior fellow at the Manhattan Institute in New York from 1993 to 2009 and a member of the Massachusetts state Board of Education for more than a decade. In 2007, Ms. Thernstrom was awarded a Bradley Prize for Outstanding Intellectual Achievement.

Ms. Thernstrom's previous study of the Voting Rights Act, *Whose Votes Count? Affirmative Action and Minority Voting Rights* (Harvard University Press, 1987) won four awards, including the American Bar Association's Certificate of Merit, the Anisfield-Wolf Book Award for the best book on race and ethnicity, and best policy book from the Policy Studies Organization, a division of the American Political Science Association.

Ms. Thernstrom is also coauthor (with her husband, Stephan Thernstrom) of *No Excuses: Closing the Racial Gap in Learning* (Simon & Schuster, 2003), which won the Fordham Foundation's prize for distinguished scholarship, and *America in Black and White: One Nation, Indivisible* (Simon & Schuster, 1997), named by the *New York Times* as one of the notable books of the year.

Her frequent media appearances have included *Fox News Sunday*, *Good Morning America*, and *This Week with George Stephanopoulos*. Her writing has appeared in *Wall Street Journal*, the *Los Angeles Times*, the *New York Times*, *The Economist*, and the *Times Literary Supplement* (London). Ms. Thernstrom received her Ph.D. in 1975 from Harvard University's Department of Government.

Juan Williams, author of the foreword, is one of America's leading journalists. He is a senior correspondent for National Public Radio (NPR) and a regular contributor to *Fox News Sunday*. He worked at the *Washington Post* for twenty-one years, serving as an editorial writer, op-ed columnist, and White House reporter. Mr. Williams received an Emmy award for TV documentary writing and earned widespread critical acclaim for his documentary *Politics—The New Black Power*. His articles have appeared in magazines such as *The Atlantic Monthly, Newsweek, The New Republic, Fortune, Ebony,* and *Gentlemen's Quarterly*. Mr. Williams has appeared on *Nightline, Washington Week in Review, The Oprah Winfrey Show, Crossfire,* and *Capitol Gang Sunday*. He serves on the boards of the Aspen Institute's Communications and Society Program, the Washington Journalism Center, and the New York Civil Rights Coalition.

Mr. Williams is the author of the highly acclaimed *Eyes on the Prize: America's Civil Rights Years, 1954–1965* (Penguin, 1988), as well as *Thurgood Marshall: American Revolutionary* (Three Rivers Press, 2000), *This Far by Faith: Stories from the African American Religious Experience* (Amistad, 2003), *My Soul Looks Back in Wonder: Voices of the Civil Rights Experience* (Sterling, 2004), and *Enough: The Phony Leaders, Dead-End Movements, and Culture of Failure That Are Undermining Black America—and What We Can Do about It* (Three Rivers Press, 2006).